DEPORTES

LATINIDAD

Transnational Cultures in the United States

This series publishes books that deepen and expand our understanding of Latina/o populations, especially in the context of their transnational relationships within the Americas. Focusing on borders and boundary-crossings, broadly conceived, the series is committed to publishing scholarship in history, film and media, literary and cultural studies, public policy, economics, sociology, and anthropology. Inspired by interdisciplinary approaches, methods, and theories developed out of the study of transborder lives, cultures, and experiences, titles enrich our understanding of transnational dynamics.

Matt Garcia, Series Editor, Professor of Latin American, Latino & Caribbean Studies, and History, Dartmouth College

For a list of titles in the series, see the last page of the book.

DEPORTES

The Making of a Sporting Mexican Diaspora

JOSÉ M. ALAMILLO

RUTGERS UNIVERSITY PRESS

New Brunswick, Camden, and Newark, New Jersey, and London

Library of Congress Cataloging-in-Publication Data

Names: Alamillo, José M., 1969- author.
Title: Deportes: the making of a sporting Mexican diaspora / José M. Alamillo.
Description: New Brunswick: Rutgers University Press, 2020. | Series: Latinidad:
    transnational cultures in the United States | Includes bibliographical references
    and index.
Identifiers: LCCN 2019044874 (print) | LCCN 2019044875 (ebook) | ISBN
    9781978813663 (paperback) | ISBN 9781978813670 (hardback) | ISBN 9781978813687
    (epub) | ISBN 9781978813694 (mobi) | ISBN 9781978813700 (pdf)
Subjects: LCSH: Sports—Mexico. | Athletes—Mexico. | Mexican American athletes.
Classification: LCC GV587.A53 2020 (print) | LCC GV587 (ebook) |
    DDC s 796.0972—dc23
LC record available at https://lccn.loc.gov/2019044874
LC ebook record available at https://lccn.loc.gov/2019044875

A British Cataloging-in-Publication record for this book is available from the
British Library.

♾ The paper used in this publication meets the requirements of the American
National Standard for Information Sciences—Permanence of Paper for Printed
Library Materials, ANSI Z39.48-1992.

www.rutgersuniversitypress.org

Manufactured in the United States of America

Para mis padres,
Rosa y José Alamillo
por su cariño y apoyo incondicional.

CONTENTS

DEPORTES

INTRODUCTION

Even before I learned about César Chávez, Martin Luther King Jr., and other civil rights leaders, I had one Latino role model—Fernando Valenzuela. As a skinny immigrant kid growing up in Ventura County, California, north of Los Angeles, I did not speak English very well. Strangers had even told me, "Go back to Mexico." To avoid being hit by racial slurs—"beaner," "wetback," and more—I used to downplay my ethnic background. But that all changed during a fateful baseball season. On April 9, 1981, Valenzuela made his major league debut as a starting pitcher with the Los Angeles Dodgers, shutting out the Houston Astros. "Fernandomania" erupted after he won his first eight starts, tossing five shutouts and posting a miniscule 0.50 ERA during that stretch. With his signature screwball and eyes-to-the-sky windup, Valenzuela earned an unprecedented National League Rookie of the Year Award and Cy Young Award while helping the Dodgers win the 1981 World Series.[1] Every time Fernando pitched when I was young, my cousins and I got together and cheered for El Toro. And afterward we always played ball. We tried throwing screwballs but were lucky if they even crossed home plate.

Apparently, I was not alone. A 1983 *Los Angeles Times* poll asked Californians to name a person they most admired, and Valenzuela ranked behind Pope John Paul II and Ronald Reagan.[2] " He is one of us," explained an East Los Angeles butcher. "I like him because he makes me feel proud. In this country, you have to be pretty good in any field to be recognized."[3] Media recognition on Valenzuela's meteoric rise to superstardom gave rise to the Fernandomania that made millions for the Dodgers franchise. Valenzuela fans bought baseball cards, magazines, jerseys, pennants, buttons, vinyl records, even boxes of gum emblazoned with their idol's image. However, something more culturally and politically significant accompanied the craze. Valenzuela inspired the Latino population of Los Angeles, immigrant and U.S. born alike. His humble demeanor, combined with his improbable success as an unassuming son of Sonora, Mexico, helped to instill a feeling of unity and optimism among Mexican immigrants, Mexican Americans, and Latino/as.

Besides uniting the Latino community, Valenzuela helped counter the anti-immigrant sentiment that seemed to reach a peak in the early 1980s. In my own family, this attitude freed my father to boast about how he had also overcome humble beginnings as an immigrant working long hours as a lemon picker and ironworker. But with hard work and a "Sí, se puede" mind-set, my father exemplified that one could accomplish anything in this country. My father is still convinced that when President Ronald Reagan invited Valenzuela to the White House for a luncheon with him and Mexico's president José López Portillo in the middle of the 1981 season, they talked more about immigration than baseball.

Perhaps my father isn't far off. One could convincingly argue that Valenzuela's success on the mound helped change attitudes toward Mexican immigrants. When Congress passed the 1986 Immigration Reform and Control Act just a few years later, it included a compromise about legalization for immigrants. The law enabled my family and nearly three million undocumented immigrants to gain legal status. My mother, who was not a big baseball fan, still believes that Fernando was "touched by God," not because he looked up to the heavens when he pitched but because he had helped change people's minds. My sisters and female cousins, who were discouraged from playing sports, even got on the Fernando-mania bandwagon. This cultural phenomenon was so powerful that it brought more women into sports spectatorship.

Valenzuela quickly became a national hero in Mexico. My relatives in Zacate-cas also referred to him as El Toro, and his popularity eclipsed the national politicians who scrambled to take a photo with the baseball celebrity.[4] Fans from the border cities of Mexicali and Tijuana made the long drive to watch El Toro on the Dodgers Stadium mound. Even this soccer-loving country started to play and watch more baseball. More than twenty thousand kids showed up to Valenzuela's baseball clinic in Mexico City. Televisa broadcasted all his games during the 1981 season, surpassing soccer matches. Valenzuela became a national hero and the "unofficial ambassador" of Greater Mexico setting a positive example for the youth and poor alike.

Why did such a talented pitcher have to leave Mexico to become a hero in his country of birth? Was he the first Mexican to make it in the big leagues? Why did it take so long for a Mexican-origin athlete to become a big sport celebrity in the United States? Why has the U.S. sports industry failed to recruit and develop Mexican talent? These questions led me to explore the historic role of sports on both sides of the U.S.-Mexico border. *Deportes* examines the sporting experience of Mexicans, Mexican immigrants, and Mexican Americans, both men and women, in Greater Mexico during the first half of the twentieth century. Although the term "Greater Mexico" encompasses all geographic areas inhabited by people of Mexican descent, I primarily focus on Southern California and its connections with Mexico. In terms of sports, I examine baseball, boxing, basketball, softball, track and field, football, soccer, and tennis at the amateur, semiprofessional, Olympic, and professional levels. I argue that Mexican-origin males and females in the United States have used sports to empower themselves and their community by developing and sustaining transnational networks with Mexico.

Sport narratives are too often centered around individual achievement, which obscures their communities of support.[5] Latino sports heroes have been made not through individual effort alone but through the support of a network of families, coaches, managers, promoters, organizations, sportswriters, and fans who have opened athletic opportunities to compete and represent their community and nation, at home and abroad. These networks are not tethered to the nation-state; rather, Mexican-origin athletes have used transnational networks to challenge racial, gender, and class barriers imposed by the sports industry, government officials, and media and in the process have created a sporting Mexican diaspora.

SPORTING MEXICAN DIASPORA

This book is indebted to the field of African American studies that pioneered the study of race and sport.[6] From the physical educator and civil rights activist Edwin B. Henderson, who wrote the first book on black athletic achievements in hopes of eliminating racial discrimination in sports, to the scholar-activist Harry Edwards, who published the groundbreaking book *The Revolt of the Black Athlete* and founded the Olympic Project for Human Rights that inspired the famous Black Power salute at the 1968 Olympic Games in Mexico City, these and a new generation of scholars have enriched our understanding of the sporting black experience in the United States.[7]

Much of sport history tends to be conducted within national boundaries. Anthropologist Alan Klein urged sport scholars to "shed national identities" to keep pace with a rapidly globalizing sports world.[8] Yet, most transnational sports history has focused between United States and Canada, rarely crossing into Mexico.[9] Recent studies on the sporting black experience have shown the utility of studying race and sport diasporically.[10] In *Race, Sport and Politics: The Sporting Black Diaspora*, Ben Carrington contends that black athletes competing in the diaspora were central to challenging white supremacy in the Western world. Building on Paul Gilroy's concept of the Black Atlantic, Carrington defines the sporting black diaspora world as "a complex, transnational, cultural and political space that exceeds the boundaries of the nation state, whereby the migrations and achievements of black athletes have come to assume a heightened political significance for the dispersed peoples of the black diaspora."[11] Similarly, I use a diaspora framework to examine the migrations, networks, and political dimensions of the Mexican sporting experience.

The term "Mexican diaspora" resembles Américo Paredes's concept of Greater Mexico, defined as all areas "where people of Mexican descent have established a presence and have maintained their Mexicanness as a key part of their cultural identity."[12] This pioneering folklorist offered an early transnational vision of Mexican expressive culture that crossed political, economic, and geographic borders.[13] Paredes reminded scholars long ago that the North American cowboy originated with the Mexican vaquero who had long participated in rodeo and *charrería* competitions along the U.S.–Mexico borderlands.[14] Since Paredes work was published, scholars have examined musical, literary, artistic, cinematic, religious, and political encounters in Greater Mexico.[15] Yet they have paid little attention to sporting practices in Greater Mexico.[16] This is not surprising since high-brow American academics have traditionally not taken sports seriously, and thus it remains "ghettoized" in many disciplines.[17]

In his critical assessment of Chicano historiography, Samuel Regalado argues that the topic of sport has remained largely "invisible" even though "Mexican American competitive sport has crossed class and regional lines, stimulated hybrid and fluid identities, and enhanced a transnational culture."[18] With *Playing America's Game*, Adrian Burgos Jr. raised the level theoretically and methodologically in the study of Latinos, race, and sports.[19] Drawing from research in Cuba, Puerto Rico, and the United States and interviews with former professional players, Burgos championed the overlooked Afro-Latinos who became "integration pioneers" in the major leagues. By transnationalizing "America's Game," Burgos proposes the writing of sport history beyond a single nation, including sources, ideologies, and frameworks from and across multiple nations. Following this lead, I trace the movement of Mexican athletes from and across Mexico and the United States to participate in a wide range of sports-related activities.

In *Deportes*, I develop the concept of "sporting Mexican diaspora" to reveal the imaginary and material interactions between athletes, team managers, and coaches across and within national borders as they organize, promote, and compete in sports-related activities. Diaspora involves the migration of Mexican athletes, teams, and sporting institutions from their once-territorial homeland held together by shared memory, loss, longing, and a sense of history and culture. This migration is anchored in social networks of affiliation, communication, and attachment across and beyond widely scattered diasporic communities that produced a vibrant sporting culture. In the face of alienation, a culture of sports has allowed athletes and their supporters to develop various forms of diasporic consciousness, whether a renewed sense of cultural and national pride, a heightened political awareness of civil rights, or a newly formed hybrid sporting identity. *Deportes* focuses on five dimensions of the sporting Mexican diaspora: (1) a physical, political, and economic displacement; (2) a transnational sporting network that has shaped political activism; (3) a sporting racial project; (4) a gendered sporting experience for male and female athletes; and (5) a diasporic consciousness that has informed the construction of hybrid sporting identities.

The first dimension encompasses the long history of physical, political, economic displacement of Mexican people as a result of U.S. imperialism. After the United States annexed Mexico's northern territory in 1848, the Mexican population found themselves physically displaced and in a precarious position where they had to renegotiate their relationship to their homeland, while at the same time trying to eke out a living in their new hostland. This new relationship was ambivalent at best. The property and citizenship rights guaranteed under the Treaty of Guadalupe Hidalgo proved to be fragile, though. Since former Mexican citizens could no longer rely on their new government for protection, they turned to family and community for support. Soon thereafter, their leisure and sporting practices came under attack by Anglo-American newcomers. In 1855, the California legislature passed a law banning bear and bull fights and other "barbarous amusements."[20] But horseracing and other roping and riding contests survived into the late nineteenth century and influenced the modern sport of rodeo.

Economic necessity also fueled displacement throughout the Mexican diaspora. When the United States exported American sports into Mexico, President Porfirio Díaz and the Mexican elite enthusiastically embraced them as part of the country's modernization program. Although the Mexican Revolution disrupted sporting activities, there was renewed growth under President Venustiano Carranza, who linked the physical betterment of Mexican citizens with building a stronger and modern nation. To bolster its international standing, Mexico competed at the Olympic Games in 1924, and although they did not win any medals, they showed the world that they could compete.[21] Despite increased government promotion of sports, the country's economic downturn during the Great Depression made it difficult to send athletes abroad. As a result, to field and sponsor teams at the 1932 Olympic Games in Los Angeles, the Mexican Olympic Committee reached out to *México de afuera* (Mexico outside) for assistance. The successful fund-raising efforts revealed how México de afuera saw themselves as members of a sporting diaspora.

The 1930s was a crucial period for the reformist administration of President Lázaro Cárdenas, who pushed for agrarian reform, public education, and state-sponsored sports programs to promote teamwork, cooperation, and nationalism. The late British historian Eric Hobsbawm recognized the role of sports in the creation of a sense of nationalism: "The imagined community of millions seems more real as a team of eleven named people."[22] This sporting nationalism reached its peak in the 1940s with the rise of Jorge Pasquel's Mexican League, which challenged the hegemony of U.S. Major League Baseball. Ultimately, sports policy was not a priority for Mexican government officials, forcing athletes to join the northward migration stream due to economic reasons. In reality, U.S. domination and influence on Mexico forced their physical displacement to the United States with dreams of becoming a professional sport star, earning higher wages to support their families, as well as creating options to stay or return home. While economic necessity kept many from returning home, Mexican athletes in the United States still found ways to build and maintain transnational ties with their homeland.

The second dimension involves building community and transnational networks for political empowerment. Institutional politics, community organizations, and family and kin networks helped facilitate the rise of a transnational sporting network within and beyond the Mexican diaspora. A network of sporting organizations (from the amateur to the professional), athletes, coaches, promoters, and sportswriters promoted a cross-border sporting culture, not limited to national boundaries. Sports provided more than recreation and entertainment that also helped offset the alienation and cultural displacement they felt in their hostland. For members of the Mexican diaspora, sports and its associated practices of gambling, drinking, and socializing provided solace from the negative social encounters they faced. Sporting transnational networks could be activated for political purposes in the Mexican diaspora. Members of the Mexican Athletic Association of Southern California (MAASC) and the Mexican Athletic Union (MAU), for example, forged ties with Mexico's sport federation during the 1930s and 1940s to provide more cross-border athletic opportunities but also to advocate for more recreation and sports programs from city officials. These networks allowed athletic organizations and their members to gain confidence in their ability to exert political influence on U.S. institutions.

The state played an important role in mediating the cross-border networks of Mexican athletes. The nation-state—through Mexican consular offices, embassies, or the Immigration and Naturalization Service and Inter-American Affairs Office—mediated these cross-border sporting networks in an attempt to control their mobility and citizenship status. To travel and compete abroad was not easy; it required sport migrants to navigate the U.S. immigration regime with assistance from a team of coaches, trainers, managers, and promoters. Before Valenzuela, many athletes had traveled north to find opportunities to play and compete, but the vast majority were not sport celebrities. Rather, these migrants were lesser-known athletes who toiled far away from the media limelight, routinely crossing national borders for a chance to compete on a baseball diamond, in the boxing ring, on a soccer field, or on a basketball or tennis court.

In the case of Mexican Americans, sports became the training ground for political activism. As high school student athletes, Bert Corona and Emma Tenayuca learned their first lessons about political organizing by playing basketball. Additionally, Mexican athletes and their supporters used their celebrity status and resources to call attention to civil rights problems affecting their community. One major civil rights issue to emerge was the battle over media representation of Mexican athletes in the sports pages. Mexican and Mexican American sports journalists played an essential role in breaking down racial barriers for athletes of Mexican descent. This book contends that sports journalists and editors writing for the Spanish-language press, with a wide circulation across the United States and Mexico, helped develop awareness of sports as civil rights in the Mexican diaspora. As Thomas Guglielmo observed, "The Mexican American civil rights struggle . . . can be known only by examining developments, institutions, and ideas on both sides of the border."[23] This includes athletes and sporting institutions that flourished across both sides of the border and were instrumental in raising awareness of civil rights within and beyond the sports industry.

The third dimension considers the sporting Mexican diaspora as a racial project. Michael Omi and Howard Winant advanced the concept of racial project to "capture how racial formation processes occur through a linkage between structure and representation."[24] Building on Omi and Winant, sport sociologist Ben Carrington coined the term "sporting racial projects" to show that the sports industry, like other social institutions, determines larger processes of race making.[25] As Carrington stated, "Sports become productive and not merely receptive, of racial discourse and this discourse has material effects both within sports and beyond."[26] In this book, I examine those sporting racial projects that constructed Mexican athletes into a "brown" racial category within the U.S. sporting world.

The sporting body that makes physical activity possible is one example of how the sports industry shapes our understanding of race. Historically, U.S. academics, travel writers, and physical educators sought to control the Mexican body through supervised play and good sportsmanship that reflected a muscular Christianity and Americanization ideology that originated in Anglo-Protestant circles. These racial discourses positioned Mexican athletic ability as lesser to that of white athletes due to a presumed inferior athleticism, smaller stature, lack of coaching, poor sportsmanship, and "uncivilized" play. These racial ideologies traveled back and forth across the U.S.-Mexico border and shaped local, regional, and state institutional practices toward Mexican migrants and Mexican Americans.

The Mexican sporting body also became a site of resistance by challenging racial assumptions about their supposed physical and mental inferiority., Through their actions on and off the playing field, Mexican athletes challenged prevailing racial assumptions about their community and nation. For example, when Mexican prizefighters defeated their opponents in the ring, they became heroes to their community at a time when they were viewed and treated as a "racial problem." These sports heroes had an affective connection with fans who instilled a sense of cultural pride and national identification.[27] In a sense, the athletic successes of Mexican athletes and their supporters were subtle attempts to subvert social hierarchies and power dynamics in society.

This book considers the spatial and relational dimensions of sporting racial projects to better understand the role of Mexican athletes within U.S. sports and society. Restrictive racial covenants and segregated schooling practices confined Mexican athletes to barrio parks and playgrounds with limited sporting facilities. George Lipsitz reminds us about the "white spatial imaginary" of publicly subsidized sports stadiums that cater primarily to white suburban spectators at the expense of impoverished black neighborhoods.[28] Despite few opportunities to recreate, Mexican athletes transformed playgrounds, gyms, sandlots, courts, and stadiums into "nonwhite spatial imaginaries" where they could they get a "fair chance" to compete, make lifelong friendships, and build solidarity with other racial and ethnic groups. To better understand the interactions and dynamics of different racialized groups, Natalia Molina urges scholars to examine race relationally, not comparatively.[29] Molina suggests that "we need to ask who else is (or was) present in or near the communities we study—and what difference these groups' presence make (or makes)."[30] By placing Mexican athletes in a relational framework, I examine interactions and connections between them and African American and Asian American athletes, even when they were not in direct or frequent contact.

The fourth dimension explores the sporting Mexican diaspora as a gendered experience. Modern sports represent a privileged arena for men that perpetuates greater gender inequities and contributes to the oppression of women athletes. Sports have provided an important vehicle for men to gain status and deploy political power, while claiming a masculine identity.[31] In a classic study of gender and sexuality in women's sports, Susan Cahn argues that sports is a site for "producing the norms that govern manhood and masculinity, womanhood and femininity."[32] Female athletes were encouraged to follow a strict definition of femininity that encouraged sex appeal and heterosexuality while discouraging "mannish" attributes to avoid accusation of lesbianism.[33]

This book also examines the relationship between masculinity, femininity, and sporting cultures in the lives of Mexican male and female athletes in order to understand how they negotiated gender identities in the sporting world. Monolithic generalizations about Latino masculinity have been criticized by scholars for ignoring changing historical and social contexts as well as race, sexuality, and class factors.[34] Recent works have adopted a more critical approach toward Mexican American masculinity in boxing and baseball.[35]

Sport has been absent in the writings of women of color. As Susan Birrell points out, "If we are to understand gender and racial relations in sport, particularly as they relate to women of color, we cannot remain in our old theoretical homes. . . . Instead we need to increase our awareness of issues in the lives of women of color as they themselves articulate these issues.[36] Sport sociologist Katherine Jamieson urged sport scholars to pay more attention to the intersectional identities and multiple feminisms of Latina athletes.[37] Few have heeded

Jamieson's call for more scholarship in "Mestiza Sport Studies."[38] In *Deportes*, I examine Mexican sporting cultures through a gendered lens to uncover the multiple forms of masculinities and femininities of male and female athletes.

Mexican women gradually inserted themselves into male-dominated sports despite widespread myths about female physical fragility and male spectators sexualizing athletic female bodies. By the 1940s Mexican female athletes had formed basketball, baseball, and softball teams and tennis clubs to compete in local, regional, and international tournaments, allowing them to exercise, socialize, and develop their own sporting networks in the diaspora. This is reminiscent of Tejanas in Houston, whom Emma Perez aptly described as "using what was available to them to intervene with their own tactics as diasporic subjects claiming survival."[39] Although most female athletes had limited travel opportunities compared to their male counterparts, they also cultivated transnational networks and embraced diasporic sporting identities. Take, for example, the Southern California shortstop Marge Villa Cryan, who played for the All-American Girls Professional Baseball League in the Midwest and during the postseason traveled throughout Latin America for exhibition games.

The fifth dimension involves the formation of a diasporic consciousness that produces hybrid sporting cultures and identities. As James Clifford explains, "diaspora consciousness" emerges out of experiences of loss, marginality, and systematic exploitation, and "this constitutive suffering coexists with the skills of survival: strength in adaptive distinction, discrepant cosmopolitanism and stubborn visions of renewal."[40] Imagined connections to their homeland and experiences of racial subordination in their hostland lead racially marginalized and disempowered people to develop a new sense of identity. As Stuart Hall suggests, "Diaspora identities are those which are constantly producing and reproducing themselves anew, through transformation and difference."[41] Sports, like music, literature, film, and visual art, makes it possible to unite dispersed populations across space and time. Consequently, sporting diasporas allow athletes to develop connections between their identities and homeland while at the same time claiming legitimacy in their new host country.

Sports provides a site for the Mexican diaspora to develop a strong sense of belonging and to forge hybrid identities. Mexicans in the United States are not fully accepted by their host country nor in their homeland. They occupy an "in-between" position that is popularity known in Spanish as *ni de aqui, ni de alla*, "neither here, nor there." Such ambiguity and blurring of borders are what Gloria Anzaldúa characterized as a "mestiza consciousness.[42] In particular, Mexican American athletes faced racial discrimination on U.S. playing fields, so they looked for playing opportunities in Mexico. While some welcomed a more relaxed racial climate for professional competition, they also faced accusations of being a "pocho" or an "Americanized Mexican." The México-El Paso semipro baseball team, for example, comprised members with mixed citizenship status who traveled back and forth to Mexico and the United States, allowing them to connect to their Mexicanness in hybrid ways.

In *Becoming Mexican American*, George Sánchez argued that children of Mexican immigrants forged a new identity as Mexican Americans.[43] In contrast, in *Rebirth*, Douglas Monroy contended that Mexican immigrants and their children constructed a Mexican national identity in the United States.[44] These two competing historical trajectories have been the subject of much debate in Chicano/a history. Throughout *Deportes*, I show how Mexican and Mexican American identities were simultaneous rather than sequential amid the sporting Mexican diaspora. Sporting diasporas can help us rethink our understanding of hybrid identity in Chicano/a history.

WHY DOES SPORTS MATTER?

In *Deportes* I demonstrate that sports are central to the making of Latino/a identity, community, and civil rights. Latino/a athletes often penetrate the consciousness of young fans as role models to emulate well before civil rights leaders. Take, for example, Julio César Chávez, the professional Mexican boxer who gained widespread popularity among Mexican youth before they learned about the civil rights leader César Chávez. The successes of Latino/a athletes, both amateur and professional, reflect a wider sense of cultural pride and belonging to a local and national community. In this regard, more resources and opportunities for Latino and Latina sport participation are needed at all levels and in a wide variety of sports. The talent exists, but collegiate and professional sports teams and national governing bodies need to develop a pipeline for Latino/a sports talent ready to seize athletic opportunities.

American sports matter for people of color who have endured a long history of oppression and marginalization.[45] As Trinidadian intellectual and sportswriter C. L. R. James observed long ago about West Indian cricketers, sports can be a source of social solidarity and group and individual pride and confidence as well as a vehicle for transformative resistance.[46] In the wise words of Nelson Mandela, "Sport has the power to change the world. It has the power to inspire, the power to unite that little else has. . . . It is more powerful than government in breaking down racial barriers."[47] However, when the public thinks of sports and civil rights, they remain stuck in a black-white binary.[48] This book will educate the public about Mexican American civil rights and sports activism prior to the well-studied period of the 1960s. Although Mexican Americans faced discrimination and marginalization in the U.S. sports world, they used sports as a venue to redress and advance their rights. By forging transnational networks with Mexico, athletes empowered themselves and their communities and gained more leverage with U.S. institutions. In effect, sports became a driving force in shaping the political consciousness of Mexican Americans.

SOURCES AND ORGANIZATION OF THE BOOK

This book makes a case for a hemispheric approach to the study of sports across national borders. I consciously sought and found primary sources, read in two languages, and engaged with scholars and historiographies in both countries. This was no easy task since few sport archives exist in Mexico. Nevertheless, I found enough sources to shed light on the little-known athletic experiences of Mexicans across national borders. The following chapters rely on presidential papers, government agency records, immigration files, YMCA records, consul and diplomatic correspondence, sports publications, newspapers and magazines in Spanish and English, sport biographies, and other archival documents. Where there were gaps and omissions in written records, especially on female athletes, I relied on oral history interviews for insight into their everyday sporting experiences.

Deportes comprises six chapters, each organized chronologically and thematically with emphasis on one or more sports. Chapter 1 examines the rise of sports in Mexico and in México de afuera communities in Southern California. It focuses on the YMCA's promotion of physical education and sports to instill a "muscular Christianity" ideology among its middle-class male membership in Mexico City. In the United States, Anglo-American reformers attempted to Americanize Mexican immigrants via sports. Mexican immigrants and their children were also introduced to sports through mutual aid organizations, the Spanish-language press, and Mexican consulate offices. Although many embraced American sports, they did so while maintaining their culture, enhancing their national identity, and constructing a unique Mexican sporting culture.

Chapter 2 focuses on boxing, one of the most popular sports in Greater Mexico during the first half of the twentieth century, and how it helped shape a sporting Mexican diaspora. It examines the relationship between U.S. immigration policy, the boxing industries, and the construction of race, gender, and nationality in the experiences of Mexican prizefighters. Mexican prizefighters navigated an increasingly rigid U.S. immigration regime that prohibited entry to some and allowed entry to others under a temporary admittance system during the 1920s and 1930s. The U.S. boxing industry, with its teams of promoters, managers, matchmakers, and trainers, acted like a transnational corporation in the recruitment of "cheap" male boxing talent from Mexico to attract larger audiences and higher profits. I show that despite encountering exploitation and racialization by U.S. immigration and boxing authorities, Mexican prizefighters used their network, mobility, and visibility to make a living and represent their community and nation in a positive manner, with the hope of becoming world champions.

Chapter 3 focuses on baseball, another popular sport in Greater Mexico, which contributed toward the making of a sporting Mexican diaspora. It explores the local and transnational connections of baseball in Southern California and Mexico in the 1920s and 1930s. By focusing on Mexico–El Paso, a semiprofessional barnstorming team from Los Angeles, I show how Mexican American ballplayers forged transnational networks with the Mexican Baseball League to overcome racial and class barriers on the U.S. playing fields. Although Mexican women were discouraged from playing baseball, considered a "man's game" in both U.S. and Mexican society, they still found ways to become part of the national pastime. Despite deeply entrenched racial, class, and gender barriers, Mexican American women became *peloteras*, and in the process gained more freedom and developed their own sporting networks. Ultimately, male ballplayers forged transnational connections to the Mexican nation to overcome racial and class barriers on the U.S. playing fields, whereas peloteras were constrained by gender expectations and patriarchal structures that limited their mobility within and across the nation-state.

Chapter 4 uses the case of the Mexican Athletic Association of Southern California (MAASC) to examine the transnational sporting networks between Southern California and Mexico. MAASC organized sports leagues, tournaments, and exhibition matches as well as secured recreation facilities, provided entertainment, and offered other athletic opportunities. A unique feature of MAASC was its transnational ties with the Mexican government and its sports federation, Confederación Deportiva Mexicana. MAASC sports forged transnational ties with Mexico that allowed mostly male athletes to adopt a Mexican national identity outside of Mexico and others to adopt a Mexican American identity that connected them more closely with Southern California and American society in general. Ultimately, they created a hybrid sporting identity that helped to instill a new confidence among MAASC members to challenge the Los Angeles Department of Playground and Recreation to provide more recreation and sports programs for their community.

Chapter 5 shifts to the international arena to examine U.S.-Mexico relations through sports during World War II. It focuses on the little-known sports office within the Office of Inter-American Affairs (OIAA), led by Nelson Rockefeller to promote the Good Neighbor Policy with Mexico and Latin America. Despite the intentions of the OIAA to promote "good neighborliness" and "good sportsmanship" with Mexican sporting institutions, U.S. efforts represented a "soft power" attempt to achieve, impose, and consolidate U.S. cultural imperialism on Mexico. This chapter shows how Mexican athletes provided a counternarrative to claims of American exceptionalism in sports and used their athletic skills during "goodwill tours" in the United States to claim real and symbolic victory against their more powerful northern neighbor.

Chapter 6 returns to Southern California to examine the sporting experiences of Mexican Americans, both men and women, during and after World War II. It profiles three organizations—the Coordinating Council for Latin-American Youth, the Mexican American Movement, and the Mexican Athletic Union—and their efforts to combat juvenile delinquency and advance a civil rights agenda through sports. Mexican American women also stepped up to demonstrate their wartime patriotism through work and play. As they became independent wage earners, they began to participate in sports in higher numbers, including joining the All-American Girls Professional Baseball League. These Mexican American women used sports to exercise, travel, socialize, and redefined gender roles within the family and community. Some even adopted a "sportswoman" identity by traveling abroad to compete and developing a strong sense of physical confidence and empowerment. These women made remarkable athletic achievements that need to be recognized for advancing gender equity in the Mexican diaspora.

1 • DEPORTES, AMERICANIZATION, AND MEXICAN SPORTING CULTURE

Lamberto Álvarez Gayou was a leading sports promoter in Greater Mexico during the first half of the twentieth century. Born to a wealthy family in Mexico City, Gayou studied engineering in college but preferred to compete in the pentathlon and gymnastics at the Young Men's Christian Association (YMCA). His passion for sports motivated him to earn a master's degree in physical education at the University of California, Los Angeles.[1] To earn extra income, he wrote for the sports pages of *El Eco de Mexico* and *El Heraldo de México*. In his spare time, he organized baseball and basketball games for Circulo Latino Americano, one of many *mutualistas* that served the recreational needs of México de afuera.

In 1926, Gayou moved to New York City to write in English and Spanish for the Associated Press on Latin American sports. He wrote for the *Pan American Union Bulletin* about Latin American athletes "who have most highly distinguished themselves in the United States, winning athletic fame for the Latin race."[2] A devoted boxing fan, Gayou wrote about the early Mexican prizefighters who traveled from Mexico City to Los Angeles and New York City to fight in the big arenas with the hopes of becoming a world champion.[3] In 1929, he moved to Mexico City to become secretary of the Mexican Olympic Committee and head coach of the Military College. A year later, Gayou moved to Tijuana to be closer to family as the government's newly appointed director of athletics for the northern territory of Baja California.

Living and working in a border town, Gayou organized cross-border sporting exchanges with amateur baseball and basketball teams from Southern California. He staged Olympic tryouts for the track and field team and hosted Mexican Olympians to train in Tijuana several months before the 1932 Olympic Games in

Los Angeles.[4] Gayou served as manager of the Mexican Olympic team in Los Angeles and even proposed a "Latin American Olympic Games" to be held in Tijuana, but the idea failed due to limited funding and facilities.[5] Despite this unfulfilled goal, though, San Diego newspaper sports columnists praised Gayou for his "ability and energy to put his plans through."[6] Gayou was a "genius" sports promoter who preached "true sportsmanship" and "clean sports," but focused primarily in developing the Mexican male athlete. He once wrote, "The boys down in Mexico are doing things. They are advancing in every field of athletics in such fashion that I confidently predict that the day is not far distant when they will be stout rivals to their neighbors to the north."[7]

Gayou was referred to as the "Father of Athletics" in Mexico for launching a "peaceful revolution" in sports and physical education during the 1930s.[8] Following Mexican president Pascual Ortiz's resignation, Abelardo Rodríguez took over the presidency on September 4, 1932, and appointed Gayou as the director of the Department of Physical Education. In his first action "to make Mexico a sports-minded nation," Gayou made the junior pentathlon mandatory in public schools and hosted the international junior pentathlon championships in Mexico City.[9]

For his next task, Gayou encouraged the formation of amateur sports clubs modeled after the Amateur Athletic Union in the United States. On July 22, 1933, President Rodríguez signed a bill to establish the Confederación Deportiva Mexicana (CDM) and appointed Gayou to lead the nation's first sports federation and "develop physically the Mexican people and enhance the prestige of the nation."[10] Gayou pushed CDM to develop transnational sporting exchanges with the Mexican Athletic Association of Southern California, which I discuss in chapter 4.

After his two-year term with the federal government, Gayou returned to Mexicali, Baja California, with his wife to begin a new engineering job while also promoting sports and physical education along the border region. Five years later, in 1940, he returned to Mexico City as technical director of physical education and met with U.S. vice president Henry Wallace to share his inter-American sports proposal.[11] Gayou proposed a series of physical education, health education, sports, and recreational programs throughout the Americas.[12] One of these was adopted as part of the U.S. Good Neighbor Program during World War II, led by Rockefeller's Office of the Coordinator of Inter-American Affairs, which I discuss further in chapter 6. The other was the creation of the Pan American Institute of Physical Education to advise Latin American countries on health and physical education.

I begin this chapter with Lamberto Álvarez Gayou's biography to show how the rise of sports in the United States and Mexico was interwoven across national borders producing a Mexican sporting culture. The first part provides a brief overview of the rise of sports in Mexico, focusing on the YMCA's role in promoting

"American" sports and a "muscular Christianity" ideology among its middle-class Mexican male membership. Mexican citizens selectively embraced American sports to develop their athletic talent and make demands on the postrevolutionary Mexican government to provide more recreational and athletic opportunities. The second part examines Euro-American reformer efforts to attack the "Mexican problem" by using sports as a vehicle to achieve immigrant assimilation in the United States. Settlement house staff, YMCA secretaries, physical educators, and municipal employees sought to "Americanize" Mexican immigrants through baseball, basketball, and other American sports to make them "better citizens." The third part focuses on three México de afuera institutions—mutual aid organizations, the Spanish-language press, and the Mexican consulate office—that helped shape a Mexican sporting culture in Los Angeles. Ultimately, I argue that U.S. institutions introduced modern sports to Mexicans on both sides of the border to advance a muscular Christianity and Americanization ideology. Although Mexicans adopted American sports, they did so while maintaining their culture, enhancing their national identity, and constructing a unique Mexican sporting culture.

THE RISE OF *DEPORTES* IN MEXICO

Like the British Empire, the United States used sports to sell American goods, ideology, and culture abroad. U.S. imperial interests created an "athletic crusade" to spread muscular Christianity, hypermasculinity, racism, and commerce in its overseas territories of the Philippines, Hawaii, and Puerto Rico.[13] Foreign visitors jotted down their impressions about Mexico and created a "culture of empire" that legitimized the U.S. economic domination of Mexico and shaped popular attitudes about Mexicans in the United States.[14] By and large, Euro-Americans viewed Mexico as culturally inferior in the arena of sports. Despite their enthusiasm for sports, Mexicans needed coaching instruction in the areas of sportsmanship, physical training, and self-discipline. For example, travel writer Stuart Chase claimed that "the [Mexican] body receives little exercise in the form of sport." He charged that Mexicans should take advantage of "opportunities for games, races, and competitions in muscular skill."[15] For Chase, Mexicans required more bodily discipline and physical training under the watchful eye of Americans.

A common complaint by foreign journalists was that Mexicans lacked "good sportsmanship." Additionally, journalist Lewis Spence claimed, "The average Mexican is more of a gamester than a sportsman . . . the sporting spirit is altogether lacking in Mexico."[16] Compared to a gamester, a sportsman is competitive and has self-discipline. Furthermore, Wallace Thompson wrote, "The Mexican does not take kindly to, nor does he usually play well, games which involve contest. He is a bad loser and to this psychological trait can be probably be traced the fact that he is very likely to cheat."[17] Thompson added, "Mexico's recreations are . . . simple, childlike, seeking pleasure and fun first, and without any understanding of the more complicated Anglo-Saxon conception that play is something that is 'good for you.'"[18] Besides lacking "good sportsmanship," Mexicans supposedly lacked an understanding of the healthy benefits of sport activity. The racial discourse of the Mexican sporting body reinforced notions of white racial superiority that began with the U.S. imperial domination of Mexico.

After the United States acquired more than half a million square miles of Mexico's northern territory in 1848, the government stepped up efforts for an economic conquest of Mexico through an influx of U.S. capital in railroads, mining, smelting, and agriculture.[19] By the late nineteenth century, Mexico had become a target of this U.S. cultural imperialism. Under President Porfirio Díaz's long rule (1876–1911), Mexico opened its doors to American businessmen as well as writers, journalists, academics, physical educators, and sports promoters. The Porfirian elite sought to "persuade" the masses to embrace the leisure and sporting pastimes of the United States and Europe, but participation remained limited to foreign nationals and Mexican elites.[20] On September 5, 1896, the *Mexican Sportsman*, dedicated entirely to sports in Mexico, premiered. This weekly magazine announced to readers that "we do not intend to leave a town or city or district unrepresented, where there is anything of interest to the sporting world. If you take any interest in sport of any kind and if you have any news that is of general interest, send it to us."[21] Published in both English and Spanish, this sports magazine reflected the U.S. influence on Mexican sporting culture.

Under the Porfiriato regime, a majority of sport activity centered around a few private athletic clubs and YMCA branches in Mexico. The Reforma Athletic Club was one of the most popular venues for cricket, tennis, baseball, and track and field events.[22] It was the YMCA, however, according to William Beezley, that was "the most persistent, and ultimately the most successful, promoter of Anglo-American sports."[23] The organization became a chief promoter of gymnastics, basketball, swimming, track and field, volleyball, and other sports in Mexico. The YMCA began operations in 1891 by serving the recreational and religious needs of the American colony in Mexico City.[24] After several years of financial instability and lack of leadership, the International Committee of the National YMCA appointed George Babcock in 1902 as general secretary of the Railroad and City Young Men's Christian Association of Mexico City.[25] Three months after opening the first Y branch, Babcock reported on how "gambling, drinking and the social evil flourish to a truly frightful extent," and while "Mexicans, for some reason, are not so easily affected or so quickly overcome by these vices, but the average foreigner goes to pieces."[26] The branch was "confined to English-speaking young men, though it hoped soon to be able to establish an Association for the Spanish speaking young men."[27] With support from Mexico's vice president Ramón Corral (who served as chairman of the Advisory Committee of the Mexico City YMCA), Babcock opened a separate "Spanish speaking branch" in 1905 with a goal of developing the "whole Mexican man—body, mind, and spirit."[28] Five years later, President Díaz helped inaugurate a five-story building to merge the English- and Spanish-speaking branches and expand its physical education department.[29]

The YMCA combined physical education with Protestantism to promote a "muscular Christianity" ideology among its upper- to middle-class Mexican male membership.[30] Although the group admitted Catholic men with "good character," they had to abide by "the ideal of the Association to be a manly man, strong physically, intellectually, spiritually, and morally; a man that tries to serve his country, his fellow men and his God."[31] To avoid the ire of the Catholic Church, however, Mexican government officials advised Babcock to keep religious proselytizing to a minimum and instead promote physical education.[32] While most Euro-American secretaries spoke Spanish fluently, they viewed and treated Mexicans in a gendered, racialized, and paternalistic manner. "The great masses of [Mexican] people were in ignorance," Babcock argued, and thus "Mexican young men . . . are at the mercy of an environment that destroys rather than develops true manhood and real character."[33] The solution for Mexico, according to a YMCA brochure, was to teach them "wholesome sports." "The eagerness of the Mexicans for wholesome sports when introduced is remarkable. Mexico City now has innumerable clubs for baseball, football, basketball, tennis and other athletics, which are taking the place of the bull fight, the cock fight, and similar diversions."[34] Babcock recruited Richard Williamson from the University of Kansas to help develop a physical education department at the Mexico City YMCA. Trained under basketball's founder, James Naismith, Williamson "took across the border the first basketball ever seen south of the Rio Grande."[35] Williamson proclaimed that basketball would inculcate the "spirit of play" and address the moral and spiritual problems facing Mexico.[36] In 1919, the Mexico City Association formed the first men's basketball league with six teams competing for the Y championship.[37] According to Professor Andres Osuna (a YMCA member who became governor of Tamaulipas), the purpose of basketball was "teaching our men how to play the game according to the rules, how to act together under a recognized authority . . . we are learning what Americans call teamwork."[38] Speaking at the YMCA branch in New York, Williamson declared that "the principal need in Mexico today is the establishment of Y.M.C.A. houses in which to educate the men of Mexico in American ways."[39]

During the Mexican Revolution the YMCA continued to offer physical education and sports programs despite a reduction in member subscriptions and Bible classes.[40] It took the Mexican Revolution to launch a "revolution in recreation" and the Mexican Constitution of 1917 to promise its citizens a "right to physical culture and the practice of sports."[41] Revolutionary leader and president Venustiano Carranza promoted sports and physical education among youth to build a healthier, stronger, and more disciplined nation.[42] Carranza built the

National Stadium, and a decade later a worker-oriented sports center was named after him.[43] In the postrevolutionary period, sports became increasingly important to unify a divided nation under the banner of Mexican nationalism and to enhance the country's international stature.[44] The Mexican government also promoted physical education in remote rural areas in an attempt to convert Indian peasants into Mexican citizens through sports.[45]

Despite the support of the Mexican government, the Euro-American YMCA leadership continued to face religious, language, and cultural barriers in Mexico. The Mexico City Association grew in membership—from 300 in 1902 to 1,334 in 1918—and 850 people participated in a physical education program with a long waiting list.[46] This increasing demand spurred a staff shortage and pushed the YMCA to train and hire Mexican "native" secretaries.[47] As a teenager, Enrique Aguirre, who was born in Cuba and raised in Mexico City, became a YMCA member. Aguirre described himself as "an undersized bundle of energy and enthusiasm" who became a prominent physical education leader.[48] In 1914, Aguirre earned a scholarship to study physical education at the International YMCA Training College in Springfield, Massachusetts, and after graduation, he returned to Mexico City to take over as director of the Physical Education Department.[49] Within two years, Aguirre had expanded its sports programs, increased enrollment in physical education classes by 50 percent, improved the gymnasium equipment, installed a new locker system, and added more showers. The YMCA gym became a popular homosocial space for Mexican men, but admission required a complete physical examination because, according to Aguirre, "it presents an invaluable opportunity for helping many young men to start upon a path of social purity and clean living."[50] The YMCA campaign for social purity was about more than improving body cleanliness and personal hygiene and aimed to impress upon the Mexican men the value of civilization and manliness.[51]

Aguirre extended his work beyond the YMCA to advise government and education officials on how to develop sports throughout Mexico. He proudly boasted about his two basketball leagues displaying "fine sportsmanlike" behavior and "total absence of rowdyism."[52] Aguirre added his observation about "how some of our native Mexican boys play just as fair and square as any of their Anglo-Saxon cousins."[53] In 1924, he helped found the Mexican Olympic Committee and traveled with Mexican Olympians to compete at their first Olympic Games in Paris. Before departing for France, he took the national basketball team on an exhibition tour in the United States and Cuba. The Red Triangles team covered over 6,750 miles to promote international friendship between neighboring countries and to showcase their athletic talent.[54] The Mexican squad surpassed expectations and defeated the best college basketball teams in Texas and other states. Aguirre wrote that his players "are a fast, clean lot of boys, of whom we are justly proud and we feel positive that they will be able to represent—worthily—the highest ideals for which we stand."[55] The U.S. newspaper coverage of their matches reinforced stereotypes about Mexicans as "invaders" and "eaters of tama-les," but commended them for their speed and shot-making ability despite their short size; team members averaged a modest five feet seven inches in height.[56] As the new director of physical education at the National Autonomous University of Mexico and the public schools of Mexico City, Aguirre established the first Central American and Caribbean Games in 1926 and continued to "attack the leisure time problem" by organizing sporting events and building recreation centers and playgrounds throughout the city.[57]

GENDER AND SPORTS PARTICIPATION

A major challenge that Enrique Aguirre and other physical educators faced was encouraging women's participation in sports. In his address to the American Physical Education Association, Aguirre expressed his frustration that "it was harder to get Mexican girls to engage in strenuous sports than boys."[58] It was due to not a lack of interest but rather a rigid gender ideology that could be traced back to the Spanish conquest: women were socially conditioned to remain inside the home for homemaking and child-rearing purposes and actively discouraged from pursuing a career, education, and recreation. Indigenous women have a long history of sport participation, from the Mesoamerican ball games to the Olympic Games. Norwegian ethnographer Carl Lumholtz observed long ago that Tarahumara Indian women also took part in long-distance running as part of their cultural and religious traditions: "It is certainly a strange sight to see these sturdy amazons race heavily along with astonishing perseverance, when creeks and water-holes come in their way, simply lifting their skirts á la Diane and making short work of the crossing."[59] This account constructed the Tara-humaras as "the white man's Indian" who were uncivilized and primitive, but performed superhuman feats of endurance.[60] The Amazon-like physical development of Tarahumara women—runners cover hundreds of miles—caught the attention of Mexican government officials who sought to enlist them in Western-style marathon races in Mexico and the United States.[61]

In 1927, three women joined the Tarahumara men on a marathon run from San Antonio to Austin, Texas, attracting media coverage and crowds that gave them a standing ovation at the finish line. The following year, the Mexican Olympic Committee sent the Tarahumara runners to the Olympic Games in Amsterdam to bolster Mexico's image abroad, but the International Olympic Committee rejected the women's marathon as an event, and only two men ran the forty-two-kilometer race.[62] "We had to baptize them as Juan and Jose," recalled Enrique Aguirre about the two Tarahumara runners who became confused when a "pedaling melee" of bicycles interfered in the race, thus causing them to finish twelfth and thirteenth. "The sudden impact of civilization on these two primitives" was too much to withstand, according to Aguirre.[63] Consequently, the Mexican government used the Tarahumara Indian races to bolster its image abroad and promote Mexican nationalism, but as Keith Brewster suggested, these motives were mere "paternalistic tokenism."[64]

Although the Mexico City Association was a masculine space for physical exercise, male bonding, and networking, it allowed women to attend Bible classes and conduct physical exercise in the gymnasium. Oscar Castillón, physical education director at the Monterrey branch of the YMCA, described the new girls' volleyball team as "the new type of Mexican feminine youth—health, happy and full of energy."[65] Besides introducing volleyball to Monterrey, Castillón also wrote a widely circulated sports column that disproved myths about women playing sports.[66] "It is not true that sports hurt a woman or make her lose all her grace," explained Castillón, "what harms her is immobility and laziness."[67] Mexican women were not lazy but rather needed their parents' permission to play sports. The Mexican secretary at the Chihuahua YMCA branch added that "they had to beg their parents to allow them to learn to play the [basketball] games."[68] Increased interest in sports among women and girls prompted the Chihuahua YMCA to "have special days and hours when the women have the exclusive use of all athletic equipment, athletic fields, the pool and the showers."[69] After some received parental permission, they joined the new women's basketball league. The league grew to twelve teams when "the girls took things in their own hands and decided to play without asking the consent of their parents."[70]

The Mexico City Association reported on the increased demand for gymnastics and basketball instruction in their gymnasium, but limited space prompted calls for opening a branch of the Young Women's Christian Association (YWCA). In 1921, the YWCA sent Caroline Duval Smith to research the possibility of opening a branch in Mexico City, but she encountered staunch opposition from the Catholic Church.[71] Two years later, Smith returned with Elena Landazuri, a former student of Jane Addams who was born and raised in Mexico City and became the first general secretary of the Mexico YWCA.[72] Developing middle-class women into homegrown leaders was crucial in developing health education, English and literacy classes, and girls' clubs. Not until they opened their own building in 1927 did the YWCA begin to offer physical education and sports programs for its largely middle-class female membership.

The postrevolutionary Mexican government encouraged lower-class Mexican men and women to take up physical exercise as part of building better bodies and a better nation.[73] Modeled after the YMCA, the National Youth Association was the first national organization to include women in their sports programs.[74] In 1923, President Obregón (1920–1924) appointed Dr. Jose Peralta as the first director of physical education under the Department of Public Education because of his medical background and physical education training in the United States.[75] This new office prepared males and females to teach physical education classes twice a week for fifty minutes at rural schools and traveling "cultural missions."[76] Historian Mary Kay Vaughan contends that the rural school system emphasized the team sports of baseball and basketball to promote hygiene, sobriety, and cooperation appropriate for the modern economy.[77] Between 1924 and 1936, the Mexican federal government integrated physical education into the public school system that reinforced gender roles. The pages of *Educación Física* magazine, for example, celebrated the male physical prowess and encouraged females to practice gymnastics to develop their femininity, grace, and delicacy.[78] The 1930 national figures revealed that over two thousand athletic clubs existed throughout Mexico with 136,618 members (one percent of the country's total population), 114,905 men and 21,713 women.[79] Two years later, women's participation had more than doubled to 54,861. This increase was in part due to the Mexican press's gradual acceptance of women's participation in sports.[80] The most popular sports among Mexican women were gymnastics, volleyball and basketball. In 1931, more women joined the newly formed Women's Basketball Federation, which quickly grew to more than thirty-one teams within three years. This new league helped develop the athletic skills of Mexican women who competed in the 1935 Central American and Caribbean Games in El Salvador where they won gold medals in basketball and volleyball.[81] Chabelita Silva, president of the Women's Basketball Federation, helped prepare the team for victory with a strict sleeping and practice routine, even though she and other female athletes had to prepare meals for the entire Mexican delegation.[82]

The widespread belief that women playing sports was a "great sin" was debunked by Lamberto Álvarez Gayou. In his 1932 address to the First International Recreation Congress in Los Angeles, Gayou asserted that "this theory has been completely exploded amongst the weaker sex, who are showing great competitive spirit and a great sporting instinct."[83] During the same year, Maria Uribe Jasso and Eugenia Escudero became the first Mexican women to participate in the Olympic Games, in javelin and fencing, respectively. Although Mexican women did not win an Olympic medal until 1968, they competed in domestic and international basketball tournaments. Writing in his monthly sports magazine *La Afición*, Fray Nano proclaimed the increased popularity of women's basketball: "Female basketball is not a just provincial element anymore, more and more women are taking up this sport."[84] In chapter 6, I discuss how the 1943 National Girls Champion Basketball team Las Politas toured for three months across the United States and Canada, all the while competing and impressing basketball opponents and sportswriters.

AMERICANIZATION, SPORTS, AND MEXICAN IMMIGRANTS

Between 1880 and 1920, American sports played a vital role in the construction of nationalism, whiteness, and masculine identity. President Theodore Roosevelt was a staunch advocate for sports and recreation for white American men in order to obtain a "vigorous masculinity."[85] To avoid "overcivilized effeminacy," Roosevelt instructed American men to take up "vigorous manly out-of-door sports, such as mountaineering, big-game hunting, riding, shooting, rowing, football and kindred games."[86] He became enamored with the heroic cowboy figure that according to Americo Paredes allowed him to "prove his manliness."[87] The strenuous exercise from outdoor sports could potentially help men prepare for the battlefield. In his famous 1899 speech, Roosevelt coined the term "strenuous life" to urge white American men to prepare for military takeovers and domination of foreign lands. The term was associated not only with America's imperialistic foreign policy but also with race and manhood. According to Gail Bederman, "American manhood—both the manly race and individual white men—must retain the strength of their Indian-fighter ancestors, or another race would prove itself more manly and overtake America in the Darwinian struggle for the world's most dominant race."[88] In particular, nonwhite people from conquered territories were considered a racial and gendered threat to white American manhood.

Mexicans that remained in the conquered territories of the Southwest had no choice but to live a "strenuous life" by working for agriculture, railroads, mining, and manufacturing industries. The Mexican body has long served as a vehicle for cheap labor for American industries, one that is overworked, underpaid, and physically strong for digging canals, picking crops, climbing ladders, and building houses. We rarely see the Mexican body performing a physical activity outside the workplace, especially in sports and recreation. A common racist belief in the early part of the twentieth century held that Mexicans were physically inferior and mentally unfit for sports competition.[89]

Scholars have shown how intelligence testing of Mexican children led to an inferior and unequal education that reinforced their subordinate role in American society.[90] Similarly, physical educators conducted athletic ability studies on the Mexican population that influenced racial thinking about their athleticism. Eugenics ideology had a major influence on the field of physical education since both were concerned with improving weak bodies for the betterment of the race.[91] Proponents of eugenics in the United States and Latin America manipulated this racist ideology for nation-building purposes and to enact strict immigration laws, forced sterilization programs and race betterment campaigns.[92] A majority of physical education research in American universities reflected a class, gender, and racial bias. Members of the American Physical Education Association (APEA), a professional organization founded to promote physical education in schools and colleges, endorsed a system of physical measurement testing to make claims about the white race as the most racially superior and physically fit. Physical educators advocated anthropometric measurement studies of the human body to establish an ideal racial type that valorized the clean, healthy white male body. The female body received attention in physical education journals but only in relation to beauty, motherhood, and femininity.[93]

Secretary of the APEA and a former basketball coach at the University of Michigan, Elmer D. Mitchell, published a three-part series titled "Racial Traits in Athletics" in the *American Physical Education Review*.[94] Mitchell made scientific observations of "15 different races" and ranked them in order of their potential contributions to athletics. Native-born white Americans were at the very top because "the American athlete is the greatest in the world . . . [and] has the physical vigor of a hustling environment and the confidence which comes from masterful success."[95] Close behind were the English, Irish, and Germans, who showed high levels of physical performance. Then, "the Latin" and "the Negro" athlete was in the second tier, excluded from the "American" category and described with the worst racial stereotypes. African American athletes were "unassertive," "lazy," and physically "heavier in the upper than in the lower part of the body." The "Latin" athlete, including the French, Italian, and Spaniard, was more emotionally driven and "vivacious, lively, and impulsive as compared with the more deliberate Northern type." Spaniards, however, had less self-control than the French and Italian, according to Mitchell, "as shown by the bullfights of Mexico and Spain."[96] The bottom tier included the "average Latin American" athlete that "while a sport lover prefers the role of a spectator to that of player" because "the Indian in him chafes at discipline and sustained effort, while the Spanish side is proud to a fault; and his pride [and] disposition makes team play difficult."[97] The mixed racial heritage of the Latin American and Mexican athletes was deemed a physical and mental impediment to their athleticism. Other physical measurement studies demonstrated how race, science, and physical education were inextricably linked with major implications for Mexican participation in school sports.[98]

THE SO-CALLED MEXICAN PROBLEM

As Mexican immigration increased during the 1920s, the so-called Mexican problem became a major concern among settlement house workers, religious leaders, educators, and politicians.[99] Historians have examined the racialized and gendered dimensions of the "Mexican problem" in the areas of education, health, nutrition, and housing, but ignored sports and recreation.[100] According to Gilbert González the phrase was already commonly used in Mexico before it crossed borders to shape U.S. attitudes and policies toward Mexican immigrants.[101] A leading proponent of this transnational discourse was Protestant missionary Robert McLean, who wrote about "the problem of Mexican ignorance and lack of initiative" in the area of recreation.[102] McLean elaborated on the Mexican "play" problem in *The Northern Mexican*, where he claimed that "the play life of the Mexican people has not been developed. Within recent years in the city districts of

Mexico, athletics have begun to take a very strong hold upon the Mexican people, but aside from bull fighting and cock fighting, the Mexican up to a few years ago has not known anything about recreation."[103] He recommended that U.S. institutions offer more "good types of recreation" in parks and playgrounds and oppose "bad" billiard rooms and dance halls to assimilate the Mexican immigrant. University of Southern California sociologist Emory Bogardus, who published widely on seemingly all things Mexican, agreed with McLean: "Wholesome recreation for Mexican immigrants is largely missing. The main amusements are talking and siestas, cheap motion pictures, playing pool, dancing, boxing matches, gambling and cock-fighting."[104] According to Bogardus, boxing was a dangerous and unwholesome sport. And yet, as the next chapter will show, Mexican immigrants still gravitated toward the boxing world.

By the 1940s, the eugenics movement began to lose influence because of the horrors of Nazi Germany, so physical educators shifted toward considering cultural, familial, and environmental factors for researching the physical development of Mexican American students. One study found that Mexican students desired to play sports but lacked parental support because they "object to their children playing because they send them to school to study and not to play."[105] Another study compared the athletic skills of Euro-American and Mexican American male students in a junior high school and found that "Anglo Americans were decidedly superior in learning basketball skills while the Latin Americans seemed to be superior on the softball throw for distance and the standing long jump."[106] A California school principal recommended forming a baseball team for Mexican boys because "these young fellows need wholesome activity and are really hungry, with the same hunger of their elders, for the better things in life."[107] Another school study found that Mexican American students have potential to become "good athletes" but "the Mexican American boy is not able to compete successfully against Caucasians and others . . . [because] he develops a defensive attitude."[108] This apparent character flaw, claimed the researcher, required "being dependent upon the physical educator being willing to help the [Mexican American] boy."[109] These researchers recommended that physical educators teach Mexican Americans athletic skills and the value of good sportsmanship.

Additionally, physical educators blamed socioeconomic conditions and traditional gender ideology. In 1945, Ed Horner, a physical educator, conducted a survey of recreation directors in Mexican American communities in Phoenix and Los Angeles. Recreation directors found that work obligations prevented sports participation because "a goodly number of the men are occupied with various types of heavy manual labor during the day. Thus, they may feel too fatigued to want to engage in recreational facilities."[110] Once they become motivated to participate in recreation activities, according to Horner, they become a "sports-loving group" choosing to play baseball, softball, basketball, boxing, and football.[111] Recreation directors must also deal with authoritarian parents who refuse to let their daughters attend a recreation center because they "feel that the young girls should be chaperoned wherever they go."[112] For this reason, most girls participate in "social recreational affairs" and "non-athletic tasks."[113] Mexican parents feared that if their daughters became "sports conscious" like their brothers they would adopt loose sexual mores and bring dishonor to the family. Despite narrowly defined gender roles, Mexican girls found ways to participate in sports.

AMERICANIZATION THROUGH SPORTS

The U.S. entry into World War I and the drive for national unity intensified Americanization campaigns to assimilate the foreign-born in public schools, settlement houses, churches, workplaces, and community centers. Americanization programs aimed at Mexican immigrants and their children have received attention by historians, but mostly focused on transforming their native language, homemaking, child-rearing, religious, and health practices.[114] We also know that California public schools became training grounds for the Americanization of Mexican children.[115] Little attention, however, has been paid to the role of sports as an Americanization agent for immigrants to the United States.[116] A wide coalition of settlement house workers, progressive educators, and municipal employees united on the need to establish playgrounds where the city's immigrants could play under supervised conditions. The playground movement began in the United States as a white middle-class response to the negative effects of industrialization on poor immigrant children from crowded tenement neighborhoods in East Coast cities.[117]

As Mexican immigrants settled into urban barrios across the United States, playground reformers were prepared to mold them into their own rigid vision of order, morality, and spirituality through organized forms of recreation. In Los Angeles, a Playground Commission was formed in 1904, with a mission of "prevention and control of juvenile delinquency and to provide wholesome and constructive play and recreation for youth, in supervised playgrounds, as an alternative to play in the city streets."[118] A year later, the Violet Street Playground opened with a clubhouse, outdoor gym, baseball diamond, basketball and handball courts, swings, sandboxes, and gardens.[119] Los Angeles playground commissioner Bessie Stoddert announced, "The community is awakening to the fact that a city should seize its opportunity to make better citizens by providing recreation of the right kind and under proper auspices."[120] The city's first playground attracted "many races," as reported by the Los Angeles Times: "One would have to travel far to find another such [Violent Street] playground, where Mexican, Negro, Japanese, Chinese, Russian, German and American children meet for recreation."[121] As Mark Wild suggested, "The integrated environment of the playgrounds stood in contrast to the enthnoracial restrictions placed on other Los Angeles recreation facilities."[122] The male playground director and female assistant encouraged interethnic mixing but separated recreational programs by gender—baseball, basketball, and volleyball teams for boys and sewing, basket weaving, folk dances, and light gym work for girls.[123] Nonetheless, in smaller cities like Oxnard white officials designed a "Mexican playground" to reinforce "mundane racism" that made segregated playing an ordinary part of life.[124]

Los Angeles recreation officials targeted immigrants in an effort to drag them away from autonomous street play and "illicit" amusements to supervised recreation centers where they could control and convert them into law-abiding, physically active, and "better" citizens.[125] "The playground had come to be a great factor in Americanization," one Los Angeles playground supervisor declared. "When an alien begins to participate with others in play he is on his way to good citizenship."[126] By 1925 voters approved a new city charter that created the Los Angeles Department of Playground and Recreation (LADPR) and funded more playgrounds and recreation centers and purchased additional miles of public beaches.[127] The city mayor appointed George Hjelte and a five-member citizen commission to reorganize the department into eight divisions: municipal sports, aquatics (beaches and swimming pools), campgrounds, music, construction and maintenance, playground and recreation centers, dramatics and pageantry, and industrial recreation.[128] Hjelte made it a priority to promote Americanization in a speech to the Friday Morning Club: "While we cannot propose a regular program of citizenship, supervised recreation centers can be a determining factor in promoting good Americanism."[129] The department's motto depicted an image of a "safe supervised playground" with the caption "The Playground—A Haven of Protection from Childhood's Dangers." In contrast to the center image of a "safe playground," eight circles contain scenes of delinquency, loneliness, unhappiness, poor health, lack of supervision, lack of cooperation, car accidents, and un-Americanism.[130] "Supervised play" was a common catchphrase used by municipal recreation officials to cloak their Americanization efforts inside playgrounds and recreation centers.[131]

The LADPR's sports division developed amateur sports programs that included athletic leagues, clubs, and tournaments. Amateur sports, as opposed to professional, aimed to keep lower classes away from country clubs and to popularize cultural ideals of American nationalism.[132] As the first director, D. Webster Lott encouraged more participation over more competition because it would "contribute to the development of good sportsmanship and citizenship."[133] Lott observed the growing interest in sports among "numerous foreign groups such as Mexicans, Slavonians, Spaniards, Germans and Japanese."[134] To encourage sport participation among immigrant groups, Lott created separate municipal associations for "international groups in Los Angeles."[135] According to the 1930 Annual Report, "The Mexicans [are] entering enthusiastically into American sports [and] taking part in municipal recreation centers ... and the city's playgrounds."[136] In comparison to immigrant groups, LADPR systematically excluded African Americans from sports programs including swimming pools. It took a two-year lawsuit from Ethel Prioleau, an African American mother of two children, to force LADPR and the City Council to integrate all city pools after the Los Angeles County Superior Court ruled in her favor in 1931.[137]

Playground supervisors relied on gendered assumptions about the physical abilities of boys and girls to shape their recreation work. Boys were directed toward recreation that emphasized masculine physical toughness, war-like behavior, and competition, whereas girls were directed toward recreation that promoted beauty, gentility, and socializing. In a study of Mexican girls' amusements in East Los Angeles, the researcher found that "the interest shown by the girls for games and for the gymnasium present an opportunity to cultivate in the girls a desire for more wholesome types of recreation than dancing or movies."[138] This presented an opportunity for the All Nations Church to introduce supervised recreation of swimming parties, picnics, and mountain hikes. Even when Mexican girls expressed interest in sport participation, they faced parental disapproval. One playground director described how Mexican parents discouraged sport participation among their daughters because "they consider indulgences in sports by girls as not becoming to their sex."[139] The "familial oligarchy" ideology used to control women's sexuality within Mexican families often extended into recreation and sports.[140]

In terms of women's sports, LADPR excluded girls and women until 1929, when they created a separate division for girls' and women's activities that included rhythmics, handicraft, athletics, social recreation, and mother clubs.[141] The division relied on the assumption that girls did not like competition, so they organized weekly "play days" at playgrounds that included archery, putting golf, swimming, and paddle tennis. According to the director of girls and women's activities, "In planning play days there is no competition of playground against playground, but rather groups of girls organized into teams at the time and playing with each other is the spirit of the day."[142] A promotional magazine featured white women playing basketball and softball but reminded readers that "participants engage in athletic events in which they play *with, not against* each other."[143] Municipal sports programs did not encourage Mexican women's participation, leaving a void for settlement houses to introduce them to American sports.

SETTLEMENT HOUSES AND YMCAS

Settlement houses were important reform institutions that extended Americanization efforts into sports and recreation programs to keep immigrant children away from criminal activity and to teach them American values of competition, discipline, and teamwork.[144] The famous Hull House, founded in 1889 by Jane Addams, sought to help immigrant families that settled in neighborhoods of Chicago. As a staunch advocate of sports and physical exercise for young men and women, Addams helped found the Playground Association of America to promote municipal recreation across the nation.[145] One of Addams's protégés was Anita Jones, who developed educational and recreational programs for Mexican youth in Chicago.[146] Jones learned Spanish while living in Mexico and returned to complete her doctorate at the University of Chicago.[147] In 1930, Jones became the director of the San Diego Neighborhood House and expanded its services to Mexican families in the Logan Heights neighborhood.[148] These services included classes in cooking, dancing, sewing, hygiene, and English language and citizenship.[149] But these services came at a price. Immigrant participants were expected to abandon their native customs, language, and loyalties and assimilate into mainstream American society. These expectations were not met as intended, as local historian Maria García convincingly argues, Mexican residents selected only those services that were pragmatic to meet their economic needs and allow them to retain their Mexican cultural values.[150] Instead, Mexican settlement members began making demands on "La Neighbor" such as adding Spanish books to the library, performing Los Pastores Christmas play, and singing Mexican songs in China poblana outfits to Jane Addams during her visit.[151]

Children of Mexican immigrants were not shy about learning to play American sports at the Neighborhood House. Mexican boys learned boxing, basketball, wrestling, and baseball under coach Bill Breitenstein, who left minor league baseball to become athletic director in the early 1920s.[152] The English sports media praised coach Breitenstein's ability to transform the rowdy behavior of Mexican boys by teaching them "the fundamentals of our national pastime."[153] According to the *San Diego Union*, "At first, he found the players rather apt to pick fights, for some of them were of the 'hard boiled' type. His idea was to teach them to play fair at all times and today the Neighborhood House team represents one of the cleanest ball teams in the city."[154] The racist implication that these boys were dirty was linked to the common perception of the Mexican sporting body as diseased, unhygienic, and physically inferior.[155] Chapter 3 will show that in fact Mexican men and women used baseball and softball to challenge this racial thinking and transform the sport.

Settlement houses introduced Mexican girls to some sporting activities as part of their services but were marginalized within physical education and recreation programs that privileged boys. At the Settlement House in Pasadena, for example, a spacious baseball, football, and basketball playing field, located in the backyard, was intended for Mexican boys "who were given coaching in various sports," but Mexican girls were instructed in crafts, sewing, and other recreational activities to "keep them out of trouble."[156] Fears that coed sports and games may lead to illicit sexual relations prompted some settlement houses to segregate them by gender. The Episcopal Church of Los Angeles built a Neighborhood Settlement House on East Ninth Street known as the Men's House, whereas the Wilson

Street settlement house was the Women's House.[157] The Men's House sponsored a baseball team known as Neighborhood A.C. that traveled to San Diego to play against a team with the same name.[158] The Wilson Street settlement house encouraged Mexican girls in participate in "suitable sports" for women. "For girls we have a volleyball and basketball team," described a 1927 annual report, but only "meet on play days with other social centers."[159] These "play days" discouraged competition and confined Mexican girls to milder team sports.[160] Mexican girls and women broke gender conventions, however, by playing baseball and other "manly" sports.

Like settlement houses, YWCA branches offered recreation and sporting activities for Mexican girls and women, but with religious overtones and a high admission fee. The International Institute of the YWCA in Los Angeles employed an international staff that spoke fourteen languages "to help the foreign born become adjusted to America and her institutions."[161] The Boyle Heights building was large enough for Bible study, Americanization classes, girls clubs and dormitories, but had little room for sports and recreation. After the YWCA opened a gymnasium and swimming pool at the Hotel Figueroa building, they developed an extensive physical education program for the "Would be Super-Girls."[162] The 25 cent admission fee, however, plus the high cost of gymnastics and swimming classes made it too expensive for Mexican girls and women who worked in low-paying jobs and contributed to the family income.[163] Nevertheless, Mexican women, like Japanese Americans and African Americans, used the YWCA for camaraderie and recreation that allowed them to develop a lively social world and extensive sporting network in Los Angeles.[164]

The YMCA duplicated its work in Mexico City across the country in Tampico, Monterey, and Chihuahua and along the U.S.–Mexico border. Servando I. Esquivel grew up at the Chihuahua City YMCA but then fled to El Paso during the Mexican Revolution and dedicated his efforts toward building a Mexican branch of the YMCA.[165] The first Mexican association was established in El Paso, Texas, in 1915 and within three years had secured its own building that served over a thousand members.[166] The success of the El Paso Mexican Y received national attention with the help of Esquivel, who established the Mexican Frontier Committee in 1919 to assist in establishing similar branches along the border. Mexican immigrants "need the touch of Christian influences of this country," Esquivel wrote, because "if they are helping to increase the wealth of this country, they are entitled to something more than wages. We mean by this better housing conditions, educational opportunities, and health and recreational advantages."[167] He convinced the YMCA leadership to allocate funding to open Mexican branches in nearby Smeltertown as well as in Metcalf, Tucson, and Miami, Arizona.[168]

In other southwestern states, the YMCA took a different approach by encouraging branch secretaries to form a Committee on Mexican Work with funding from the Pacific Southwest Area Council, a regional division covering California, Nevada, Utah, Arizona, New Mexico, and West Texas. In a 1934 speech to the Pacific Southwest Area Council meeting, secretary Forrest Knapp reminded delegates that while the YMCA had "been generous in extending service to the young men in foreign lands," they "should also help meet the needs of similar groups of young men in the home field." He cited a Mexican immigrant's complaint directed to a YMCA supervisor: "The YMCA will serve us in Mexico, but when we reach the United States it does not seem to be interested in us."[169] In response, the area council formulated a plan for California Y branches titled the "Mexican YMCA Program for California," authored by Richard Williamson, former general secretary of Mexico YMCA, that outlined a series of best practices. These included organizing boys' clubs, promoting athletics and health education, conducting youth conferences, sending them to a summer camp, organizing friendship tours to Mexico, assimilating Mexican youth into church groups, and developing "a limited number of leaders for community work among their own nationality."[170] The YMCA Committee on Mexican Work produced a trifold brochure with a Mexican boy on the cover with the caption "Mexican Youth ... Whither Bound?"[171] The insert included photos of committee members, the boys' camp, a football championship team, and Mexican Youth Conference attendees and conference leaders dressed in suits with a Y triangle.

Although the YMCA professed a belief in "Christian brotherhood," they maintained Jim Crow separatism with African Americans, who built their own associations and cultivated their own leaders.[172] The LA black community raised enough money to build their own YMCA building on Twenty-Eighth Street and Central Avenue.[173] Unlike African Americans who maintained more autonomy over their own association, Mexican Americans were more dependent on the YMCA. This did not mean they failed to assert their agency or make demands on the YMCA. Take, for example, the cases of Tom García, Juan Acevedo, and Gualberto Valadez. García was born and raised in Van Nuys, California, and became active in the San Fernando YMCA branch and worked as the director of the Delano Street Playground before attending Whittier College.[174] García approached Knapp for financial support to attend the YMCA training school at Whittier College and received a scholarship. After graduation, the YMCA hired García as the executive secretary of Mexican YMCA clubs of Southern California. One of García's duties was to help organize Mexican clubs within YMCA branches and serve as an advisor for the Mexican Older Boy's Youth Conferences, which began in 1934.

Gualberto (Bert) Valadez, who had previously worked at the San Francisco YMCA, organized the Mexican Y Club at the Downtown Los Angeles YMCA in the early 1930s. He wrote in the *Mexican Voice* about how twenty-five Mexican members did not know each other until they were brought together at the Mexican Youth Conferences.[175] After he left his job at the YMCA Los Angeles, Valadez became the director of physical education at La Jolla Junior High School, in

Placentia, California, where he used sports to keep Mexican students in school and coached an all-Mexican girls' softball team and boys' basketball team that won several county championships.[176] Club president Juan Acevedo, an art student and track athlete at UCLA, stressed the "spiritual, mental, social, and physical condition of the Mexican young men" in order to "improve the condition of the Mexican people."[177] The club's athletic program became a model for other YMCA branches and participated in the annual basketball tournament at the Mexican Youth Conference. The YMCA-sponsored Mexican Youth Conferences became the forerunner of the Mexican American Movement, a college student organization incorporated in 1942 whose motto was "Progress through Education."[178] From Mexico City to Los Angeles, Mexican secretaries transformed the YMCA into a vehicle for sport participation, cultural expression, and ethnic identity formation. The bilingual *Mexican Voice* publication and Mexican American Movement emerged from the Mexican YMCA conferences and promoted not only education but also sports for Mexican American youth.

MEXICAN SPORTING CULTURE

During the 1920s the Spanish-language press, mutual aid organizations, and the Mexican consulate office promoted a transnational *Mexicanidad*, one that encouraged the Mexican immigrant population to maintain their language, show loyalty to the Mexican government, and most of all remain firmly rooted in Mexican culture and identity. The term *México de afuera* initially applied to political exiles in the United States who fled the Mexican Revolution and later was extended to economic migrants who came in larger numbers after the revolution.[179] Although both groups intended to return to their homeland when conditions improved, others opted to remain and (re)imagine and (re-)create Mexicanidad within a U.S. local or regional context.[180] Mexican migrants turned to Mexican folklore, Spanish-language theater, cinema, and musical traditions, and Fiestas Patrias and other cultural celebrations as way to reidentify with Mexico and with becoming Mexican. According to Douglas Monroy, sports also became a "passion" of México de afuera communities.[181] The major institutions that helped shape a Mexican sporting culture included mutual aid organizations, the Spanish-language press, and the Mexican consulate office.

La Opinión's sports page played an important role in the rise of sports in Greater Mexico. Its coverage of athletes and sporting events in Greater Mexico countered the negative stereotypes about the sporting Mexican body. The female athletic body, however, was highly sexualized and evaluated according to physical appearance and dress, as opposed to actual athletic skill or talent. Like mainstream American newspapers, *La Opinión* devoted more sports news coverage to increase subscription rates and advertising revenue during the golden era of sports. Ignacio Lozano founded the paper in 1926 after noticing an increase of

Los Angeles subscribers to his San Antonio newspaper, *La Prensa*, and rapid growth in the Mexican population.[182] *La Opinión* printed a daily sports page titled *Deportes*, covering league standings, athlete profiles, team scores, and international sporting events. A content analysis of *La Opinión* editorial and news coverage between 1926 and 1929 found 29 percent of headlines related to sports, radio, and entertainment, compared to 28 percent Mexican news, 13.7 percent U.S. news, and 11.5 percent Mexicans in the United States.[183]

Sports editors and writers at *La Opinión* played an essential role in Mexican participation in sports, from the amateur level to the professional. Lozano recruited sports editors from Mexico City to appeal to a wider readership beyond Los Angeles and to reflect its largely middle-class ideology. He hired Ignacio F. Herrerías as the first sports editor who wrote a weekly column, *Comentarios Deportivos* (sports commentary), under the pen name "Kayo."[184] Two years later he changed the column to *Por El Mundo Del Deporte* (the sporting world), writing about international sporting events. Herrerías reprinted entire columns from his friend Fray Nano, who covered the Central American and Caribbean Games in his sports newspaper *La Afición*.[185] Herrerías returned to Mexico City in 1932 to write for *El Excélsior* and start his own sports magazines, *El Gráfico* and *Mujeres y Deportes*.[186] After Herrerías, Rafael Ybarra became sports editor and reported on the 1932 Olympic Games.[187] A year later, José Hernández Llergo joined the editorial staff and wrote the popular *En La Maraña del Deporte* (in the tangle of sports) column under the pen name "Makanazo."[188] Llergo remained at *La Opinión* for ten years, then returned to Mexico City to join the staff of *Hoy* magazine, founded by his brother Regino and cousin José Pagés, who also worked briefly as *La Opinión* staff reporters.[189] These sport editors espoused a "racial uplift" message in their writings, encouraging readers to learn the values of self-help, good sportsmanship, and patriarchal authority through sports participation.[190]

La Opinión journalists also covered the local sporting scene and developed a close relationship to readers. Boxing fans looked forward to reading the weekly column of Luis Magaña, considered one of the best boxing writers in Los Angeles. Born in Morelia, Michoacán, Mexico, Magaña grew up in Los Angeles playing sports, especially baseball and boxing. He recalled his first visit to the newspaper's headquarters "with a desire to get his team's results published on the sports page, so that their baseball experience was widely recognized."[191] Although he played baseball, he loved boxing even more. He founded the Evergreen Boxing Club and organized fights every Wednesday night.[192] It was Magaña who convinced Herrerías to devote more coverage to boxing shows staged every day of the week, except Sunday, across Southern California. After he joined the sports staff in 1930, he began covering the boxing scene at the Olympic Auditorium.[193] When he arrived with his press pass, he was denied entry and was told to purchase a ticket: "They told me that they only granted that privilege to 'American' newspapers." Itching to pick a fight, Magaña threatened that he and fellow reporters would give them no publicity because of their racist behavior: "Curiously, it was a bad boxing card with few spectators, but they believed it was the fault of La Opinión. So, the next day Olympic officials showed up with press passes."[194] Soon thereafter, he was hired to oversee public relations and outreach to the Latino community.[195] Magaña became known as "Mister Olympic" and was responsible for bringing Hollywood movie stars like Gilbert Roland, Lupe Vélez, and Anthony Quinn to the fights. Magaña also became the official interpreter for prizefighters from Mexico.[196] "He would go to Mexico to have them sign the contracts," recalled his nephew. "He did everything including working the ticket booths."[197]

Another sports journalist who joined La Opinión was Rodolfo "Rudy" García, who wrote a popular weekly column called Esquina Neutral (neutral corner) from his corner newsroom office. Born in Monterrey, Mexico, to a large family, García started working as a newspaper boy, lottery ticket vendor, and shoe shiner at an early age. After his family moved to San Antonio, Texas, he continued selling newspapers until he met Lozano, who offered him a job in Los Angeles. After moving there he worked his way through the newspaper from printing press assistant to sports reporter. Although he started writing about boxing with his "Sombras de Fistiana" column, he later switched to write more about baseball.[198] On April 25, 1943, García stepped in to become sports editor when José Hernández Llergo announced his departure to Mexico. After World War II, García shifted to covering Latino players in the Pacific Coast League and major leagues.[199]

La Opinión encouraged its readers to be proud of their Mexican heritage through a variety of "culturally reinforcing activities" that included Mexican sports leagues and figures.[200] The newspaper also understood the practical reality of adapting to life in a foreign environment, such as learning English and American habits and forming clubs and organizations.[201] La Opinión sportswriters encouraged the formation of sports clubs and reminded athletes to conduct themselves in a manner that reflected positively on both their local Mexican community and the Mexican nation. In a 1930 column titled "The Organization of Sports Clubs Is Missing in Los Angeles," Llergo lauded the YMCA and Carranza Sports Center as exemplary sports institutions in Mexico City and instructed readers to follow "the good sports organizing that exists in the capital of Mexico" because it would "be a great education for the fans in Los Angeles" and "a priceless value if only our compatriots could organize similar institutions."[202] This column revealed the interconnections between Mexico City and Los Angeles in shaping a Mexican sporting culture. The call for more sporting institutions to serve the recreational needs of México de afuera communities then grew louder with the advent of the 1932 Olympics in Los Angeles.

Female sports journalists were absent from the male-dominated sports department of La Opinión and other Spanish-language newspapers across Greater Mexico. Despite the rise of the "modern" woman in the 1920s, Ignacio Lozano criticized women who engaged in masculine activities, including sports.[203] This meant not that Lozano's two newspapers ignored women but that the sports coverage was more concerned with female spectators, sexualized bodies, appropriate women's sports, and athletic performances that subscribed to a narrow definition of femininity. One *La Opinión* article prescribed swimming, tennis, and basketball as more appropriate for women and discouraged track and field because "makes females acquire an aspect of *marimachismo* that is obviously repulsive."[204] Besides privileging female athletes who subscribed to a heterosexual femininity, stories appeared on the sexualization of the sportswoman. For example, *La Opinión* and *La Prensa* published articles that claimed that sports enhanced women's beauty and charm.[205] Another article praised the increased participation of "las guapas chicas" (pretty girls) in swimming, volleyball, and basketball, but then added, "This desire of the Mexican woman to take an active part in the practice of sports, will certainly serve to create a new strong and healthy generation because the girls will be the mothers of sons of tomorrow ... [who] will be born robust, intelligent and good."[206] This press coverage shows that sports were not simply intended for women's enjoyment but rather aimed to enhance women's sex appeal and improve their reproductive system to fulfill their roles as girlfriends, wives, and mothers. These entrenched gender ideologies and practices in the sports pages also extended to mutual aid organizations.

Also known as *mutualistas*, mutual aid organizations offered immediate care, relief, and protection for the Mexican community in the United States. Scholarship on mutualistas has highlighted their relief work and insurance coverage as well as their social functions and patriotic celebrations that promoted Mexican culture and identity.[207] Missing, however, are mutualista recreation and sports activities that helped shape a Mexican sporting culture. In a survey of community organizations in California from 1927 to 1933, Nelson Pichardo found that mutualistas organized recreational activities and youth sports teams "to bring the community closer together."[208] One of these mutualistas, La Unión Patriótica Benéfica Mexicana Independiente (UPBMI), sponsored a men's baseball team that traveled throughout Southern California to play other teams.[209] As one of the largest mutualistas in the United States, Alianza Hispano Americana (AHA) grew from offering life insurance and social activities to defending the civil rights of its members.[210] AHA also supported athletic activities for its members as a way to build lodge unity and promote ethnic pride.

On April 30, 1927, AHA leaders congregated inside *La Opinión*'s office for a photograph and announced a new sports organization, Asociación Deportiva Hispano Americana (ADHA), to "promote and stimulate athletic activities in the Hispanic American communities."[211] The pan-ethnic label reflected the diversity of members from Mexico, Spain, Chile, and Argentina. A photograph of the all-male ADHA's Board of Directors made the front page and included the president, Ignacio Herrerías, vice president Agustín Álvarez, treasurer José Torres, and secretary Luis Alvear.[212] For a thirty-cent monthly fee, middle-class Latino professionals joined the ADHA, which in three months had attained 182 members. Within one year, the ADHA accomplished two successes: a gymnasium and soccer club. The construction of the gym, located on the first floor of Hotel Natick, required five months of fund-raising events, including "smokers" and "Bailes del Deportista."[213] The dances raised more money because they featured prizefighter Bert Colima, Hollywood celebrities Ramon Novarro and Dolores del Río, and diplomats from Latin American consulates.[214] At the grand opening, Herrerías spoke to attendees about the significance of this new gym: "Gentlemen, the gym is not elegant, it does not have a nice floor, porcelain showers, or expensive equipment, but at least it belongs to us. . . . It was built from the ground up by the efforts by a group of sport enthusiasts and help from many friends. Now it depends on you all and the Hispanic American youth that will grow it into a powerful institution."[215] The gym lasted just two years; the Wall Street Crash of 1929 cost the ADHA its main source of funding, forcing it to dissolve.

The ADHA formed one of the early Latino soccer clubs, Hispano Americana Football Club, due to the efforts of José "Pepe" Torres, considered by La Opinión as the "Angel of soccer in Los Angeles."[216] In the early 1920s Torres arrived in Los Angeles to join his brother Alejandro, who was appointed vice consul of Spain and began playing goalkeeper for several soccer clubs. He organized the first Hispano Americano Football Club in 1921 and several others with the same name. The main reason for organizing a pan-Latino team, according to Torres, was that he could field better players who "cannot be defeated [and] . . . would be more to the liking of fans from different nationalities."[217] In 1927, ADHA asked Torres to organize another Hispano Americano team with younger players from Spain, Mexico, Chile, and Argentina.[218] Torres and other AHA members encouraged Mexicans to identify not only with Mexico but also with Latinos in the United States.[219] His claim was substantiated when Hispano Americano competed and won the Greater Los Angeles Soccer League and California Soccer League titles during the 1928–1929 season.[220] After winning these titles coach Torres accepted an offer to play exhibition games in Mexico City, but a lack of funding prevented the team from making the journey.[221] The team lasted until 1931, when it lost ADHA as its financial sponsor and the economic depression forced players to quit or join other teams.[222] Compared to baseball and boxing, soccer remained a marginal sport in Mexican Los Angeles until the postwar era, when Torres formed a powerhouse soccer club, El Club Deportivo Pan Americano, affiliated with the Greater Los Angeles Soccer League.[223]

The Mexican consulate office of Los Angeles played a significant role in promoting sports in México de afuera communities in the United States. Scholars have studied the role of Mexican consulates in protecting their compatriots from discrimination and other injustices, organizing the community along nationalist lines to ensure loyalty to the Mexican government, repatriating those who could not find employment back to their homeland, and organizing patriotic celebrations to maintain a sense of Mexican cultural identity.[224] The Mexican consulate's role in the arena of sports, however, remains understudied. Mexican consulate representatives made their presence known at sporting events by delivering a congratulatory speech to the winning team, taking photographs with athletes, or throwing the ceremonial first pitch at baseball games. For example, F. Alfonso Pesqueira, Mexican consul of Los Angeles from 1925 to 1930, routinely accepted invitations to throw the first pitch at White Sox Park.[225] Even staff members of the LA Mexican consulate got involved by forming Club Deportivo del Consulado to compete against other company-sponsored sports clubs.[226]

Apart from organizing charity organizations and patriotic committees, the Mexican consul also tapped into recreational clubs to use sports for fund-raising opportunities and project a positive image of the Mexican diaspora. In attempt to help distressed compatriots during the Great Depression, the Mexican consulate stepped up fund-raising efforts for the new charity organization, Comite Beneficencia Mexicana (CBM).[227] Mexican consul Rafael de la Colina sent a telegram to the Mexican military requesting an exhibition soccer match between their team, Marte, and St. George Soccer Club in Los Angeles.[228] The proposal included 33 percent of the gate receipts donated to CBM and the remaining funds split between the opposing teams. Additionally, de la Colina enlisted the help of social and recreation clubs to raise funds for CBM. One of these was the Bohemia Athletic Club, founded in 1929 by mostly young men from East Los Angeles. The club president, Fernando Miranda, worked closely with the Mexican consulate and the Los Angeles Playground and Recreation Department to organize an annual Mexican fiesta featuring music and dance performances, a queen coronation ceremony, and a basketball match.[229] De la Colina reported on the second annual event held at Echo Playground to the secretary of foreign affairs; despite multiple obstacles, it became "a source of pride for the Mexican colonies in the state of California."[230] With more than a thousand in attendance, the fiesta's success was attributed to the "absolute integrity" and "extraordinary organizing" of Miranda, who later was charged with organizing a parade to welcome the Mexican Olympians to Los Angeles.[231] After the 1932 Olympic Games, the Mexican consulates helped facilitate transnational ties between U.S. and Mexican sports federations, discussed in more detail in chapter 4.

CONCLUSION

Sports enabled Mexicans on both sides of the border to come to terms with American culture. The United States influenced the development of sports south of the U.S.-Mexico border during the Porfiriato era, but participation was limited to elite men until the Mexican Revolution brought more personal freedom to workers and peasants. The YMCA played a key role in establishing a physical education movement to bring young Mexican men closer to Christianity while improving their moral character and physicality. Mostly middle-class Mexican males took advantage of YMCA programs to develop leadership skills and affirm their masculinity and national identity. Enrique Aguirre and Oscar Castillon were two Mexican YMCA secretaries who pushed the Mexican government to form a National Olympic Committee, host international competitions, and build the Venustiano Carranza sports center. In 1933, the postrevolutionary Mexican government formed CDM, a sports federation that governed seventeen organized sports and resembled the Amateur Athletic Union of the United States. These developments, according to Lamberto Álvarez Gayou, constituted a "peaceful revolution" that transformed the nation from a "sleepy unsophisticated Mexico" to a "seething hotbed of athletic action."[232] It was not until decades later, when Mexico City hosted the Olympic Games in 1968, that Mexican sports reached its peak as an expression of national pride.

Sports was not a mere reflection of the uneven power relations between the United States and Mexico, but an active racial project that shaped commonsense understandings of the Mexican sporting body. Mexican sports promoters asserted that building a stronger body could improve the "Cosmic Race" and by extension the national body. They also saw the physical potential of Tarahumara Indian runners at the Olympic Games but were "too primitive" to compete at international competitions. On the other hand, American writers, researchers, and other observers of Mexican athletes constructed a transnational discourse about the Mexican sporting body as racially inferior to whites.

Although some believed that Mexicans' physical ability was a sign of biological inferiority, others attributed their physical condition to environmental and cultural factors. This latter group, composed of settlement houses, the YMCA, and municipal playground officials, introduced "American" sports to Mexican immigrants and their children, and this segued to lessons in discipline, "good sportsmanship," and assimilation to American culture. Indeed, Americanization was the overriding ideology and practice during the interwar years, and consequently the Mexican population came to be viewed and treated as a racial problem. Americanization was a contested term, however, and Mexican immigrants derived their own understanding of themselves and their new country through sports participation. In turn, Mexican participation at the YMCA and in playground and municipal sports became opportunities for community building and organizing as well as remaking their own culture and identity.

Mexico and the United States adopted a similar approach of excluding, marginalizing, and trivializing women's sports. Female athletes were tracked into sports—tennis, gymnastics, swimming, volleyball, and basketball—deemed more appropriate to maintain their femininity and physical beauty. In other words, men were evaluated based on their athletic skills, whereas women were sexual objects to look at. The few stories that appeared in Spanish-language newspapers featured their sports attire, physical attractiveness, and potential for motherhood.

Sports helped Mexicans ease their transition into American society and helped them to reconnect with Mexican culture. The Spanish-language press, mutual aid organizations, and the Mexican consulate office were three México de afuera institutions that helped form a Mexican sporting culture, one that challenged stereotypes about physically unfit Mexicans and celebrated Mexican sports stars as positive role models. One of the first sports celebrities was Bert Colima, a prizefighter from Whittier, California, who attracted large audiences to big arenas to see one of his 195 fights between 1919 and 1933. After he became the middleweight champion of Mexico, Colima was treated like royalty by Mexican government officials and Angelenos. Mexico won its first Olympic medal in boxing in part due to the transnational networks developed by prizefighters, managers, promoters, and fans in Greater Mexico.

2 • *EL BOXEO*, IMMIGRATION, AND THE "GREAT BROWN HOPE"

El boxeo (Mexican boxing) has always been a family event. On boxing nights, my uncle would walk around the packed household of male and female relatives soliciting a ten-dollar bet for the *quiniela*. Quiniela is a gambling tradition from Mexico that has become a family tradition on pay-per-view boxing nights at my uncle's home in Oxnard, California. Before the fight, my uncle uses a makeshift hat with a full number of rounds written inside a piece of paper, then each person exchanges a ten-dollar bill for a randomly selected slip. If the fight ends, either by knockout or by decision, during your selected round, then you win the entire pot of money. Depending on the number of participants, the winning pot could reach over two hundred dollars. The bigger the family, the more money one can win. At the end, everyone pitches in money for the pay-per-view cost.

One match stands out. During the Oscar De La Hoya versus Julio César Chávez match, the family was divided along generational lines. While my parents, aunts, and uncles were cheering for the ferocious Lion of Culiacán who represented all things Mexican, my cousins and I cheered for the elegant Golden Boy who embodied a Mexican American identity.[1] My uncle proudly reminded the younger generation that Mexico has produced more world champions than any other country. This match was more than a clashing of boxing styles and personalities—the bout reflected ethnic, class, and generational divisions within the sporting Mexican diaspora.[2]

Most will recognize Julio César Chávez and Oscar De La Hoya as two great champions of boxing, yet we know very little about the early boxers of Greater Mexico. This chapter recovers the early history of boxing in Greater Mexico by examining the relationship between immigration, race, and masculinity among professional Mexican and Mexican American prizefighters. First, I examine how boxing emerged as a racial project with black and white boxers competing for the world heavyweight championship. Mexican and Mexican American prizefighters occupied an in-between racial position in the U.S. boxing industry, encountering varying forms of acceptance and marginalization. One of these was Bert Colima, a first-generation Mexican American from a working-class family in Whittier who emerged as the first boxing superstar in Southern California and a national hero in Mexico. Second, I examine the immigration case of two Mexican prizefighters, Rodolfo Casanova and Luis Villanueva, who navigated an increasingly rigid U.S. immigration regime that prohibited their entry at the U.S.-Mexico border. I show that despite the boxing industry's desire for foreign athletic talent from Mexico to attract larger audiences and big purses, immigration authorities and nativists racialized Mexican prizefighters as "brown bodies" who supposedly threatened the livelihood of Euro-American boxers. Third, I follow the boxing career of Alberto Arizmendi, who began prizefighting at a young age in Tampico, Mexico, and then moved to Los Angeles to pursue professional boxing in hopes of becoming Mexico's first world champion.

Ultimately, in this chapter I argue that for some prizefighters boxing became a way to remember and represent their homeland and develop a Mexican national identity, but for others it meant gaining acceptance by American society. These Mexican and Mexican American professional boxers, with help from promoters, trainers, sportswriters, and fans, gave rise to the sporting Mexican diaspora.

THE RISE OF BOXING IN GREATER MEXICO

From the beginning, a sharp color line existed in the sport of boxing. White supremacy in boxing was essential to maintain and uphold manhood for white males. According to Gail Bederman, heavyweight boxing "was so equated with male identity and power that American whites rigidly prevented all men they deemed unable to wield political and social power from asserting any claim to the heavyweight championship."[3] White boxers refused to fight against any blacks, denying their ability to make money. When John Sullivan became the first world heavyweight champion and America's first sports superstar, he publicly declared, "I will not fight a Negro. I never have and never shall."[4] The "whites-only" policy continued until Canadian Tommy Burns stepped into the ring against Jack Johnson in Sydney, Australia, and took a severe beating. As the first black world heavyweight champion, Johnson broke the "global color line" and, according to Theresa Runstedtler, "pried open an imaginative space for utopian dreams of black freedom."[5] His masculine bravado and preference for white women angered the white public, who initiated a worldwide search for the "great white hope." Johnson's subsequent defeat of white boxers from 1908 and 1913, including Jim Jeffries, America's great white hope in what was billed as the "fight of the century," led to race riots initiated by angry whites and forced his exile from the United States.

In effect, the removal of Jack Johnson from U.S. boxing opened the opportunity to restore the color line and pushed for the legalization of boxing. When Jack Dempsey defeated Jess Willard in 1919 for the heavyweight championship, he reassured white America that he would not fight against black opponents. As Jeffrey Sammons observed, "The failure of boxing or governmental authorities to facilitate and perhaps force acceptance of a black challenger for a period of twenty-two years indicates institutional racism and conspiracy."[6] Dempsey's declaration greatly enhanced his popularity during the 1920s, making the so-called golden age of sports a preserve of whiteness.

Boxing emerged as global sport rooted in the migration and mobility of people who crisscross nations in search of the next ring contest.[7] Between 1880 and 1914, boxing spread across Britain, Australia, and the United States largely due to its fluid, multiple, and loosely structured transnational networks.[8] As prizefighting increased in popularity on the East Coast of United States, social reformers stepped up efforts to outlaw this "barbaric sport." With states passing anti-boxing legislation, the sport moved to the West Coast and along the U.S.-Mexico border where fewer regulations existed.[9] U.S. novelist Jack London recognized the sport's popularity among Mexican migrants when he visited El Paso to report on the Mexican Revolution. In 1911, London published a short story, "The Mexican," that focused on eighteen-year-old Felipe Rivera, who joined revolutionary rebels fighting to liberate their country from a dictator. Rivera journeys from Veracruz, Mexico, to El Paso, Texas, to join Junta Revolucionaria Mexicana and become a prizefighter. To secure more funds for the revolutionary cause, he takes on a winner-take-all match against a legendary Anglo-American contender in California. The fight lasts seventeen rounds and although badly outmatched, he fights even harder when recalling the death of his parents by anti-revolutionaries. Rivera eventually triumphs, allowing "the revolution to go on," in London's own words.[10] London's story highlights how Mexican boxing became an important expression of nationalist, racial, and masculine pride on both sides of the U.S.-Mexico border. The story also reveals the transnational boxing networks that emerged across national borders that pulled disadvantaged young men from Mexico to make the reluctant journey to Los Angeles with dreams of fame and money.

Much earlier than other professional sports, boxing in Los Angeles began in the 1880s, producing its own homegrown boxing clubs, gyms, arenas, and world champions. With the founding of the white, middle-class Los Angeles Athletic Club (LAAC) in 1880, government officials, newspapers, and boosters attempted to attract top boxers and trainers to make this growing city into a world renowned "fight town."[11] Black members were excluded from LACC and other white-owned athletic clubs, forcing them to join the United Republic Club or the Manhattan Club. These black-owned athletic clubs hosted weekly fights until city health officials closed them down.[12] Fearing that blacks would control the boxing scene, the City Council attempted to prevent interracial fights, but boxing promoters kept the sport alive. Considered the city's first big boxing promoter, Tom McCarey established the Century Athletic Club and staged world championship bouts at Hazard's Pavilion in Downtown Los Angeles that featured all-black and mixed-race bouts. McCarey's preference for black talent earned him the nickname "Uncle Tom," but according to historian Louis Moore, it also generated a "white backlash" among white progressives who sought to eliminate interracial boxing.[13] McCarey also featured Mexican American boxers in boxing cards, but they did not stir up the same controversy as black boxers because they were legally classified as "white" and could claim Spanish ancestry.

For example, when McCarey's Pacific Athletic Club hosted the world lightweight title match between Aurelio Herrera and Battling Nelson, the public eagerly awaited this battle between the Danish and Mexican during Los Angeles Fiesta Week.[14] Although the English-language press portrayed Herrera as a "Castilian" with good English-speaking and -writing skills, he was racialized as "little brown-skinned greaser" and blamed for the failed title fight because of problems with weight scales.[15] Herrera defended himself in print, claiming that "the most opprobrious epithets have been applied. 'Indian,' 'low brow,' 'greaser,' 'Good for nothing,'" and asserted that "I may be an Indian. If so, I command a certain respect as a scion of an ancient race. . . . I maintain that my knowledge of the world and a command of language is certainly up to the standard observed by the average knocker who is flattening my name on this anvil."[16]

When the Los Angeles City Council banned world title bouts in 1908, boxing moved to the city of Vernon, where former railroad worker and bartender Jack Doyle had built an outdoor arena, training camp, and gigantic saloon. José Ybarra, who fought under the name Mexican Joe Rivers, drew large crowds, especially on July 4, 1912, when he was winning handily against Ad Wolgast for the lightweight title until the thirteenth round, when a "double-knockout" occurred.[17] Instead of counting down on both, the referee counted Rivers out while helping Wolgast to his feet. This controversial decision outraged Rivers fans who hissed and poured into the ring to protest. Certainly, racial bias was a factor in the referee's actions, and this outcome prompted calls for more oversight and regulation of the sport. In 1914, California legislators passed an amendment that restricted boxing matches to four rounds and to offering no more than twenty-five dollars in prize money. Between 1914 and 1925, the four-round era of boxing in California encouraged more young men to join boxing clubs with the hope of getting onto a weekly boxing card and earning prize money under the table (usually called "medals").

White-owned athletic clubs allowed Mexican American boxers to join and train in their gyms because of their intermediate racial status compared to black boxers.[18] One of these was Joe Salas, born and raised in Elysian Park, Los Angeles, who befriended Joe Rivers in his neighborhood and started training in his backyard gym until he joined the LAAC. "The Los Angeles Athletic Club was a nice club," recalled Joe Salas in an interview. "I got membership through a friend [George Blake]. They had good training facilities."[19] Blake trained young promising amateur fighters like Salas, Fidel La Barba, Jackie Fields, and Ad Allegrini, all of whom earned a spot on the U.S. Olympic boxing team for the 1924 Olympic Games in Paris. Salas reached the finals in the featherweight division against Jackie Fields, a childhood friend from his neighborhood, and although it was an evenly matched fight, Fields won gold and Salas brought home the silver medal. Although considered the first U.S.-born Latino Olympian, Salas still faced questions about his race and citizenship aboard the USS *America* ship.[20] He was not the only team member feeling marginalized within the U.S. Olympic team. When he observed white teammates ignoring a black athlete, he said, "The hell with this stuff, I went up to him, shook his hand and said, 'Hi I'm Joe Salas'—we became friends."[21] After the Olympic Games, Salas turned professional, earning a respectable living with a 42–6 record, before retiring in 1927. Salas continued to teach boxing at El Sereno Boys Club and served as a training assistant for the U.S. boxing team at the 1932 Olympics.[22]

On November 4, 1924, California voters passed Proposition 7 that permitted boxing and wrestling for prize money and created the California State Athletic Commission to regulate contests and to license professional and amateur boxers. To the delight of boxing promoters and fighters, the new law also permitted bouts to extend to ten rounds, even twelve if there was no decision. Once the ten-round law was implemented, new boxing clubs and arenas emerged, including the 10,400-seat Grand Olympic Auditorium that opened its doors on August 5, 1925, "ready for its baptism of black eyes and bloody noses."[23] Boxing shows appeared every day of the week in different boxing arenas across Southern California, and by 1929 there were a thousand professional boxing shows staged in the state.[24] The sport's popularity during the 1920s attracted young working-class Mexican boys who gravitated to neighborhood boxing clubs and makeshift fighting rings. One research assistant reported to sociologist Emory Bogardus about large crowds that gathered in backyards of Mexican homes: "It seemed that rings sprang up all over this neighborhood and clubs of fellows would get together and train and fight all the time."[25] This finding signaled to Bogardus a potential cultural malady among Mexicans who "like the more brutal sports as wrestling, boxing and tumbling."[26] A staunch opponent of legalized prizefighting, Bogardus warned about the dangers of boxing, its association with gambling, and its "hindrance to the growth of team games."[27] He recommended instead the national pastime of baseball that "acquires a new meaning for teamwork."[28] To the contrary, boxing and its network of gyms, clubs, and arenas brought together managers, trainers, cutmen, and other personnel to prepare a boxer to compete. As boxing historian Gregory Rodriguez suggested, the network of neighborhood boxing clubs brought the community together "to socialize, to express ethnic pride, [and] to escape the indignities of a hostile environment."[29] For Bogardus, boxing somehow hindered the Americanization of the Mexican immigrant, but for immigrants and their children boxing was a ticket out of poverty and racial oppression.

During the 1920s, Mexican American prizefighters emerged as sports heroes to a growing Mexican immigrant community in Southern California. "Above all other people the Mexicans are national hero worshippers," explained a Los Angeles playground director, precisely because "nearly every Mexican boy has the ambition to be a great boxer. This is the main thing he thinks about until he gets married and has to go to work digging ditches or working for the railroad."[30] Mexican boys looked up to Mexican prizefighters as male role models who performed a masculine identity in their public display of physical strength and aggression inside the ring. Outside the ring, they crafted themselves as self-made men who could make money and provide financially for their heterosexual family in a labor market that forced them into low-paying jobs. Boxing for Mexican prizefighters also served to shatter the racist myth of Mexican physical and mental inferiority. The sporting press played a key role in constructing Mexican prizefighters as the first sports heroes of the Mexican diaspora. One of the most discussed in sports pages, in both English and Spanish, was Bert Colima (see Figure 2.1). Epifanio Romero was born to a large family on a farm near Whittier and started at an early age doing ranch work, which prepared him physically to become

FIGURE 2.1. Bert Colima (left) sparring with Everett Strong (right) prior to their fight at Wrigley Field on Oct. 23, 1926. Colima won in a 10-round decision. (Courtesy of the Department of Special Collections, Hesburgh Libraries, University of Notre Dame)

a future boxer. His father was a fan of Joe Rivers and brought home boxing gloves so his boys could fight each other and neighborhood kids. His uncle noticed his interest in boxing, so he bought him gym clothes so he could begin training at the Western Athletic Club. His parents were initially opposed to his pursuit of a professional boxing career, but he convinced them that he could use his footwork, speed, and accuracy to avoid getting hurt badly. After winning thirty-five of thirty-seven fights, he attracted the attention of George "Dutch" Meyers and Jack Doyle, who convinced him to change his name and to fill the Vernon Arena, respectively. He chose "Bert" because it was closely linked to "Bird," a nicknamed earned while walking the Whittier streets whistling; "Colima" was in honor of his grandmother's home state in Mexico.[31]

The Spanish-language press extensive coverage of Colima's training regimen at Main Street Gym, and boxing performances from 1919 to 1933 reflected a kind of "heroic masculinity" that reflected positively on the Mexican population. On February 9, 1928, *La Opinión* devoted front-page coverage to his fight against Joe Anderson at the Vernon Arena that ended in a dramatic finish: "We had never seen him step on a ring with such confidence and courage with which he did last night," wrote sports editor Ignacio Herrerías. He added, "We had never seen Colima use both hands with equal ease, nor deliver blows with such precision, speed and strength."[32] After being pounded all over by Anderson, Colima attacked him with a barrage of punches in the last rounds to win by a close decision. Afterward, Colima credited his victory to his fans. "If I have triumphed, I owe it to the determined help and cooperation that I have always received from my compatriots, all Mexicans in California. Your faith in me, your confidence in my abilities and your shouts of encouragement, strengthened my spirit continuously, and so I could dominate my dangerous adversary."[33] When insulted for his race and manhood by opponents, Colima beat them soundly. His son recalled how "[Ray] Pelky heaped abuse on Colima, calling him everything from a chili-picking Mexican to a yellow hound" in the sixth round at Dreamland Rink in San Francisco. He responded with his "fists smashed squarely over his mouth and he hit the floor with a thud and was counted out."[34] To the delight of Mexican fans, when Colima fought and defeated Euro-American boxers, it was more a surrogate victory against a racist society that denied them equality.

Colima trained at the Main Street Athletic Gym, where he met and befriended other boxers to spar with and mentored young prospects.[35] In 1926, Carlo Curtis opened the Main Street gym at 321 South Main Street for local amateur and professional boxers to train for their upcoming bouts. The gym staged a weekly boxing card on Saturday night that became popular among Mexican fans.[36] The Mexican Press Association of California organized a special boxing exhibition on April 6, 1927, featuring ten of the best Mexican and Mexican American prizefighters.[37] Although aggression, competition, and other masculine behaviors characterized the homosocial world of the boxing gym, male friendships developed across race and class differences. *La Opinión's* boxing writer Luis Magaña reflected on regular visits to the gym to report on Saturday night fights. He wrote, "I remember the old and beaten up gym, climbing up windy stairs and arriving to see a tall, skinny man, Al Lang, who charged 25 cents to see white, brown and black figures searching for a breakthrough in life with their fists."[38]

Outside the ring and gym, Colima's marriage to Leonor Olea and subsequent birth of their daughter helped him develop a respectable form of masculinity as a responsible husband and father.[39] Beyond his family, Colima offered his services to help community groups to raise funds for social causes. For example, to commemorate his ten-year professional boxing career, the Asociación Deportiva Hispano Americana awarded Colima a diploma and honorary membership to their new gym.[40] At the invitation of the Union of Mexican Journalists, Colima visited the offices of *El Heraldo de México* to discuss his exhibition at the upcoming festival at Capitol Theater in Downtown Los Angeles.[41] The newspaper staff wrote that "we were very impressed of this young Mexican who so effectively and within his sphere, is fighting for the prestige of our race."[42]

Colima's popularity extended beyond Southern California to border towns and Mexico City. He fought eight times in Mexico, twice along the border cities of Tijuana and Mexicali, and six times in Mexico City, where he received the most publicity. Upon arriving by train on March 12, 1926, Colima told one *Excélsior* reporter that "when treading the soil of my homeland, I feel happy because the opportunity has come to present myself to the cultured Mexican fans."[43] Although government officials treated Colima like royalty, fans were disappointed when he fouled Arturo Schackels in the first round and demanded their money back. He made up for it, however, by knocking out Buck Holley and Bobby Corbett, both in the second round, in consecutive matches. Colima's son recalled his first visit to Mexico City: "They had great respect for the fighter and his accomplishments. Given that he was first-generation Mexican-American, the Mexicans identified with him and were honored to be at his side either socially or at ringside."[44] Two years later, Colima returned to Mexico City to fight Tommy White for the middleweight championship on October 7, 1928, at the Plaza de Toros.[45] In front of twenty-five thousand attendees, including president-elect Emilio Portes Gil and other government dignitaries, Colima won in twelve rounds by a judges' decision. The foreign press, including the *New York Times*, disagreed with the decision, feeling White was the "aggressor" against the "flashier fighter," but according to Mexican sportswriter Alejandro Aguilar Reyes, better known by his pen name Fray Nano, Colima won because of his longer reach, his weight advantage, and "the great sympathy the public has for him."[46] Colima's fights in Mexico sparked more interest in boxing and helped usher in Mexico's first golden age of boxing.

An early form of boxing originated in ancient Mesoamerica for rain ceremonies and mountain worship, but its modern form emerged under the Porfiriato regime for the Mexican elite and foreign residents in the capital city.[47] Boxing also flourished along the Gulf port cities and the U.S.-Mexico border, where promoters staged illegal bouts without permission from government officials.[48] As the Mexican Revolution spurred interest in fighting, military colleges and academies took up boxing to train young men for combat. When the revolution ended, the nation's economy was left in shambles, its political system was in disarray, and boxing went unregulated. Fed up with defrauded boxers and disgruntled fans, the Mexican press called for a boxing commission.[49] When working for *El Universal*, Fray Nano helped organize the first boxing commission, which lasted just two weeks due to "corruption that was immediately installed by members who allowed it to be handled by the great interests of politicians and businessmen."[50] In 1925 the Mexican Boxing Commission appealed to the California State Athletic Commission for help in "keeping the fight game clean" and to adopt a reciprocity agreement to enforce suspensions and barring of fighters.[51] The *Ring* praised this agreement and added, "With a competent commission of twelve good sportsmen in control of the boxing situation, the better boxers are confident of coming to Mexico and getting a fair deal."[52] Even President Portes Gil offered his help by being "present at the last fight and promised to aid in building up the game."[53]

The visits of heavyweight champions Jack Johnson and Jack Dempsey helped to boost the popularity of boxing in Mexico.[54] Mexican fans and sportswriters embraced Johnson when he arrived in Mexico City on May 26, 1919, because of his flashy style and racial conflict with white Americans. As Theresa Runstedtler put it, "Johnson emerged as a symbol of anti-Americanism in the eyes of his Mexican supporters."[55] It must be noted, however, that Johnson still faced antiblack racism in Mexico. When a restaurant refused service to Johnson, it provoked a public outcry and a rowdy crowd yelled in unison, "Viva Johnson, Viva Mexico." After the 1920 assassination of President Carranza, whom Johnson had befriended, he returned to the United States to surrender to federal agents after seven years in exile. Five years later, Jack Dempsey arrived in Mexico City to a large enthusiastic crowd that nearly trampled him. Dempsey staged an exhibition match against Jack League at El Toreo in front of thirty thousand persons jammed inside the country's largest bullring. According to the *Ring* Dempsey "received more attention while in the Republic than any champion bull fighter every received."[56] Dempsey's popularity can be attributed to his "whiteness" and masculinity that supported the postrevolutionary state's racial and gender ideology of building white muscular and athletic male bodies to represent Mexico abroad.[57]

Even *La Opinión* devoted coverage to Dempsey. Working as a shoeshine boy in his hometown of Monterrey, Mexico, sportswriter Rodolfo García recalled how he met Dempsey, his sports idol.[58] One morning in 1927, an American man requested a shoe polish, and within five minutes, a crowd gathered around his famous customer calling him "El Asesino de Manassa!" and "Champion!" After adding an extra shine to his famous shoes, Dempsey gave him a twenty-five-cent coin. He remembered vividly, "It was the first time I had received such a large tip and I kept the coin for about two months until I had to get rid of it at the market." That weekend he got a chance to watch Dempsey in an exhibition match at the Plaza de Toros, and "that's when I fell in love with boxing and sports," he explained. Years later when he became a sports reporter for *La Opinión* he recounted this story to his friend Gus Wilson, a boxing manager and trainer, who then reintroduced the two at a Los Angeles press conference. Dempsey called over the photographer and told Wilson, "Now I'm going to clean García's shoes." A photo showed García with his shoe on Dempsey's knee and telling him that "he wants them very shiny, Mr. Champion."[59]

The search to find a Mexican Dempsey began during a period when rebuilding the nation and improving the Mexican race became major concerns. Anthropologist Manuel Gamio advocated for the "civilizing" and racial betterment of the indigenous population in Mexico.[60] In his collection of testimonies of Mexican immigrants, Gamio interviewed Eduardo Huaracha, whom he described as light-skinned with light eyes and a strong body. Born to a poor family in Yurécuarao, Michoacán, Huaracha played all sports but liked to box because he was strong and could instill fear among his classmates. He moved to Mexico City and later Los Angeles with an ambition to become a professional boxer. He shared his dream with Gamio: "I expect to make a small fortune as a boxer and to get my name in the Mexican and American newspapers. When I accomplish this, which I think is only a matter of a few more years, I will aim to fight Mexican or American boxers in the diverse plazas of Mexico until I reach the capital, in where I hope to crown my career by becoming the Mexican middle-weight champion."[61] Since he could not afford a manager, he worked at a packinghouse during the day, trained at night, and arranged his own fights. Spanish-language newspapers referred to Huaracha as El Caballero (the gentleman) because he sent money to his parents, attended church regularly, and offered to help community groups.[62]

Inside the ring, however, Huaracha showed an aggressive masculinity and knocked out opponents, prompting some to call him the "Mexicano Jack Dempsey."[63] Huaracha confessed to Gamio that he preferred to dress in the American style, which caused confusion about his identity. "During my fights, people get confused by thinking I am an American, because they see me as white and with light brown hair." So, he reminded promoters to announce that he was "Mexican, so that la raza realizes that I am Mexican." Huaracha embodied the racial and gendered ideal of a Mexican boxer who represented his nationality with pride, but had little success inside the ring and retired early after losing Mexico's light heavyweight title.

By the late 1920s, professional boxing had reached a new level of maturity, with over three hundred licensed boxers in Mexico City ready to lace up their gloves and fight in one of four major arenas.[64] Associated Press sportswriter Lamberto Álvarez Gayou informed readers that "el boxeo or the sport of the padded mitts is becoming the national pastime south of the Rio Grande . . . and a brand new language has been devised to describe their activities."[65] As evidence, Gayou cited the widespread use of Spanglish words such as *noqueado* (knockout), *opercoot* (uppercut), and *faoool* (foul) in the Mexican boxing world. Besides the hybrid sporting language, Gayou drummed up support for the first title fight in Mexico City between defending champion Panama Al Brown and Mexico's bantamweight champion, Blas Rodriguez.[66] Additionally, Mexico sent its first boxing team (Alfredo Ganoa, Fidel Ortíz, Raúl Talán, and Carlos Orellana) to the 1928 Summer Olympics in Amsterdam, and although they did not receive a medal, they proved they could compete at the international level. Four years later, at the Olympic Games in Los Angeles, Fernando Cabañas Pardo brought home the country's first medal in boxing.[67]

Boxing is one of the most masculine of sports, offering a space for men where traditional physical aggression dominates. But female boxers have also entered the ring despite being banned from boxing gyms and amateur tournaments by governments around the world. In Mexico, boxing is a powerful symbol of nationalism that extends only to male boxers, at the expense of women who receive no support from the government, entrepreneurs, or the media.[68] One of these women who battled for equality in boxing was Margarita Montes, known also by her ring name La Maya. Born near Mazatlán, Sinaloa, to a poor farming family of eight, Montes left school to work and a found stable job at a corn mill that sponsored a girl's baseball team. Her stellar pitching and batting helped her team Cervecería Díaz de León win the state championship in 1928. Two years later, she switched to boxing when she learned she could make money and receive training from prizefighters Joe Conde and Raul Talán. After defeating Josefina Coronado in Mazatlán's Teatro Rubio to earn the Pacific Coast Championship, she traveled all over Mexico and the United States, accompanied by her brother and manager.

Overall, during the 1930s Montes fought thirty-three professional fights—five against women and twenty-eight against men.[69] She became friends with Talán, who after retiring from boxing became a journalist for *El Nacional* and wrote two books on Mexican boxing. In *En El 3er Round*, Talán profiled Montes, who engaged in some tough fights and never gave up, especially when male opponents and fans would laugh and mock her. But, Talán wrote, "this woman is braver and macho than many men."[70] Her story was featured in *Ripley's Believe It or Not* column: "She is not a clever defensive boxer as you might think, but is the real slugger type, with a knockout wallop in either arm."[71] Montes asserted a "masculine femininity" inside the ring that challenged notions of Mexican nationalism and masculinity exclusively reserved for male boxers.

Yet in the end, the entry of women into boxing threatened the Mexican government such that President Alemán Valdés, who signed a decree on December 5, 1946, to ban women's boxing.[72] The Great Depression hit the boxing scene very hard in Mexico, forcing the Mexican Boxing Commission to convene a special meeting among boxers, managers, and journalists to discuss how to revive it. In attendance was Fray Nano, who founded *La Afición* in 1930 to cover national and international sports; he recommended they enlist the help of Jimmy Fitten, Mexican American matchmaker, and put together a top boxing card at National Arena. Born to a Mexican mother and Jewish American father in Oakland, Fitten was a former professional boxer turned trainer, manager, promoter, and matchmaker in Mexico City.[73] As a boxer, Fitten had shown "unsuspecting fineness," but "as a promoter he shows a soft hand in negotiation of top fights." Fitten fondly recalled his first boxing show in Mexico City: "[I] said to myself after the show was over, Jimmy this is it! These folks instinctively love boxing and if only the Mexican kids can be taught just a little bit about the art of fight promotion here will be a business, a big business."[74] Soon thereafter, Fitten started training kids in his garage and later opened the National Arena, an indoor venue dedicated solely to professional boxing and wrestling. "Mexicans instinctively are good ringmen," observed Fitten, "they love to fight for fighting's sake, and they have plenty of courage. . . . They catch on rapidly; they are mature fighters at an early age."[75] Fitten invited Bert Colima to return to Mexico City with a young light heavyweight prospect Alejandro "Sandy" Garrison Casanova for a boxing demonstration. Fray Nano also convinced entrepreneurs to work closely with Fitten to put up prize money, but it was his newspaper that helped create the golden age of boxing by covering every fight and profiling the newcomers to the ring.[76] Several of these included Luis "Kid Azteca" Villanueva, Rodolfo "Baby/Changó" Casanova, and Alberto "Baby/El Generalito" Arizmendi.

A MEXICAN PROBLEM OR MEXICAN VOGUE?

By the late 1920s, the rise of the "Mexican problem" combined with the stock market crash led to stricter immigration policies and increased enforcement along the U.S.-Mexico border, which markedly reduced immigration from Mexico. Even though the 1924 Immigration Act exempted Mexico from the quota system, this did not preclude the State Department from using administrative means to restrict Mexican immigrants through head taxes, literacy tests, medical examinations, and Border Patrol arrests and deportations and by enforcing the contract labor ban. Immigration historian Mae Ngai asserts that the imposition of border control and administrative measures functioned to racialize Mexicans as "illegal aliens."[77] Once settled in the United States, Mexican immigrants faced legislative bills and judicial rulings that attempted to strip them of their rights to become U.S. citizens.[78] To add insult to injury, the 1930 U.S. census reclassified Mexicans from "white" to "a race all their own," causing discrepancies in immigration registration listings along the U.S.-Mexico border.[79] The anti-Mexican movement reached its peak in the early 1930s with the mass deportation and repatriation of more than four hundred thousand Mexican immigrants and their U.S.-born children back to Mexico.[80] According to Natalia Molina, the U.S. immigration regime used several racial scripts to construct Mexican immigrants as a separate race to deprive them of a sense of belonging in American society.[81] These racial scripts and immigration practices also affected the experiences of Mexican prizefighters, as revealed by the immigration cases of two Mexican prizefighters in the next section.

At the same time nativists complained about the supposed "Mexican problem" in the late twenties, Americans developed an "enormous vogue" with Mexican art, literature, music, and culture.[82] For example, Christine Sterling, known as the "Mother of Olvera Street," began her campaign to create a Mexican marketplace to save the Los Angles Plaza from demolition but also to attract tourists and romanticize Mexican folk culture.[83] Even Hollywood studios looked to Mexico and Latin America as potential lucrative markets to produce and distribute films.[84] A fascination with "things Mexican" also emerged in the boxing arenas of Los Angeles. Los Angeles managers and promoters considered Mexican boxing a sporting event that could draw the biggest audiences and generate a six-figure purse. Sports journalist Ignacio Herrerías, based in Los Angeles and Mexico City at that time, defined the situation as follows: "A Mexican boxer is a real gold mine in California, since it has been perfectly proven since the time of Bert Colima that every time he shows up in a stadium around five or six thousand people follow with him with amazing regularity, that is, five or six thousand dollars at the box office."[85] Cheering for their favorite Mexican boxer, fans, according to Douglas Monroy, "[saw] themselves more and more as Mexicans."[86] Boxing was not associated with Americanization, according to Gregory Rodriguez, but "came to be identified with 'Mexicanness,' with Mexican guts, Mexican spirit, and Mexican victories."[87] This "Mexicanness" was closely linked with public performance, style, and commodification. But this sporting phenomenon also occurred within a transnational network of prizefighters, promoters, trainers, matchmakers, and fans that linked the boxing worlds of Mexico City and Los Angeles.

In an attempt to capitalize on the "Mexicanization" of prizefighting, Todd Faulkner, a Scottish-Irish boxer from Huntington Beach, appropriated the Mexican label by adopting the nickname of "Kid Mexico" to attract matchmakers, albeit to the utter confusion of fans and sportswriters alike. "Kid Mexico is the most wrong-named fighter who ever stuck out a fist," declared the *Los Angeles*

Times. "Announce him and the audience expects to see a Herrera, a Rivers, and Ortega. He isn't Mex at all, He is Scottish and Irish." Faulkner explained that he adopted the nickname to support his three little sisters and for personal ambition. "I want to get some place—be a success—in boxing or business. If I'm not a fighter I want to find it out right now and try something else."[88] After Colima whipped him twice inside the ring, Faulkner retired from boxing in 1932 and became a wealthy businessman in Signal Hill.[89]

The English-language sports media published contradictory depictions of Mexican male boxers. On the one hand, they were deemed threatening like revolutionary bandits who had invaded the boxing arena; but on the other, they were characterized as primitive and childlike with references to their inferior physicality. Newspaper articles frequently used the moniker "little Mexican boxer" when discussing their body size or explained why so many were in lighter weight divisions.[90] By adopting an emasculated, docile image of Mexican boxers, sportswriters quelled the fears of the white boxing world. Promoters and matchmakers' preference for ring names that began with "Baby" and "Kid" also served to emasculate male boxers. "Perhaps it is the Aztec influence," claimed one sportswriter. The author continued, "They have tried out a number of Tarahumaras, long distance mountain runners, as heavy weight prospects, [but] while they have all the physical requirements, were utterly incapable of mastering the finer points of boxing."[91] The short size combined with their "fiery Latin" temper made the utter Mexican boxers incapable of winning a world title.[92] According to one Associated Press article, "Boxing fans in this country are waiting in hopeful suspense for the outcome of three ring battles in the United States within the next month in which three dark-skinned little fighting men will engage in crucial contests which may decide whether Mexico is to realize its ambition for the first world championship in any sport."[93]

When Bert Colima announced his retirement on September 16, 1926, it became headline news for *La Opinión* in the Spanish-language newspaper's inaugural issue on Mexican Independence Day, creating a stir among fans and promoters about the future prospects of Mexican boxing.[94] Although Colima did not retire until 1933, Los Angeles boxing promoters worried about finding boxers to replace Colima. The *Los Angeles Times* put it bluntly, "Promoters of California have been trying for years to develop another Mexican boxer who could pack an arena like Bert Colima. It has proven to be an endless chain of disappointments so far."[95] The solution was to look to Mexico. "There is gold down in Mexico," announced the *Los Angeles Times*, which described how a "young school of fighters that country was developing" and advised Los Angeles boxing promoter Jack Doyle to "start importing them for the Olympic [Auditorium]."[96]

La Opinión sarcastically pointed out that like "in the prosperous years, from 1920 to 1925 there was demand for Mexican braceros that came to sweat in the fields of farmland, in the coal mines, in the railways or industrial houses, now

there is demand for Mexican boxers."[97] The first bracero program was established during World War I to solve labor shortages but was extended until 1922
because employers became addicted to cheap labor. The same *brazos* (arms)
used for picking fruit were also effective for sparring and fighting in the ring. "It
is not rare, therefore, to see Los Angeles managers and promoters so interested
in obtaining our [boxing] element," declared *La Opinión*, "because apart from
being good box-office magnets, they are flourishing in these moments in a matter
of courage, endurance and aggressiveness."[98] Even the boxing industry's leading magazine the *Ring* applauded the increased popularity of boxing in Mexico
and warned, "Our southern neighbor has taken up this boxing business in a serious way and is serving notice on the world that in the future the Mexican must
be reckoned in the championship accounting."[99] In the early 1930s, Luis "Kid
Azteca" Villanueva and Rodolfo "Baby Face" Casanova were two Mexican professional boxers hoping to make it big in the boxing arenas of Los Angeles (see
Figure 2.2).

In Mexico, Rodolfo Casanova was nicknamed "Changó" (monkey) because
of his "mangoloid face of an Indian," but in the United States the sports media
anointed him "Baby Face" or "Baby" because of his youthful features.[100] Casa-

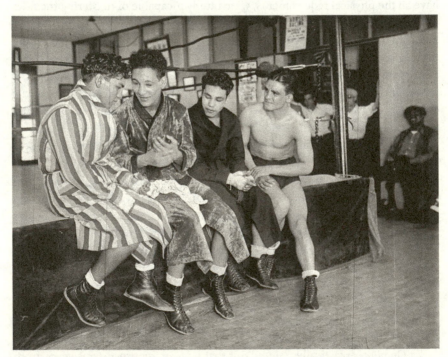

FIGURE 2.2. (left to right) Alberto Arizmendi, Luis Villanueva, Rodolfo Casanova, and
unknown boxer. (Courtesy of the Department of Special Collections, Hesburgh Libraries,
University of Notre Dame)

nova was born in León, Guanajuato, and after his father's death he moved the family to Mexico City in search of work as a street food vendor. Casanova rose from poverty to become a professional boxer at the age of sixteen. He shocked the boxing world when he defeated top-ranked Filipino boxers, first Speedy Dado in November 1932 and then Sid Torres in February 1933 in Mexico City. A few months later, promoter and matchmaker Jimmy Fitten persuaded the Mexican bantamweight champion to make the journey to Los Angeles to fight for a big purse and a world title.

Luis Villanueva also caught the attention of Los Angeles promoters. Villanueva grew up in the working-class neighborhood of Tepito, Mexico City, which became famous for boxing gyms and trainers that produced world champion boxers.[101] As a young fifteen-year-old, Villanueva began his professional career under the name "Kid Chino" (curly kid) in Nuevo Laredo, Mexico, while he worked as a tailor's apprentice. In 1931, he substituted for another boxer called "Kid Azteca," and after an impressive ten-round win decided to keep the ring name.[102] A year later, he won Mexico's national welterweight championship by defeating David Velasco in Mexico City. The next year, Jimmy Fitten convinced the Mexican welterweight titleholder to join Casanova in a boxing tour to Los Angeles.

BOXED INTO A CORNER: MEXICAN PRIZEFIGHTERS REFUSED BORDER ENTRY

On June 20, 1933, boxing fans waited anxiously for the arrival of Casanova and Villanueva in Los Angeles, but U.S. immigration inspectors denied them entry at the El Paso–Ciudad Juárez border crossing. Inspectors classified them as "alien contract laborers" and held them in custody for violating the 1885 Alien Contract Labor Law.[103] The Olympic Auditorium, LA's leading boxing venue, had scheduled Villanueva to fight Cerefino Garcia on June 27 and Casanova to battle Young Tommy on July 11, but now the card remained uncertain. Also in custody was trainer Rafael "Tio" Torres-Lopez, who along with Casanova and Villanueva waited anxiously for their Board of Special Inquiry hearing.[104]

At the hearing, both boxers testified that they were making a "pleasure trip to California." According to Casanova, "We are coming to the United States to go to Los Angeles on a vacation. We are coming here to rest." However, when inspectors presented the boxers with newspaper articles announcing their upcoming bouts, they accused the pair of lying under oath. The *Los Angeles Examiner* explained that Casanova had signed a contract with promoter Tom Gallery for three fights: "It is expected the Mexican will work at the San Francisco Dreamland as well."[105] Casanova repeated that he "did not know anything about it" because his manager dealt with contract negotiations. The inspector asked him, "Would it not seem strange to you that a contract for three fights for you would be signed by your American manager and you would not be advised?"[106] Again, immigration inspectors accused Casanova of making "false and misleading statements before this Board." El Paso boxing promoter Joe Corona came to his defense and testified, "Casanova is the most sensational fighter since Jack Dempsey, and they have heard about him all over the world." Corona explained why Casanova had not signed a boxing contract yet: "In these days, in order to obtain publicity for their fighters, the promoters and publicity agents, a lot of times will write things which have not happened or will not happen and are not the truth. I likewise have done so at times, under the guise of 'ballyhoo' to gain publicity."[107] Despite Corona's explanations, U.S. immigration authorities remained unconvinced.

Professional boxing is one of the most international sports and welcomes participants from all over the world. Foreign boxers, however, have confronted immigration problems, whether being denied a visa, being held in detention, or facing deportation. The U.S. Immigration and Naturalization Service (INS) treated foreign boxers as contract laborers under the 1885 Alien Contract Labor Law (also known as the Foran Act), which prohibited the importation of foreign laborers under contract.[108] This law helped fuel racist and nativist sentiments among labor unions and native-born European American workers who blamed immigrants for taking their jobs and driving down wages. Although the law exempted "professional actors, artists, lecturers, or singers," it did not stop nativist forces from demanding stricter laws against foreign entertainers. In response to demands from the entertainment industry and American audiences, the Bureau of Immigration created a "temporary admittance" procedure that according to Krystin Moon sought "to balance the need for foreign entertainment with nativists' and racists' concerns."[109] This procedure allowed foreigners to stay temporarily under bond (five hundred dollars) and to depart by a specific date, or else risk losing the bond and undergo deportation proceedings.

As immigration regulations became more stringent during the 1920s, the temporary admittance procedure was selectively enforced based on race. U.S. immigration officials at border crossings and ports of entry sought guidance and instructions from the Bureau of Immigration on how to treat foreign athletes. INS commissioner Edward Shaughnessy reminded district employees about certain sports exempted under contract labor law: "The present policy of the Central office is to hold that aliens applying for admission to this country as professional tennis, football, baseball, hockey and soccer players . . . [pay] a suitable bond to guarantee status and departure."[110] The INS directive did not include boxing, thus allowing immigration authorities more discretion when considering the entry of Mexican prizefighters.

During the second day of hearings, the Board of Special Inquiry chairman asked Casanova and Villanueva why they had not obtained proper immigration visas. In fact, both had applied for visas at the U.S. consul in Ciudad Juárez but had been denied—"No proof existed that they are professionals."[111] Since they could not obtain a work visa as professional boxers, they sought entry as tourists.

When questioned again, Villanueva admitted that they were coming to the United States for boxing matches. Ultimately, the chairman ruled that Casanova and Villanueva should remain "aliens excluded" for perjury and "not in possession of immigration visas in violation of the alien contract labor provisions of the immigration laws."[112] The immigration ruling that "prizefighting is work" and "Mex Champs barred" reached media outlets throughout the country. In response to the board's decision, Corona advised Casanova and Villanueva to appeal to the U.S. Department of Labor and asked for their release under his supervision. The board approved their parole to Joe Corona's residence while they awaited a final decision.

News about the Mexican boxers' exclusion generated public support from nativists. In a telegram to the U.S. Department of Labor, an Anglo male argued that immigration officials should deny Mexican prizefighters' entry in order to "Give American Boxers a Break." He wrote, "These Mexicans are coming to this country under contract to fight for Jack Doyle and Tom Gallery in Los Angeles and to the detriment of American boxers." He added, "California right now has a surplus of cheap boxers from Mexico and something should be done to prevent the entry of others." He urged the federal government to do more to protect white American workers from "alien Mexicans" and concluded, "It certainly is not proper in these hard times that good capable American boxers should be made to lie around in idleness, shabbily dressed and without sufficient sustenance, while imported boxers from Mexico get the principal engagements and live in comfort. An American boxer cannot compete with imported cheap trash from Mexico."[113] This nativist discourse characterized white boxers as hardworking and humble, while Mexican boxers were ungrateful intruders into the sport. The power of whiteness in sports continues to valorize white athletes at the expense of their black and Latino counterparts.[114]

Blacks and Mexicans faced differential forms of discrimination and exclusion in the sport of boxing. The Texas legislature barred black boxers from fighting whites in interracial matches, and this ban remained until 1954 when African American boxer I. H. "Sporty" Harvey launched a successful lawsuit to desegregate the sport.[115] Unlike blacks, Mexican prizefighters were legally constructed as "white" and were therefore allowed to participate in mixed-race matches despite facing subtle to overt forms of discrimination based on race, class, and citizenship. For example, Mexican prizefighters were considered a threat to the "white hopes" of Texas boxing. The U.S. immigration office in Galveston, Texas, received complaints about the importation of boxers from Mexico, supposedly intended to lower wages and reduce opportunities for white American boxers. One San Antonio resident complained about the "wholesale passage of Mexican Boxers from across the river at Laredo."[116] He explained that boxing in San Antonio was "in a very bad condition" because the local newspaper owner and promoter had established a monopoly where they import boxers from Mexico "while the local [white] boys sit around idle." He wrote, "The promoter used to pay Americans $35 to $50 dollars for semi-finals but now he uses Mexicans for Ten Rounds instead of Eight Rounds for $20 to $30 dollars." He recommended that the San Antonio immigration office investigate and offered his help "to put a stop to this violation in trying to give the fans and especially the [white] boxers on our side a fair deal." As a result, this racialized language—"cheap" undocumented Mexican workers "stealing American jobs"—led to concerted efforts by federal, state, and local officials targeting Mexicans for deportation and repatriation during the early 1930s because of the mistaken belief that they were a burden on the welfare system and stealing American jobs.

The popular image of Mexicans as "illegal aliens" and "invaders" in the print media contributed to Mexican boxers' problem at the border. A United Press article, "Mexican Boxers To Invade Los Angeles," circulated around the country and described Casanova and Villanueva as "two of Mexico's young but seasoned ring warriors that will invade Los Angeles."[117] A *Los Angeles Times* headline did not help their cause by using the language of invasion: "Rival Gymnasiums Squabble over Invading Mexican Boxers."[118] One boxing enthusiast wrote to *Ring* and claimed, "Too many foreigners have come to our shores in hordes, have taken thousands of dollars from us and have given us little in return but trouble."[119] According to historian Natalia Molina, nativists constructed a racial script of "Mexican invasion" to recast Mexican immigrants as a racial problem and thus justify legislative and judicial efforts to place them on a quota system and deny them citizenship.[120] When these efforts failed, anti-immigrationists turned to the "deportable Mexican" script as a more viable solution.

THE GLOVES ARE OFF: THE PUBLIC CAMPAIGN FOR MEXICAN BOXERS

News of the barring of Mexican boxers from the United States reached LA boxing circles. In response, boxing promoters quickly postponed the upcoming bouts and kick-started a publicity campaign to pressure the Department of Labor for a favorable ruling on the appeal. The ruling was bad news for former silent film actor Tom Gallery, who was making his debut as the new promoter and matchmaker for the Olympic Auditorium. Gallery had lined up two "Mexico City-versus-Manila" bouts, expecting to generate huge amounts of cash for the venue and promoters. These matches were certain to sell out, reasoned Gallery, "since the Mexicans are champions in their nation. The Filipinos hold California titles."[121] Filipino and Mexican boxers were formidable rivals according to at least one observer: "The harder they are pressed, the better they fight."[122] Like Mexicans, Filipinos developed feelings of anger fueled by acts of racial hostility and nativist backlash in Depression-era California. Nevertheless, as Linda España-Maram asserts, "Filipino pugilists sought a legitimate place within organized sport by defying its assumptions about race and ability."[123] To be sure, though, promoters fueled this rivalry by assigning separate seating for Mexican and Filipino fans.[124] Olympic Auditorium promoter Jack Doyle decided to have separate ticket windows and seating for Mexican and Filipino fans because "the feeling between Mexican and Filipino fans is at such a high pitch."[125] Since the border incident threatened a huge loss in revenue, Gallery publicly lobbied to win a favorable ruling: "Bringing Casanova and Azteca from Mexico City gave the fights international publicity. [Until] the two Latins got their feet caught in the immigration bridge between Juarez and El Paso. It took extra work to get them on a plane headed for Los Angeles."[126]

Furthermore, Gallery enlisted the help of Salvador Baguez, a Mexican artist for the *Los Angeles Times*. Baguez published a drawing of Casanova's somber face next to Villanueva with slumping shoulders, sad face, and strapped fists with no gloves (see Figure 2.3).[127] Combined with the headlines "On the Outside Looking In" and "Mexico's Best Bets Denied Admission," the drawing sought to generate sympathy for the Mexican boxers who were "forced to camp" for ten days while they

On the Outside Looking in   -   -   -   -   -   By Salvador Baguez

FIGURE 2.3. Luis "Kid Azteca" Villanueva and Rodolfo "Baby" Casanova in a *Los Angeles Times* cartoon drawing (June 22, 1933) by Salvador Baguez. (Courtesy of Salvador Baguez and *Los Angeles Times* Staff)

waited for a final decision from Washington, DC.[128] Baguez published the same drawing in *La Opinión* to generate support from *los paisanos* (their compatriots).[129] While Villanueva and Casanova waited for their appeal, *La Opinión* called for the postponing of Villanueva's match against Ceferino Garcia because he needed more time to train: "This encounter is important and they should not risk losing."[130] Los Angeles boxing promoter Jack Doyle told the *Los Angeles Times* that he was confident that Villanueva could still make the fight if released immediately. Since Villanueva had been training in El Paso, "he saw no reason why the show would not be held."[131]

It took Gallery's political connections to convince Department of Labor officials to grant them approval. On June 22, Gallery sent a telegram to his former Cathedral College classmate and *Chicago American* reporter Ed Gorey, asking him to intervene. Gorey explaining the situation in writing to James Farley, U.S. postmaster general and close friend of President Roosevelt's: "It seems their Mexican manager for some unknown reason listed them as tailors although Gallery has posted $500 bond listing them as boxers and guaranteed their return in the usual manner and custom prevailing on the west coast apparently the difference in listing caused the authorities to detain them. Gallery flew in for brief visit with me and plans to fly back Sunday, shall appreciate the favor greatly if anything can consistently be done to straighten out the matter."[132] On June 28, after a week in limbo, Villanueva, Casanova, and Torres received approval to be formally admitted under a sixty-day temporary visa with a five-hundred-dollar bond to ensure their return home.[133] Not mentioned in the English print media is the role of the Spanish-language press and Mexican American leaders who sought to help Kid Azteca and Baby Casanova gain entry.

LA's largest Spanish-language newspaper, *La Opinión*, played an important role in publicizing their detention. When Villanueva and Casanova failed to arrive on their scheduled day, the newspaper expressed concern and asked the Mexican consul to inquire about their delay. The vice consul from Los Angeles, Benjamin Hill, immediately sent a telegram to the consul general at El Paso, requesting that "all necessary steps be taken for Casanova and Villanueva and not suffer any delay when subjected to immigration requirements."[134] "Don't the immigration authorities understand how far they have to travel far before their match," complained *La Opinión* sports columnist Rafael Ybarra, who continued, "They are making them go around and around and spending money right and left on telegrams." He reminded readers of Gilberto Rodríguez, who attempted to cross through San Pedro but was detained and forced to sleep overnight on his boat while he waited for an appeal. This, according to Ybarra, illustrates "the cold face and unshakable heart of the immigration authorities."[135]

In another column, Ybarra blamed the incident on their manager Jimmy Fitten, who wrongly advised them to enter as tourists but rather "should have stated their [boxing] profession." He accused Fitten of naïveté for failing to understand that "in this country they don't believe there is such a thing as dark-skinned Mexican tourist with decayed suitcases."[136] Even if they had had a boxing contract there was no guarantee they would be allowed entry because of INS reports alleging that Mexican immigrants had been using "fraudulent boxing contracts" to enter the United States, which led U.S. immigration inspectors to further scrutinize those claiming to be boxers and trainers.[137] Accusations of fraudulent contracts served to mark Mexican prizefighters as untrustworthy and suspicious of manipulating the immigration system for their own gain.

Mexican American prizefighters in Los Angeles heard about the border incident and sought to defend Casanova and Villanueva. Upon hearing about Casanova and Villanueva, Bert Colima called his former manager, Dutch Meyers, to intervene on their behalf by calling U.S. immigration officials in El Paso. Meyers reportedly spent a hundred sixty dollars on telephone calls to El Paso, Washington, and Chicago.[138] After his final retirement in 1933, Colima remained close to the boxing world by attending the fights and mentoring younger fighters. Bert W. Colima recalled how his dad "would go to the Main Street Gym and talk to the boxers and managers about up-and-coming boxers. He would offer his help, or anything else he could do stay close to the game. Everyone in the gym always received Colima with great affection, greeting him with 'Geeve it to heem Colima' as he entered the gym."[139] The slogan was popularized by Mexican actress Lupe Vélez, who was an ardent fan of Mexican boxers and revealed how much fans loved to cheer for Colima.

Mexico City newspapers followed the border incident with special concern for Casanova and Villanueva. *El Excélsior* questioned why "the popular Mexicans settled for saying they were going for a walk when they knew they were going to fight Los Angeles."[140] They blamed the promoters (Fitten and Gallery) for not advising them correctly and offering them a contract and bond in advance.[141] The incident reminded readers about Casanova's first match in Los Angeles when he battled Filipino boxer Speedy Dado on November 15, 1932, and lost in ten rounds before ten thousand spectators at the Olympic Auditorium. Casanova's defeat led *El Gráfico* to launch a Stay at Home campaign for Mexican boxers who were sent to the United States only "to be victimized."[142] One Mexican doctor cautioned against sending Mexican boxers to the United States "until they are ready to defend themselves not only against their opponents but against the maneuvers of referees as well."[143] He suggested, "A Mexican to win in dollar-land must knock out or overwhelm his opponent to win."[144] The Stay at Home campaign abruptly dissipated, but it revealed Mexican leaders' increasing interest in developing athletes to compete effectively at the international level. Thirty years later, however, the new head of Mexico City's Boxing Commission, Luis Spota, prohibited Mexican boxers from fighting in California until they received fair matches, a medical exam, and equal opportunities to fight in both Mexico and California.[145]

FIGURE 2.4. Hollywood actress Lupe Vélez was an ardent boxing fan who cheered at ringside for her favorite Mexican boxers at the Olympic Auditorium. (Courtesy of the Lozano family/*La Opinión* Collection, The Huntington Library, San Marino, CA)

Mexican prizefighters' biggest fan and supporter was stage and screen actress Lupe Vélez, who attended boxing matches on Friday nights at the Hollywood Legion, frequently occupying a front-row seat where she would stand, yell, and cajole Mexican boxers to knock out their opponents (see Figure 2.4). Vélez defended Mexican boxers when they were wrongly denied a victory in the ring. *La Prensa* recounted an incident when Vélez jumped into the ring to hit the referee with an umbrella after her favorite Mexican boxer was denied a win.[146] Although it cost her a thousand-dollar fine, she earned a reputation as a loud champion of Mexican boxers. When Vélez committed suicide with a drug overdose on December 13, 1944, the *La Opinión* sports editor wrote, "The death of Lupe Vélez caused more sensation in the boxing circles of Los Angeles than in the artistic world where the number one boxing fan reached international fame."[147] Through her attendance at boxing bouts, Vélez expressed nationalist loyalty to Mexico and challenged traditional gender norms. It was considered inappropriate for Mexican women to fight or to encourage others to fight for prizemoney. But according to Gregory Rodriguez, a large number of Mexican females attended boxing bouts during the interwar years, often with a male chaperone, and "found a freedom that broke with social convention and defied gender conformity."[148]

Besides Vélez, other early Mexican movie stars with Hollywood ties were also boxing fans, including Ramon Novarro, Gilbert Roland, and Anthony Quinn. In his autobiography, Quinn recounts how he himself became a boxer and befriended Mexican boxers.[149] Fighting under the name Tony Quinn, he won nine welterweight fights and earned twenty to thirty dollars per fight, until he got knocked out by an African American boxer. He retired early from the sport because he lacked "a killer instinct." It is interesting to note that Quinn used his brief boxing career to deliver a remarkable performance as a boxer in the 1962 film classic *Requiem for a Heavyweight*.

After a weeklong publicity campaign, the U.S. Department of Labor on June 29 approved Villanueva and Casanova to enter for only sixty days as "nonimmigrants."[150] Upon hearing the good news, *La Opinión* announced their pending arrival at Burbank Airport, where "representatives of the fighters, some athletic groups and numerous sympathizers, will attend in order to welcome them. It is expected that their presence in these parts will inject animation to pugilistic activities."[151] Upon arrival, Villanueva and Casanova began training at the Ringside Gym for their rescheduled double-feature match on Tuesday, July 11. Fans congregated around the gym to catch a glimpse of their boxers. One sports reporter observed that, "They have packed the gymnasium day after day to watch the workouts of the Latins."[152] Jimmy Fitten announced his arrival to Los Angeles prior to the match to "personally take care of his boys." Ybarra jokingly reminded readers about the proverb, "The master's eye makes the horse fat," which means that looking after one's possessions will bring good results.[153] It was a mixed result, however, as Young Tommy soundly defeated Casanova in ten rounds and Villanueva scored a ten-round decision over Ceferino Garcia before eight thousand fans. One of the loudest fans was Vélez, who shouted at Villanueva to knock out Cerefino Garcia.[154] According to the *Los Angeles Times*, she was also "doing one of those hot-cha dances as her Mexican idol put the Filipino in his place."[155]

Because of their negative experience with U.S. immigration authorities, Casanova and Villanueva decided to return to Mexico City.[156] Six months later, when Casanova returned for a rematch against Speedy Dado, he was again detained at El Paso while U.S. immigration authorities investigated the "alien status" of the "little Mexican battler."[157] After several days, he received temporary admission for six months after immigration authorities ruled that his profession was "unusual" and "unique."[158] In part because of their immigration problems, Casanova and Villanueva remained living and working in Mexico City, where they enjoyed more success and popularity. Casanova left his manager and trainer because they "mismanaged" his funds and "injured" his health by forcing him to make weights out of his class.[159] After his retirement, a Mexican film, *Campeón sin Corona* (1946), largely based on his life story helped to bolster his image as a masculine role model. Although mythologized as a "champion without a crown," Casanova wrestled with alcoholism, mental health problems, womanizing, and an unstable family life, ultimately costing him his life.[160]

THE SEARCH FOR THE "GREAT BROWN HOPE"

After Casanova and Villanueva returned to Mexico, promoter Jimmy Fitten tried to convince world bantamweight champion Al "Panama" Brown to fight one of his boxers in Mexico City because "Mexico must have a champion no matter who, provided he is Mexican." Fitten declared to *La Opinión*, "It is time for Mexico to have a world boxing championship to show the boxing world that this manly sport is no longer in diapers in our country."[161] In 1929, Panama's Brown became the first Latin American world champion in the sport of boxing, followed by Cuba's Eligio Sardiñas Montalvo, better known as Kid Chocolate, who became feather and junior lightweight champion in 1931.[162] Two years later, on February 20, 1933, José "Battling Shaw" Perez Flores defeated Johnny Jadick in New Orleans to claim the world light welterweight belt and become "the first Mexican boxer to win a ring title."[163] He kept the title through two defenses until he lost to Tony Canzoneri three months later. The National Boxing Association refused to recognize his title because they considered the weight class a "synthetic division" and Jadick had already relinquished the title prior to the fight. Although newspapers and boxing records referred to him as "Battling Shaw of Mexico," he was born in Laredo and considered himself a "Texas boy."[164] Because he was not born in Mexico, according to *La Opinión*, "he is not genuinely Mexican and spent his first days in the State of Texas."[165] The Spanish-language newspaper's strict definition of Mexican was based narrowly on birthright citizenship. Previous Mexican American contenders like Aurelio Herrera, Joe Rivers, and Bert Colima had fought, but lost world title fights.[166]

The search for a "great brown hope" who could deliver a world championship for Mexico continued in the 1930s. Alberto Arizmendi emerged as the next contender. Born to a working-class family in Tampico, Arizmendi overcame a mild case of polio and school yard bullying by taking boxing lessons from a family friend who taught him to defend himself. He used his fighting skills to stand up to bullies and soon thereafter became a leader of a gang who called him "El Generalito" (little general), a nickname that followed him throughout his boxing career in Mexico. At the age of thirteen Arizmendi became the youngest professional boxer when he debuted in Laredo. He then moved to Mexico City and won a string of victories in 1931, including Mexico's bantamweight title by defeating Kid Pancho, after which he received offers to fight in Los Angeles. Before he arrived there, his manager Bert Morse encouraged him to adopt the nickname "Baby" because of his youthful looks and marketing appeal.[167] After Arizmendi defeated Speedy Dado on February 9, 1932, at the Olympic Auditorium to earn the California featherweight title, he became "the new Mexican sensation" in the sports media.[168] One reporter attributed Arizmendi's fighting ability to his "Aztec ancestry along with the fire which warms the Spanish blood in his veins, the brown idol of Old Mexico and Little Mexico alike."[169] The *Ring* concurred when describing Arizmendi as a "two fisted puncher" with "an Aztec stolidity in his face."[170] A state title was not enough for Arizmendi, as one sports columnist noted: "This little brown son from below the border wants to establish his claim on the world's championship."[171] His opportunity to fight for a world title came on February 28, 1933, when Freddy Miller agreed to a ten-round bout at the Olympic Auditorium.

Anticipation over the Arizmendi-Miller confrontation began to take shape in the pages of *La Opinión* when readers expressed their opinions about the upcoming title fight. The newspaper published over 140 letters and telegrams from readers as far away as Chicago and Mexico City.[172] A majority predicted Arizmendi to clinch the world title, but only "if there is a fair referee," explained one fan. They continued, "Unfortunately, we have always been victims of the referees, when it comes to serious contests in which a Mexican participates."[173] For this reason, fans believed that he could win only by knockout. The racial overtones of the fight were evident when one fan wrote, "The Aztec eagle will win easily because the courage of a Mexican Indian is undoubtedly superior to the German Miller."[174] Another fan invoked the historic battle of Tenochtitlan when he wrote that Arizmendi resembled "the agility and courage of Cuauhtémoc . . . and Miller will mourn his defeat like Hernan Cortes."[175] A dozen female fans wrote letters offering their support and prayers for Arizmendi. One female reminded him that "the Mexican nation is behind you waiting for you to ring its name in exile."[176] Two days before the title fight, Arizmendi responded with a published letter: "Although the hopes of my countrymen have obliged me to do my best. I can assure you that you will not be disappointed in your hopes, for even in defeat you will always see me fight like men." He reaffirmed his national and masculine pride by stating that "he is not afraid of the champion" and expects "to give my people the satisfaction of a world championship."[177]

Although Arizmendi was favored to defeat Miller, he lost in a ten-round decision before twelve thousand spectators. Miller dominated the fight, winning seven out of ten rounds, while Arizmendi later claimed that he was ill twenty minutes before match time.[178] The referee's decision angered fans, who threw bottles, seats, and other projectiles toward the ring causing, some injuries. The English-language sports press accused Mexican fans of causing a "near riot" with their "fiery Latin blood" causing injury to four people.[179] One boxing reporter proclaimed, "It was the wildest scene recalled in modern California ring history."[180] Additionally, the press described Mexican fans as irresponsible gamblers. For example, a cartoon portrayed a naked Mexican fan—crammed inside a wheelbarrow—strolling away from a bookie. The caption read, "Mexican fight fans are rabid. They will bet all they own on their idols."[181] The Spanish-language press warned readers that the actions of a few "passionate fans" have contributed to the racialization of "all Mexicans" in the mainstream press. *La Opinión*'s Rafael Ybarra scolded those "passionate fans" who threw bottles at innocent spectators and "signified that perhaps the Mexican people are not yet qualified to have a world champion." Ybarra argued, "We must teach ourselves to be good losers" and urged all Mexican fans to conduct themselves that reflected positively on the Mexican nation.[182] This criticism reflected the middle-class bias and racial uplift ideology of La Opinión staff members.

After losing to Miller, Arizmendi faced more battles outside the ring. On May 5, 1933, U.S. immigration authorities denied entry to Arizmendi at the Tijuana border station because he was classified as an "undesirable alien."[183] Equipped with a temporary visa, Arizmendi visited Tijuana for a boxing benefit show, but when he attempted to return he was denied entry because of a thirty-five-hundred-dollar judgment filed by his former girlfriend in LA Superior Court.[184] The previous year, seventeen-year-old Frances Armenta had sued Arizmendi for "betraying her under the promise of marriage" and endured "disgrace and mental suffering" as a single mother with his infant son. Arizmendi denied that he was the father and asserted that she brought the suit for "the purpose of embarrassing him because he was engaged to marry another girl."[185] "Arizmendi has hit another snag," reported one sports columnist. "It looks as though his affair with the 17-year-old is going to prove costly in other ways than paying out 3,500."[186] With the help of his new manager, Cal Working, who translated, Arizmendi appealed to the U.S. Department of Labor, which ruled he could to return, but only if he paid the judgment to Armenta.[187] La Opinión's Ybarra speculated that perhaps "[immigration] won't let him return to the United States because they don't want foreign champions here."[188] After a few days, he paid the money and was allowed to reenter the United States, but his problems with Armenta continued. Years later Arizmendi admitted that he was the father of Armenta's son Raul, after a paternity test forced him to plead guilty to a charge of failing to provide child support. Armenta told the court that she did not need the money. "All I want is that he admits he's the father—he's been so stubborn."[189] Arizmendi's problems with women stemmed from his masculine behavior reinforced by boxing's association with toughness, aggressiveness, and physical prowess that extended beyond the ring. Unlike Casanova and Villanueva, who returned to Mexico, Arizmendi remained in the United States after marrying Henrietta Herold.

Arizmendi's problems at the U.S.-Mexico border raised questions of race and citizenship. Sports cartoonist Werner Laufer illustrated his battle with U.S. immigration officials in a cartoon titled "Aztec Assassin," distributed around the country.[190] Arizmendi, the "hot tamale on the featherweight trail," is depicted as a short, scrawny boxer who challenges a black boxer named Chocolate and white boxer named Miller to a prizefight. Chocolate tells Miller, "We Nordics Shouldn't Play with Those Mex Latins, Fred!" Laufer positioned Arizmendi as a perpetual foreigner attempting to gain entry to the black-and-white boxing world. Another sombrero-wearing caricature of Arizmendi is running away from Uncle Sam, who is pointing his finger and shouting "Scram." The caption reads, "The Babe had a tough time getting Uncle Sam to okay him—Now that he's a citizen he wants his chance." Laufer incorrectly stated that Arizmendi had renounced his Mexican citizenship to gain U.S. citizenship. The cartoon portrays Mexican boxers as a perceived threat to color line, fearing that if Arizmendi is given just one opportunity to become a citizen, he will become the next featherweight champion. Upset about the racist and xenophobic cartoon, Mexican boxing fans wrote to *La Opinión* to express their opinions. One San Francisco fan accused the cartoonist of "trying to play politics with our own idol."[191] Another fan related that "we have the absolute certainty that Arizmendi is very Mexican, but we believe that this illustration can cause him some difficulties." Arizmendi repudiated this "citizenship change" allegation and declared to *La Opinión* that "I'm very proud of being Mexican." Although the language barrier inhibited Arizmendi from speaking directly to Laufer, he directed his manager Cal Working to contact Laufer. Laufer apologized for the citizenship error and claimed to be an admirer of Arizmendi. Despite Laufer's mea culpa, the vast circulation of this controversial cartoon contributed to the racialization of Mexican boxers. However, Arizmendi's and fans' responses revealed their agency to make their own claims about belonging in the boxing world.

After the border and cartoon controversy, Arizmendi refocused on his training for the next big title bout in New York City. On August 30, 1934, he squared off against Mike Belloise at the Dickman Oval baseball stadium and easily captured his first world featherweight title.[192] The New York State Athletic Commission recognized Arizmendi as the new holder of the title previously vacated by Kid Chocolate, although the National Boxing Association still recognized Freddie Miller as the world featherweight champion. After the win, Arizmendi approached Miller for a rematch but Miller refused, thus denying Arizmendi a shot at the National Boxing Association title. Nevertheless, Arizmendi became the first Mexican boxer to win a world championship. *La Opinión* ran the headlines "Arizmendi, World Champ" and "He Reached the Goal, Finally!" on the front page of its August 31 issue with a picture of Arizmendi with a wide-brimmed straw hat and serape blanket.[193] Even the *Los Angeles Times* praised "the brown skinned 'Little General' from below the Rio Grande" for winning eleven out of fifteen rounds.[194] "I went up to the ring remembering my homeland," Arizmendi told *La Opinión* in a telephone interview. He dedicated his victory to all Mexicans on both sides of the border: "The thought was that my supporters and friends in Los Angeles and Mexico had all their hopes on me, that they wanted to see me come back to Los Angeles bringing them the world featherweight championship. So I had to win it with blood and fire in the ring."[195]

Arizmendi was already a "Mexican hero" in the eyes of Mexican fans who wrote poems, plays and *corridos* (folk ballads) expressing their devotion to Arizmendi (see Figure 2.5).[196] Fans lined up at Teatro Hidalgo to watch a new play, *El Establo de Arizmendi* (Arizmendi's stable), by Daniel Venegas, on the early life of

FIGURE 2.5. Mexican boys admiring their boxing hero, Alberto Arizmendi (right) before his fight against Jackie Wilson at Wrigley Field on May 17, 1941. (Courtesy of the *Los Angeles Herald Examiner* Photo Collection, Los Angeles Public Library)

Arizmendi.[197] Another example is a famous corrido titled "The Ballad of the Famous Mexican Champion—Baby Arizmendi," written by F. T. Franco:[198]

> There's a lion in a California
> And he wants to be a champion
> And he's covering with glory
> The Mexican flag.

Arizmendi is a good rooster
Wherever he paints and stripes
He is like a lighting hurricane
And of shrapnel

This corrido extols the masculinity and national pride of Arizmendi. Comparing him to a lion and a rooster who "knows no fear [and will] fight with anyone" conveys the masculine duty of Arizmendi to protect and defend the Mexican nation.[199] The corrido, typically depicting male outlaws of the Mexican Revolution and the Texas-Mexico border region, was now for the first time dedicated to a male sports hero. As Américo Paredes observed long ago, the corrido represented the heroic struggle against oppression in Greater Mexico.[200] In effect, Franco's corrido had galvanized Mexican fans to cheer for Arizmendi as he battled for recognition in both the boxing world and American society.

In 1942, Arizmendi retired from boxing and enlisted in the U.S. Navy, serving in the Pacific during World War II. After the war, Arizmendi opened a popular restaurant, California Café, at 1558 Sunset Boulevard in the Echo Park district of Los Angeles. He used his popularity to attract patrons and offered a space for retired boxers to reminisce about their old fighting days. One advertisement announced to *Sport Page* readers to come "Meet Popular Baby Arizmendi at the California Café."[201] Sometimes, however, scuffles would break out between boxers who tried to resolve old grievances or promote their next fight.[202] Arizmendi remained a restaurant owner until he died of diabetes-related complications in 1963, at the age of forty-eight.

CONCLUSION

Mexican and Mexican American prizefighters embodied the racial hopes and fears of their community and nation during the Roaring Twenties and the Depression. They entered the boxing world as neither black nor white, but as the next "great brown hope" who could win a world championship title for Mexico. Boxing promoters and matchmakers searched far and wide for Mexican prizefighters to fill arenas and build a loyal fan base. Reflecting on the fifty years of Mexican boxing in Los Angeles, *La Opinión*'s boxing journalist Luis Magaña concluded that "Bert Colima, born in Whittier was one of the first great idols . . . before the Aztec boxers began arriving in California."[203] Colima emerged as a celebrity sports hero for challenging prevailing stereotypes of "lazy," "dirty," and "diseased" Mexicans that fueled nativist calls for harsh immigration restrictions. Even in Mexico, Colima won over new fans and was treated like royalty by Mexican government officials.

Boxing emerged as a transnational sport in Greater Mexico despite attempts by social reformers and government officials to regulate the mobility of Mexican prizefighters. Under the direction of managers, trainers, and promoters, boxers moved from Mexico City to Los Angeles to fight for money and glory, but because of restrictive immigration laws, they were briefly denied temporary entry. The immigration problems faced by Rodolfo Casanova, Luis Villanueva, and Alberto Arizmendi revealed their economic vulnerability and racialization. Immigration authorities racialized Mexican prizefighters as "brown bodies" who supposedly threatened the livelihood of Euro-American boxers. Although the U.S. immigration regime treated Mexican boxers as a racial and economic threat, the public campaign waged by promoters, sportswriters, and fans forced their release and temporary admittance. Temporary admittance became an "in-between" category in U.S. immigration law that limited the rights of migrant athletes and sometimes made them vulnerable to exploitation in the boxing industry. Boxers in the Mexican diaspora could challenge their own marginality, not only through their public identity but through hidden maneuvers, activating their sporting networks and political connections, and seeking compassion and solidarity from supporters. By making themselves visible to fans and sports media, however, Mexican boxers challenged the production of their illegality and deportability.

U.S. immigration officials also denied entry to baseball players from Mexico. On March 21 1932 José "Chile" Gómez was refused admittance into the United States by the Immigration and Naturalization Service after trying to travel to Memphis, Tennessee.[204] Gómez was born in Villa Union, Sinaloa, and at the age of ten he immigrated to United States with his family. His family settled in south Los Angeles near John Adams Junior High, where he began playing sports. He excelled in football and track and field at Polytechnic High School, but it was in baseball where he got the nickname "Chile" for his quickness and fielding skills.[205] After high school graduation, he played second base for the México-El Paso team for one season until he joined Club Aztecas in Mexico City.[206] After playing several seasons with the Mexican Baseball League, he was signed by a Memphis baseball club, but did not make spring training because he was detained at the U.S.-Mexico border. Gómez was disgusted by immigration officials' refusal "to allow him to cross the border." He told the *New York Times* that he would try again, but "if he failed he will rejoin the Aztecas."[207] Ultimately, he did return to the Aztecas until 1935, when the Philadelphia Phillies came looking for a second baseman. Gómez impressed the Phillies with his "brilliant fielding game" and was offered a contract. He became the second Mexican player to join the Big Leagues.[208]

3 • PLAYING *BÉISBOL* ACROSS BORDERS

On June 5, 1955, former ballplayers of the El Paso Shoe Store team gathered at the Hotel Statler in Downtown Los Angeles to share memories about the best years of their lives. Billed as "El Banquete de Recuerdos" (a banquet of memories), this reunion of semiprofessional baseball players was the brainchild of baseball player and promoter Tony Gamboa, who had expressed a desire to honor "these Mexican players from the Golden Age of Baseball."[1] In attendance were former team owners Arturo and Rodrigo Castillo and coach Tony Galindo, accompanied by a majority of original team members.[2] Formed in 1926, the El Paso Shoe Store team changed its name to México-El Paso in 1930 to emphasize its transnational ties with Mexican baseball. In its fiftieth anniversary edition, *La Opinión's* sportswriter Luis Magaña touted México-El Paso as "the most powerful team at the time [1920s and 1930s] . . . composed entirely of Mexican players."[3] "This nine-man team was so popular among Mexican fans," recalled another sportswriter, that "many came to White Sox Park from all over the city."[4]

Built in 1924, White Sox ballpark in South Los Angeles became the center of nonwhite semiprofessional baseball, where Negro League, Japanese American, and Mexican American teams faced each other in front of cheering fans. México-El Paso hosted teams from Mexico and barnstormed throughout Mexico, in search of opportunities to both play and develop a transnational sporting network. For Mexican Americans, playing baseball in Mexico provided an opportunity to play on a more level playing field. It allowed ballplayers to visit their homeland and renew their ties with family and friends. And while baseball historians have documented the Negro League players who migrated to the Mexican Baseball League during the 1930s and 1940s, they have failed to consider that Mexican Americans also made a similar journey.[5] To capture the transnational experience of ballplayers, we must follow their footsteps. As baseball historian Adrian Burgos reminds us, "[A] geographically determined notion of identity fails to take into account the role of migration as a critical aspect of Latino experience and identity in the twentieth century."[6]

Mexican American women also joined baseball and softball teams during the same period, albeit in lesser numbers because they faced greater barriers than their male counterparts. Women faced enormous societal pressure to play softball instead of baseball—a larger ball, a shorter distance between bases, and smaller fields. Although they faced strict parents and limited sponsorship opportunities, Mexican American women formed teams of their own with fierce yet feminine names like Las Debs, Las Aztecas, Los Tomboys, Vixies, and Señoritas. They became *peloteras* by playing baseball and softball on women-only teams with an all-male coaching staff. These peloteras competed in citywide and regional tournaments but were neither allowed nor encouraged to travel abroad and play in Mexico. Although these Mexican American women are inconspicuously absent in baseball and softball histories and newspaper remembrances, they nevertheless found ways to insert themselves into the history of the national pastime.[7]

This chapter examines the local and transnational connections of baseball and softball in Greater Mexico during the 1920s and 1930s. It focuses on the experiences of male and female ballplayers—spanning from amateur to professional—who crossed racial, gender, and national borders to play ball. Sport historians have tended to focus more on male ballplayers. Therefore, I trace the participation of Mexican American women in the amateur softball leagues of Southern California. Ultimately, I argue that male ballplayers forged transnational connections with Mexico to overcome racial and class barriers on U.S. playing fields, whereas peloteras were constrained by gender expectations and patriarchal structures that limited their mobility within and across the nation-state. Nevertheless, Mexican American baseball and softball women contributed to the formation of a sporting Mexican diaspora and advanced gender equality in their families and communities as well as making great strides in the histories of women, sports, and Latinas.

THE RISE OF *BÉISBOL* IN GREATER MEXICO

In 1911, sporting goods mogul A. G. Spalding declared that baseball should "follow the flag."[8] In particular, American writers fashioned an imperialist discourse about how if Mexico wanted to become a modern nation, its citizens needed to replace the barbaric sport of bullfighting with baseball. An American tourist observed that bullfighting "is a brutal, degrading sport, which the authorities have done much to discourage, but it has a very strong hold on the vulgar herd."[9] Despite the Mexican elite's attempts to ban bullfighting, this spectacle continued to be popular among the working class until after the Mexican Revolution, while Americans heavily promoted baseball.[10] A series of baseball exhibitions sought to introduce to Mexico the American ideals of competition, teamwork, and discipline. An American traveler who had stumbled upon one of these games observed that Mexican ballplayers lack "Yankee alertness manifested in their playing, as you see in the picture some of the players are standing with arms folded, or leaning against the chimney."[11] This observation revealed American racial thinking about Mexicans as mentally and physically unprepared to play modern sports. Ban Johnson, president of the American League, visited Mexico City several times to donate a championship trophy to the winning team "in the interest of good sportsmanship between the United States and Mexico," but also "to displace the cruel and savage bullfight with the clean American sport of baseball."[12] By the 1920s, baseball was surpassing bullfighting in popularity. The YMCA general secretary in Mexico stated, "It is difficult in Chihuahua to get up a lively interest in bull fighting because the Mexican men and boys have taken up baseball and are playing with enthusiasm."[13]

In June 1925, the first organized baseball league debuted in Mexico City precisely around the same time that an amateur and semipro Mexican American baseball movement was emerging in Los Angeles. Sportswriter Alejandro Aguilar Reyes, who wrote under the pseudonym Fray Nano, joined forces with baseball promoter Ernesto Carmona to form the Mexican Baseball League.[14] The league began with five teams—all located in the capital city—but inconsistent play, mostly empty ballparks, and erratic schedules plagued the early years.[15] By 1930, the league enlisted the help of baseball promoter Homobono Márquez, who had formed a powerhouse team, Club Fabriles (later renamed Aztecas), and organized exhibition matches against teams from Cuba, the Negro Leagues, and Mexican American semiprofessional teams in the United States.[16] In 1932, President Abelardo Rodríguez, a former varsity baseball player for the University of Arizona, created the country's first sports federation to promote sports and physical education. A year later, Baldomero "Melo" Almada, a Mexico-born player who grew up in Los Angeles, was drafted by the Boston Red Sox and during the off-season accepted President Rodríguez's invitation to play exhibition games in Mexico City.

Americanization influenced the coverage of baseball in the Spanish-language press. Norman Hayner recognized the increased use of a new hybrid language in Mexico City newspapers. For example, *El Excélsior* adopted the words *un jit, jonrón, fual,* and *straiquaut* in their baseball coverage.[17] The use of hybrid terms also appeared in *La Opinión* during its coverage of the World Series. Some words used included *wild pitch, base por bolas,* and *un doble play.*[18] Mexican conservative journalists opposed the spread of *pochismo* in the Spanish language by organizing Anti-Pochismo week in August 1944.[19] They accused Mexican sportswriters of using "bastardized works which are neither Spanish or Yanqui."[20] Defenders claimed that there were few equivalent terms in Spanish to describe American sporting activities. Sports editor of *La Opinión* Ignacio Herrerías reflected on the use of the term *pochismo* and questioned why fans call athletes *pochos* as an insult. In his opinion, "There is no basis for our countrymen, those born in Mexico, to confront our brothers born here simply because they are not responsible for their parents emigrating to the United States."[21] Herrerías correctly noted the problem with disparaging a person's identity without recognizing the historical and structural factors that create a hybrid language and identity in the Mexican diaspora.

By the early 1940s, millionaire Jorge Pasquel sought to build a full-fledged baseball league by luring top professionals away from Major League Baseball to the Mexican League. His recruitment plans included enticing Negro League stars to Mexico's more welcoming racial climate. U.S. sportswriters characterized Pasquel's operation as an "outlaw" league seeking to "raid" the major leagues and setting off a "baseball war" between both countries.[22] The *New York Times* declared, "Mexico is out to destroy the United States monopoly on baseball."[23] In 1946, Pasquel signed white American players, a move that upset baseball commissioner Albert "Happy" Chandler and prompted a five-year ban against all major leaguers who jumped their contracts to play for Pasquel's league. Still, eighteen major leaguers defied the ban. "No one in the world loves baseball more than the people of Mexico, and millions of our fans deeply resented the use of the word 'outlaw' to describe the Mexican League," wrote former ballplayer Mario de la Fuente in his provocative memoir, *I Like You, Gringo—But!*.[24] By 1949, Pasquel's short-lived plan had failed to live up to players' expectations when their salaries decreased and stadiums began to deteriorate. Five years later, Pasquel died in a plane crash and left the Mexican League in disarray. Even though the new league had folded, Mexico's integrated baseball system helped pave the way for racial integration of American baseball.

As Mexican immigrants journeyed to the United States seeking economic security for their families, they brought their passion for baseball with them. Once they secured a steady job and cozy home, their children spent their leisure time at movie theaters, dance halls, and playgrounds.[25] It was on the diamond, however, rather than at church, where many preferred to be on Sundays.[26] Although many were already familiar with baseball in Mexico, they found better facilities at the schools and parks. Young boys and men also became "star struck" with sports heroes in a consumer-driven economy that gave rise to the golden age of American sports.[27] Chief among them was George Herman "Babe" Ruth, who frequently excited fans with his home runs and outgoing personality. Ruth frequently visited Los Angeles during the off-season because he could earn extra money making public appearances and taking promotional photographs with Hollywood stars.[28] English- and Spanish-language newspapers covered his whereabouts in the city.[29] *La Opinión* devoted extensive coverage of Ruth especially during the 1927 season when "he connected 60 home runs setting a record that lasted 34 years."[30] The golden age of sports narrative rarely includes African American and Mexican American athletes.[31]

Because of the entrenched color line in U.S. professional baseball, it was the black sporting press that informed readers about Leroy "Satchel" Paige and other great Negro League players. Unlike their black counterparts, fifty-three light-skinned Latino players, mostly from Cuba, played in the major leagues between 1882 and 1947. Several of these were of Mexican descent and became sports heroes to members of the Mexican diaspora. Fans followed their baseball careers in the Spanish-language sporting press. *La Opinión* in particular encouraged baseball coaches to report their team scores, player names and positions, and play-by-play for games. One newspaper delivery agent praised Herrerías for the baseball coverage of his city's teams; the agent also noticed that newspaper sales had increased along with interest among youth: "The enthusiasm that has been awakened by the entire [Mexican] colony for baseball is evident, because every Sunday hundreds of people attend to watch the games, who are interested to see the news in *La Opinión* as much or more than the players themselves."[32] While *La Opinión* helped bolster baseball's popularity among Mexican boys and men, it encouraged girls to participate in "feminine" sports. One *La Opinión* article asked readers about which sports women should practice—results showed that readers deemed swimming, tennis, and dance "more suitable" compared to football, boxing, wrestling, and other sports "that requires a violent effort or needs a brutal attitude."[33]

Although the golden age of sports of the 1920s opened more opportunities for women's sports participation that led to the first wave of athletic feminism, there was little coverage of women's sports in *Deportes*.[34] American girls capitalized on the pleasure-seeking flapper to shatter gender expectations and gain new social freedoms.[35] No longer did women have to settle for "lady-like" sports like tennis or swimming, instead gravitating toward vigorous competitive sports like baseball. American women have been playing baseball since the late nineteenth century, joining "bloomer girl" teams and barnstorming across the country, playing against semipro and minor league teams.[36] In fact, the Chicago Bloomer Girls, owned by Madame J. H. Caldwell, directly challenged men's teams. Caldwell boldly declared, "Our women are voting now, so why not be able to play a real game of baseball?"[37] Sports journalists, however, still considered bloomer baseball a novelty and found it acceptable as long as the girls maintained their femininity.[38]

Lured by the bourgeoning U.S. consumer culture that produced shifting gender norms and new freedoms, Mexican female adolescents were determined to gain control over their leisure time.[39] Sport participation offered a new venue for Mexican girls to adjust to American life and challenge traditional gender expectations that pervaded their families and community. However, female sporting options were highly circumscribed by limited economic resources and male authority. Companies established baseball teams to develop a sense of cooperation, team spirit, and loyalty among their male employees.[40] Daughters of male employees sought the opportunity to play alongside their brothers and male relatives.

The earliest women's baseball teams emerged in company towns where they could be closely watched by male authorities. Since its founding in 1905, the Simons Brickyard Company sponsored a semiprofessional baseball team at its company town in Montebello, California.[41] Every Sunday the entire family headed to the ball field to cheer for the team known as the Mexican Nine.[42] Alejandro Morales's *The Brick People*, a historical novel of El Pueblo de Simons, narrates the story of Nana, a girl who persuades her father to allow her to attend the ballpark, only to watch the brickyard team lose a hard-fought battle and witness upset fans throw bricks at the visiting team.[43] Yet being a spectator was not enough for Maggie Montijo and Mary Cano, both of whom wanted to join the Simons team. Surely, Simons women were passionate about baseball as both spectators and participants. However, sportswriters were concerned about the "masculinizing" effects of competitive baseball on Mexican female bodies, so they pushed them toward the more "feminine" sport of softball. A 1915 photograph features both teenagers in a baseball uniform embracing each other and holding a bat, glove, and hardball.[44] It is unclear whether they were accepted onto the men's team or if the company formed a women's team.

EL PASO SHOE STORE ZAPATEROS

Baseball had been a love affair for the Orozco and Salazar families. Alonzo "Pops" Orozco and David "Sally" Salazar were best friends and teammates for El Paso Shoe Store, one of the best semiprofessional baseball teams in Southern California during the 1920s and 1930s. Orozco played outfield and led the team in hitting, while Salazar was the team's star pitcher. Both became closer when Orozco married Salazar's niece Rosemarie Salazar in 1935, even though her father disapproved because he was older and he would leave her behind as a "baseball widow" during his many barnstorming tours. This did not bother Rosemarie because she loved baseball and her husband, so much so that she kept a scrapbook of his long baseball career.[45]

The El Paso Shoe Store team was the brainchild of brothers Rodrigo and Arturo Castillo, who moved from El Paso to Los Angeles in 1920 to set up shop at 144 Main Street. To advertise their shoe business and promote their favorite sport, they formed a baseball team with their store name emblazoned on the jersey (see Figure 3.1). Fans and sportswriters shunned the team's original White Sox name and preferred Los Zapateros (the shoemakers) because of their baseball sneakers provided by their sponsor.[46] Beginning in 1926, Zapateros won several league championships across Southern California and traveled to play exhibition games in Mexico. The team underwent a transformation in the 1930s with a new name, new coach, and younger ballplayers, several of whom continued playing in the U.S. and Mexico professional leagues.

FIGURE 3.1. Zapateros baseball team inside the El Paso Shoe Store in the 1920s. The ballplayer behind the bat boy is Alex Orozco, his older brother Alonzo "Pops" Orozco is behind him in the white shirt. (Courtesy of Elisa Orozco-O'Neil and National Museum of American History)

The Castillo brothers hired Manuel Regalado as team manager because of his successful managing experience in El Paso and Ciudad Juárez. *La Opinión* nick-named Regalado as the "McGraw of Mexican American baseball" because of his keen baseball mind that resembled that of John McGraw, the hall-of-fame New York Giants manager.[47] From 1926 to 1929, Regalado led the Zapateros team to three league championships, but when he lost one game in particular, fans turned against him. After Zapateros committed two errors that cost them the game against Shell Oil, "the fans were shouting at Regalado for losing the game."[48] *La Opinión* defended Regalado against fan criticism, even praising him as a man of "great qual-ity and firmness of conviction."[49] Promptly after this backlash, though, automotive dealership owner Julio Perez recruited Regalado as manager for his new baseball team, Club México, which lasted only a year, after which it merged with El Paso Shoe Store. Regalado passed his love for baseball to his daughter Nellie and four sons. As a standout shortstop at Glendale High School, the youngest son, Rudy Regalado, earned a baseball scholarship to the University of Southern California, which prepared him for a professional career with the Cleveland Indians.[50]

The importance of family in Mexican American culture was central to building team chemistry for the Zapateros, who won three consecutive Spanish American

League championships.[51] The Castillo brothers treated the players like family, referring to them as *hijados* (godchildren) and rewarding them with a *tamalada* party for their hard-earned victory.[52] As an incentive, the Castillo brothers awarded a new pair of shoes to the player with the highest batting percentage.[53] Matches became fund-raisers for a baseball player who was injured or experienced a death in the family.[54] For example, when Orozco's mother died, his team observed a minute of silence before a game and donated a percentage of the gate receipts to offset funeral expenses.[55] The generosity extended even to rival teams. For instance, when an automobile accident badly injured a rival player, the Zapateros helped raise money for his medical costs.[56] To motivate each other, teammates repeatedly used the Spanish phrase *ponte las botas* (put on your boots), which translated to "put extra effort and energy into playing ball."[57]

When the Zapateros needed a home field for practices and hosting games, David Salazar's brother, Mike Salazar, offered his backyard—a dirt-filled lot behind his home in San Gabriel. The sandlot was located at South Mission Drive and Broadway Avenue, near the San Gabriel Mission Playhouse.[58] The players rolled up their sleeves to build their own diamond surrounded by chicken-wire fence and makeshift bleachers. Games advertised in the *La Opinión* newspaper referred to the sandlot field as "Los Terrenos de San Gabriel."[59] When they needed to baseball equipment, they stitched together some leather to make a glove and gathered used wood to make their own bats. For families like the Salazars, fabricating their own equipment was part of a Chicano working-class aesthetic of "making do" with materials at hand and using wit and ingenuity to create sports artifacts.[60] Baseball managers created innovative ways to publicize their games. For example, a 1928 leaflet encouraged Zapatero fans to come early and receive a free bar of soap before the match against the Mission Bell Soaps.[61] They played the majority of their games at the San Gabriel field, until Rodrigo Castillo reached a leasing agreement at White Sox Park.

In 1924, Italian American brothers John and Joe Pirrone used earnings from their wholesale fruit business to build the seven-thousand-seat White Sox Ball Park on the corner of Thirty-Eighth Street (now Forty-First) and Compton Avenue in South Los Angeles.[62] The Pirrones built the park for Negro League clubs to compete against the best semipro teams as part of the California Winter League.[63] Unlike the Pacific Coast League that barred black teams from playing in their stadiums, White Sox Park became a "showcase for Negro League Baseball."[64] Los Angeles African American newspaper *California Eagle* explained, "Colored fans feel that [White Sox Park] is their institution" because "Colored teams can play there year round . . . and Colored men and boys form the large personnel of employees at the grounds. No other place in the city has year-round colored employees."[65] Additionally, White Sox Park welcomed interracial games between African American, Japanese American, and Mexican American teams. Generally, White Sox Park represented the formation of a nonwhite spatial imaginary in which racialized teams transformed a segregated baseball stadium, produced by racist institutions and practices, into a visionary place of freedom "where everybody is somebody."[66]

On September 16, 1928, the Pirrone brothers invited the Zapateros to play a doubleheader against the Wilmington Tigers and Ortiz Fords at White Sox Park.[67] In an interview with *La Opinión*, Joe Pirrone told readers, "I recognize that many talented [Mexican] ballplayers have not developed to their fullest potential because of limited opportunities. Additionally, fans have not seen them in action because there are no facilities to watch comfortably . . . for this reason I would be very happy for the Mexican clubs to play in my park."[68] Pirrone praised the athletic abilities of Mexican baseball players and predicted, "There will be least five to ten players going to the big leagues every year."[69] His prediction proved correct. Three former Zapateros—Melo Almada, Jose Luis "Chile" Gomez, and Joe Gonzalez—joined the major leagues in the 1930s.

During the 1927 season, the Zapateros clinched the Spanish American League Championship and boasted to *La Opinión* "they were the best organized baseball team in the Mexican community."[70] When the *La Opinión* sports editor declared the Zapateros as the best Mexican baseball team in Southern California, the San Fernando West Merchants protested to the editor claiming that their team had a comparable winning record and deserved a chance to play for the title of "Best Mexican Team in Southern California."[71] The highly anticipated match took place on Sunday November 18, 1928.[72] With the game tied at three in the ninth inning and two outs, a Zapatero player hit a single, driving in his teammate from second base. The plate umpire called out "safe," but the first base umpire called him "out." This conflicting call created controversy between rival newspapers. *La Opinión* declared Zapatero the winners, while *El Heraldo de México* called it a draw.[73] Inadvertently, this controversy helped generate more publicity and excitement for a rematch.

The rematch doubleheader on February 24, 1929, at White Sox Park would determine the "true" champion of the Spanish American League. Ignacio Herrerías, sports editor for *La Opinión* and correspondent for *El Excélsior* in Mexico City, raised the ante by announcing that the winning team would receive round-trip tickets to Mexico City.[74] The winner would play against the Mexican Baseball League's champion Club Fabriles and be declared the "baseball champion of all México."[75] This transnational championship series would serve as a first step toward bridging two baseball leagues. The doubleheader was highly publicized in newspapers and handbills throughout Southern California. The handbill announced Mexican consul Alfonso Pesqueira throwing the ceremonial first pitch with boxers Bert Colima and Eduardo "Caballero" Huaracha, taking turns at bat. Mexican film star Raquel Torres made a surprise appearance as the newly appointed "godmother" of the Spanish American League (see Figure 3.2).[76] Occasionally,

BASE BALL GAME
For The Champion Ship
Of The
"SPANISH-AMERICAN LEAGE"
SUNDAY FEBRUARY 24th 1929 AT 1 P. M.

EL PASO SHOE STORE VS San Fernando MERCHANTS
AT THE "WHITE SOX PARK"
38th and Ascot Ave.   Take "B" Car
Two Games for the Price of One
FIRST GAME WILL START PROMPLY AT 1 P. M.
First Ball will be pitched by the Mex. Consul Mr. F. A PESQUEIRA
and cought by Mr. BERT COLIMA with
Mr. CABALLERO HUARACHA at bat

EL PASO SHOE STORE   144 N. MAIN St.
LOS ANGELES, CALIF.

FIGURE 3.2. 1929 Handbill of Spanish American Baseball League Championship Game inside the Salazar and Orozco Family Scrapbook. (Courtesy of Elisa Orozco-O'Neil and National Museum of American History)

baseball promoters recruited Hollywood celebrities to drum up publicity for big games and take part in the first-pitch ceremony.

Before five thousand spectators at White Sox Park, the Zapateros defeated San Fernando 7–1 and 14–4 in a doubleheader. Zapateros' David Salazar recorded a stellar pitching performance—he allowed only five earned runs—and Lefty Ocampo hit a grand slam in the second game. Consul Pesqueira praised the *beis-*

bolistas at the celebration banquet, where he announced, "Not only do you serve as examples for the development of sports among our people, but also with your sportsmanship, you are bringing out the best quality among all of us. Your attitude is affable and I can only but admire and encourage you to continue your athletic contests that will make us all better, physically and morally as Mexicans."[77] The Mexican elite viewed baseball as a civilized and modern sport that would boost industrialization and the country's international status. The consul's speech interlinked nation building and the construction of a masculine identity with the team's athletic success.

Baseball played a central role in the promotion of Mexican culture and identity. On May 5, 1929, the Castillo brothers convinced Joe Pirrone to organize a Fiesta Beisbolista at White Sox Park to commemorate the historic Battle of Puebla. The Castillo brothers aimed to attract celebrities, dignitaries, mutual aid societies, and spectators from the Mexican community. The event began with the Mexican consul general Alfonso Pesqueira participating in a first-pitch ceremony, then president of Sociedad Mutualista Mexicana spoke about the historical significance of Cinco de Mayo. The event concluded with performances from two bands.[78] After the festivities, the Zapateros played a doubleheader against the Greater Southern California Baseball Association champions, the Pacific Electric team. *La Opinión* observed the large attendance of "compatriots at White Sox Park which is the most numerous that has been registered to date."[79] Although they split the doubleheader, Zapateros showed that they could compete against teams from other leagues and mobilize their community to celebrate their Mexican heritage. After the successful Fiesta Beisbolista, the Castillo brothers convinced Joe Pirrone to organize a summer Mexican Baseball season featuring the best teams from Mexico competing against the best local Mexican American teams. During the 1930s White Sox Park became the center of transnational béisbol where Mexican fans could enjoy a game of baseball, musical entertainment, and delicious food options (see Figure 3.3).

Baseball victories against white teams had greater social significance during the late 1920s, when nativists cited the "Mexican problem" to justify restrictionist immigration policies against Mexico.[80] The Southern California Baseball Association invited Zapateros, after three consecutive Spanish American League titles from 1927 to 1929, to play in the Summer League against all-white American baseball teams. The owners of El Paso Shoe Store positioned their "Mexican team" as the chief rival against "white teams" of the Southern California Baseball Association. On March 24, 1929, *La Opinión*'s sports section ran the headline "Today the Mexicans versus the Americans at White Sox Park" in anticipation of the Zapateros' tough match against the Cudahy Puritans, composed of Cudahy Puritan Meat Packing Company employees.[81] Despite the 3-to-2 odds against the Zapateros, they beat the Puritans 3–1 in a hard-fought match. *La Opinión* reported that an "infinity of fans stormed the field to hug the ballplayers some

FIGURE 3.3. Food vendors in front of White Sox Ball Park on 38th Street and Compton Avenue in south Los Angeles, 1939. (Courtesy of The Huntington Library, San Marino, CA)

almost kissing them. . . . It was a victory that was shared with frenzy while American players and their supporters slipped out the back door."[82] The Puritans captain blamed their "first loss to a Mexican team" on "bad luck" and refused to leave the ballpark until he scheduled a rematch the following week.[83] After the victory they received an invitation to play at Wrigley Field for the first time.

Considered the largest ballpark in pre-WWII Los Angeles, Wrigley Field hosted minor league baseball teams, boxing, and other sporting events. The first boxing card at Wrigley Field took place in 1926 when Bert Colima defeated Everett Strong. The presence of Colima combined with several Mexican players already playing in the Pacific Coast League (PCL) helped to facilitate their inclusion at Wrigley Field. Prior to their November 10, 1929, game against the Pacific Electric team, the Castillo brothers announced in a special *La Opinión* advertisement that "El Paso Shoe Store has the privilege of being the first Mexican team to occupy the Wrigley Park diamond, which is usually reserved for professional teams of the Major Leagues."[84] The *Los Angeles Times* failed to mention this local integration story but did announce that "the Mexican Consul, Alfonso Pesqueira, is to be present at the game with several Latin-American movie stars."[85] Even though they were now welcomed at Wrigley Field, the Zapateros felt more at home at White Sox Park, especially when hosting teams from Mexico.

Racial restrictions kept African Americans from playing in PCL team rosters and ballparks in Southern California. Chewing gum magnate and owner of the Chicago Cubs William Wrigley Jr. purchased the PCL Los Angeles Angels in 1921 and four years later built Wrigley Field in South Los Angeles.[86] The Angels owner and manager refused to give African Americans tryouts with the team, even though many talented players lived near the stadium. Not until 1947 when Jackie Robinson joined the Brooklyn Dodgers did the PCL reconsider its racist practice. A year later the San Diego Padres became the first PCL team to integrate their roster by adding John Richey, a homegrown catcher with a cheerful personality.[87] Compared to African Americans, several Mexican-origin players circumvented the PCL color line before Richey.[88] Although these players were not officially banned by the PCL, some were made to feel unwelcome. David Salazar's nephew Ernesto Salazar refused to join the Hollywood Stars after he was offered a contract because, according to his daughter, "he felt they were not ready to accept Mexicans like him."[89] Instead, he opted to play for the Mexican Baseball League, where he felt more accepted.

BARNSTORMING ACROSS BORDERS

During the 1930s, baseball offered a counterpoint to the grim material realities that working-class Mexican Americans encountered at work and in communities across the United States; indeed, Mexican Americans used sport to reclaim their cultural pride and advocate for civil and labor rights.[90] The deportation and repatriation drives that had ensued during the Great Depression reminded Mexican Americans of their second-class status and tenuous place in American society.[91] While amateur baseball was mostly for recreation and entertainment, some players used sports as an extra source of employment. Semipro players earned a monthly salary of thirty to a hundred fifty dollars, depending on how many games they played. In addition, teams that craved success paid talented pitchers more money. Although team owners feared that gate receipts would decline in economic hard times, fans still came out to the ballpark, if only to temporarily forget about their troubles.[92] Despite widespread racial discrimination and nativism, Mexican Americans turned to baseball, the one area they could exert more control over their lives. Teams and leagues, ballparks, sportswriters, and business sponsorships were all crucial components for the development of a sporting Mexican diaspora that extended beyond Southern California.

In order to make money during the offseason, the Zapateros traveled across the Southwest and Mexico in a barnstorming tour during the 1930s. Before they embarked on their trip to Mexico, the Castillo brothers merged their team with Club México to become "México-El Paso" The players for Club México, formed in November 1929 by Julio Perez and managed by Manuel Regalado, proudly showed off their national pride at the precise moment when Americans raised concerns about the so-called Mexican problem.[93] These changes were also part of a broader effort by middle-class Mexican progressives to promote all things Mexican to a growing Mexico de afuera community to strengthen transnational ties with Mexico.[94] The Castillo brothers worked closely with La Opinión sports-writers and the Mexican consulate office to arrange teams from Mexico to travel to Los Angeles to compete against the best local Mexican teams at White Sox Park. Besides boosting cultural pride and forging closer relations with their homeland, another reason for the name change was to take advantage of the ris-ing interest in baseball in Mexico.

On September 5, 1930, Castillo and Perez agreed to appoint Carlos "Tony" Galindo as the manager and coach.[95] Galindo, a former captain of the USC base-ball team, became a teacher and coach at Roosevelt High School in Boyle Heights in 1929 and lasted until 1944.[96] Galindo encouraged student athletes to pursue college scholarships; Joe Madrid Gonzalez obtained a baseball scholar-ship to USC and later pitched for the Boston Red Sox during the 1937 season.[97] Because of Galindo's impressive coaching experience, the owners agreed to give him complete control of the team. Galindo thanked the owners and reassured everyone, "From this moment, there are no players from either México, or El Paso and we have left behind the rivalry and distancing. From here on we are going to defend one single name 'México-El Paso,' that is more than a blending of two teams, the name is a symbol that represents a bond of Mexican elements that combined resources to channel our efforts in a single direction to achieve better results."[98] This merger led to an eighteen-player roster with the best Mexi-can baseball talent poised to compete and win against the best teams in the big-gest stadiums.

One of the principal objectives of the newly formed team was to strengthen its relationship with the Mexican Baseball League by inviting teams and star players for exhibition games. México-El Paso invited Mexican League pitcher Fernando Barradas to start in their team's debut at Wrigley Field against the Los Angeles Nippons.[99] Barradas gained popularity at the 1930 Central American Games when his stellar pitching helped Mexico defeat the Cuban team.[100] In an interview with La Opinión, Barradas explained that his visit would "start an exchange of Mexican athletes between Los Angeles and Mexico."[101] Barradas was impressed with the local Mexican baseball talent and believed that "very soon we will proudly see Mexican players in the Big Leagues."[102] Galindo instructed his players to arrive early in the evening to receive their new uniforms and pre-pare for the night game against the best Japanese American semipro team in Southern California.[103] During the game, Barradas struck out fifteen batters as he led México-El Paso over the LA Nippons 7–5 under newly installed lights and before seven thousand Mexican spectators seated in the lower deck.[104] La Opin-ión applauded its owner, Ignacio Lozano, for throwing the first pitch to Raquel

Torres, a Mexican film actress dressed in a México-El Paso uniform.[105] Unlike the Spanish-language newspaper coverage, the *Los Angeles Times* reported, "Night baseball has not only made a hit with the American baseball fan, but from the turnout at Wrigley Field last Monday evening the foreign element of Los Angeles has also been taken by the night baseball bug."[106]

Visiting ballplayers and teams from Mexico helped strengthen the relationship between the Mexican Baseball League and Mexican American baseball. In late September 1930, México-El Paso hosted the Mexican Baseball League champion, Club Fabriles (later renamed Aztecas), for a seven-game exhibition series at White Sox and Wrigley Field.[107] Founded by Homobono Márquez, the "czar of Mexican baseball," the team had been on the road for a month playing exhibition games in northern Mexico and across the U.S. Southwest before arriving in Los Angeles.[108] *La Opinión* publicized these exhibitions with daily updates on practice sessions, play-by-play coverage, and results. The stadium reached full capacity on Sunday afternoon, November 21, as spectators watched Zapateros lose the first game 5–4 but then rally to win the second 8–5.[109] The next day, Joe Pirrone told *La Opinión* "that since building this stadium, yesterday had the greatest amount of fans, and what was so extraordinary was that all of them were Mexican."[110] Despite the economic downturn, Mexican attendance at baseball games remained high because they were family and cultural events that offset the grim realities of the Great Depression. Park admission was seventy-five cents for adult males and free for women and children.[111] To accommodate more fans, the third game was moved to Wrigley Field. The following weekend, the Zapateros came back from a 2–1 deficit to win the series with some hard hitting and clutch pitching.[112] Homobono Márquez confessed to *La Opinión*, "I never imagined that [Mexicans in LA] played such high quality of baseball in Los Angeles."[113]

On November 22, 1930, eighteen players of México-El Paso left Los Angeles to play against Club Fabriles for "the baseball championship of México" in Mexico City. The *La Opinión* sports editor observed, "The players left, all with confidence in bringing back to California the championship title of the Republic of México."[114] This confidence stemmed from a previous victory against the visiting Fabriles. Joining the team was Luis Almada as interim manager. Despite his family's advice to accept a scholarship to the University of Southern California, Luis decided to sign a five-thousand-dollar contract with the New York Giants in 1927. Unfortunately, Luis became severely ill during spring training, ending his brief major league career before it had even started. He returned to California to play in the PCL and joined México-El Paso during the off-season to develop his skills and visit his family.[115]

Upon arriving in Mexico City on December 4, 1930, the Mexican Baseball League owner and government dignitaries welcomed the players with musical entertainment.[116] After a few days to practice, México-El Paso debuted at Delta

Park in a best-of-seven series, but the city's high altitude made it difficult for them to play their best. The LA team barely won the first match 6–5. Additionally, *El Universal* newspaper reported an incident during the first game that threatened their goodwill visit.[117] The pitcher hit Alonzo "Pops" Orozco, who in a fit of anger retaliated by throwing his bat at the pitcher. The spectators erupted in a storm of disapproval, calling for the manager to suspend Orozco from the game. Despite the public censure, Orozco remained in the game. This incident, however, contributed to the team losing four consecutive games and ultimately the series, five games to one.[118]

Mexico City baseball fans were disappointed with the visiting team, who "were tainted with bad luck."[119] "Bad luck seemed to have followed México-El Paso," explained *La Opinión* Ignacio Herrerías, but he also cited the high altitude and player illnesses and injuries as the main reasons for the loss.[120] During the awards ceremony, Fabriles manager Homobono Márquez received the Juan Jose Rio Trophy (named after a Mexican revolutionary soldier turned politician).[121] Despite the team's loss, players enjoyed sightseeing and visiting museums around the city. A few players accepted an invitation to stay longer and play exhibition games with the Mexican Baseball League. This series led to a friendly rivalry between both teams and forged closer relations between the Mexican Baseball League and the Mexican Baseball League of Southern California.

On the eve of the Olympic Games in Los Angeles, several semipro teams got together to form the Mexican Baseball League of Southern California (MBLSC). The MBLSC invited Ernesto Carmona to throw out the first pitch at the México-El Paso versus Carmelita opener at White Sox Park on Sunday, August 7, 1932.[122] Seven years earlier, Carmona and sportswriter Alejandro Aguilar Reyes (Fray Nuno) had cofounded the first Mexican Baseball League in Mexico City. Carmona had been visiting Los Angeles as part of the Mexican Olympic delegation in preparation for the Olympic Games. Spectators received a free Olympic Games program in Spanish as they watched México-El Paso and Carmelita split the doubleheader.[123]

The MBLSC's eight founding teams included México-El Paso, Carmelita Provision Company's Chorizeros, San Fernando Missions, Hernandez Sastres, Belvedere Bus Lines, Roger Jessup Dairy Farm, Chevy Chase, and Carta Blanca. Carmona spoke with Ignacio Herrerías, sports editor for *La Opinión*, about how impressed he was that over seventy teams played every week in Southern California; Carmona recognized a possibility for future international exchanges between Los Angeles and Mexico City: "Leagues of California and México begin approximately at the same time and the winner of each of them would dispute the Championship in a series of seven meetings. The first year the Mexican team of California would go to the city of México, and the other, México would come to Los Angeles, taking turns in the same order in successive years."[124]

Peloteros from both countries would improve their skills and the winning team would receive a free round trip.

México-El Paso barnstormed throughout the Southwest and northern Mexico during the 1930s. In May 1934, they were invited to play a three-game series against the state championship team in Cananea, Sonora, a copper-mining town known for the 1906 strike that became a rallying cry for the Mexican Revolution. Upon México-El Paso's arrival on May 19, El Circulo Social Anáhuac, the city's leading sports club, held a special dance at a recreation center in honor of their baseball guests.[125] The next day, government offices and businesses closed so their employees could attend the game. The México-El Paso team underestimated the Cananea team, however, and lost the series two games to one. "We were very surprised about the baseball knowledge they deployed," explained México-El Paso team owner Rodrigo Castillo. "They are clearly one of the best teams in Mexico."[126]

Furthermore, Coach Galindo attributed their loss to the "bad sporting spirit" of Mexican fans. Galindo explained how many players were insulted for being *pochos*.[127] "It seems that it is our fault to having been born on this side of the border instead of Mexico," wrote Galindo in a guest column for *La Opinión*. He elaborated, "They called me names from thief to the most disgusting names in our beautiful language." In comparison, he defended his team's record of "good sportsmanship" and stated, "I am willing to raise the sport of baseball among our people and that is why I suffer all these things and contribute my knowledge and humble efforts to baseball."[128] Galindo's defense raises the question of identity in the sporting Mexican diaspora. Mexican American ballplayers and other Mexican-origin athletes developed a hybrid sporting identity in which they drew on aspects from one or both cultures depending on the situation in which they found themselves. Before they departed Mexico, they invited the Cananea team to Los Angeles for a five-game series. This time, México-El Paso exacted revenge on Cananea by winning all five games at White Sox Park. Before Cananea returned to Mexico, México-El Paso organized a special banquet at Blackie's Place restaurant to show their appreciation and "good sportsmanship."[129]

Baseball historians have noted that Negro League players frequently opted to play in Mexico for higher pay and a more welcoming racial climate.[130] This was also the case for hundreds of Mexican American ballplayers who desired to play professional baseball in their parents' homeland. Impressed with the high-quality of Mexican American baseball players in Los Angeles, Mexican Baseball League owners scouted and recruited them to join their rosters. A majority of these players chose to play in Mexico rather than the United States for various reasons: (1) the opportunity to play more, (2) the chance to visit with family and friends, (3) greater news coverage about their athletic achievements, (4) opportunities to coach and manage teams, and (5) the generally less prevalent racial discrimination. Playing ball also reaffirmed their language and culture and gave them cultural legitimacy regarding their Mexican heritage. Some players also forged friendships, found love, and engaged in transnational marriages. Using the most complete statistical records on the Mexican Baseball League, I have found at least fifty Mexican Americans from the United States who played for the Mexican Baseball League during the 1930s.[131] Several of these included México-El Paso teammates David "Sally" Salazar, Al "Pops" Orozco, Alex Orozco, Ernesto Salazar, and Robert "Lakes" Lagunas.

David Salazar never reached the major leagues, even though he showed great potential to become a professional pitcher. "He was Mexican, and in those days that was like being black. Those guys never got a fair shake," argued his grandson, Darrell Evans, who debuted with the Atlanta Braves in 1969, just five years after his grandfather died; Evans played professional baseball for twenty years.[132] Born in 1895 in Atwater Village near Glendale, California, to an immigrant family from Jalisco, Mexico, Salazar began playing baseball with his older brothers and cousins. He developed into a stellar pitcher and solid hitter, which earned him a tryout for the PCL. The San Francisco Seals signed Salazar for the 1924 season, but he pitched in only one game. According to his son, Carlos Salazar, "He only pitched two innings and was not given a chance to develop. He would have gone further to the big leagues, but he was born at the wrong time when there was discrimination big time."[133]

While playing for the Nogales Crows team during the 1922 season, Salazar received an offer from the governor of Sonora to play for the cross-border team in Nogales, Sonora. Because they could not pay Salazar a comparable salary with Mexico's pesos, they offered him a job as a border guard patrolling the Arizona-Sonora border. He would be paid three hundred pesos per month. The details of the job were sent in a letter stating, "Your commission is to monitor the border to prevent smuggling because according to reports it has been very often to the great detriment of our treasury."[134] It is unclear whether Salazar accepted this offer, but he did accept offers to play exhibition games in Mexico.[135] President Obregón invited Salazar and other all-star Arizonan ballplayers to compete in a series of games in Mexico City.[136] Homobono Márquez, manager of the Sonora Baseball Club, pleaded with Salazar to respond to his initial request: "WHEN WILL YOU BE READY TO COME TO PLAY FOR MY TEAM AND WHAT IS THE LAST WORD ON YOUR SALARY YOU LIKE TO GET." He concluded the letter by reminding him of the Mexican president's request. "I'm the manager of the Mexico Baseball club and this club now belongs to the President Obregón, he likes the club because all the players are all Mexican boys and he is the one that is asking me about you every time he sees me."[137]

Ultimately, Salazar signed for the 1925 season with the Mesa baseball club in the Arizona-Texas League, where he became "one of the best-known baseball pitchers of Arizona."[138] Sportswriters shortened Salazar to "Sally." According to

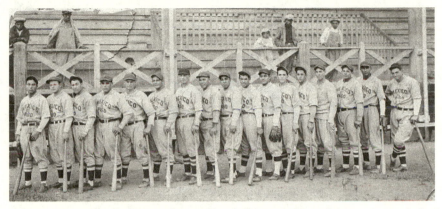

FIGURE 3.4. Los Angeles semiprofessional baseball team, México-El Paso, at Parque Delta in Mexico City, Mexico 1936. (Courtesy of the Salazar Family and Latino Baseball History Project, Pfau Library, CSU San Bernardino)

the *Arizona Republic,* "Sally was a fixture in Arizona baseball circles for many years, and the fans were always willing to play the board straight across when the husky Mexican twirler was on the hilltop."[139] When he won games for the Mesa team, he received lavish praise—fans and reporters alike called Salazar the "master of the speed ball" and "the Mexican twirling ace."[140] At the end of the 1926 season, though, Salazar became the center of a contract dispute. When his club refused to pay his full salary, he signed as a "free agent" with a rival baseball team, forcing league officials to meet and settle the dispute "over the ownership of Salazar."[141] In 1928 Mesa traded Salazar to the El Paso Texans of the Arizona-Texas League because of his bad "temperament but ended up winning 20 or more games in four consecutive seasons."[142]

During winter seasons, Salazar returned to Los Angeles and pitched for México-El Paso until he joined the barnstorming trip to Mexico City. A photo taken at Delta Park shows the entire team posing in their uniforms while leaning on their bats (see Figure 3.4). Before leaving El Paso, David Salazar recruited his nephew Pete Salazar to the Miami Miners of the Arizona-Texas League. On May 16, 1930, the nephew beat his uncle in a pitching duel, with Miami topping El Paso 6–1.[143] Upon returning to Los Angeles in September 1930, David Salazar easily regained the top pitching spot for México-El Paso as they prepared to battle Club Fabriles in Mexico City.

In 1936, David Salazar recruited his best friend's younger brother, Alex Orozco, and nephew Ernesto Salazar to play for the Aztecas (formerly Club Fabriles) as they barnstormed throughout the U.S. Southwest. After contract negotiations with the PCL's Seattle Indians failed in 1933, Ernie Salazar signed with the Mexico City Aztecas (see Figure 3.5).[144] Homobono Márquez recruited Mexican American and Afro-Cuban players to join his Aztecas baseball club, which earned a reputation for defeating visiting U.S. professional teams.[145] Before Ernesto left

FIGURE 3.5. Mexico City's Aztecas baseball team in a U.S. barnstorming tour. This photo was taken on March 7, 1936, at El Corralón ballpark in Colton, CA. Alonzo "Pops" Orozco is first from left and Ernesto Salazar is third from right. (Courtesy of Elisa Orozco-O'Neil and Latino Baseball History Project, Pfau Library, CSU San Bernardino)

for Mexico City, he challenged his sisters that he would buy a silver bracelet for the one who wrote the most letters to him. Rosemarie accepted the challenge and composed hundreds of letters to her little brother. Hence, Ernesto returned with a silver bracelet with embossed roses for his older sister. Ernesto enjoyed his time in Mexico City because he earned a better salary, played in larger stadiums, and played alongside his uncle, who would take him on weekend excursions to visit relatives. This was not the case for Alex Orozco, who was homesick even though he earned a high batting average in the Mexican Baseball League.[146] Although Salazar never reached the major leagues, they would pass down their love of the game onto his children and grandchildren.

Additionally, Robert "Lakes" Lagunas was David Salazar's teammate during barnstorming trips to Mexico. Born in El Paso, Lagunas began playing at a young age, often crossing over the international bridge to play ball in Ciudad Juárez.[147] When he joined the Waco and Mexia clubs of the Texas League in the early 1920, his teammates nicknamed him "Lakes," the meaning of his last name in Spanish. As the only dark-skinned Mexican American on the Mexia baseball club, Lakes Lagunas encountered vehement racial hostility. A Mexia newspaper article recounted how fans treated Lagunas: "Baseball fans as a rule are rather unjust. Lagunas is generally made the target of abuse by fans of rival cities when playing away from home, which is very unfair, unjust, and does not smack of the best of sportsmanship."[148] Lagunas was considered "one of the best shortstops in town" and a "leading hitter," even though he had to endure racial slurs on the playing field.[149] His son, Bob Lagunas, recalled how his father was called "greaser and spic by fans and threw things at him. This affected him emotionally."[150] Tired of being harassed by fans, Lagunas had to develop a thick skin and fight back by showing off his baseball skills, but sometimes his temper got the best of him. One newspaper account described him as "the Mexican boy would be given a tryout with the Hollywood club, but temperament is his main difficulty."[151]

Another response to the racial discrimination Lagunas faced was to break his contract and play baseball in Mexico. During the late 1920s, he played for baseball clubs in Ciudad Juárez, Hermosillo, Tampico, and Torreon. On several occasions, Lagunas jumped his contract for another team in Mexico; he used Gonzalez, his mother's maiden name, to avoid detection. Lagunas played "outlaw baseball," that is, he left his original team to play for another team under a false name. For Lagunas, playing "outlaw baseball" in Mexico was much better than the hostile racial climate in Texas. Lagunas understood the few opportunities available to young Mexican American ballplayers, so he would recruit and take them to play in Mexico. When Lagunas managed a Chihuahua baseball team of the Mexican Baseball League, he would organize exhibition games with Negro League players at White Sox Park.[152] His younger brother, Raymond "Monchy" Lagunas, was one of these promising players who joined his Chihuahua team in 1940. Then, Raymond signed with Torreon for the 1941 and 1942 seasons. Former México-El Paso teammate Melo Almada, who ended his major league career early to become a Mexican League manager, had recruited Raymond to Torreon's Algodoneros (cotton pickers). During his last season, Raymond recorded the highest batting average in the Mexican League of .392. But tragically, within a year of being married to a Mexican woman, Raymond died of a severe illness.[153]

The "baseball widow" was not unlike the women left behind, often with children, in Mexico by their bracero husbands and had to find ways to make ends meet.[154] While their husbands traveled abroad with their barnstorming team, women stayed behind to raise families. For example, the wife of Lakes Lagunas endured the emotional and economic costs of long-term separations. During the early 1930s, Lagunas moved his family to Pico Rivera, California, where he found a job picking oranges, but during summers he left home for Mexico. As Bob Lagunas remembered, "It was difficult for my mom because she was a baseball widow since dad was always gone playing or managing baseball in Mexico during the summers."[155] His mother communicated with her husband through letter writing and survived through the support of extended family members.

PELOTERAS IN PARADISE

During the 1930s, Mexican American women actively participated in softball because of increased sporting opportunities and the freedom to experiment with new gender roles and behaviors, despite the close sexual policing by male coaches and family members. While the Great Depression worsened economic conditions for the Mexican community, it also created new opportunities for women. In 1930, the percentage of working Mexican women was 14.8 percent, compared to 22 percent of all women in the U.S. labor force.[156] Mexican women played a prominent role in the labor movement through organizing and leading strikes at pecan-shelling plants, steel plants, and the garment industry.[157] Their unemployed husbands did not always embrace these changes because their already bruised egos made it difficult for them to relinquish their breadwinner role. Some husbands compromised and allowed their wives and daughters to work for wages and even join the neighborhood softball team.

Despite the shifting gender roles during the 1930s, the patriarchal system of chaperonage extended into softball, thus making the sport more acceptable for Mexican parents. Opportunities to join a softball team increased with the formation of the Amateur Softball Association and the National Softball Association in 1933. Soon thereafter, softball replaced baseball as the preferred sport for women throughout the nation.[158] As a modified form of baseball, with its large "soft" ball and short base paths, softball emerged in late nineteenth-century Chicago as an indoor winter sport and gradually gained popularity in settlement houses and school playgrounds.[159] While boys were encouraged to play baseball, girls' softball was lauded by physical educators for its health benefits and moral ethical character.[160] At first companies formed softball teams as part of their industrial recreation program, and then playgrounds, churches, businesses, schools, and cities formed their own leagues.[161] By 1935, more than sixty thousand organized amateur softball teams and one thousand lighted parks had spread across the United States.[162] Three years later, a sports survey of the Los Angeles region found "no less than nine thousand softball clubs within Wrigley Field."[163] These teams emerged from diverse ethnic neighborhoods, where female Mexican teams competed against black, white, and Asian American teams.[164]

The earliest female baseball teams emerged in settlement houses where they received free equipment and coaching by male coaches.[165] These teams were part of the Americanization campaigns carried out through various sporting activities. Mexican female participants in sport programs, however, did not abandon their language and culture, but rather selectively appropriated resources for their own benefit. The case of the Valentina "Tina" Hernandez illustrates how young Mexican girls took advantage of Americanization sports programs to play ball. Hernandez was born to a large family of ten girls and four boys in Barrio Logan in Downtown San Diego. The Hernandez siblings started playing baseball at the Neighborhood House baseball field, under the supervision of coach Bill Breitenstein. All of her brothers played for the Neighborhood House team—one of the top semi-pro teams in San Diego—including her older brother, Manuel "Nay" Hernandez, who played for the San Diego Padres in the PCL.[166] Hernandez could not play baseball because her mother had forbidden it. She would admonish her, "Baseball is not for women, you need to learn to make tortillas instead." Mexican American families had strictly defined gender expectations for young girls to remain inside the home and could leave only when they got married. Gone was the "new woman" of the 1920s. The women of the 1930s had had to yield to marriage and motherhood. Her brothers and father came to the rescue, however, by defending her athletic skills and persuading her mother to allow her to play. Unlike the boys who played sports all day at the Neighborhood House, Mexican girls were restricted to attending cooking, craft, and sewing classes and had to return home immediately every day. This gender double standard did not sit well with Hernandez, so despite her mother's objections she played on a boys' team and in 1936 formed an all-Mexican girls' team. She recalled, "My mother would get mad because I went around trying to organize a team and some parents would not let them play."[167]

But Hernandez's efforts at community building persevered; she persuaded Settlement House supervisor Anita Jones to offer more sports for Mexican girls. This push was aided by New Deal funding to purchase more open space and hire fifty-five State Emergency Relief Administration workers at the Neighborhood House.[168] Anita Jones conceded because "she championed [programs] to make the daily lives of the community a little better."[169] One of the ways to get their minds off their bad financial situation was to expand their recreation and sports activities. A 1937 study of Neighborhood House reported on the new girls' team and added, "The staff acknowledge that learning team play was one of the first steps in true American citizenship."[170] Hernandez's friend Concha Estrada joined the girls' team without her parents' permission—she strategically wore shorts under her skirt or pants and removed them by the time she arrived at the diamond.[171] Because her brother was the coach, she was forgiven for defying her parents' wishes. On some occasions, even though Estrada and her team were ready to play, the opposing teams "refused to play the Mexicans so the game was canceled, not forfeited."[172] Although they faced racial and gender barriers on and off the field, they were not discouraged from playing ball.

Despite the support of her father and brothers, Hernandez could not join any teams because by the mid-1930s baseball had been replaced by softball as the main sport for women. As a softball player Hernandez became one of the best catchers in San Diego County. She proudly boasted that "I was very good at catching men's pitches."[173] For the 1939 season, she joined the Coronado Lime Cola softball team at the age of fifteen and hit an impressive .515 in nineteen of twenty-one games. In fact, Hernandez "was rated one of the finest feminine softball players in the county."[174] Compared to her Anglo teammates, she was the smallest player but fierce behind the plate, throwing out runners on a consistent basis. The Coronado Lime Colas won the 1939 championship against an Oakland team. The *San Diego Union* printed a photo of her in a catcher's stance with her nickname "Val Hernandez" and the tagline "She's a threat at the plate or behind it."[175]

Several of the early female softball teams also emerged within voluntary associations and political organizations that fielded a men's baseball team. In the early 1930s, the Los Angeles chapter of Partido Liberal Mexicano (PLM), an anarcho-syndicalist organization founded by Mexican intellectuals to support the Mexican Revolution, formed a baseball team called Los Politicos.[176] A year later, the

PLM announced the formation of a female softball team called México-Líbre (free Mexico), a slogan that inspired PLM's revolutionary imagination to fight for Mexico's freedom against U.S. political and economic influence. On March 11, 1934, the team debuted at El Porvenir Park on Brooklyn Avenue (renamed Belvedere Park in 1949) against their male counterparts from the PLM.[177] The team's captain and pitcher, Felicitas Gomez, described as an "enthusiastic sports woman," informed the newspaper that they were prepared to compete against the best female teams in the Mexican community.[178] Gomez was one of several Mexican women who gained power and leadership within the PLM and articulated a "third space feminism."[179]

As mentioned earlier, the Salazar family's love for baseball extended to all members. In 1934, Carmen Rose and Mercedes Salazar lobbied their uncle David Salazar to help them form a team. They got their wish when México-El Paso agreed to sponsor their new team, El Paso Femenil, and recruited Margarita Rodriguez as manager and older brother Ernesto Salazar as coach.[180] Rodriguez promptly announced to *La Opinión*, "We are willing to play with any female team in Los Angeles, whether Mexicans, Japanese, Chinese, or black etc. . . . but especially the players of México-Líbre."[181] When México-Líbre declined to play against El Paso Femenil, Rodriguez complained to *La Opinión*, "They were the ones that challenged any team to a game."[182] Instead, Rodriguez scheduled their debut match against Club Athenas, a black women's team from Los Angeles.

Although *La Opinión* publicized the first women's baseball game in White Sox Park history, the coverage reflected a male bias.[183] On April 15, 1934, the women's match preceded the México-El Paso–Hermosa Mexican match and lasted just four innings to allow enough time for the men's match.[184] *La Opinión* provided extensive play-by-play coverage of the México-El Paso victory, but not the women's match.[185] Furthermore, *La Opinión*'s sports columnist reported on a pregame meeting whereby female players discussed their sexual attraction to pitchers Ernesto Salazar and Zurdo Carrizosa. Rather than asking them, he wrote, "Perhaps it's better to say that [Ernesto] Salazar is more 'good looking' than [Zurdo] Carrizosa, at least in the opinion of the girls that will debut today at White Sox Park."[186] Once again, these female athletes had been reduced to "Baseball Annies" or female groupies who sought sexual relations with male baseball players.[187]

In the early 1930s, Mexican women joined any women's softball league that would allow them the opportunity to play. In 1934, the Mexican Señoritas joined the Central Softball League, an integrated women's softball league with two black teams (Eastsiders and Athenas) and a "Mexican, Russian and Caucasian team."[188] *California Eagle* sports editor Harry Levette had founded the women's league and reported the play-by-play and scores three times a week from White Sox Park.[189] Levette described the large crowds at the Athenas–Señoritas match: "Surprising the good-sized crowd by their speed, cleverness, earnestness and knowledge of baseball, a girl's baseball team composed principally of and named the Athenas beat the crack team of Mexican girls at White Sox Park with a score of 6 runs and 9 hits to 2 runs and 6 hits."[190] "Crack team" was meant as a compliment for their quickness and overall strong performance. *La Opinión* noted that a black-Mexican rivalry would boost fan attendance: "With all certainty that these games will be interesting and arouse the enthusiasm of the fans and it is not difficult for the new *peloteras* to soon win the sympathy of the public that attends Sunday to Sunday at White Sox."[191] The Spanish term *peloteras* refers to female baseball and softball players whose stories have been missing from historical narratives. In *Making Lemonade Out of Lemons*, I stumbled upon a women's softball team while researching peloteros in Corona, California.[192] A Corona Athletics ballplayer mentioned that he played catch with his sister, who later joined the Corona Debs team. I interviewed several members of the Corona Debs who fondly recalled the sense of community and the expansive female support network they built within their team, despite an all-male coaching staff. In some cases, Mexican parents permitted their daughters to play, but only under male supervision. According to Sandra Uribe, the common practice of chaperonage extended into women's amateur softball teams throughout Southern California.[193] In the case of the Orange Tomboys, Uribe found that sisters were chaperoned by their younger brother who also served as assistant coach. However, these peloteras found ways to evade and resist chaperonage on and off the field.

Sisters Ramona and Della Fonseca evaded chaperonage if they completed all their domestic chores prior to playing their favorite sports.[194] When their parents divorced in 1935, their mother became stricter, but they convinced her to allow them to practice after school and play only weekend matches. Both joined the Girls Athletic Association (GAA) and played baseball, basketball, and volleyball at San Fernando High School. In 1936, they joined a new all-Mexican girls' softball team named Aztecas (see Figure 3.6). Mexican American baseball and softball teams adopted the name "Aztecs" or "Aztecas" to affirm their connection to Mexican indigenous culture while asserting their right to play America's pastime. The Rotary club sponsored the team and assigned a male coach. The team uniforms included long pants that, according to Della, "were old fashioned and donated by merchant sponsors." Ramona recalled, "We played against different teams from North Hollywood and Van Nuys and different towns out of San Fernando." The sisters' ability to travel, though, was seriously hampered by their lack of an automobile and a strict single mother. Despite their limited geographic mobility, Della proudly stated, "Even when my husband went into the army, I stilled played baseball."[195]

Another way peloteras asserted their agency was in naming their teams. Mexican American women's softball teams frequently chose names that defied gender norms. For example, Carmen Cornejo Gallegos, who grew up in the Cypress

FIGURE 3.6. Las Aztecas, a girl's baseball team from Pacoima, CA, circa 1930s. Della Fonseca Ortega is standing, second from right. (Courtesy of Shades of L.A. Collection, Los Angeles Public Library)

Street barrio of Orange, California, recalled how she and her five sisters formed a "team of our own" and cleverly called it Los Tomboys as a way to emphasize their cultural roots and stretch the boundaries of gender.[196] Other names emphasized women's fierce competitiveness while maintaining their femininity. Ramona Valenzuela remembered how she came up with team name Vixies for her North Hollywood team. "I thought of Vixen, which is like a female fox, and because women can run like foxes. Vixies is short for Vixens."[197] Another meaning of the term refers to a hotheaded woman with a fierce temper. Valenzuela admitted that she was stubborn, and this suited her well as team captain, but she still allowed the team to decide, and all agreed that Vixies suited them well. Sometimes women accepted traditional feminine names chosen by male coaches. In the late 1930s, Gabe Castorena named and coached the Colton Mercuries and the Colton Mercury Señoritas. Because he worked for the city parks and recreation department, he secured equipment and fields for both teams.[198] This arrangement worked fine for Carmen Lujan, who had wanted an opportunity to play at the age of twelve with the 1936 Señoritas team and continued playing while working at Norton Air Force Base during World War II.[199]

Another women's team emerged with the same name around the same time but was sponsored by a local Catholic Church parish. In 1934, the Cristo Rey Catholic Church sponsored the Señoritas team for parish girls who lived in the local Mexican barrio called Toonerville.[200] Former México-El Paso manager and

Snappy Spanish Senoritas Play Pelota Muy Buena

FIGURE 3.7. The Glendale Señoritas softball team featured in the *Los Angeles Times* (April 29, 1936) under the heading: "Snappy Spanish Señoritas Play Pelota Muy Buena." From left to right, Emma Perez, Vera Terrazone, Ruth Mendoza, Sally Hernandez, and Frances Valle. (Courtesy of *Los Angeles Times* staff)

parish member Manuel Regalado helped coach the team, which included his daughter Nellie, who also played for the Glendale High School softball team. The church's sponsorship, according to his grandson and baseball scholar Sam Regalado, helped temper parents' concerns about their daughters playing in the evening and traveling across Southern California.[201] The team's traditional uniform of white pants and a sweater with a white collar helped to put parents at ease.[202] The Señoritas demonstrated a "respectable femininity" by conceding to a strict dress code and a male coach, as long as they could play ball.[203]

Two years later, an all–Mexican American team joined the Los Angeles League, a seven-team association that played under American Softball Association rules at Loyola Stadium.[204] Hollywood celebrities—including Jeanette Mac-Donald, Clark Gable, Jean Harlow, and Spencer Tracy[205]—helped promote the women's league by throwing out first pitches and watching from the stands. A *Los Angeles Times* photograph featured the Señoritas team in their new uniforms with the tagline, "Snappy Spanish Senoritas Play Pelota Muy Buena" (see Figure 3.7).[206] The caption described how "a bevy of *Spanish beauties* from Glendale have organized their own softball team and are now battling for the feminine softball championship at Loyola Stadium." Because the church's Spanish American Civic

Group sponsored the team, they were identified solely by their Spanish heritage, even though they were of Mexican descent. The headline implied that despite being fashionable and stylish dressers with their silk shirts and short shorts, they could still play good softball.

Furthermore, this photo shows these smiling girls squatting and holding baseball bats in a sexualized way, and therefore their athletic skills are delegitimized at the expense of their sexuality. While *La Opinión* praised the Glendale team for representing the Mexican community in the all-white women's softball league, they also participated in the sexualization of these female athletes.[207] Before their impending exhibition match at White Sox Park, the team visited the *La Opinión*'s offices for publicity photos with wrestler Vincente Lopez.[208] One photo portrayed a smiling Lopez surrounded by Glendale teammates. The headline warned Lopez that his upcoming title defense could be in jeopardy because "he surrounds himself with a group of beautiful softball players."[209] In this case, the Glendale Señoritas were lauded in the pages of *La Opinión*, but for their physical appearance as opposed to their athletic skills.

Although *La Opinión* began to promote women's softball in the late 1930s, sportswriters considered female players not as serious competitors but rather as sexualized objects for entertainment purposes. Sports columnist José Hernandez Llergo, writing as Makanazo, speculated, "The public is more attracted by the beauty and grace of the female players than the game itself."[210] After all, he added, "their uniforms look more like swimsuits than baseball uniforms."[211] Even Francisco Costello, representing the Mexican Athletic Association of Southern California (MAASC), suggested, "It would not be bad for more sports and social clubs to organize a Mexican League of this sport, so that the pretty girls of our colony can compete."[212] Even though women's softball was considered a novelty attraction for male spectators, it had the potential to generate revenue. On May 23, 1937, former El Paso Shoe Store owner turned baseball promoter for White Sox Park Rodrigo Castillo announced a preliminary game by "novenas de muchachas Mexicanas" before a men's match between a visiting team from Mazatlán, Mexico, and a local team.[213] The Spanish term *novena* has a religious connotation that refers to women's groups who gather to pray the rosary and in turn helped to allay parental fears about their daughters as respectable and honorable while playing softball. The all-Mexican Four Star Eagles battled against their rival, the all-white Baldwin Park Girls, in a close game of seven innings of "interesting" play.[214] After the Eagles defeated the Baldwin Girls, *La Opinión* commented, "Hopefully, the enthusiasm of the young girls who form the Four Star Eagles, will find support among the public at the White Sox, and that the development of softball among our young girls will progress this season, because in truth it is healthy and attractive."[215] Eventually, the rising popularity of women's softball in Southern California and other parts of the country led to the formation of the All-American Girls Baseball League in 1943.

THE "FIRST MEXICAN" IN THE BIG LEAGUES

Fernando Valenzuela was the not first major league baseball player who garnered hero status on both sides of border. Baldomero "Melo" Almada became the first Mexican-born player to play in the U.S. major leagues becoming a sports celebrity in Mexico and Los Angeles. On June 14, 1931, Melo Almada made his debut with México-El Paso against the Los Angeles Colored Giants, pitching six innings, giving up only two runs, and striking out the best hitters.[216] *La Opinión* sportswriters lauded his performance and forecast, "Melo Almada left us fully convinced that he has all the necessary material to make himself into an excellent pitcher in organized baseball."[217] After one season with the México-El Paso, eighteen-year-old Almada followed his older brother Lou to the Pacific Northwest.[218] The Almada brothers were star football and baseball athletes at Los Angeles High School. Their father was a big baseball fan and encouraged sons and daughters to play sports, including Nellie and Carmen Almada, who played softball during high school.[219] The brothers were offered athletic scholarships to the University of Southern California but declined because of their family's deteriorating financial situation during the Great Depression. The Almada brothers played for the Seattle Indians of the PCL, but it was the younger brother who impressed the coach with a .325 batting average and thirty stolen bases.

The Seattle Indians invited Melo for another season, but heeding the advice of his older brother, he refused to sign until they raised his salary. When the team owner demanded a cut on his contract, Lou refused and the Indians traded him to the San Francisco Mission Reds.[220] Melo remembered feeling guilty, though: "It hurt to the soul, so much that I cried like a child, but that was the kind of man that was my brother."[221] By his third season, Melo had won over many local fans, including a scout for the Boston Red Sox. Lou Almada recalled, "Boston was about to buy him, and he could have made himself some money. Well, somebody called [Bill] Klepper and told him that my brother was going to be a free agent. So Klepper brought cash over and paid Mel all he owed him. About four days later, he sold him to Boston for $25,000. Klepper was able to catch up on his debts and pay off the rest of the players with that."[222] Melo could have made more money if he had remained a "free agent" instead of having the Boston Red Sox buy his contract for less money. Melo called his brother and then called home with the exciting news; his mother broke down in tears because "he would be far away and for a longer period from home."[223]

Although Melo Almada became popular with many fans, the Seattle newspapers repeatedly misunderstood his ethnic identity, referring to him as a "Spanish athlete" and changing his name to "Mel." Before his departure, fans arrived early to Civic Stadium to celebrate Mel Almada Night. The *Seattle Post-Intelligencer* wrote, "The nineteen year old Spanish athlete will be honored by home-town boosters on the eve of his departure for Boston, where he will join the Red Sox, who purchased him from Seattle more than a month ago."[224] The "Spanish" term emphasized his European heritage and light features, which allowed him to occupy an in-between racial position in Major League Baseball's color line. Misrepresentation of his ethnic identity would continue to haunt him throughout his major league career.[225] When news of Almada's signing with the Boston Red Sox reached Los Angeles, the *Los Angeles Times* reported, "Now it's 'Viva Almada' with local Mexican sports fans that can turn their attention from the prize ring to the baseball diamond where they have a new idol in Melo Almada."[226]

On July 23, 1933, *La Opinión* and *Los Angeles Times* sportswriters organized a special celebration at Wrigley Field in Melo's honor before the doubleheader between the Seattle Indians and Hollywood Stars. Melo Almada Day featured family members, former coaches and teammates, Hollywood celebrities, Mexican prizefighters, and Mexico consular officials. Mexican actress Rosita Moreno began with awarding Melo a golden baseball trophy donated by Mauricio Calderón, Dr. Reynaldo Carreón, and Dr. Manuel Servín. The Associated Press photo featured Moreno hugging Melo Almada with the caption "Thees for you, Señor."[227] The stereotypical use of broken English gave readers the false impression that Mexican people were foolish and lacked formal education.

At another moment on Melo Almada Day, Luis "Kid Azteca" Villanueva, a Mexican prizefighter, handed Melo his boxing gloves imprinted with "Tuesday, July 11, 1933," the day that Azteca had defeated middleweight champion Ceferino Garcia.[228] Perhaps best of all, former teammates from México-El Paso joined the twenty thousand spectators to celebrate Melo's athletic accomplishments. "To show how the local Mexicans are getting behind 'Almada Day,'" reported the *Los Angeles Times*, "Rodrigo Castillo, manager of the local México-El Paso nine, has canceled a double header scheduled for today so all of Melo's countrymen can come out and pay him homage."[229] Castillo awarded Melo with a signed bat inscribed with "México-El Paso."[230] Teary-eyed Almada thanked his family, former teammates, and fans. He told the press, "I can't express how much I appreciate the efforts of the local Mexican colony in putting on a day for me . . . and I only hope I can give them something to cheer about."[231]

On September 8, 1933, Almada made an impressive debut at Fenway Park, batting .341 in fourteen games and hitting the only home run in his first season. Most impressive was when he got 3 hits and 2 walks against 38-year old Babe Ruth at Yankee Stadium.[232] These were the last hits that Babe Ruth gave up as a pitcher before retiring. Outside the locker room, moreover, Almada had to correct some misconceptions about his ethnic identity. Boston sportswriters mistakenly characterized him as an Italian player because of his last name and appearance. After a home game, Almada approached a *Boston Globe* sportswriter to make a special request: "I wanted to thank you for your kind attention you have given me, but I want to plead with you and the public that I'm not only of Mexican descent, but I was born in Huatabampo, Sonora, a state in México along the Arizona-México border." He explained that he was proud of his Mexican heritage and it bothered him that the press misrepresented him as Italian.[233] In an interview with *La Prensa*, he recalled how "one of the teams [Boston Red Sox] wanted to announce him as an Italian, but he flatly refused and told them loudly to the four winds that he was Mexican and was proud of it."[234] The team intended to market Almada as an Italian because of his last name and the large Italian fan base in Boston, so he complained to the manager that it bothered him when they misrepresented his identity. He spoke English and Spanish fluently and reminded critics of his Mexican American upbringing. In a profile in the *Sporting News* he explained why his family left Mexico during the Mexican Revolution and emphasized that "My father always wanted us children to have an American education . . . I was then only a year and one-half old, so you see, I am very much an American."[235] Almada embraced a hybrid ethnic identity that varied according to the social situation, who he was with, and the time period in which he found himself. To the American public Almada defied the short and dark Mexican stereotype. *Collier's* admitted that to their surprise, "although proud of his Mexican lineage and completely loyal to it, he doesn't even look like a Mexican, being taller, broader and considerably fairer than most of the citizens of our sister republic."[236]

The U.S. sporting press continued to rely on long-standing racial stereotypes about Mexicans in the film industry.[237] The *Sporting News* attributed his effective base stealing technique to running long jump and hurdles in high school, but then included a stereotypical cartoon with the caption "AH-A Mexican jumping bean."[238] The *Boston Herald* used terms like "fireball" and "hot-blooded" in describing Almada. One article claimed he had special magical powers: "Almada brought down Mexican curses on the head of Powell in the second inning."[239] Whether based on Catholic doctrine or some kind of witchcraft, Melo's nationality was used to explain his behavior and temperament. Sportswriters applied the "good field, no hit" stereotype to Almada, often applied to Latino players because of their graceful fielding skills but poor hitting.[240] For example, the *Washington Post* described Almada as "the only full-blooded Mexican in major-league baseball [had] his best season in 1935 when he batted .290 but his hitting deficiencies [were] partly offset by his speed and cleverness in the outfield."[241] Despite these stereotypical descriptors in the sports press, Almada continued to excel in both hitting and fielding. Almada spoke fluent English and got along with teammates in the dugout, including hall of famer, Bobby Doer (see Figure 3.8).

During the 1933 offseason, the Almada brothers reunited in Los Angeles to play with former teammates. When the México-El Paso manager approached them to help raise funds for the victims of the September 16, 1933, Category 5 hurricane in Tampico, México, which killed hundreds and caused massive flooding, they accepted without hesitation. Melo explained why he decided to help: "I could not forget about that immemorial tribute that my compatriots organized at Wrigley Field before I left to the East [Coast] . . . so it is important that I play

FIGURE 3.8. Baldomero "Melo" Almada, wearing a Washington Nationals uniform, is posing with former Red Sox teammate and hall of famer, Bobby Doer, 1937. (Courtesy of Eduardo B. Almada)

with my fellow countrymen."[242] The widely publicized exhibition match on October 24, 1933, featured Melo Almada for the San Fernando Missions and Luis Almada for México-El Paso. Conchita Montenegro, a Hollywood actress who starred in *Cisco Kid* (1931) and *The Gay Caballero* (1932), threw the first pitch for the opening game.[243] The exhibition game raised several hundreds of dollars for the hurricane victims, and the Almada brothers received much praise from the Mexican consul. After accepting the funds, Alejandro Martinez admitted, "I expected a generous offer to the victims of Tampico from our Mexican community, but I did not expect it would come from our Mexican athletes." He added, "This benefit will not only help the Tampico victims, but will it create enthusiasm for the king of sport, baseball."[244]

On November 22, 1933, Mexicans President Abelardo Rodríguez invited Melo Almada to play exhibition games against teams from the Mexican Baseball League in Mexico City.[245] Before he accepted the offer, Melo requested to have his brother accompany him because Lou had visited Mexico City previously with the México-El Paso team. Melo also had to request permission from the baseball commissioner, Kenesaw Mountain Landis, who explained why he approved the request: "As a courtesy to México, and understanding that the Aztec nation there exists a bright future for the king of sports, I granted Melo Almada to visit the capital to take part in some exhibition games and upon watching a great baseball player like Almada in action, the Mexicans will dedicate themselves more to the sport."[246] The commissioner viewed the Mexican Baseball League as inferior to Major League Baseball, even though top-notch Afro-Latino and African American ballplayers excelled in Mexico in part because they experienced less racial discrimination.[247]

From November 24 to December 10, 1933, the Almada brothers played several exhibition games in Mexico City. The city's newspapers highlighted Melo's big league achievement and called him "an idol to all Mexicans."[248] Ignacio Herrerías, former *La Opinión* sports editor now writing for Mexico City's *El Excélsior*, highlighted "his youthfulness and modesty and his enormous accomplishments in less than a year in the Pacific Coast League and then recruited into the big leagues, has become a hero to millions of Mexicans at home and abroad." Upon arrival on November 24, Mexico's political establishment held a dinner banquet and dance to honor the Almada brothers.[249] Pedro Almada, who lived in Mexico City, joined his nephews at the welcoming festivities.[250]

At the opening game at Venustiano Carranza Park, a jazz band played while Tirso Hernandez threw the first pitch to begin the three-game series. Luis played for the 1933 championship Comintra team and Melo for the runner-up Delta team. In front of five thousand spectators, Melo stole several bases and hit "one of the longest homeruns ever hit at Parque Carranza."[251] With the teams tied at one win apiece, the Almada brothers asked Carmona to offer free admittance to women and children.[252] Carmona approved the request, and after Delta won the game he raffled signed balls from the Almada brothers.

As "México's baseball ambassador," Almada showed his nationalist loyalty to the Mexican nation by playing exhibition games in Mexico City. Because of his popularity among fans, Ernesto Carmona asked Commissioner Landis for a week extension so that the Almada brothers could play with Delta against the Aztecas.[253] Formed by Homobono Márquez, the Aztecas team comprised Mexican, Mexican American, and Afro-Cuban players. Unfortunately, the Azteca-Delta three-game series was delayed because of a dispute over umpire selection. The Aztecas suggested two Cuban umpires, but Delta insisted that umpires should be of Mexican origin. Carmona sided with Delta and argued that the "Mexicanization of baseball" should begin with the umpires.[254] "Let's leave this umpire issue in peace," Melo told both teams, "what matters most is that we prepare ourselves and show our best effort on the field."[255] Ultimately, each team selected its own umpire, and the series ended with the Aztecas defeating Delta two games to one.

The night before their return to Los Angeles, a special dance was held at Club Deportivo Chapultepec in honor of the Almada brothers, who extended their visit in order to help develop professional baseball in México.[256] El Excélsior editorialized that the Almada brothers' visit should serve as a reminder that Mexican ballplayers have the potential—when provided with more support and opportunities—to follow in the footsteps of Melo Almada.[257] When a journalist asked Almada why there had been few Mexicans in the major leagues, he faulted "the lack of suitable coaches and the failure of American scouts visiting Mexico. It's a shame, because I know there are many good players."[258]

Upon returning to Los Angeles, his sports celebrity status landed him in several Hollywood motion pictures, mostly for release in Mexico. Almada admitted that he was not "another Ramon Novarro," and "they gave me a small speaking part occasionally, because I took Spanish in school and talk it fairly well."[259] His movie cameos were cut short however, when he had to report to spring training. At the end of his major league career in 1938, Almada was batting .342 for the St. Louis Browns, but after a poor start they traded him to the Brooklyn Dodgers. After a salary dispute with the Dodgers, Almada decided to retire and return to California. He played for the Sacramento PCL team until 1942, when he retired from baseball. Almada reflected, "I feel more comfortable playing in the Pacific Coast League because in most of the cities we play there are many Mexican fans. . . . This upcoming series against Los Angeles, we have Jesus Flores as pitcher, and Chico Hernandez as catcher, and with the two speaking Spanish I feel more at home."[260]

While Almada preferred to play closer to his Mexican fan base, his brother Luis cited another reason—racism. Melo got tired of being hit by pitches because of his ethnicity. He would complain to his brother, "They're throwing at me because I'm a Mexican."[261] Additionally, his son Eduardo Almada recalled how "there were occasions when he did suffer racism because he was Mexican from other players and fans, especially in the American South."[262] Almada once told the Arizona Daily Star that he did encounter situations where he was discriminated against and humiliated. "Every so often, we'd be out for a drink and suddenly someone would say, 'Hey, you god-dammed Mexican . . . what makes you think you can act like an American?'"[263] After Mexico's nationalization of the foreign oil, Almada's loyalty was questioned by teammates. According to his son, Almada became "the subject of taunts from the bench of the other teams. They would call him a thief. They would want to know, 'What kind of country are you from.'"[264] Despite the privilege he enjoyed from his lighter skin and English-language fluency, Almada occupied an in-between racial position in American baseball—neither black nor white. Consequently, Almada encountered a different form of racism based on his exoticism, foreignness, cultural difference, and outsiderness in the American pastime.

After playing in the PCL for a year, he returned to México to coach and manage teams in the Mexican League. Jorge Pasquel hired him to manage the Union Laguna team in Torreon, but he quit midseason because of a conflict with a few players who thought he was too "Americanized." One Cuban player claimed that Negro League players in the Mexican league hated Melo Almada because of his light skin privilege that allowed him to play in the major leagues. He returned to live in the United States, joined the Army Medical Corps during World War II, and became a permanent resident. After the war, Melo Almada returned to Sonora. He coached Los Mayos de Navojoa in the Mexican Pacific Coast League from 1953 to 1957.[265] When Almada died in Caborca, Sonora, on August 13, 1988, there was little mention of his death in mainstream U.S. newspapers. Unlike U.S. baseball, Mexican baseball honored Almada with the Mexican Pacific League Rookie of the Year trophy in his name and selecting him to the Mexican Hall of Fame.

CONCLUSION

This chapter has focused on peloteros and peloteras in Greater Mexico in the 1920s and the 1930s, from the amateur level to the professional, who crossed racial, gender, class, and national borders in search of opportunities to play ball. Family became central to building good team chemistry among players and encouraging them to compete and sometimes win championships. The family bond was evident in the El Paso Shoe Store team, who changed to México-El Paso to represent the Mexican nation and forge closer ties with the Mexican Baseball League. México-El Paso underwent another major change when it merged with Hermosa Mexico during the 1935 season, becoming Hermosa-El Paso. This merger lasted for just one year; the Castillo brothers returned the team to its original name when veteran players like Salazar, Lagunas, and Orozco were reunited.[266] The team continued playing against teams from the Mexican League, the Negro League, and the PCL until 1940, when it finally dissolved. *La Opinión*'s sportswriter described México-El Paso's legacy: "Sunday through Sunday, instead of going to the movies or having fun on the beach, the amateur fan preferred to attend the park on 38th street to see his favorite sport. It was in this way that the veteran organization of Mexican baseball here, infiltrating the hearts of the fans to make it the most popular Latino organization that has existed in the United States."[267] Two establishments were key to the rise of Mexican American baseball in Los Angeles: White Sox Park and *La Opinión*. White Sox Park invited México-El Paso and local teams to play in the California Winter League and inaugurated the Summer Mexican Baseball Season that pitted visiting teams from Mexico against local teams. *La Opinión* sportswriters devoted extensive coverage to play-by-play, scores, and schedules, profiles of teams and players, and ballpark advertisements. This semiprofessional team won several championship titles and produced some of the best Mexican baseball players who entered the U.S. major leagues.

In general, the success of teams relied on a network of owners, coaches, managers, family members, sportswriters, ballpark owners, and fans. Some of these fans included mothers, daughters, and wives who received free admission to cheer on their favorite team. Women were not mere spectators, but also played baseball and softball. They formed their own teams often with the help of businesses, settlement houses, churches, and civic groups. Fathers, brothers, or male relatives often acted as chaperones to Mexican American women's softball teams. These teams garnered sporadic coverage from Spanish and English newspapers and were often portrayed as sexualized and feminized athletes who supposedly played a novelty sport. The opportunity to travel beyond their city and region was not available for most softball players. Despite these economic, racial, and gender barriers, Mexican American women became peloteras as a means to empower themselves to gain more freedom and develop networks. With the arrival of World War II, Mexican American women entered the workforce in larger numbers, thus creating more opportunities to play professional softball and baseball.

Considered the first Mexican-born player to enter the big leagues, Baldomero "Melo" Almada became a national hero in Los Angeles and Mexico. Melo Almada never turned away his family, community, coaches, and México-El Paso teammates who helped him to develop into a major league player. Mexico embraced Almada as one of their own who rose to prominence, inspiring future baseball players. His visits and coaching career in Mexico represented the athletic aspirations of a Mexican nation still insecure about its baseball program and seeking credibility in the international arena of baseball. In 1973, Mexico's Salón de la Fama (Hall of Fame) in Monterrey selected Almada as one of eleven notable players in Mexican baseball history. A *New York Times* reporter visiting Mexico's Cooperstown noted the "symbiotic" relationships between the two countries with "players crossing the border in both directions season after season after season."[268] He concluded that "baseball is not the American game but rather the game of the Americas."

4 • FORGING TRANSNATIONAL SPORTING NETWORKS

José Arteaga was born in Baja California, Mexico, moved to Los Angeles during his teenage years, and in 1921 teamed up with Lamberto Álvarez Gayou to form the first all-Mexican basketball team, "Bohemia." Gayou eventually became the president of Mexico's first sports federation, and Arteaga became a basketball player and coach in the city's new amateur athletic association. Arteaga coached several teams, with only the best players chosen to play exhibition games in Mexico. His criteria for selecting his all-star Mexican basketball team included height and weight standards—a minimum height of five feet eight inches, weight of less than a hundred sixty pounds—good sportsmanship, technical knowledge and ability, and "patriotism and love for Mexico." On the last requirement, Arteaga praised his players as "representing the sporting spirit of México de afuera."[1]

Like Arteaga, Juan Acevedo was another amateur athlete who sought to increase recreational opportunities for Mexican-origin youth. Acevedo was born in East Los Angeles and became a star cross-country runner at Roosevelt High School and Los Angeles City College. Between 1933 and 1936, Acevedo held the city's three-mile record 17:20. Unlike Arteaga, however, Acevedo advocated for the use of the term "Mexican American." Acevedo asserted, "Racism toward Mexicans was deeply rooted [in the United States] . . . we had to confront the reality of our situation that we had to call attention to our U.S. citizenship."[2] These two athletes, Arteaga and Acevedo, had different ideologies that coexisted within the new amateur athletic association, the Mexican Athletic Association of Southern California (MAASC).

This chapter examines the local and transnational politics of sports in Greater Mexico through the activities of MAASC, which spanned the period from the 1932 Olympic Games to World War II. The Los Angeles Olympics provided an opportunity to bring city recreation officials, Mexican government representatives, and Mexican and Mexican American leaders together to form an amateur athletics organization to promote sports in the *barrios* and *colonias* of Southern California. MAASC organized sports leagues, tournaments, and exhibition matches; it also secured recreation facilities, provided entertainment, and offered other athletic opportunities. A unique feature of MAASC was its transnational ties with the Mexican government's sports federation, the Confederación Deportiva Mexicana (CDM). This chapter argues that MAASC and its related activities forged a sporting Mexican diaspora. MAASC sports maintained transnational ties with Mexico that allowed some athletes to adopt a Mexican national identity outside of Mexico and others to adopt a Mexican American identity, which in turn connected them more closely with Southern California and U.S. society in general. Ultimately, Mexican-origin athletes adopted hybrid sporting identities that helped to instill a new confidence among MAASC members to challenge the racist paternalism of the Los Angeles Department of Playground and Recreation (LADPR).

1932 LOS ANGELES OLYMPIC GAMES

During the 1920s, Mexico organized its own domestic athletic tournaments to produce athletes capable of representing the country at international tournaments. In 1924, Mexico sent a team to compete in the Olympic Games in Paris, followed by Amsterdam in 1928 and then Los Angeles in 1932.[3] Despite a worldwide economic depression, the Los Angeles Olympic Organizing Committee ignored calls for cancellation and pressed ahead to stage the world's biggest sporting event. In particular, though, foreign countries faced financial difficulties in sending their athletes to Los Angeles. The Mexico Olympic Committee reached out to México de afuera in Los Angeles for assistance. Enrique Mexia, commercial agent for the Mexican government, formed a subcommittee with local businesspersons and professionals to raise funds for Mexico's Olympic team.[4] The new subcommittee, the Mexican-American Olympic Committee (MAOC), appealed to the patriotism of readers of La Opinión: "What a beautiful opportunity to show our government officials and compatriots that live in Mexico that the dividing line and distance are purely geographic because, when it comes to uniting our people, we help out with such big endeavors in the name of Mexico." Mexia urged compatriots to purchase a one-cent Mexican Olympic Stamp from Mexican-owned businesses to defray the costs of Olympian athletes from Mexico (see Figure 4.1).

Mexia instructed readers to place the stamps on their house and car windows as a "symbol of solidarity with La Raza."[5] Female members of México de afuera were also enlisted to sell Olympic stamps at a rate of one cent per vote.[6] Josefina Olea sold the most stamps and earned the title of Queen of the Mexican Olympic Team. Olea helped welcome the Mexican Olympians to the Olympic Auditorium and expressed her gratitude to her friend, Baby Arizmendi, who helped her sell votes.[7] Mexican American women used their fandom of boxing and other sports to claim public space.

Despite nationalist appeals, Mexia encountered problems raising money from a community simultaneously suffering high unemployment and nativist

FIGURE 4.1. *México en la Olimpíada* stamp designed by Roberto Silva, 1932. (Courtesy of Roberto Silva)

hysteria. Mexia recruited prominent Anglo Californians as honorary members, including Governor James Rolph, Los Angeles mayor John Porter, Hollywood cowboy star Will Rogers, *Los Angeles Times* publisher Harry Chandler, and superintendent of the LADPR Raymond Hoyt. Mexia also solicited help from recreational clubs and athletic organizations in Mexican communities. Fernando Miranda, president of the Bohemia Athletic Club, responded to Mexia's call by convening a meeting with his members at Evergreen Playground. Bohemia proposed an exhibition modeled on the Olympic Games, with over twenty-five athletic clubs competing. Mexia and Miranda approached Hoyt for financial support. Hoyt enthusiastically supported the request and instructed his employees to publicize this "special athletic program to be held at Evergreen Playground on May 8th." Mexica declared the "Mexican pre-Olympic event a big success," attracting over three hundred spectators and one hundred athletes competing in different track and field events, with each champion earning an Olympic-like medal.[8] Besides defraying the costs for the visiting Mexican Olympians, the participating athletic clubs used the event to seek additional support from the city recreation department.

To generate additional funds, MAOC announced a qualifying tournament for local amateur boxers to earn a spot in Mexico's Olympic boxing squad and compete at the 1932 Olympics. After receiving support from the state boxing commissioner and the Los Angeles Athletic Club, MAOC staged the pre-Olympic boxing tournament at the Olympic Auditorium on July 11, 1932. The *Los Angeles Times* reported, "Several amateur scrappers from Old Mexico are here to compete against the best Mexicans of Southern California for the five positions on the Mexican ring squad."[9] Mexican American boxer Bert Colima offered to coach the Mexican boxing team during workouts.[10] This contest generated so much excitement that another pre-Olympic event was held for track and field athletes at White Sox Park. Attendees paid twenty-five cents to watch athletes from Baja California compete in eleven track and field events against local athletes from Southern California. Nicknamed the Mexican Olympic Fiesta by the *Los Angeles Times*, this pre-Olympic event featured a night baseball game, a Mexican army band performance, the crowning of the Mexican Olympic Queen, and a guest appearance by Mexican Hollywood actress Lupita Tovar.[11] In a letter to Superintendent Hoyt and LADPR commissioners, Mexia expressed his appreciation: "We wish to thank you for your most splendid cooperation given to our [Mexican American Olympic] Committee for the meet between Los Angeles and Baja California athletes at White Sox Park."[12] By the time the Mexican Olympians arrived on July 23, 1932, MAOC had raised over three thousand dollars.

Prior to these events, Mexican Olympians had encountered problems crossing the border at El Paso, not unlike Mexican Prizefighters discussed earlier U.S. immigration officials did not allow them to enter unless they underwent medical inspection and vaccination.[13] Despite claims of diplomatic immunity and complaints to the Mexican consul, the team reluctantly accepted the vaccination in order to arrive in Los Angeles on time. Seventy-three Mexican athletes (two of them women), accompanied by officials and coaches, were escorted to the Olympic Village in Baldwin Hills by a caravan of six hundred automobiles and were greeted by five thousand spectators lined up along Crenshaw and Vernon avenues, waving Mexican flags.[14] The caravan included female Mexican Olympians for the first time, including Maria Uribe Jasso competing in the javelin throw and Eugenia Escudero in fencing.[15] That same night, MAOC held a special welcome dinner and dance for the Olympic team at the Shrine Auditorium, with "more than 600 Mexican athletes, and members of Southern California athletic associations in attendance."[16]

Despite all the fanfare and excitement, however, the *Los Angeles Times* relied on a series of racial stereotypes to describe the visiting athletes. One article called them "Mexican caballeros [who] bring color to [the Olympic] village" carrying "the blood of the Aztecs and the Continental Spanish in their veins" and enjoying a strict diet of "frijoles." Racialized images of "frijole-eating" athletes did not surprise Mexican American leaders who were already feeling besieged by a climate of racial discrimination. According to the newspaper, "The Mexican Olympic forces were a bit surprised and the local Mexican papers are indignant, over reports that the ever-popular frijole bean is the predominant dish in the training diet of the visitors from the neighboring republic. The only thing conspicuous about the frijoles in the Mexican camp is their absence, the athletes say." Despite the negative press, the athletes received strong support from Mexican American fans during the games. They won silver medals in boxing and shooting.[17] In a show of transnational solidarity, the Mexican Olympic team invited athletes from México de afuera to accompany them as they circled the Coliseum waving the Mexican flag during closing ceremonies.[18]

The international appeal of the Olympic Games offered an opportunity for immigrants living in Los Angeles to display their ethnic nationalism by hosting and cheering for their compatriots.[19] Like the Los Angeles Japanese Association, the MAOC hosted, entertained, and rooted for visiting Olympic athletes from their homeland.[20] The Mexican government, however, sought to recruit athletic talent from México de afuera to achieve Olympic victory on the international stage. The *Los Angeles Times* observed, "Names rather familiar to Southern California sport fans are found on the list of athletes who will represent old Mexico in the Olympic Games. Six boxers and five track men all received their preliminary athletic training at Southland high schools."[21] One of these athletes was Los Angeles–born Manuel "Midget" Martinez, who, after winning the flyweight division in the pre-Olympic boxing tournament, earned a spot on Mexico's boxing team. Several years later Martinez served as the amateur boxing commissioner for the MAASC and as founding editor of the *Sport Page*.

The Olympic Games brought together Los Angeles city officials, Mexican government representatives, and local athletic clubs for the first time, laying the groundwork for a new amateur association to coordinate and promote athletic events throughout Southern California's barrios and colonias. Consequently, one cannot overestimate the significance of the Olympics in spurring athletic interest in the Mexican diaspora. Labor and civil rights leader Bert Corona later recalled, "The Olympics in 1932 had also attracted many Mexicanos, especially to see the Mexican and Mexican-American athletes who participated in the running events."[22] In a letter to Mexican President Abelardo Rodríguez, the president of Club Atletico México, expressed such excitement in watching his *paisanos* compete in the Olympics that he offered to bring his "basketball team to beloved Mexico for a tour to lift up the sporting spirit of his brothers and to help them prepare for the next Olympics [in Berlin]."²³ He argued that sports could help strengthen transnational ties between athletes of the Mexican diaspora. "We have the conviction that a trip of this nature would strengthen relations between brothers of the Mexican race."²⁴

MEXICAN ATHLETIC ASSOCIATION OF SOUTHERN CALIFORNIA

Three months after the 1932 Olympic Games, MAASC held its first meeting in the LADPR office to approve a new constitution, organizational structure, and executive board. Its constitution outlined its main objectives:

(1) The object of this association shall be to organize, conduct, and promote the physical and cultural, social intercourse and recreational athletic activities in Latin-American communities in accordance with the rules of the Amateur Athletic Union of America. (2) To unite, co-ordinate, and enlarge the athletic programs of the Latin-American communities. (3) To advance and improve amateur athletic relations between the United States and Mexico. (4) To inculcate the spirit of true sportsmanship among Latin-Americans and to bring greater cooperation among the organizations, thereby fostering fellowship and goodwill among them and the community in general.²⁵

The organization's first president invoked the phrase "a union hace la fuerza" (unity is strength) to remind members about building unity among athletes, coaches, and spectators. In fact, the MAASC logo featured an eagle biting a serpent that resembled the Mexican flag, reflecting the association's transnational ties to Mexico. The city's sports supervisor Dudley Shumway praised MAASC's members for "filling a big gap in the local Mexican community." Shumway added, "I sincerely believe that [MAASC] will be a powerful influence in uniting all the branches of sport in Southern California's Mexican community."²⁶

The organizational structure included three executive board members (president, secretary, and treasurer), a small group of advisers, several standing committees, sport commissioners, and members who belonged to community sports clubs. The executive board appointed a commissioner for each sport to be in charge of the tournament schedule, managed the budget, and enforced rules of sportsmanship according to the Amateur Athletic Union. The advisory board consisted of Shumway, the Mexican consul of Los Angeles Alejandro Martinez, and "professional Mexican business men, who were held in high esteem in the Mexican colony."²⁷ The standing committees included the Olimpíada Mexicana (Mexican Olympic Games) held annually with a Cinco de Mayo festival, the Gymnasium Committee, finance, and publicity. Each sport commissioner filed a report on tournament results, the names of the winners and participants, and a list of suggestions for improvement. MAASC members had to pay an annual fee of twenty-five cents and have "at least one parent of Latin American descent."[28] While the purpose of the racial eligibility clause was to promote athletics among Latinos, it proved difficult to enforce and sometimes became controversial when athletes did not appear Latino, as problematic and assumption-filled as that thinking was.

The MAASC executive board consisted of a mix of male athletes of Mexican descent. Some members were born and raised in Los Angeles, grew up playing in the city's playgrounds, completed their high school and college degrees, and became professionals and civic leaders. These included Juan Acevedo, Ralph Romero, Juan Alonso, Roberto Ortiz, Pedro Despart, and Ray Sánchez. Others, like José Arteaga, Arturo Flores, Juan de la Vega, and Guillermo Eddy, were born in Mexico and arrived in the Los Angeles area as youth with every intention of playing their favorite sport in México de afuera.[29] Sportswriter Francisco Costello was a member of MAASC's executive board and wrote a weekly sports column for *La Opinión*. Costello played a key role in MAASC's publicity efforts by reporting on their activities and monthly meetings.

Former YMCA member Acevedo became one of the active members and prime movers behind MAASC, serving as secretary between 1933 and 1939 and designing the logo (see Figure 4.2). In the early 1930s, Acevedo founded the Club Deportivo Atenas and competed in the Junior Olympics, cross-country races, and marathons. Acevedo organized the annual track and field events for the Olimpíada Mexicana. In 1939, he joined the cross-country team at the University of California, Los Angeles (UCLA) on an athletic scholarship. After returning from military service, he took a job as a social worker and soon joined the 1947 campaign to elect Edward Roybal to the Los Angeles City Council. Acevedo gained important leadership and organizational skills with MAASC that later extended to the Mexican American Movement, Mexican American Political Association, and the California Youth Authority.[30]

Ralph Romero attended Polytechnic High School and played baseball and basketball; after graduation in 1923, he worked for the city public works department. During the Olympics, Romero joined MAASC as the representative of the Hazard Latins sports club, for which he served as treasurer and president in 1934 while he attended law school at the University of Southern California. A former student-athlete at Belmont High School, Ray Sánchez joined MAASC as the basketball commissioner.[31] In 1936, he led a Mexican American political club in support of Franklin D. Roosevelt's reelection campaign and named his basketball team On with Roosevelt.[32]

A chief proponent of Mexican nationalism in México de afuera, Arteaga coached and managed the Club Deportivo Los Angeles, which fielded several basketball teams, including Bohemia, LA Mexicans, and Arriola A.C. Arteaga joined MAASC in order to organize an amateur basketball league tournament and travel to Mexico to compete in exhibition games. In 1932 Arteaga wrote an editorial, "The

FIGURE 4.2. Mexican Athletic Association of Southern California logo. Courtesy of © Juan Acevedo/*La Opinión*. From the *La Opinión* Newspaper Records, CSRC-2015-007. Courtesy of the UCLA Chicano Studies Research Center.

Momentum of Sports in México de afuera," in which he expressed commitment "to help President Rodriguez develop sports in Mexico."[33] He reasoned, "By play-ing [exhibition] matches in border towns, it will inspire and stimulate our [Mexi-can] brothers to take up sports." Arteaga also reported on basketball tournaments and amateur athletes for *La Opinión*.[34] He warned readers about unscrupulous sports promoters who intended to "make money from our athletes by paying them misery wages and dropping them when they could no longer profit from them" and cited an incident in which a promoter had defrauded members of Club Atlet-ico México with the promise of financing their exhibition trip to Mexico City.[35]

MAASC promoted various types of amateur sports, beginning with track and field and basketball and later swimming, tennis, football, boxing, and softball. During its early years, MAASC set forth an ambitious agenda to appoint com-missioners and organize leagues for each sport, secure playing fields for practices and tournaments, and instruct athletes on the rules of "good sportsmanship." By 1933, MAASC claimed 115 athletic clubs, 38 baseball teams with over 500 total participants, 66 basketball teams in leagues with over 450 participants, 16 softball teams with 225 players, 5 track and field events with 425 participants, and more than 1,600 spectators.[36] Some of these clubs reflected both México de afuera and Mexican American ideologies.[37]

Men held all leadership positions within MAASC. A combination of Mexican masculinities, from traditional to modern migrant forms, contributed to the group's male orientation and promotion of "manly" sports.[38] Women were allowed to participate in traditional feminine sports like tennis, softball, and gymnastics. Dudley Shumway, head of the Municipal Sports Division, emphasized the sports' masculine character: "This is the moment in which we should lend our support to all Mexican amateurs who have great abilities to convert themselves into great athletes. . . . Athletics has proven to be the best means in which to make good male citizens."[39] MAASC's president used similar gendered language: "Instructing athletes to be truly sportsmanlike, competing honorably and with fair play, and being truthful noblemen when they win or lose."[40] Since the late nineteenth century, sports had been a social institution through which "masculine hegemony" was constructed and reconstructed by linking specific sports with male aggression and by allowing men to govern sports organizations.[41]

MEXICAN OLYMPIC GAMES

MAASC's first athletic event was a track and field meet at Evergreen Playground, held in conjunction with Cinco de Mayo festivities. The event was called Olimpíada Mexicana for its resemblance to the Olympic Games. Shumway praised the two hundred fifty athletes and six thousand spectators for their participation and "for lifting the spirits of the Mexican Athletic Association and their magnum opus." *La Opinión* sportswriters credited MAASC officials for "their unselfish undertaking in trying to unite the Mexican colony" and remarked how the "Chicanitos" of Club Trojan won first place in a majority of races.[42] The Spanish-language sporting press referred to young male athletes of Mexican descent as Chicanos or Chicanitos. These athletes navigated the cultural tensions within a sporting world that emphasized American values and norms while also maintaining aspects of Mexican culture and identity, thus adopting hybrid sporting identities.

MAASC organizers sought to use sport participation to present a positive image of a Mexican population that was still considered a "Mexican problem" during the mid-1930s. Olimpíada Mexicana became a larger event the following year (1934) because city mayor Frank Shaw helped secure the Los Angeles Memorial Coliseum, the largest sports venue in the city; events included a polo game, a soccer match, music, an awards ceremony, dancing, and the coronation of the Olimpíada Mexicana queen. MAASC organizers recruited over forty athletic clubs from across Southern California (principally Orange County and the San Fernando Valley), over four thousand athletes (between the ages of fifteen and twenty-two), and over twenty thousand spectators. MAASC invited special guests, including Hollywood celebrities, boxing champions, the mayor and police chief of Los Angeles, and the California governor. One MAASC organizer reminded *La Opinión* readers to wear their best Mexican costumes and arrive with "proper enthusiasm so that we can demonstrate to the [Anglo] American audience that our [Mexican] colony will not only be the largest population locally, but the most powerful in culture, athletics, and discipline."[43]

Another MAASC objective was to showcase the athletic talents of its youth so that they might earn athletic scholarships to colleges or universities. In fact, Bert Corona arrived at the University of Southern California on a basketball scholarship. "On certain game trips outside of El Paso, we encountered quite a bit of harassment," recalled Corona. He elaborated, "We got booed and called all kinds of dirty names. These places where Mexicans weren't liked hated seeing their home teams beaten by Mexican athletes."[44] Acevedo was an example of a MAASC athlete who had earned a college scholarship to UCLA. One community college coach admitted, "Those Mexican boys are bringing much strength into the current sport movement, and in the long run, will gain more honors than those [white] American boys in the universities, colleges, and high schools of Los Angeles."[45] Both Corona and Acevedo helped organize YMCA-sponsored Mexican Youth Conferences and the Mexican American Movement that promoted education and athletics to build leadership skills among men of Mexican descent.

La Opinión sportswriters consistently defended Mexican-origin athletes when they were misrepresented by American academics and physical educators. The short size of Mexicans was frequently cited for their poor basketball skills. In a physical ability study of Anglo-Americans and Latin Americans, the researcher found that "Anglo Americans were decidedly superior in learning basketball skills while the Latin Americans seemed to be superior on softball throw for distance and the standing broad jump." Latin Americans scored lower in basketball skills because of their shorter size, but excelled in the "dribble test."[46] The inventor of basketball even suggested the elimination of the tip-off "because of the short stature of the Mexican players" during a match between University of Kansas and University of Mexico teams.[47] Even though Mexican basketball players had a size disadvantage, it did not prevent them from excelling in speed, dribbling, and rapid delivery as well as accurate shooting and tenacious defense.

The sports pages of *La Opinión* praised the skills of basketball teams coached by José Arteaga, who traveled with his all-star team to Mexico for exhibition matches. At the 1936 Olympic Games in Berlin, Arteaga attributed Mexico's basketball bronze medal to the transnational exhibition matches that Arteaga had helped organize.[48] In an article titled "Los Mexicanos 'Son Chiquitos pero Picosos'" (short but spicy), *La Opinión* sportswriters appropriated the term "spicy" to counter the common stereotype about the short size of Mexican athletes. The article highlighted the achievements of basketball athletes at local high schools and community colleges: " Mexican athletes who attend Los Angeles institutions have not only distinguished themselves in first, second and third teams, but they have shown that despite being small they are speedy and spicy."[49] Mexican basketball players have achieved success in other high schools. For example, the Lanier High School basketball team from San Antonio's West Side overcame racial and class barriers to win two state titles and prove that "Mexicans could also play ball."[50]

In February 1937, Occidental College invited Centinelas Athletic Club, the winners of the MAASC basketball tournament, to play an exhibition game. Before the match, the Centinelas were "boasting [to be] the most powerful Mexican aggregations ever gathered in Southern California."[51] Centinelas lived up to their reputation by defeating the Occidental Tigers, 50–36.[52] After Centinelas roundly defeated Occidental College's Tigers by fourteen points, the *Los Angeles Times* took notice of their top guard, José Placencia, who was "considered one of the best players in all Mexico and was selected to play on the Mexican Olympic basketball team which went to Berlin [in 1936]."[53] Placencia won numerous accolades for representing Greater Mexico in the Olympic Games and the Amateur Athletic Association (AAU) basketball league, where he led his Mexican All-Star team to victory and in 1942 became the top AAU basketball scorer.[54] "Maybe representatives from the University, who are always looking for new material, will finally take notice of our athletes," declared *La Opinión*.[55] Placencia's athletic achievements generated publicity for the MAASC basketball tournament and showed the general public that Mexican American athletes were capable of competing and winning at the collegiate level.

Even though MAASC leaders insisted on "good sportsmanship," the competitive nature of sports made this policy difficult to enforce during matches. Still, only on rare occasions did fights erupt. During the 1934 basketball season, controversy arose when Club Minerva's coach, Benito Montoya, threatened to leave the tournament because of false accusations. When Club Iris was about to lose a match, its members accused Club Minerva of fielding a "negro player," in violation of MAASC rules allowing only players of Latin American descent. Montoya defended Kenny Washington's ethnic identity, claiming that he was the son of a black father and a Mexican mother, had grown up in a Mexican neighborhood, and spoke Spanish fluently. Montoya complained that "Club Minerva players forfeited the game and ridiculed Washington, who felt embarrassed as he walked off the court in silence."[56] MAASC leaders mishandled the incident by neglecting to take disciplinary action against Club Iris for its "anti-sportsmanship" behavior. This conflict revealed the contested meaning of Mexicanidad, which has been narrowly defined as a mixture of indigenous and European heritage, ignoring the African presence in the Mexican diaspora.[57]

CONFEDERACIÓN DEPORTIVA MEXICANA

International sporting exchanges between Mexico and the United States are not a recent phenomenon; since the 1920s both countries have competed in the

Olympic Games, FIFA (Fédération Internationale de Football Association) soccer tournaments, and "goodwill" exhibition games.[58] By the 1930s Mexico's post-revolutionary government sought closer ties with México de afuera through the country's new sports federation. Mexico developed its national sports program much later than the United States, when in January 1933 President Abelardo Rodrí-guez established the nation's first sports federation, Confederación Deportiva Mexicana (CDM), with the chief aim of promoting physical exercise, discipline, and nationalism.[59] President Rodríguez appointed Lamberto Álvarez Gayou as director of physical education, in charge of making Mexico a "sports-minded nation." As discussed in chapter 1, Gayou studied physical education at UCLA and after graduation became a sportswriter and sports promoter on both sides of the U.S.-Mexican border.[60] "Mexico realizes that its athletic future lies with its youth," wrote Gayou. He continued, "So it is on youth that it is concentrating its intensive campaign to develop physically and morally the Mexican people and enhance the prestige of the nation."[61] His first action was to introduce a junior pentathlon program, modeled after the one in Los Angeles.

Just one year later, Mayor Shaw of Los Angeles praised President Rodríguez for hosting the first international junior pentathlon meet: "We are pleased to know that your government has adopted this program as a regular part of the cur-riculum in your public schools."[62] Despite the rising interest in sports, according to Gayou, "we lack trained physical educators and coaches. . . . There are no sports clubs in Mexico like the Los Angeles or the New York Athletic clubs." Using the Amateur Athletic Union as a model, Gayou pushed for the creation of the CDM.[63]

Like Gayou and Rodríguez, President Lázaro Cárdenas understood that Mex-ico could learn much from American sports, so he sought to strengthen athletic ties with México de afuera. During the mid-1930s, Cárdenas expanded physical edu-cation, parks, and sports programs as part of his populist and nationalist agenda.[64] He viewed sports as a form of racial uplift for the individual and nation.[65] On March 17, 1937, Cárdenas sent two CDM athletes, Jose de Anda and Fernando Campo, to meet with MAASC president Ralph Romero to discuss ways "to tighten our sporting relations."[66] The visitors received a special dinner, hosted by MAASC and the Los Angeles Mexican consul.[67] At dinner, de Anda invited MAASC ath-letes to compete in the Mexico City trials for the 1938 Central American Games. De Anda explained how impressed they were with MAASC athletes: "We have a great desire to include the best athletes living in Southern California to compete for a spot in the [Mexican] national team for the 1938 Central American and Carib-bean Games in Panama City."[68]

Two months later CDM's president, Gustavo Arévalo Vega, invited MAASC leaders to become partners with their sports federation.[69] Vega emphasized, "It is our fervent desire to be united with our brothers who live outside of our coun-try."[70] CDM offered to defray a portion of transportation costs for MAASC ath-letes who wished to participate in the Mexico City trials.[71] Acevedo led the team of eight track and field athletes to Mexico City, but only three runners (Francisco Lopez, Adolfo Curiel, and Roberto Madrid) earned a spot on Mexico's national team for the Central American and Caribbean Games scheduled in Panama City for February 10 to 23, 1938.[72] Adolfo Curiel won a silver medal in the four hundred meters.[73] "The most important thing for us," wrote Makanazo, "is that the Mexican colony of Los Angeles sent a small contingent to reinforce the delegation of our [Mexico] country."[74] *La Opinión* sportswriters made a persuasive argument that given the opportunity and resources, Mexican athletes could compete at the national and international levels. After agreeing to work with the CDM, MAASC appointed Guillermo Eddy as its official CDM representative in Mexico City.[75]

After forming a binational partnership, MAASC and CDM cosponsored a series of exhibition basketball games in Mexico. As discussed in chapter 1, the YMCA had introduced basketball to Mexico, and by 1934, according to one physical education director, the game had become "the most popular sport with a total of 40,000 players."[76] Mexico made a strong showing at the 1936 Olympics in Berlin when its basketball team won a bronze medal. To practice for the Olympic Games, CDM and MAASC cosponsored the Centinelas team to travel to Mexico for ten exhibition games. Coached by MAASC advisory board member Dr. Angel Antonio Loyo, the Centinelas team won seven games and lost two against a Chihuahua team. Impressed with the Centinelas' playing style, the Mexican Olympic Committee asked Loyo if the team's top player, José Placencia, could join Mexico's Olympic basketball team. The Centinelas exhibition tour, according to Loyo, demonstrated that MAASC had "extended its jurisdiction to the other side of the border, making possible that our boys from our jurisdiction get recognized for their worth."[77] Gaining international recognition for their athletic talent was significant, given prevalent racial beliefs in the United States about the supposed mental and physical inferiority of Mexican immigrants.[78]

To strengthen their athletic partnership, MAASC leaders also invited CDM athletes to compete in their 1938 Olimpíada Mexicana event at the Los Angeles Coliseum.[79] The fifteen visiting athletes from Mexico surprised local observers by winning first place in eleven competitions.[80] The following year MAASC recruited "the cream of the crop" from Los Angeles City College to compete against Mexico's top athletes.[81] Described as "the crack squad of athletes from Mexico" by the *Los Angeles Times*, "the boys from Mexico were the pick of the southern republic. Some of them won championships at the Central American Latin Olympic Games in Panama last year."[82] Each year the number of visiting athletes increased, attracting more spectators to the Los Angeles Coliseum eager to watch this international competition, but the gate receipts were not enough to offset MAASC expenses.

By the late 1930s, financial problems threatened to cancel MAASC-sponsored athletic events. When CDM and MAASC proposed the first annual international amateur boxing tournament between Mexico and California, the California State Athletic Commission, the agency that regulated boxing, denied their request.[83] MAASC leaders appealed the decision, arguing that this tournament would improve "goodwill relations" between both countries.[84] After receiving approval, MAASC officials now had to secure the financial backing for the boxing event on November 20, 1939, at the Olympic Auditorium. MAASC's boxing commissioner Midget Martinez proposed to President Cárdenas that if CDM paid the Mexican athletes for travel to Tijuana, MAASC would cover the remaining cost to Los Angeles. Cárdenas approved Martinez's request, stating, "I have already given instructions to the Confederación Deportiva Mexicana to take care of this request."[85] Mexico's boxers won all divisional titles in front of packed boxing arena.[86] To improve MAASC's poor performance for next year, Martinez recruited prize-fighter Bert Colima to help train amateur boxers and organize an elimination tournament.[87] Building transnational ties with the Mexican government and local ties with sports promoters and homegrown organizations not only allowed MAASC to support its athletes but also infused leaders with more confidence to challenge the city's recreation department.

LOS ANGELES DEPARTMENT OF PLAYGROUND AND RECREATION

Early Americanization efforts in the city's public health programs and recreational playgrounds had treated Mexicans as capable of assimilation but also as racialized subjects in need of guidance and direction.[88] The LADPR resembled the Los Angeles Bureau of Music in its "racial paternalistic" approaches toward immigrant and racial minority residents.[89] When the city's recreation department announced the formation of MAASC, there was some suspicion, if not mistrust, about the city's intentions. LADPR superintendent George Hjelte proclaimed during a keynote speech to the Friday Morning Club that "supervised recreation centers can be a determining factor in promoting good Americanism."[90] "Supervised play" was a common catchphrase used by municipal recreation officials to cloak their Americanization efforts. Dudley Shumway, LADPR's municipal sports division supervisor, reassured La Opinión readers that "the importance of this relationship is that the municipal government does not intend precisely to 'Americanize' its affiliate [Mexican] groups but only to apportion the necessary measures so they can develop their athletic faculties."[91]

Three years later, however, the relationship between MAASC members and Shumway began to break down. On September 21, 1935, LADPR sponsored an exhibition football game between National University of Mexico and Occidental College at the Los Angeles Coliseum.[92] To earn one-quarter profit of total ticket sales, MAASC agreed to sell tickets, decorate the stadium with Mexican flags, broadcast the game in Spanish, and sit in the "Mexican section to cheer for their football players from Mexico."[93] Although MAASC acquiesced to this segregated seating arrangement, members of the organization expressed disappointment with the racist portrayal in the *Los Angeles Times* of Mexico's football players as "Mexican jumping beans" and "Latin Leviathans."[94] Using a series of racial stereotypes for Mexican athletes, the newspaper reported that "a band of Mexican footballers aren't much to look at. They're light. They're small. But like chili con carne, they have a lot of pepper."[95] To counter the negative press coverage, Mexican fans hoped for an underdog victory against the more powerful Occidental football squad, but, despite over six thousand Mexican spectators cheering for their compatriots, the Mexican team lost by twenty-one points.[96]

Losing the football game was disappointing, but even more upsetting was not receiving a share of the profits. When MAASC president Juan Alonso inquired about the missing funds, Shumway told him there was no money left, due to a hundred-fifty-dollar debt. "We believe this is a great injustice," Alonso angrily complained to the press, "because the members of [MAASC] spent at least $200 to promote this event." Shumway denied that he had promised one-quarter of total ticket sales to MAASC. Soon thereafter Alonso resigned in protest and urged MAASC members to sever ties with Shumway.[97] After Alonso's resignation, several sports clubs also declared their independence from the city because of Shumway's disrespect for MAASC.

Momentum to split from the city grew the following year when Shumway once again exerted his authority over MAASC leadership. MAASC's basketball commissioner Armando González complained that Shumway had arbitrarily disqualified a basketball team because it failed to turn in an eligibility list before the deadline. According to González, "[Shumway] undoubtedly thinks that he can expel any team that does not abide by the rules, but the only one that can do that is me, as head commissioner of the [MAASC] basketball league." During a heated confrontation with Shumway, González accused the city recreation department of "trying to command the membership of the Association with an iron hand." The final straw came when Shumway financed the travels of his favorite basketball team (Centinelas) for exhibition games in Mexico, even though they had lost the basketball tournament.[98] This move angered the winning team, Club Deportivo Mexico, which urged the new MAASC president, Roberto Ortiz, to take action against Shumway and to "work hard to separate from the Department of Recreation and Playgrounds."[99]

During a "heated and sensational" meeting on March 28, 1936, MAASC members voted to oust Shumway from the advisory board and to move their meeting location from City Hall to Evergreen Playground in East Los Angeles. "This move," declared Ortiz, "was one step in breaking definitively from Mr. Dudley Shumway who has been governing the destinies of our Association since its founding." Ortiz clarified that the battle was against Shumway, but he also held the city recreation department responsible for not taking any disciplinary action.

"Now that the Association is free," *La Opinión* columnist Francisco Costello reminded its members, "We need to prove to Shumway that we are very capable of doing a good job of bringing sports to the Mexican youth of Los Angeles." Costello urged former members—Juan Alonso, Ray Sánchez, Arturo Flores, and José Arteaga—to return to MAASC to prove to Shumway that they could organize their own events. Juan Acevedo attributed the success of Olimpíada Mexicana to the organization's newfound independence. "After the Association was freed from the yoke of the Department of Recreation," Acevedo observed, "we have come to see the spirit and willingness of the various parts of the Association working together much better."[100] The Olimpíada Mexicana event took on greater significance since it allowed MAASC members to prove to themselves and their peers that they were capable of working together and organizing a successful large-scale sporting event.

Several months later, Shumway retaliated by revoking MAASC's use permit for the Evergreen Playground and Recreation Center's gym that hosted the annual basketball tournament. "Once again Shumway has demonstrated his prejudice against the Association for having liberated itself from the yoke of his department," wrote Francisco Costello in his weekly column. This move created logistical and financial problems, forcing MAASC to postpone the tournament. A basketball player complained about Shumway to *La Opinión* accusing him of "doing destructive work among the ranks of the Association and by denying us permission to practice in the gymnasium." Then, to add insult to injury, Shumway threatened to retrieve the city trophy awarded to the winning team of the MAASC basketball tournament. "Is it really necessary to be prejudiced against the MAASC?" asked one *La Opinión* sports columnist. "It looks really bad for a high-level city official to try to take away a trophy that his own department donated." Shumway's retribution served as a wake-up call for MAASC to become more financially independent. "Shumway has tried to harm us by closing the gates to the city's playgrounds," declared MAASC basketball commissioner Ray Sánchez. "Now is the time for all [MAASC] members to be extremely united to show Mr. Shumway that Mexicanos know how to work well together and can succeed financially."[101] Sánchez enlisted the help of the Mexican consul of Los Angeles, who then complained to Mayor Shaw, forcing Shumway to back away from his threat.

MUJERES WHO STEPPED ONTO THE COURT

In the late 1930s, MAASC facilitated sporting opportunities for female members of Greater Mexico in basketball, softball, and tennis. In 1938, MAASC made an announcement in *La Opinión*'s social clubs section, encouraging Mexican women to take part in the seventh annual Mexican Olympics at the LA Coliseum.[102] MAASC president Rafael Romero made a special plea for more female participants in track and field and basketball and even promised them trophies like their male counterparts. Romero appealed to women's patriotism to their homeland in his call: "It is time for our young women to participate in a purely Mexican sporting event, organized by Mexicans for the Mexican public, on a date that is glorious for all of us, so I do not doubt that our athletes will respond to our desires."[103] The athletic program featured 143 registered athletes representing ten athletic clubs competing for the *La Opinión* and Cantu Lara trophies, but none included a female.[104] Alma Joven and Club Ideal de Señoritas, two Mexican American women clubs, responded to the call by forming all-female basketball teams and holding practices at the Evergreen basketball courts, but did not compete at this event for unknown reasons.[105] Two years later, an all-Mexican female basketball league formed with six teams competing at Echo Park Playground, but MAASC failed to support the league, so it lasted only one season.[106] Other sporting organizations in the Southwest were more successful in supporting Mexican American women's basketball.

In San Antonio, Texas, the Spanish American League formed a more successful girl's baseball and basketball league made up entirely of Mexican American women from the West Side barrio.[107] San Antonio's English and Spanish newspapers reported on the basketball league play and score results. Through his many articles on the sporting successes of the West Side barrio, Frank Trejo of the *San Antonio Light*, according to a high school principal, "did more to improve Anglo-Latin relations in Bexar County."[108] *La Prensa*'s Frank Jasso wrote a sports column, "El Deporte Entre Nuestra Colonia" (sport in our colony), that described the sporting activities of La Liga Femenino Hispano-Americana de Basketball (the Spanish American women's basketball league). La Liga included teams with names like What Next, Modern Maids, Orquídea, Lulac, and Tuesday Night.[109]

Each team was led by a Mexican American male head coach and assistant. All their practices and matches were held at Sidney Lanier High School on the West Side of San Antonio. The Lulac team referred to the first major Mexican American civil rights association, League of United Latin American Citizens, founded in 1929 in Corpus Christi, Texas.[110] The team name was adopted because many of the players and their parents were members of the LULAC San Antonio chapter. Indeed, LULAC's team captain was Berta Alderete, known as a *brillante jugadora* (brilliant player) because she was the top league scorer for 1932 with eighty-nine points.[111] It was not only Berta's shooting skills that caught the attention of *La Prensa* sports reporter; she was a "beautiful captain who masterfully led the team to a brilliant victory against Tuesday Night squad."[112] This description reveals how sports writers and spectators continued to sexualize female players, reinforcing gender inequality in sports.

In the 1930s, women's basketball rules were modified to allow players to dribble only once and pass the ball twice before taking a shot.[113] Women were discouraged from aggressive guarding and physical contact in order to protect their femininity. As Susan Cahn contends, "The 'aggressive' and 'uncharming' woman who pursued highly competitive basketball risked association with sexual as well as athletic deviance."[114] Despite these restrictions, Mexican American women played their own style of basketball. Ernestine Navarro recalled how she had loved playing basketball, but not by women's rules. Oxnard's high school basketball rules required girls to play half court, whereas men played full court. Navarro recalled, "We could only dribble the ball one time, and pass it three times before shooting a basket . . . but I liked to be aggressive and would steal the ball, I never liked been held back."[115] For Navarro, using physical strength and endurance while playing basketball was part of her working-class upbringing, which did not match middle-class ideals of femininity. As the "modern woman" gained the right to vote and to work outside the home, they began to assert themselves in the world of sports. Similarity, second-generation daughters of Mexican parents coming of age during the 1920s and 1930s began to push social and cultural boundaries through sport participation, but usually under the protectiveness of male coaches and male-dominated athletic organizations.

La Liga was sponsored by mutual aid societies, fraternal lodges, and voluntary associations from San Antonio's Mexican community. But when teams were short of funds for uniforms and traveling expenses, players would organize a special dance at the West Side recreation center.[116] These women acquired leadership skills playing on the court that could be transferred to fund-raising or any other area of life. Take, for example, Emma Tenayuca, who played guard for the Modern Maids team from 1932 to 1934.[117] The team emerged from the Modern Maids Club, founded in 1931 as a social and recreational club that referred to themselves as Muchachas Modernas (modern girls).[118] After high school graduation in 1934, Tenayuca became a labor organizer and joined the Worker's Alliance and Communist Party.[119] This "Radical Tejana" first learned how to organize players on the basketball court before organizing workers inside the workplace and union hall. As a point guard Tenayuca held an important leadership position on the court. The point guard position is often viewed as an extension of the coach on the floor, requiring not only dribbling and passing skills, but excellent communication skills to get the ball to teammates and into the basket. For her tenacious playing ability, Tenayuca was selected in 1933 to all-city girls' basketball team.[120] Tenayuca also played baseball for the Spanish American Girls Baseball League alongside Eva Garza, who later became a famous singer around the world.[121] Basketball and baseball taught her invaluable leadership skills that became crucial for organizing workers in San Antonio's pecan shelling industry. Tenayuca was known as a "troublemaker" by the Mexican American middle-class establishment in San Antonio, but before passing judgment *La Prensa* reminded readers about her athletic record. "The young female labor leader who has appeared in the headlines of the local newspapers for demonstrations in the municipal palace, was once a notable female baseball player and basketball player with the Modern Maids part of the first women's basketball league from the [Mexican] colony."[122] To note, the sporting experiences of Tenayuca and other Mexican American labor and civil rights leaders have yet to be told.

Compared to La Liga, MAASC had more success encouraging women to play tennis. On November 3, 1939, a small group of male and female tennis enthusiasts formed the Mexican Tennis Club to "promote tennis among youth of both sexes from the Mexican colony of Los Angeles."[123] The club received approval from the city's parks and recreation department to reserve their home courts at Echo Park Playground for Sunday practices.[124] Within a year the club grew to ninety members, with a male leadership that delegated organizing the club's festivities to female members.[125] Stereotypical gender roles followed Mexican American female tennis players on and off the courts. At the 1940 tennis tournament at Griffith Park, *La Opinión* sportswriters referred to Latina tennis players as *señorita* when describing Margarita Gomez's singles title.[126] Sportswriters spent more ink describing the femininity of Latinas rather than their tennis game or technique.[127] Although tennis was considered socially acceptable for women, they were not taken seriously, received less prize money, and were discouraged from making tennis a career.[128]

FORGING TRANSNATIONAL SPORTING NETWORKS

After MAASC broke its ties with the city's recreation department in December 1936, the group faced major challenges in organizing athletic events for the Mexican population, but it still managed to forge a sporting diaspora by using local and transnational sporting networks.[129] The first problem was finding a location to hold its monthly meetings. Since its inception, MAASC had worked closely with the Mexican consul of Los Angeles, who served on their advisory board, made guest appearances at athletic events, and granted permission to hold meetings at the consulate office.[130] In addition, the Mexican consul helped sponsor MAASC athletes to compete in exhibition matches in Mexico. Los Angeles consul Joaquín Terrazas explained that "if we want our sons to grow up wholesome and strong, we should make sports part of their activities . . . and [let them] compete in athletic tournaments."[131] The Mexican consul helped MAASC organize the Olimpíada Mexicana at the Los Angeles Coliseum. The consul negotiated a low stadium price with Ralph Chick, head of the LA Coliseum, and awarded trophies to the winners.[132] The newly appointed Mexican consul of Los Angeles, Renato Cantú Lara, donated the Cantú Lara Trophy for the winner of the ten-thousand-meter race for the 1938 Olimpíada Mexicana. He also sent a special bulletin to *comisiones honoríficas* (honorary commissions) throughout Southern California, instructing them to send athletes to attend "the [MAASC] sport festival, which will be colorful and overflowing with enthusiasm."[133]

To make the 1937 Olimpíada Mexicana a success—even without the city's help—Ralph Romero and Juan Acevedo (MAASC leaders from 1936 and 1942) forged stronger ties with the Mexican consul, Hollywood celebrities, Spanish-language print media, sports promoters, and Mexican American organizations. Acevedo resolved the problem of late registrations by publishing the form with rules and regulations in *La Opinión* sports pages. Acevedo also solicited three new trophies for the winners: one donated by *La Opinión's* owner, Ignacio Lozano, one by the Mexican consul, and one by Mayor Fletcher Bowron. In addition, Acevedo invited Hollywood actor Leo Carrillo to serve as the master of ceremonies.[134] Carrillo's debut was a huge success, attracting over forty thousand attendees and much praise from athletes.[135] Two years later, MAASC invited athletes from Mexico City, Baja California, and Arizona to compete in the largest sport festival to date. The *Los Angeles Times* praised the event as "one of the gayest of the Mexican celebrations, the holiday witnessed a gala fiesta and track meet at Memorial Coliseum . . . one of the largest and most colorful programs ever presented by the Mexican colony."[136] In a dramatic showing of "good neighbor" relations, the Mexico consul hoisted the U.S. flag while Mayor Bowron raised the Mexican flag. Bowron declared, "It is an inspiring spectacle to witness this celebration of the people of a nation which, like our own, loves peace, liberty, and independence. We hope that Mexico and the United States may be in peace as long as their flags shall wave, and may they wave forever."[137]

Government officials were not the only ones to evoke the official Good Neighbor Policy; MAASC leaders also used the rhetoric of inter-American cooperation to gain support for their athletic events. On September 4, 1939, MAASC teamed up with boxing promoter Henry von Stumme to organize a Labor Day Sports Fiesta at his outdoor arena in the San Fernando Valley. The event featured eight amateur bouts, a women's softball game, a baseball game, and the selection of a *Reina Mexicana del Deporte* (Mexican sports queen), followed by a jitterbug dance contest.[138] According to MAASC, the event's purpose was to create "a fund which will make possible the goodwill exchange of athletes of Latin descent with those of the neighboring [Mexico] republic." Besides raising money to send a "Mexican-American ring team" to Mexico City for an international boxing competition, the boxing show featured "Latin American ring greats" Bert Colima, Joe Rivers, Alberto "Baby" Arizmendi, and Joey Silva who "mingle[d] with outstanding prospects for the future."[139] As historian Monroy has pointed out, "The Mexican boxers quickly became an important presence in the arenas of California and provided a central means by which men's ethnic consciousness was formed."[140]

MAASC TENNIS AND HOLLYWOOD CONNECTIONS

In 1933 Ray Sánchez, MAASC tennis commissioner, organized the first tournament with singles and doubles matches at Evergreen Playground courts. Two years later, several tennis clubs were formed to compete in the third annual tennis tournament at Exposition Park.[141] Club México's Ernesto Peña battled against Felix Romero of Club Juarez for the singles title and to represent MAASC in the international tennis league and travel to Baja California to play exhibition matches.[142] Because of the close proximity to Mexico, MAASC forged a transnational relationship with Mexico's tennis federation to arrange matches between their top players. The Mexican Davis Cup arrived on Oct 1 1939 to play five exhibition matches at Griffith Park against "some of the best local Mexican aces."[143]

When MAASC leaders encountered problems securing tennis courts and trophies for their tennis tournament, they asked Hollywood Mexican actor Gilbert Roland for assistance. Roland responded generously by donating a singles trophy for the male winner and offering to use his celebrity status to generate publicity. He also helped MAASC to gain access to the much larger tennis courts at Griffith Park. Roland himself was an elegant tennis player who agreed to an exhibition match against the visiting Mexican Davis Cup team.[144] Trained to be a bullfighter by his Mexican father, Roland used his graceful athletic posture inside the tennis courts and flashy celebrity persona outside to generate publicity for MAASC tennis tournaments. Roland was routinely featured in the sports pages of *La Opinión* newspaper awarding the trophy to the winners.[145] Roland developed an on-court rivalry against Fernando Isais, who won back-to-back singles titles from 1938 to 1940, and also became a world champion horseshoe pitcher.[146] In fact, these MAASC tennis tournaments played a significant role in developing future tennis star Richard "Pancho" González discussed in the last chapter.[147]

DECLINE OF MAASC

After MAASC cut its ties with the city recreation department, the association was forced to pay higher fees for private sport facilities and high school gyms where its programs took place. In February 1937, therefore, MAASC embarked on its most ambitious fund-raising project to build its own gymnasium. A special gymnasium project committee was formed to raise money and put on a special banquet to honor the association's biggest supporters.[148] The first step was to consult with advisory board member and attorney Manuel Ruiz Jr. about seeking non-profit status. Using gendered language, Ruiz drafted the application outlining its main purpose: "To promote the physical, cultural, social intercourse and recreation of its members and to encourage all proper and *manly* sports and pastimes."[149] Once MAASC acquired non-profit status, Ruiz proposed that the organization request the Los Angeles Board of Education to grant an exemption from paying service fees for high school gyms. In a letter to the school board, Ruiz explained that MAASC had "for some years engaged in character-building activities for young Mexican boys in athletics . . . [which] has directly contributed to the partial solution of the juvenile delinquency problem."[150] Ruiz requested that the school board rescind the charge of service fees for use of gymnasiums because it "has imposed such a hardship that the athletic schedule this year cannot be carried forward." One week later, MAASC received a letter from Ruiz that the "Board has rescinded its action and has withdrawn the charge involved in the use of school gymnasiums. Congratulations!"[151]

Despite this small victory, MAASC remained frustrated that three years later there was little progress in building MAASC's own gymnasium.[152] According to José Arteaga, "The Association still does not have a suitable place to carry out its sports program," complained Arteaga, who blamed the city's recreation department for its lack of support and for contributing to the "pachuco problem." "At one time, [MAASC] had a remedy for the pachuco problem," he asserted in *La Opinión*, "but the selfishness of city employees with the power in their hands ruined a noble effort, and if they had given more to support them [MAASC athletes] there would not have existed a pachuco problem."[153] Most scholars have attributed the "pachuco" and "zoot suit" hysteria to wartime anxieties, Los Angeles police arrests, and newspaper stories, but none have considered how the discriminatory actions of municipal recreation officials may have also contributed to the rise of juvenile delinquency.[154]

Amid these financial worries, a powerful struggle emerged within MAASC's leadership in which some board members tried to oust Pedro Despart. During a summer trip to Mexico City, Despart accused MAASC executive board members of holding elections in his absence; after protesting the results, he resigned and, along with Ray Sánchez, formed a rival organization in 1940, the Mexican Athletic Union (MAU).[155] MAU held its first meeting at Downey Playground and even invited MAASC's foe, Dudley Shumway, to say a few words in support of MAU activities. With the exception of football, MAU competed with the MAASC in offering similar sports programs. This caused confusion among local athletes and Mexican government officials. In a sharply worded letter to both athletic organizations, Mexico's Director of Physical Education Ignacio Beteta advised the two organizations to put aside their differences and "unite their forces to work together for the improvement of sports among the Mexican youngsters who live outside of Mexico."[156] Los Angeles Vice Consul Eduardo Zembrano convened a special meeting with both groups to resolve their differences but met with little success. It took the arbitrations skills of attorney Manuel Ruiz Jr. to bring the two rivals together. After a lengthy meeting at Evergreen Playground, *El Espectador* reported, "It was decided in this meeting that both athletic organizations will cooperate to the fullest extent with each other's activities and not encourage friction between both organizations which will disrupt the relationship now established."[157] Both organizations decided to coordinate a master schedule and offer separate sports programs; MAASC coordinated track and field, tennis, adult basketball, and swimming, whereas MAU organized football, women's softball, amateur boxing, and junior basketball.[158]

After helping to resolve the conflict with its rival athletic organization, MAASC worked more closely with Manuel Ruiz Jr. to reestablish relations with the city recreation department to combat juvenile delinquency.[159] Ruiz had been the Manual Arts High School's valedictorian, debate team captain, and track star who received a scholarship to attend the University of Southern California. After college graduation, he opened a law practice and offered legal advice to several Mexican American organizations.[160] As a former high school athlete, Ruiz strongly supported the use of sports to combat juvenile delinquency among Mexican American youth. He understood that "delinquency" was neither a biological nor cultural attribute associated with Mexican American youth, but a product of racism, economic factors, and social marginalization. In an article in *Crime Prevention Digest,* Ruiz blamed sensationalist newspaper reports, police mass arrests, job discrimination, segregated schools, lack of recreational opportunities, and "racial theories imported form the deep South" as the chief causes of juvenile delinquency.[161] Furthermore, he made recommendations to the city, including opening indoor school gyms for recreation at night and on weekends; providing athletic equipment, lockers, and organized programs at recreation centers; hiring Spanish-speaking supervisors for playgrounds and recreation centers; and establishing more youth leadership camps.

In September 1940, Ruiz made his first attempt to restore relations between MAASC and the city recreation department. In a letter to Superintendent Hjelte, Ruiz acknowledged that "certain past misunderstandings have occurred between the Mexican Athletic Association and particular individuals employed by the Department of Playground and Recreation." Now, however, MAASC members expressed a desire to put these past issues aside and refocus on combatting juvenile delinquency through recreation. Ruiz proposed, "For the purpose of eliminating future confusion, to designate one or two persons from its group, as clothed with the authority of dealing with your department." Ruiz couched his argument in the rhetoric of the Good Neighbor Policy, stating that this new relationship would "foster goodwill and a spirit of international cooperation between Latin Americans and other elements of our body politic."[162]

During the early 1940s MAASC struggled to sustain its sports programming amid the Sleepy Lagoon court case and Zoot Suit Riots, but persistent financial problems and limited access to municipal playgrounds, combined with several members enlisting in the U.S. military, made it difficult to sustain organizational unity. The last chapter will examine how the MAU and Coordinating Council for Latin American Youth superseded the work of MAASC by expanding sports programs and recreational opportunities for Mexican American youth. One last attempt to revive MAASC occurred in September 1945, when returning veterans Juan Acevedo, Rafael Romero, Juan Alonso, and Roberto Ortiz held a reunion at the Casa del Mexicano in Boyle Heights. They invited all interested athletes to help "reorganize the Association and reinstate sports among our youth once again."[163] With only a few attending the meeting, MAASC leaders decided to part ways and pursue other interests.

CONCLUSION

Why have American sports not cultivated more talent from within Mexican American communities and Mexico? MAASC, with its transnational ties with Mexico, represented an opportunity for U.S. sports to tap into the athletic talent, but it failed to do so. MAASC played a significant role in promoting and organizing sports in Greater Mexico from the Great Depression to World War II. Even Chicano scholars have ignored the role of sports and the making of a transnational community. They have focused on Mexican American campaigns for fair employment, school desegregation, public housing, unionization, and civil rights but have ignored the transnational politics of sports in Southern California and Mexico. In a hostile climate of high unemployment, repatriation campaigns, immigration restrictions, and racial discrimination, MAASC forged a sporting diaspora by mobilizing community-based sports clubs and athletes of Mexican descent to participate in a wide variety of sports. To be sure, sport participation did more than highlight athletic talent on the playing fields. Just as importantly, sports have served to present a more positive image of the Mexican diaspora. For MAASC athletes, the organization also offered a training ground for political leadership and community activism. Juan Acevedo, José Arteaga, Ray Sánchez, Juan Alonso, Francisco Costello, Pedro Despart, Ralph Romero, Manuel Ruiz Jr., and other athletes all developed important leadership skills that transferred into political and other social arenas, at least for men. MAASC, and its sports programming, was a masculine space, with men dominating at every level. Mexican American women and young girls were steered toward more socially acceptable sports like softball, basketball, and tennis.

With or without the city's assistance, MAASC achieved some success in steering youth toward athletic, educational, and political pursuits. Becoming Mexican American and becoming Mexican were simultaneous occurrences within MAASC. By building transnational ties with the Mexican government and its sports federation (CDM), MAASC was able to offer more athletic opportunities to its members and, in the process, connected them to an emerging Mexican national identity. By allowing México de afuera athletes to join Mexico's Olympic team or to compete in other athletic events, the Mexican government sought to extend its influence into Mexican communities abroad. MAASC and its related athletic activities simultaneously raised the consciousness of a sporting Mexican diaspora among its members while also connecting them to a network of municipal, high school, and college sports in Southern California. By forging close ties with Mexico's sports federation, MAASC positioned itself as a chief promoter of Good Neighbor Policy relations through organized sports, thus gaining political power and the confidence to challenge city recreation officials. MAASC demanded that the city government provide more recreational resources for Mexican-origin youth who faced segregated schooling, negative press coverage, intimidating police officers, and prejudiced city recreation officials.

5 • BECOMING GOOD NEIGHBORS THROUGH WARTIME SPORTS

In the May 1943 issue of *Modern Mexico*, a publication of the Mexican Chamber of Commerce in the United States, *Novedades* sports editor Fray Kempis declared, "Baseball Makes Good Neighbors."[1] Kempis continued, "It is the fact that the ball, the bat, and the glove have conquered Mexico completely, as it has not been conquered since a tough no-rules team of Spaniards." And since then, according to Kempis, "baseball has become a great common denominator of inter-American understanding and friendship." He recounted how American baseball heroes have become household names in Mexico, including in small villages like Tlaquepaque, Jalisco, where "every man, his son and his brother, is at once a potter and a *beisbolista*. Every woman, her daughter and her sister, is a fan." Baseball has seeped deep into the Spanish language and introduced new words like *fildeo* and *un jónron* and into the Mexican consciousness by "substituting confidence and genuine neighborliness for the former fear and inferiority complex toward the Colossus of the North."

Indeed, World War II was not the only reason bringing countries together, but also "because we have discovered we love the same games and subscribe to the same sport standards and enthusiasms. Through sport the Johnny Browns and the Juan Morenos are getting together and understanding one another." Kempis romanticized the U.S. conquest of Mexico through baseball and promoted a sporting universalism that disguised baseball's color line and gender discrimination. Furthermore, this magazine article carried "considerable weight" among officials with the Office of Inter-American Affairs as they carried out "goodwill missions" in baseball and other sports.[2]

This chapter takes a hemispheric approach to examine the role of the U.S. federal government in promoting "American" sports in Mexico and Latin America. Using records from the Office of Inter-American Affairs (OIAA), I critically analyze the gendered and racialized discourse of OIAA officials and coaches who viewed Latin American athletes as "primitive," exotic, and effeminate. Despite the short tenure of the OIAA Sports Office, the U.S. government used sports as a "soft power" diplomatic approach to undermine anti-Americanism and promote a racialized and gendered version of the American way of life to win over the loyalty of Mexico and other Latin American countries. I argue that Mexican athletes provided a counternarrative to claims of American exceptionalism in sports and used their athletic skills during "goodwill tours" in the United States to claim real and symbolic victory against their more powerful northern neighbor.

GOOD NEIGHBOR POLICY AND PAN AMERICAN GAMES

The U.S. government used sports as an instrument of Franklin Roosevelt's Good Neighbor Policy toward Latin America during World War II. For much of history, relations between the United States and Latin American countries have been plagued with tension and distrust. In his inaugural address on March 4, 1933, Franklin D. Roosevelt introduced his approach, "to dedicate [the United States] to the policy of the good neighbor, the neighbor who resolutely respects himself and, because he does so, respects the rights of others."[3] Being a good neighbor became linked to Roosevelt's policy, aimed as it was at curtailing military intervention and promoting cooperation in trade and mutual defense. The Good Neighbor Policy ensured that the United States would remain dominant in Latin America by deploying "cultural diplomacy" or a "soft power" approach.[4] U.S. diplomatic efforts in Latin America have focused on building cultural connections through literature, arts, print media, and film to "promote mutual progress and understanding in the Americas" that will ultimately lead toward more trade and commercial cooperation.[5] Sports also emerged as a good opportunity for the United States to forge good relations with its southern neighbors.

Before the Good Neighbor Policy, Pan Americanism, the idea that Western Hemisphere countries should promote goodwill and friendly relations because they share common interests, helped spur interest in sporting exchanges.[6] By presidential proclamation, Herbert Hoover authorized April 14 as Pan American Day, calling it an "outward symbol of unity . . . for the republics of this hemisphere."[7] A year later, Representatives of Latin American countries met at the Olympic Games in Los Angeles to discuss the establishment of a regional tournament to be held in the Western Hemisphere every four years and alternating with the Olympic Games. The Mexican delegation proposed creating a sports organization to govern and organize these games. At the 1940 meeting of the Pan American Sports Congress, which represented sixteen nations, participants selected Buenos Aires to host the first Pan American Games in 1942, but World War II forced the postponement of the games until 1951.

Most historians cite the 1951 Pan American Games as the first international sporting exchange in the Western Hemisphere, but the failed 1942 games are often overlooked.[8] Five years earlier, an Olympic-style sporting festival in Dallas was organized by football franchise owner George Preston Marshall under the sponsorship of the Greater Texas and Pan-American Exposition. The Dallas Games, according to Mark Dyreson, inspired the Pan American Games movement.[9] The Good Neighbor Policy also played a key role in the Pan American Games movement. President Roosevelt endorsed the Pan American Games by declaring, "I have long felt that friendly competition in sports is one of the finest methods of stimulating closer relationships and good-will between individuals and nations."[10] Before the 1942 postponement, the OIAA worked closely with Avery Brundage, president of the Pan American Games Committee and the U.S. Olympic Committee, to make preparations and send a delegation of U.S. athletes to Buenos Aires. Asa Bushnell, director of the OIAA's Sports Office, was charged with organizing a series of international sporting exchanges as lead-up events to the Pan American Games in Buenos Aires.

Once the Pan American Games were canceled, concerns were raised about the future of the Sports Office within the OIAA. A main criticism was that "American sports" could generate Yankee animosity and anti-Americanism. Sports columnist Henry McLemore criticized Rockefeller's Sports Office as part of the Good Neighbor Policy because it will "breed ill-will, not love."[11] McLemore claimed that "the athletes of the United States can't miss winning. This won't help friendship one bit." He added, "If South America is to have any chance to win, they will have to cheat in the approved international fashion. The South Americans will have to add such events as llama clipping, Andes climbing, Speaking Spanish without an accent and doing the rhumba. If this is done, then we'll get mad." McLemore cited the behavior of Nazi Germany at the 1936 Olympics, when the host nation cheated its way to first place, ostensibly to ensure racial supremacy and military prowess. McLemore concluded with a staunch warning: "If Mr. Rockefeller is allowed to bring the North and South American athletes together, he is going to pave the way for South America's delivery into the hands of the Nazis."[12] Despite using stereotypical language, McLemore made critical points about the negative side of sports competitions.

Given this criticism, moreover, the OIAA Sports Office had to be more careful in using sporting events to build trust and friendly relations among its Latin American neighbors. After hearing the news of the cancelation of the 1942 Pan American Games Bushnell wrote to Avery Brundage, "The [Sports] office has, however, lost none of its belief in sport's value in the development of lasting friendship, and it will continue to make use of athletics in its activities to whatever degree is in keeping with changing conditions."[13] Ultimately, the Sports Office sought to use a kinder approach in an attempt to win over the loyalty of Latin American countries.[14]

SPORTS DIPLOMACY AND OFFICE OF
INTER-AMERICAN AFFAIRS

The "cultural turn" in the social sciences and humanities inspired historians to examine the cultural dimensions of the Good Neighbor Policy. Scholars have documented the entertainment industry's efforts to produce films with a more positive spin on Latin American countries and their citizens, even though these films perpetuated stereotypes of Latin American Otherness.[15] The main reason why sports have been overlooked is the OIAA organization's small size and short tenure; from 1940 to 1942, its activities remained obscured under larger divisions. Sports historian Barbara Keys briefly mentioned that U.S. diplomats resisted mixing sports with politics until the creation of the OIAA to promote the "interchange of athletes, teams, coaches, and demonstration groups."[16] In her in-depth account of OIAA cultural initiatives, Darlene Sadlier overlooked the crucial role of sports in cultural diplomacy.[17]

A new collection on the OIAA broadens our understanding of this wartime agency by focusing on the "Latin American part in the equation of inter-American relations" and closely examining the role of Coordination Committees.[18] Coordination Committees in each Latin American country were established as field representatives who would carry out the work of OIAA, sometimes working closely with the U.S. embassy and other times acting independently.[19] By focusing on Coordination Committees at the local level, Thomas Leonard uncovered a wide array of cultural activities and sporting activities in Central America.[20]

Concerns about the spread of Nazism and disruptions to trade and U.S. investments in Latin America led the Roosevelt administration to create the Office of the Coordinator of Inter-American Affairs (later renamed the Office of Inter-American Affairs, or OIAA) on August 16, 1940.[21] Under the leadership of Rockefeller, the OIAA engaged in a vast range of activities that required the cooperation of government agencies, businessmen, media executives, educators, and field experts who resided in Latin America for several years and developed considerable local expertise. With the support of the U.S. embassies, these field experts— including U.S. company employees, military officials, journalists, and athletic coaches—were organized under local "coordinating committees" that helped implement programs, activities, and athletic games, and they reported to the OIAA on the successes or failures of these events.[22]

In January 1941, Nelson Rockefeller created a Sports Office under the Cultural Relations Division (later renamed the Science and Education Division) to develop an Inter-American sports program to send Anglo-American athletes and coaches as "goodwill ambassadors" to spread pro-American propaganda in Latin America. Rockefeller understood, according to one researcher, "that sports were a major in interest in Latin America, so he worked to increase inter-American competitions."[23] He enlisted the help of U.S. amateur sports organizations to organize goodwill exhibition tours, coaching missions, and a U.S. tour for Latin American sportswriters. Rockefeller also instructed the Sports Office to conduct a sports survey of Latin American countries on the eve of the 1942 Pan American Games in Buenos Aires, Argentina.[24]

OIAA used a sporting diplomacy to bring countries together for athletic competitions. "Sporting diplomacy," according to Jeremy Goldberg, allows countries "to break down stereotypes, increase understanding, and confine battles to the playing field rather than the battlefield. They are a 'safe' way to ease a country out of isolation, acting as a first step of engagement."[25] In particular, there was considerable discussion about the purpose of the Sports Office among his closest associates. John Clark was one of Rockefeller's closest assistant who directed the Information Division and outlined a three-step process: (1) select a "big name figure-head" chairperson and an executive secretary with experience in managing sporting events and athletes; (2) develop an Inter-American Sports Program with short-term and long-term objectives; and (3) address the question of media publicity. As a former editorial writer for the *Washington Post*, Clark presented a case for bringing Latin American teams and players for exhibitions in the United States because "we can control the events, the conduct of our own people, and insure against the embarrassment which will naturally result from the uneven competition which would occur in Latin America."[26] OIAA officials had to be careful not to emphasize competition in their sports program because it could produce anti-American sentiment. One newspaper columnist criticized Rockefeller's sports that will "breed ill will, not love."[27] The columnist reminded readers that, after all, "athletes of the United States can't miss winning. That won't help friendship one bit." Clark further proposed inviting Latin American sportswriters to accompany their country's team because "they can wire stories down there just as our reporters now follow the various baseball teams."[28] In addition, exerting tight control over the Latin American press during the Second World War was a major concern of the OIAA and the State Department in an effort to counter a well-oiled Nazi propaganda machine that strategically characterized the United States as the enemy of Latin America.[29]

During the summer, OIAA officials met to discuss the main objectives of the Sports in the Hemisphere Defense Program, or what was later called the Inter-American Sports Program. The program's short-term objectives included (1) to offset anti-U.S. influences exerted particularly on younger groups through foreign language schools and through subsidized foreign coaches and traveling athletes in the other American republics; (2) to inspire pro-U.S. enthusiasts in persons of Latin Americans who might be brought to the United States; (3) to promote the United States; and (4) to promote U.S. mindedness of players and spectators who may have contact with U.S. sports representatives. The long-term objectives were to assist Latin American physical education and develop Latin American interest in U.S. sports concepts.[30] The discussion group ranked sports according to the most popular (baseball, basketball, track and field, soccer, boxing), more exclusive (tennis, golf, polo, skiing), and noncompetitive or exhibition (jai alai, horse racing, and shooting). The last part of the discussion raised questions about which sports deserve priority, what countries deserve special consideration, how teams, coaches, and athletes would be selected, and whether preference would be given to amateurs over professionals in inter-American sporting exchanges. Some of these questions were answered by closely examining the Inter-American Sports Program below, but others remained unanswered.

On August 1, 1941, Rockefeller decided to forgo the "figure-head" position and appoint Asa Bushnell as executive director of the Sports Office.[31] Rockefeller selected Bushnell for his considerable experience in planning and managing athletic programs as the founding director of the Central Office of Eastern Intercollegiate Athletics, the country's biggest collegiate athletic association, and he later became secretary of the U.S. Olympic Committee. Although not an athlete himself, he managed the Princeton Athletic Association and other athletic groups and earned a reputation as a "financial wizard" for keeping amateur sports programs out of financial debt.[32] Bushnell told the New York Times that "Inter-American Athletic relationships offer an opportunity to heighten mutual interest and increase common participation in the national sports of the twenty-one American republics." After all, Bushnell added, "sports lovers in all countries speak the same language." However, the majority of "Inter-American" contests were reserved for "sportsmen" despite "the benefits derived by all sports devotees throughout the hemisphere."[33] Women athletes were included only in swim meets, basketball, and tennis tournaments.

INTER-AMERICAN SPORTS PROGRAM

Before the United States entered World War II, most Inter-American Sports Program activities comprised bringing Latin American athletes and teams to conduct "goodwill tours" throughout the United States. There were a few exceptions where U.S. athletes participated in "goodwill tours" in Latin America. Another activity was sending American coaches as "athletic consultants" to Latin American countries, but only if they were invited by the country's physical education department or universities. The main reason for this program was concern that some Latin American countries lacked "sufficient number of trained coaches" and would not be ready for "Inter-American competition in a large number of sports" prior to the 1942 Pan American Games in Buenos Aires.[34] Furthermore, after Japan's attack on Pearl Harbor and the U.S. declaration of war against the Axis powers, the OIAA pushed to cancel the Pan American Games. After December 1, 1941, the OIAA curtailed its "goodwill athletic tours" and redirected its activities toward donations of athletic equipment, radio broadcasts of U.S. sporting events, and distribution of U.S. sports films throughout Latin America.

During the first two months, Bushnell spent considerable time studying suggestions from sports leaders across the country and determining the proper role of the Sports Office in Latin America. He decided to prioritize amateur athletes and work closely with amateur sports organizations. Avery Brundage, president of the Amateur Athletic Union (AAU) and the U.S. Olympic Committee, advised Bushnell to avoid sending touring athletes because they would appear like "propaganda tours" and "our Latin American friends are not children, and are not easily fooled." Rather, he suggested "building goodwill among the other American nations through amateur sports groups."[35] Bushnell agreed that the Sports Office should avoid outright propaganda tours and "instead devote its energies to cooperation with established sports groups in the conduct of undertakings of theirs which can do so much towards the attainment of the common goal."[36] By allocating money to amateur sport organizations, they would avoid criticism for producing propaganda resembling that of Nazi Germany.

Bushnell recruited sport's leading governing bodies such as the AAU, Eastern Intercollegiate Athletics Association, U.S. Golf Association, U.S. Lawn Tennis Association, U.S. Football Association, U.S. Polo Association, U.S.A. Baseball Congress (amateur baseball organization), U.S.A. Sports Federation, and National Ski Association of America (NSAA).[37] The first project was allocating seven thousand dollars to the NSAA to bring a Chilean ski team to visit major ski resorts across the United States for a two-month period.[38] Considered the first winter sports team to visit from South America, six members of the Chilean Ski Association arrived on January 27, 1941, to a welcome reception by Brooklyn city officials and Eugene DuBois, chairperson of the NSAA Chilean Ski Team Committee.[39] Dubois reminded NSAA members, "It is very important that the Chileans be treated as honored guests wherever they go and that they be given comfortable lodgings. We are anxious to avoid having them considered as 'charity' cases, which, of course, they are not."[40]

During their tour, John C. Jay, an American ski filmmaker, served as their official escort and produced a ninety-nine-minute color film, *Ski Here, Señor*, about the visiting Chilean skiers. Jay showed the film to ski clubs throughout the United States and later distributed it in South America through the OIAA Motion Picture Division.[41] The Chilean team's final event on March 20 was to compete in the Pan American Ski Meet at Sun Valley, but injuries kept two skiers from competing.[42] "Last year I followed the tour of the Chilean ski team with much interest," wrote Edwin Hilbert in a letter to the *New York Times* sports editor. He questioned why the OIAA started with the exclusive sport of skiing to "further our good neighbor relations with the peoples of South America" since it "is a relatively minor sport in South America." He asked, "What is being done in the one sport that can be truly called the national sport of all our Southern neighbors—association football [soccer]?[43] Soccer officials criticized the Good Neighbor sports policy for its bias toward track and field, American football, baseball, tennis, and golf. "We have promoted and played American games in which we naturally excel. . . . How much wiser for us to develop a game which those to the south already play as well as any people in the world."[44] This criticism raised the idea of a survey to determine which sports are more popular in certain countries and regions throughout Latin America.

On April 11, 1941, Rockefeller and assistant coordinator Carl Spaeth met with former Boston Red Sox catcher and assistant coach Morris "Moe" Berg to discuss his potential role in the new sports program.[45] "Nelson Rockefeller and I are particularly anxious to have you work with us on this program," wrote Spaeth to Berg as he awaited his reply to accept his diplomatic mission as a "Goodwill Ambassador."[46] Fluent in Spanish, Portuguese, Japanese, and six other languages, Berg was a son of Jewish parents and was considered a gifted linguist who had worked as a spy for the Office of Strategic Services while coaching baseball in Japan. Berg was considered the perfect candidate to "make a survey of sports in the other American Republics and to establish the preferences of each country . . . create interest in the other American Republics in starting sports programs themselves."[47] With four thousand dollars in funds, Berg spent six months in South and Central America hopping from military base to playing fields, observing athletic events, studying health and physical fitness programs, and sending detailed reports back to OIAA. Besides studying sports, Berg was also a spy sent on a covert operation to infiltrate Latin American governments to counter the Nazi influence in South America.[48] Berg first became a spy while traveling with the Major League Baseball all-star team in Japan, from which he took home movies and photographs of the Tokyo skyline that were used for bombing raids. In Latin America, Rockefeller instructed him to observe the playing fields and pay close attention to "the reactions of all levels of the people as they watched the games."[49]

OIAA Sport officials carefully selected those sports that would produce more "goodwill" between the United States and Latin American governments as well as Anglo American male athletes that would not offend Latin American elite sensibilities. For example, boxing was considered too risky, breeding more "ill-will" than "goodwill" because of its association with violence, hypermasculinity, and gambling. When former heavyweight champion boxer Jack Dempsey wrote to Rockefeller expressing his willingness to serve as a "goodwill ambassador" to the Inter-American Sports Program, his offer was rejected.[50] In comparison, soccer received minimal assistance from OIAA officials because it was considered an "un-American" sport associated with immigrants and socialism. As discussed later in this chapter, Latin American soccer officials appropriated the Good Neighbor Policy language to organize international soccer matches displaying superior athletic skills. Despite the widespread popularity of boxing and soccer in Mexico, the Caribbean, and Central and South America, the Sports Office preferred those sports that the U.S. athletes dominated. "It is admitted that some sports are not particularly fitted to promote peaceful relations in any direction," wrote a *New York Times* sports columnist. "But golf, baseball, track and field, tennis and some other sports promote more good-will than bad feeling when our competitors go abroad or foreign competitors come here to take part in such games."[51]

The Inter-American Sports Program excluded nonwhite athletes as part of its official goodwill tours to Latin America. One proposal submitted to the Sports Office, intended to "assist a group of Negro and Filipino athletes in a trip to Latin America," was rejected with no explanation.[52] This proposal raised some questions for OIAA officials about their selection process: "Can Negro athletes form the U.S. make a special contribution? Conversely, will Negro athletes from Latin America constitute a special difficulty? How can the matter best be handled?"[53] In a confidential brief to the Sports Office, Winston Guest outlined the sports program for Mexico with American football as a top priority, followed by track and field, tennis, polo, basketball, and baseball. For track and field athletes, however, Guest stressed "the importance of them being white."[54] OIAA officials were concerned that African Americans like Jesse Owens, who had won four gold medals in the 1936 Olympic Games, would somehow cause controversy in Latin America, especially since Jim Crow extended overseas in the U.S. military and Foreign Service during wartime.

Not sending African American or nonwhite athletes, however, could potentially backfire. An American sportswriter, John Nash, who lived and traveled throughout South America, observed that a "certain hostility on the part of the masses has been fanned by [Nazi] propaganda, on the score of unfair treatment of Negroes in the U.S.A. In Brazil, equality is enjoyed between colored and white, and the former enjoy much influence. This opposition must be met, and a good way to do it would be to include Negroes on sports teams that we would send to Brazil."[55] Nash also reminded OIAA to not forget about Latin American women whose "knowledge of American womanhood is very limited and is usually distorted through impressions received in the movies ... and would be vitally interested in the spectacle of basketball, swimming, tennis teams made up of women from the U.S.A." Although Nash exaggerated Brazilian color blindness and mischaracterized Latin American womanhood, he called for more racial and gender diversity in OIAA's goodwill athletic tours.

The U.S. Lawn Tennis Association (USLTA) recruited three top-ranked women to join three men in an all-star tennis team tour to South America, Mexico, and Cuba from October 19, 1941, to January 1, 1942, with the objective to "give large athletically minded groups there creditable impression of U.S.A. athletes and sportsmanship."[56] Team captain Elwood Cooke kept a diary of the team's tennis clinics, exhibition matches, and social gatherings. In Rio de Janeiro, Cooke was surprised about the popularity of tennis clinics with Brazilian women. He wrote, "There were more girls than boys at the clinic which is quite unusual."[57] In Buenos Aires, however, they found overzealous fans in packed stadiums cheering for Argentines to beat the Americans. When Mary Teran beat

Katherine Winthrop, "she was applauded with some vigor by the spectators."[58] And when Alejo Russell and Heraldo Weiss defeated Elwood Cooke and Donald McNeill in five bitterly fought sets, there was "delirious joy from the 3,000 spectators, who threw hats, cushions, programmes and themselves into the court after it was all over."[59] Aside from the nationalistic pride exhibited by Argentine fans, "the trip was an unqualified success," reported the USLTA at its annual meeting. "The democracy of sport brings thousands of people closer together in friendly relations and this is especially true of tennis, which helps to develop good fellowship and sportsmanship, mutual respect, and understanding."[60]

Members of Coordination Committees made requests to send Latino and Latin American athletes abroad on goodwill tours. For example, the Coordination Committee in Colombia requested tennis players Francisco "Pancho" Segura and William Talbert to play some exhibition matches in Bogotá and Medellín. Alfonso Londono argued, "There is a great deal of interest in seeing Segura against Talbert here and their visit would contribute enormously towards the development of the game in this country."[61] The interest stemmed from Segura's 1943 defeat of Talbert to win the Pan American championship in Mexico City. Born to a large poor family, Segura left his hometown of Guayaquil, Ecuador, for the University of Miami on a tennis scholarship. With his unorthodox but devastating two-handed forehand, Segura won three consecutive national collegiate titles (1943–1945) and became the third-ranked American player.[62]

In particular, the print media highlighted his exotic, dark-skinned features and short size and referred to this new tennis star as a "colorful caballero," "Good Neighbor with a Racquet," and "Goodwill Kid," as well as the racially charged "Good Neighbor Tennis Threat" to a staunchly white American tennis establishment.[63] Despite Segura being considered as "the best tennis Ambassador of Good Will for Latin America," Rockefeller rejected Londono's proposal because "we feel that there is a very real danger of criticism by Latin Americans in the case of such projects as this."[64] Due to wartime manpower needs, contemporary critics felt that "men in good physical condition and well enough to indulge in active sports should be in the armed forces of the United States rather than on an athletic field."[65] After the Pearl Harbor attack, though, the OIAA backed out of participating in the Pan American Games, discontinued inter-American sports exchanges, and shifted toward sending American coaches on "missions" to train Latin American athletes, donating sports equipment to poorer countries, and using motion pictures and shortwave radio to disseminate sports programs.

AMERICAN FOOTBALL COACHING
MISSIONS IN MEXICO

In spring of 1942, the Sports Office organized the Athletic Coaches Missions to Chile, Ecuador, Mexico, Peru and Uruguay for three to six months.[66] Since sporting exchanges were discontinued, the project's main objective was to help physical education departments in Latin American countries during wartime. "With teams to be made ready for Inter-American competition in a large number of sports," wrote Rockefeller, "it is felt that some of the countries may be facing difficulty in finding a sufficient number of trained coaches within their own boundaries to handle all the work entailed."[67] Another objective was to help in "the growth of the sport in other American Republics as a means of developing the physical fitness, leadership, competitiveness, and stamina indispensable to the effectiveness of inter-American solidarity in the present crisis."[68] The U.S.A. Sports Federation assisted the OIAA in carefully selecting three coaches to teach three or more sports per country. A questionnaire was administered to gauge each country's interest and what sports they preferred. While most countries responded favorably, a few had no response, and some rejected coaches. For example, Cuba indicated that coaches were "not desirable" and "superfluous."[69] Bolivia was more straightforward: "Carrying out such a program now would indicate to South Americans that U.S.A. is either whistling in dark or can't face realities."[70] The first coaching mission including the following countries (with their preferred sports): Chile (basketball, track, swimming), Ecuador (gymnastics, baseball, basketball, swimming), Peru (track, basketball, swimming), Uruguay (basketball, swimming, and track), and Mexico (American football, basketball, tennis).

Mexico was the first country to receive athletic coaches in the sport of American football. National Autonomous University of Mexico (UNAM)'s Pumas football team was founded in 1927 by a group of students led by two brothers, Roberto and Leopoldo Noriega, and in 1933 it became the official Pumas varsity team.[71] The same year President Roosevelt appointed former newspaper editor Josephus Daniels as ambassador to Mexico; he sought to implement the Good Neighbor Policy with a friendlier approach, compared to the more antagonistic style of the State Department. Daniels supported the Mexican plan to expand public education and sports. Working closely with former polo player and close confidant of Rockefeller Wilson Guest and International News Service bureau chief Arthur Constantine, Daniels sent a proposal to OIAA requesting a football coach for the UNAM football squad from September 10 to November 30, 1941. Bushnell supported the proposal, arguing that "the University plays an American style of football, due in large measure to the fact that they were coached at one time by Reggie Root of Yale. They are anxious to carry on this coaching tradition."[72] A State Department official also expressed his support for a "coaching mission" because it "would improve athletics and sportsmanship in Mexico."[73] On August 29, 1941, the proposal received approval "to propagate United States standards of play and conception of sportsmanship among college undergraduates and sport followers in Mexico."[74] The original proposal requested the University of North Carolina's football coach Paul Severin, but he was not available, so officials selected former Dartmouth quarterback Bernard Hoban as the athletic consultant and football coach to UNAM.

Before Hoban there were several American football coaches who attempted to develop the sport in Mexico. In September 1929, Reginald Root arrived in Mexico City to begin coaching a squad of eleven *futbolistas* from UNAM. He faced many challenges, including the language barrier, a shortage of football equipment, and a lack of university funding.[75] Root's salary was paid by a combination of checks from American oil industrialist Harry Sinclair and donations from college football teams. Root's biggest challenge, according to one American sportswriter, was not being "acquainted with the Latin temperament." "He knows that the Mexican is at times slow and easy-going, but that he has a vast amount of potential surplus energy, which may explode at any moment."[76] Within a year, Root's team had played six games, winning three, tying one and losing two, both against U.S. college teams. Although they lost against Occidental College in front of twenty thousand spectators at the Los Angeles Coliseum, according to the president of the Los Angeles Chamber of Commerce, they "exhibited the best sportsmanship and played a clean game throughout."[77] After Root returned to a coaching position at Yale, Dixie Howell took over as head coach for two years, but a lack of financial support stalled the development of football in Mexico.[78]

Anglo-American coaches like Root, Howell, and Hoban promoted themselves as football trainers and teachers of "good sportsmanship" to Mexican athletes. When Hoban arrived in September 1941, he made an immediate impression by leading the Pumas team to two successive victories against rival colleges. In his weekly report, however, he complained that "there have been many incidents of an unpleasant nature, sometimes on the field and more often among the partisan supporters of the team."[79] To remedy the problem of "bad sportsmanship" by players and fans, he "insisted on meeting all the coaches of the teams we play and shaking hands with them in the center of the field before and after the game." Hoban realized that "one must learn all about and study the Latin and Mexican temperament to do this job well."[80] Being culturally aware helped because, he later wrote, "I think some progress toward better sportsmanship has already been made."[81]

After winning four consecutive games against other college teams, Hoban wanted stronger competition, so he requested an additional five thousand dollars in funding for three international games, against the University of New Mexico, Mississippi College, and Louisiana College, to be held in Mexico City. The request was rejected because the Sports Office was concerned about "direct promotion of athletic events of any sport" that would potentially result in ill-will, instead of goodwill. An advisor to the Sports Office suggested instead bringing Mexican football teams to U.S. exhibition games because "participation in this country would be much less expensive," and will generate "favorable reception to Latin American players."[82] "The Pumas team was anxious to schedule an "Inter-American athletic program," wrote Rockefeller to Adolf Berle, assistant secretary of state for Latin American affairs, "so it is hoped that the athletic managers of the various colleges involved will be able to finance them through gate receipts and without the necessity of outside aid."[83] After securing thirty-five hundred dollars in private funding from foreign investors, the Sports Office approved the international match between UNAM and Louisiana College, scheduled for January 1, 1942.

This was the seventh game between both schools since 1929, and according to Louisiana's coach Philips, "It is the longest international rivalry in football."[84] The New Year's football game was publicized as the Orchid Bowl, the [National Autonomous] University of Mexico's first bowl, probably named after Baby Kate Roosevelt, granddaughter of Franklin Roosevelt, who had a new seedling orchid named after her.[85] Before seven thousand spectators at Necaxa Stadium, both teams battled on even terms during the first half, until the Louisiana team scored a field goal and a touchdown near the end to win 10–0.[86] "This was the best game of American football ever played in Mexico," wrote Hoban, in his final report to the OIAA sports director. He continued, "The University team averaged 161 lbs. while Louisiana College averaged 186 lbs. This tremendous weight advantage gradually wore down the smaller Mexican players and they succumbed after a gallant fight."[87] The weight and size disadvantages were often invoked in news coverage of Mexican teams' losses to American college teams.

Despite the smaller size and weight, Mexican football players used their speed, and their passing, kicking, and throwing skills to excel on the gridiron. They developed a unique playing style, according to one sportswriter: "The Mexicans have a varied attack, but their longest gains against heavy competition frequently are made by the hidden ball trick, [at] which they are experts."[88] An assistant at the U.S. embassy in Mexico City visited the team during a scrimmage and observed, "The ball handling on spinner plays and forward passes coupled with laterals is something which makes one sit up and take notice."[89] He was mostly impressed with their kicking skills, carried over from their favorite sport of soccer. "The punting is excellent, both in the matter of distance and placing." In *The Quarterback Who Almost Wasn't*, Jorge Prieto recalled how his team from the National Polytechnic Institute was outmatched against the El Paso High School team. "They were so much taller and heavier than us that we knew we were in for a rough afternoon. In a game of constant physical encounters such as football, size can be decisive. It really was a gross mismatch since they outweighed us by more than 20 pounds per man."[90] Another disadvantage, according to Prieto, was that "[Mexican] coaches were not allowed money for travel to the so-called 'football clinics' in the U.S. until the late 1940s, and thus they were unprepared for what [Prieto] faced in that Texas Team."[91] The aggressive masculine behavior of players also hindered team discipline. Prieto admitted that "display of flamboyant, arrogant manliness is one of the worst vices of Mexican males."[92] For Prieto, playing against Mexican American football teams in South Texas also presented a big challenge. According to Jorge Iber, Mexican American football players from the Rio Grande Valley challenged stereotypes by their excellent athletic performance on the field.[93]

Furthermore, Hoban encountered problems during his coaching mission. In the beginning he had to overcome distrust and suspicion as well as "some feeling evident against the University because they along have an American coach." He admitted, "On the surface all has seemed serene and friendly, but I know that I have been resented, at least at first." After three weeks, though, he began to "secure the friendship of the boys" by accepting invitations to their homes.[94] Language and cultural barriers also presented problems for Hoban. He expressed initial difficulty learning Spanish to communicate with his players. He also canceled practices during the December religious festival because "I realized that the tradition behind 'Las Posadas' was much stronger than football."

Another problem Hoban faced was the lack of resources. Since the football team received no financial support from university administration, they battled a shortage of equipment, were forced to use an outdoor locker room with a limited hot water supply, and had to share a playing field with soccer and baseball teams. Finally, the biggest problem was getting the team to practice on time. "The boys love to play in games, but do not like to practice," Hoban wrote. "We must practice between 1 and 3 P.M. (the siesta hour). Some boys arrive ready for practice at 1:30 or 1:45, and some must leave by 2:30 or 2:45. One uninterrupted hour for practice is all that can be hoped for."[95] By and large, poverty was the principal factor that kept players from attending practice. Hoban observed, "Most of the players are poor and there is some question if all of them get enough to eat."[96]

But the end of his term on January 5, 1942, Hoban had made friends with players, university administrators, sportswriters, and coaches, including critics of American football. A U.S. embassy official commended Hoban for making an excellent impression in local educational and athletic circles.[97] UNAM's Provost agreed and added that "Mr. Bernard Hoban's services were most useful in developing this sport among the Mexican youth."[98] Fray Kempis, sports editor, wrote, "A one hundred percent amateur sportsman is gone. Bernard Hoban's favorite idea was to promote good relations between our Republic and the powerful northern neighbor. He leaves behind a host of friends."[99] Writing to Bushnell, football team manager Leopoldo Noriega had requested an extension of Hoban's contract for the 1942 fall season especially during wartime. "I believe that now, more than ever, the American continent should be united and the best way of strengthening relations between the U.S. and Latin America is by means of sports. Sports is a more efficient propaganda than any form of propaganda statesmen could device."[100]

After the new U.S. ambassador to Mexico, George Messersmith, denied the request for Hoban's return, a group of UNAM students sent a petition to Rocke-feller.[101] Rockefeller supported the return of Hoban for the 1943 season because "he did an outstanding job on his previous assignment and while we are not carrying on a sports program as such, we feel that the request made by the UNAM should be granted."[102] The executive secretary of the Coordination Committee for Mexico declined the proposal to return Hoban to Mexico City and cited war-time restrictions on travel and expenditures.[103] It was the football players, how-ever, who put pressure on Rockefeller and the committee by sending fifty-one cablegrams calling for the return of their coach.[104] Ultimately, Hoban returned for the 1943 and 1944 seasons without a salary and paying for his own expenses; he reasoned, "I like boys, I like football. I like Mexico and I like international friendship. That is why I am down here. If we can get Mexican youth to know about the United States and like us, I believe we are on pretty solid footing and football will help do that."[105] Upon his return, he won back-to-back champion-ship titles. But in his last game, the Sun Bowl at El Paso, Texas, on New Year's Day 1945, Southwestern University defeated UNAM 35–0.[106]

Mexican football players and teams appropriated the rhetoric of the Good Neighbor Policy and made demands on the OIAA Sports Office. For example, football team captain and chemical engineer student Eliot Camarena requested assistance from Hoban and the U.S. embassy in applying for graduate school at the Massachusetts Institute of Technology. "He has all the earmarks of a leader," wrote Dudley Easby, assistant at the U.S. embassy, "and will undoubtedly be a prominent man in Mexico, so that anything we can do to help him realize his ambition to go to M.I.T. will be well worth the effort."[107] In his final report, Hobart recommended that OIAA "make every effort to assist Mexican football players to receive scholarship aid or assignment to study in the U.S."[108]

Besides educational opportunities, Mexican football teams made requests to the OIAA Sports Office for equipment donations. For example, Club Wacha Chara football players from the National Preparatory School visited the U.S. embassy in Mexico City and requested thirty-five football uniforms with helmets and shoes because unlike the university football team, they were an independent organization and could not afford them. The team had arranged an exhibition match against Lanier High School in San Antonio, but "the young men added that it is particularly embarrassing for them to play before United States spectators in the patch work uniforms that they now have."[109] Ambassador Josephus Dan-iels emphasized that Club Wacha Chara was a "strong pro-American nucleus within the school" compared to other students with their "emotional nationalism that makes them easy prey for anti-American agitators." "It must be remem-bered," Daniels argued, that "these Preparatory students will go out into all the professional branches of the University within the next year or two, and that eventually some of them will become the professional and intellectual leaders of Mexico."

Furthermore, this statement reveals the hidden agenda behind promoting American football to cultivate pro-American sentiment among Mexican youth. Daniels concluded, "It is my firm belief that there is no better way of developing cultural relations in Mexico than by encouraging these 'American football' teams to play a game which was born in the United States."[110] This opinion resembled the discourse of YMCA secretaries, discussed in chapter 1, who viewed Mexican youth as vulnerable to anti-American propaganda and in need of coaching in "good sportsmanship" and American ideals.

GOOD NEIGHBOR SPORTS TOURS IN THE UNITED STATES

Compared to the more popular American sports of baseball, football, and basketball, soccer has been considered the marginal sport of immigrants and foreigners.[111] The marginalization of soccer was evident in the promotional sporting activities of the OIAA despite requests from soccer clubs and promoters. Even sportswriters questioned this neglect. Burton Benjamin observed, "If sports are to have a role in the promotion of Pan-American good-fellowship, U.S. athletic brass hats had better forget track and fields, American football, baseball, tennis and golf and concentrate on soccer."[112] Compared to twenty-five thousand amateur soccer players in the United States, "five times as many compete in Mexico alone," Benjamin reminded officials. He added, "Soccer replaced bull-fighting as the national pastime south of the Rio Grande."[113]

On May 7, 1942, the New York Americans, founded by Erno Schwarz, a Hungarian American player-manager who became a leading soccer promoter during the middle of the twentieth century, requested financial assistance from the OIAA Sports Office to bring Mexico's recently crowned national champions, Club Atlante, for a "Good Neighbor Soccer Tour."[114] Bushnell responded with lukewarm support: "The Sports office has had and will have no part in the inspiration of, arrangement for, or management of the tour, but it has given some slight assistance to the responsible parties in their efforts to find a suitable site for the New York game, because of a desire to have the Pan American Day program carried out in the best possible surroundings and with the greatest possible change for benefit to the cause of Inter-Americanism."[115] Because of the "Pan-American Angle," Bushnell reluctantly approved half of the amount ($175) requested to hire a band for halftime ceremonies. Since its founding in 1916, Club Atlante was popular among Mexico City's working-class population, which nicknamed it the People's Team, and had acquired national fame during the 1930s for beating visiting foreign powerhouse teams.[116] This was not their first U.S. visit; in 1940, the club went on a seven-game tour across the United States without losing a game against the best soccer teams. This time, however, they would come up against all-star players from four American Soccer League teams and would have to participate in Pan American Day ceremonies. The day before, a special luncheon was held for the visiting squad, and Rafael de la Colina, Mexican consul general of New York, U.S. Football Association officials, and Bushnell were all in attendance.[117] Bushnell greeted the players and expressed his hope that their visit would result in "a stronger solidarity among the people of the Americas, something needed now more than ever due to the rough conditions in the world."[118] On New York's official Pan American Day—Randall Island's Triborough Stadium was adorned with twenty-one flags flying above ten thousand spectators, including nineteen Latin American consul generals. And as for the actual game, with just two minutes remaining, Club Atlante's captain Martí Ventolrá headed a shot into the corner of the net to help end the match in a 3–3 draw.[119] A soccer fan wrote to the *New York Times* surprised by the "invasion of our shores by foreign athletes . . . all young, clean and courageous."[120] This would attract many fans because "soccer is a common ground on which we can learn to know our Latin-American neighbors better. It is one mutual contact which has its own language."[121] There was little common ground, however, when fights broke out during a hotly contested match at Starlight Park.[122] In the second half, two opposing players started fighting, and immediately thereafter "several hundred fans stormed the field"; after twenty minutes "this free-for-all was broken up by special police." After the two players were ejected from the match, Club Atlante suffered their first shutout. They rebounded in Baltimore, however where they "put on a dazzling exhibition of speed and dexterity" as they defeated the Baltimore Soccer Club 6–3.[123] After a record of two victories, two ties, and two losses, Atlante's soccer tour was canceled on June 15, 1942, because of the war situation, player injuries, and depleted funds.[124]

New York's *La Prensa* covered the welcoming reception of Atlante players hosted by the Mexican consulate office and praised the soccer skills of "futbolistas from the south of the border."[125] As Mexican soccer players exerted their athletic skills on the soccer field, they claimed real and symbolic victory against their more powerful neighbor. Athletic competitions always seemed to result in "good sportsmanship"; however, they sometimes erupted into bitter rivalries and conflicts between countries revealing the competing national and masculine identities that extended beyond the playing field. For Mexican soccer players, the Good Neighbor sports tours opened a space from which they could show off their athletic abilities in the colossus of the North.

Visiting Mexican athletes faced discrimination in the United States that revealed cracks in the Good Neighbor Policy. When Perry Jones, head of the Los Angeles Tennis Club and also known as the "czar" of Southern California tennis, visited

Mexico City, he was treated "like a brother" by the Mexican Tennis Association (MTA).[126] To return the favor, he initially invited a tennis team from the MTA to participate in the annual Pacific Southwest Tennis Tournament on September 14, 1941, but then treated them like "bad neighbors." First they were refused tennis balls to practice, were denied access to country club amenities, and were the only foreign team taken off the bleachers.[127] According to team captain Manuel Grey, "Our team was humiliated by Mr. Jones in every possible way . . . [we] were isolated to the point where our players had no place in which to sit."[128] Feeling very upset, "Mr. Grey asked Mr. Jones for the return of the Mexican flag, presented to him in Mexico, because they are consider unworthy to be floating in a stadium where they treated Mexicans badly."[129] The U.S. embassy expressed concern about the unflattering Mexican newspaper coverage than about the incident itself, and consequently requested the Coordinator's Office to "ascertain the true facts."[130] Upon returning to Mexico City, Manuel Grey launched a complaint with the MTA to demand an apology from Perry Jones. Eventually, Jones apologized and wrote a series of letters "praising everything Mexican to the skies" in order to "obliterate the offenses of his Los Angeles [tennis] club staff."[131]

Mexican males were not the only ones showing off their athletic skills in Good Neighbor U.S. tours. Mexico's 1942 female basketball championship team toured the United States and Canada, overcoming gender barriers and a lack of financial assistance from the OIAA. On October 27, 1942, Angel Rosas from the Mexican embassy in Washington, DC, contacted Wallace Harrison of the OIAA requesting assistance with fuel costs for a three-month tour for the National Girls Champion Basketball team called Las Politas. He argued that the tour would "greatly benefit the existing friendly relations between Mexico and the United States."[132] The request was held up for several weeks because it contained some ambiguity. In an interoffice memo, Harrison wondered whether "the only specific type of assistance requested is obtaining gasoline, but I didn't ask more about what they needed as if might sound too encouraging."[133] This comment revealed the reluctance to support any more Good Neighbor sports tours because of the ongoing war. Rosas, however, noted that the Mexican government would pay for all travel expenses, except fuel, and that the proceeds would go to the War Relief Fund.[134]

Inaction from U.S. government officials did not hinder their tour. On January 1, 1943, the basketball team left Mexico City for their first game in St. Joseph, Missouri. The team was composed of female students enrolled at the Instituto Politécnico Nacional and employees from Mexico's Department of Labor. Formed in 1933 by manager and coach Antonio Lavin, the team's original name was Partido Nacional Revolucionario—the forerunner to Mexico's ruling party, Institutional Revolutionary Party (PRI)—but after 1938 was changed to Politécnico, which evolved into Las Politas.[135] Politas won first place at the 1938 Central American and Caribbean Games in Panama City. During the tour, the English-language newspapers characterized them as "Mexican Señoritas" who "appeared both attractive and healthy" and did more than play, but "entertain with Mexican music and dancing."[136] Even *La Opinión* published a photo of Las Politas dressed in traditional charro attire wearing white sombreros that resembled halos.

Politas did not hold back when playing competitive ball, however, especially in close matches. One newspaper reported, "Star Politas [Elsa] Gamborino, who was knocked out for fighting in the fourth quarter, remained in the game to become the high scorer for the Mexican team."[137] As they traveled from town to town, according to *La Prensa*, "they left a great reputation among a crowd of sympathizers who watched their showmanship, great speed and very Mexican courage."[138] At the St. Louis Arena, Politas battled against the national AAU champions from Davenport, Iowa, in front of 3,115 fans who braved below-zero weather to watch women's basketball.[139] Luis Fernández MacGregor, Mexican consul in St. Louis, described how Politas came from behind to eke out a victory, 21–19. He wrote, "The game was in favor of American girls in the beginning, but as it progressed, the speedy Mexican girls turned it around and proved to be true champions of the sport."[140]

Although they lost more games than they won at the end of their basketball tour, "the 13 girls remember this is a good will trip, and ration their complaints to the officials—who probably couldn't understand them anyway."[141] Las Politas made up for their shorter size with speed, passing, and aggressive play that defied gender expectations as defined by spectators, physical educators, AAU and OIAA officials. Concerned that Latin American female basketball was not playing according AAU's rules, Bushnell requested that the Publications Division to work closely with the National Women's Basketball Committee of the AAU to translate the women's basketball rules pamphlet into Spanish because "at present women's play there [Latin America] is conducted under men's rules, and many unnecessary accidents occur in consequence."[142] Mary Hall, professor of physical education at Wellesley College, visited South America and "was amazed to learn that the women students there had no knowledge of basketball for girls." She suggested to Mary Winslow, an advisor on women's affairs to Rockefeller, that "the translation should be made in the U.S.A. as I know of no one in South America who has sufficient knowledge of basketball for women to undertake this important task."[143] This condescending attitude was indicative of the problems with U.S. physical educators and sports officials trying to teach Latin American women how to play by their own rules.

BECOMING GOOD NEIGHBORS?

Baseball was a popular sport organized by Coordination Committees because it best symbolized the "American way of life." Baseball has been integral to America's foreign policy as a way to sell and export the American dream.[144] In a letter to Rockefeller, the Coordination Committee of Venezuela claimed, "Baseball is one of the best means available to our government for promoting closer friendly relations and better understanding between the people of the U.S.A. and those of the Latin-American countries."[145] Congressman Charles Clason advised Rockefeller to consider Leslie Mann's proposal to send a U.S. team to compete in the 1941 World Baseball Cup in Havana.[146] Former professional baseball player Mann founded the International Amateur Baseball Federation in 1938 as a world-wide governing body of amateur baseball; this organization lobbied for baseball to become an Olympic sport and organized the annual Baseball World Cup (later renamed World Baseball Classic, which still takes place every four years).

The 1942 baseball team representing the United States finished in last place, prompting some "constructive criticism" from W. S. Link, a sports promoter and member of the Coordination Committee for Venezuela. "The sending of a weak team to represent the U.S.A. was a tactical error from a 'Good Neighbor' or 'Public Relations' point of view," wrote Link, because "by sending inferior material against them . . . it implies condescension in our part in the minds of these [Latin American] people, with consequent resentment."[147] He warned Rockefeller of spurring anti-Yankee sentiment since "we have underestimated the playing ability of the Latin-American players, which in turn indicates a lack of interest on our part in the analyzing of sports and players outside our own borders—a reflection of U.S. egotistic self-sufficiency."[148] The Sports Office denied any role in the selection of the baseball team and agreed that "all our activities in the other Americas should be free from any feeling of condescension or lack of interest in the peoples or events of those countries."[149]

The Coordination Committees in Central America organized baseball tournaments attracting large crowds and extensive publicity. In Guatemala, the committee sponsored a baseball tournament in honor of President Jorge Ubico that included a U.S. Army baseball team and eight Guatemalan teams.[150] The championship game between the U.S. Army and Victor on April 18, 1943, "brought out a crowd in excess of 7,000—the largest on record—to watch these two teams battle for the flag and the first prize of 15 uniforms." Although the U.S. Army team won 7–5 in a very tight game, the Guatemalan players showed that they "are good players and who will come along further with more experience."[151] A member of the Coordination Committee was so impressed with Guatemalan players' athletic skills that he suggested sending "one or two outstanding players of the Guatemalan boys for a try-out with some of the minor or major leagues" or asking major league clubs to send scouts to Central America.[152] In a letter to William Harridge, president of the American League, John Akin of OIAA reiterated the idea of sending scouts to Central America because "they have some first rate players" and baseball is played year round so "the players are always in good condition."[153] But major league failed to act; rather, the OIAA donated baseball equipment and films to be distributed throughout Latin America.

After 1942, sports films became one of the ways that the OIAA promoted sports in Latin America. An OIAA official appealed to the sports director that "many of the Coordinating Committees have urged us to send more films on sports.... In fact, by a recent survey we made of all Coordinating Committees, sports films were requested more often than any other kind."[154] One of the baseball films promoted by OIAA was *The Ninth Inning* directed by Lew Fonseca, a former big-league baseball player who led the American League in batting in 1929 turned filmmaker.[155] Fonseca's 1942 film was dedicated to Lou Gehrig, the New York Yankees legend who died of amyotrophic lateral sclerosis (ALS), a neurodegenerative disease that later became widely known as Lou Gehrig's disease. The film's title derives from the All-Star Game at which the National Leaguers thought they had the game in the bag until Boston's Ted Williams came up in the ninth and slapped a homer out of Briggs Stadium in Detroit. The film was distributed nationwide to civic groups and schools and overseas to U.S. military bases, Coordination Committees, and national sport offices in Latin America. Puerto Rico's sports commissioner wrote to Fonseca requesting permission to "exhibit your film in all towns and cities of the island, [so] our youth may have the same opportunities to learn and enjoy playing baseball that Continental American boys have."[156] The forty-five-minute film faced some obstacles: since it was available only in English, the instructional scenes were too technical for a wider audience, and the high distribution cost further limited access.

Sports films remained racially exclusive, showing only Euro-American athletes. Although attempts were made to enlist Hollywood studios to produce sports films, they primarily focused on cartoons, families, melodramas, westerns, and musicals.[157] One significant problem was the skewed representation of baseball players, ignoring Latino major league players like Melo Almada, Chile Gomez, Hiram Bithorn, Alejandro Carrasquel, Roberto Estalella, and Roberto Ortiz. Although the Latino presence in the major leagues increased during the 1930s and 1940s (the majority from Cuba), Fonseca featured only the game's most prominent Euro-American ballplayers.[158] Although "many of the Coordination Committees have urged us to send more films on sports," explained Maurice Ries, liaison officer of the Motion Picture Society of the Americas, there remained a need for diverse sports films.[159] Ries suggested to the Motion Picture Division a newsreel-type picture of Latin American athletes in U.S. sports. He noted that "there are baseball-players from Cuba, Venezuela, Mexico of whom there are quite a few engaged in present or recently past baseball careers in the United States; tennis players like Pancho Segura; boxers of who there are also quite a lot; [and] perhaps basketball players etc."[160] To emphasize the point, Ries attached a *Washington Post* column by Shirley Povish that discussed Joe Cambria's recruits from Cuba. "The Nat[ional]s are prepared to field a team next season with a heavy Spanish accent," wrote Povish. He continued, "For nearly 10 years Cambria has been stomping through the Cuban hinterlands corralling the native kids for Griffith, and no longer are the other big-league clubs ridiculing his safaris."[161]

At the end of World War II, the Good Neighbor Policy and Major League Baseball became increasingly tested by Jorge Pasquel's Mexican League. The *New York Times* expressed concern about the rival Mexican League by publishing a series of articles and cartoons depicting the "baseball war" with Mexico.[162] When Pasquel's league began to challenge Major League Baseball, suddenly Mexico became a "Bad Neighbor." The *New York Times* quoted Jorge's brother Bernardo that "Mexico is out to destroy the United States monopoly on baseball."[163] The *New York Times Magazine*'s Jack Markow published a cartoon with racial caricatures of Mexican ballplayers dressed with sombreros and serapes with the headline "If 'Beisbol' Should Cross the Border."[164] The caption warned readers about what would happen if "the Mexican version of the game might someday alter the scene in the big-league stadiums of the United States." Each image relied on long-standing racial stereotypes about Mexican athletic inferiority. It was not only Mexico that accused Major League Baseball of violating the Good Neighbor Policy. Cuba's sports director accused A. B. Chandler of "slamming the door against efforts to establish a four-nation baseball federation that would include Venezuela, Mexico and Cuba." He attributed Chandler's rejection to the "the commercial, imperialistic monopoly that is organized baseball in the United States."[165]

CONCLUSION

The 1932 Olympic Games and the Good Neighbor Policy stimulated interest in Pan American competitions to strengthen relations between the U.S. and Latin America, but when World War II forced the cancelation of the hemispheric sporting festival, U.S. officials turned to the Nelson Rockefeller's Sports Office. On April 10, 1946, President Truman abolished the OIAA and transferred its remaining functions and responsibilities to the State Department. Even though the Sports Office was fleeting, it used "American sports" as a "soft power" approach to maintain and continue its political and economic influence over Latin America. Good Neighbor sports diplomacy facilitated continued U.S. domination of the Western Hemisphere because since we are "good neighbors," the United States argued, we have a right to your political loyalty, natural resources, cheap labor, and athletic talent. As sports historian Barbara Keys has suggested, international sports acted as a forum for nationalist rivalry that governments manipulated to further their own agenda, but sport's existence as an international system was also used by private groups to forge transnational ties and further their own agenda.[166] During World War II, sports took on a highly politicized role in the international system. The U.S. sought to ensure that nations in Latin America were joined in the Allied war effort and not remotely associated with the Axis or communist sympathizers. Although a majority of Latin American countries sided with the Allies—except Argentina, who was declared a "bad neighbor" for its neutrality that resulted in a breakdown of trade and diplomatic relations with the United States—the Good Neighbor sports program did not alter the asymmetrical relationship with the Colossus of the North. At best, the Good Neighbor sports program allowed countries to tolerate the U.S. hegemony in the region, and for some Latin American athletes and teams, through sporting exchanges, it provided a forum to which they could make claims for better coaching, sports equipment, and training.

This chapter revealed the U.S. government's use of sports through the OIAA to manipulate Latin American perceptions of the United States as a "Good Neighbor" and symbol of democracy and freedom. The treatment of Mexican and Latin American athletes, however, did not match the promises of the U.S. Good Neighbor Policy and its Sports Office. The Sports Office used a gentler approach to further their political and economic conquest of Mexico and Latin America. Instead of accepting the desired message of U.S. government officials, Mexican and Latin American athletes and teams appropriated the "goodwill" rhetoric to provide counternarratives of racial discrimination, class exploitation, and gender oppression. To be sure, these athletes exerted their agency and were not victims of Yankee imperialism; indeed, Mexican athletes took advantage of the American football coaching missions, sporting exchanges, and touring opportunities to the United States to show off their athletic talent, especially in soccer, the one sport in which they knew they could beat the Americans. Through their participation in U.S.-sponsored sports programs, Mexicans helped grow and expand the sporting Mexican diaspora.

6 • SPORTING A NEW IDENTITY IN POSTWAR AMERICA

After Valentina Hernandez said goodbye to her four older brothers who joined the U.S. military at the onset of World War II, she returned to the ballpark to play for the Coronado Lime Cola team. When Valentina married a baseball pitcher in 1942, she defied another gender norm—she refused to stop playing ball.[1] She told her husband that she wanted to continue playing until she got pregnant. However, her physician diagnosed her with an iron disorder that prevented pregnancy, an issue that contributed to their divorce. To support herself, Valentina left her low-paying housekeeping job for a high-wage defense job at the Rohr Aircraft plant in Chula Vista, near San Diego. Valentina became one of many Mexican American women who found jobs in the wartime defense industries to advance economically and expand their social networks. Although "Rosie the Riveter" became the iconic image of the wartime white female worker, Mexican American women also labored in defense industries albeit with far less recognition.[2] At Rohr, she developed lifelong friends at work and play. She formed a company softball team, the Sheet Metalettes, and played for many years. "I was good at everything, both playing ball and in my defense job," declared Valentina. Valentina remained at Rohr for thirty-three years; at one point she received a hard-earned promotion to become a supervisor, but she declined because it interfered with her softball coaching on weekends. Despite this unfulfilled opportunity for a work promotion, Valentina fondly recalled traveling with her teammates for tournaments across state lines.[3]

While playing in Tucson she met softball star pitcher Amelina "Amy" Peralta, who helped the Phoenix Ramblers win three American Softball Association championships. "Even men had a hard time hitting against her," recalled Valentina. After the game, Peralta told her, "You are a good catcher, why don't you get on our team? But my mother would not let me go that far."[4] Valentina's mother refused to allow girls to travel without a chaperone, unlike her older brothers who traveled across the country and overseas to play baseball. Throughout it all, her brother Manuel "Nay" Hernandez, who joined the San Diego Padres in 1944, was her biggest supporter. But within three months of being drafted into the U.S. Army, he was killed in battle at Ludwigshafen, Germany, on March 24, 1945.[5] With the help of a San Diego baseball historian, Valentina fulfilled her wish to have the San Diego Padres recognize her brother for his sacrifices to both the sport and country during a 2010 game.[6]

This chapter examines the sporting experiences of Mexicans and Mexican Americans, both men and women, on the U.S. home front during World War II. First, I examine how Mexican American leaders mobilized through Coordinating Council for Latin-American Youth (CCLAY) to tackle the problem of juvenile delinquency through sports. CCLAY attempted to hold city officials, law enforcement, and print media accountable for unequal treatment of Mexican and Mexican American athletes. Second, I recover the hidden history of Mexican American women who flocked to the diamond to play softball and baseball during World War II. After finishing their defense work and family obligations, these "Rosita the Riveters" joined sports teams and leagues to demonstrate their wartime patriotism through sports and in the process redefined gender roles within their family, work, and community. Some even became professional athletes, like Marge Villa Cryan, who joined the All-American Girls Professional Baseball League (AAGPBL) and traveled across the country and Latin America playing baseball. Finally, I focus on how the Mexican Athletic Union (MAU) became the leading amateur sports organization in the postwar years, organizing cross-border competitions in northern Baja California. Ultimately, I argue that Mexican American athletes and organizations advocated a broader civil rights agenda that included sports and recreation as part of the sporting Mexican diaspora.

SPORTS AND JUVENILE DELINQUENCY

World War II had a profound impact on Mexican Americans in Los Angeles. While thousands of men and some women joined the U.S. armed forces to defend their country, others remained and continued working and playing sports to boost civilian morale on the home front. When the mainstream press fanned fears of rising juvenile delinquency and crime, law enforcement responded immediately by targeting black and Mexican American youth. Disaffected Mexican American youth facing extreme poverty and racial discrimination turned to *pachuco/a* and zoot culture as way to rebel against American society. Besides mobilizing law enforcement to combat juvenile delinquency, city and county officials enlisted the help of middle-class Mexican American leaders. In July 1941, Los Angeles mayor Fletcher Bowron and City Council members formed the Coordinating Council for Latin-American Youth (CCLAY), composed of middle-class Mexican American professionals, which sought to develop "a constructive delinquency prevention program for Mexican youth."[7] Historians have documented the history of CCLAY as part of a politicized Mexican American generation who fought against school segregation, employment discrimination, and police harassment, but have overlooked its work in the arena of sports.[8] Mayor Bowron appointed political activist Eduardo Quevedo as president and attorney Manuel Ruiz Jr. as executive secretary of CCLAY.[9] While Quevedo mingled with influential political leaders and delivered public speeches, Ruiz handled the day-to-day operations and correspondence of the organization.

On August 14, 1941, CCLAY formed the Athletics Committee to use sports as a delinquency prevention strategy.[10] Bill Lopez, athletics director for the Los Angeles Department of Education, led this new committee with members from sports clubs, playground recreation centers, YMCAs, and other athletic organizations.[11] Retired prizefighter Bert Colima joined the committee to use his boxing program as a model on how "to keep the kids off the streets and out of trouble."[12] As the only female in a male-dominated committee, Hortenzia Perez served as the treasurer and captain of a women's basketball team.[13] At its first meeting at Evergreen Playground, the committee formulated a constitution with rules and regulations about membership, sportsmanship, and eligibility. For instance, teams playing football were allowed "2 non-Mexican or Latino players."[14] *La Opinión* praised the committee's effort to convince "heartless gangs to become sports teams in softball, baseball, football, basketball and even boxing and wrestling, and the supreme winner will be decided in the sports field, not in city streets with stones and punches."[15] All this work required money, however, so members visited Mayor Bowron at City Hall to request financial support. Bowron offered only moral support and use of municipal sports facilities. Without city funding, they faced a serious financial challenge that required creative fund-raising efforts and assistance from local sports organizations and the Mexican government.

For their first fund-raiser, CCLAY organized a boxing exhibition at Eastside Arena to send a team of Mexican American athletes to compete in the Mexican Revolutionary Games in Mexico City from November 4 to November 20, 1941. The fund-raising committee included representatives from CCLAY, the Mexican Athletic Association of Southern California (MAASC), the Mexican Athletic Union (MAU), and *La Opinión*.[16] In their request for a boxing permit from the California State Athletic Commission, they invoked the Good Neighbor Policy by claiming, "Funds are being raised to send a goodwill athletic team to Mexico City for its coming Mexican Olympiad. The contingent will be in the nature of a good-will mission in keeping with the Federal policy of fomenting close Inter-American relations for better Pan-American solidarity."[17] After receiving approval, the fund-raising committee confirmed with John Doyle about using his boxing venue at no expense.[18] CCLAY member Ernest Orfila used his connections with Hollywood Legion Stadium promoters to secure Mexican professional boxers to participate in six boxing matches of three rounds each. The boxing card featured Luis "Kid Azteca" Villanueva, Rodolfo Ramirez, Ricardo Lemos, and

Juan Zurita, as well as Alberto "Baby" Arizmendi and Bert Colima, serving as referees.[19] Ticket prices were reduced for minors under twelve years of age to encourage them to attend with the hope that they would be inspired to join boxing programs. The boxing event generated enough funds to support the travel of twenty-two athletes to Nogales, Arizona, and back, so they turned to the Mexican government for the remaining funds.[20]

CCLAY members skillfully drew on their transnational connections with the Mexican government to secure additional funding. They contacted Rodolfo Salazar, Mexican consul of Los Angeles, and Guillermo Eddy, MAASC representative at Confederación Deportiva Mexicana (CDM), for assistance.[21] After receiving approval from President Manuel Ávila Camacho, CDM paid for round-trip railroad transportation from Nogales to Mexico City, along with food and lodging. Eddy reassured the Los Angeles delegation that "they will be welcomed and treated as if they were from another state in the Republic of Mexico."[22] Modeled after the Olympic Games, the two-week Revolutionary Games were meant not only to celebrate the thirty-first anniversary of the Mexican Revolution but, according to President Camacho, "to strengthen the ties of national unity that must exist between the inhabitants of all the States and Territories."[23] Camacho added that "the games will provide the great masses a healthy distraction of exemplary discipline and physical strength, necessary qualities to fight effectively against the old, inherited vices."[24] The president's statement aligned with CCLAY's efforts to combat vice among the younger Mexican population in Los Angeles. Each Mexican state sent a delegation to participate in the Revolutionary Games, along with a Los Angeles delegation that arrived in Mexico City three days late and with little time to practice for the twenty-five sporting events.[25] In the end, the Los Angeles delegation competed in tennis, swimming, and track and field and returned with a few medals.[26] By building transnational ties with the Mexican government, CCLAY helped foster hemispheric solidarity through sports. The organization, however, was less effective in combating juvenile delinquency without addressing the structural causes of poverty and discrimination.[27]

Another major focus of CCLAY was to counter negative portrayals of Mexican and Mexican American athletes by the mainstream press. Ruiz felt that Anglo Americans routinely conflated Mexican immigrants and Mexican Americans under the racial category of "Mexican" instead of using "Mexican extraction."[28] Thus, the racialization of the term contributed to their negative media portrayal. CCLAY members complained to Ruiz that this anti-Mexican bias in mainstream English-language newspapers extended to athletes.[29] After they discussed the issue, Ruiz wrote to Manchester Boddy, chief editor of the *Los Angeles Daily News*, expressing his displeasure with sports columnists Bob Hebert and Gordon Macker for "consistently making statements derogatory to the character and ability of Mexican boxers."[30] For example, Hebert criticized Mexican sportswriters for selecting Juan Zurita as athlete of the year even though he "did not fight once in Mexico last year."[31] Hebert also referred to Baby Arizmendi as "the sawed off little firecracker from Mexico."[32] Additionally, Macker questioned why Pedro Ortega was scheduled to fight against Cecil Hudson if he "fought here five or six years ago and was such a flop that he was suspended by the state athletic commission for 'the good of the game.'"[33] Macker downplayed Ortega's credentials and called him a "Little Pancho" and "Floppo Pancho." The word "Floppo" refers to a fat, lazy person, and "Pancho," although commonly used as a nickname for Francisco, in this case was used in a racist and derogatory manner.

Additionally, Ruiz attached a letter from the State Athletic Commission's chief inspector confirming that they never suspended Ortega: "Since 1935 Pedro Ortega has improved so much that he defeated the following men and this latter record certainly places him in the position today of being a capable main event attraction in any club in California."[34] Ruiz concluded the letter by stating, "Feeling that you, as Editor of this great daily newspaper, are doing all you can to promote friendly relations with our neighbor to the South, we request that you call attention of Bob Herbert and Gordon Macker to please desist in publishing statements which are without truth and foundation and which tend to break down the morale of these boys who are here to perform for the benefit of our boxing public. We would like them to feel that this Country welcomes them so that when they return to Mexico, they will not feel that they have been discriminated against because of their race."[35] Ruiz's letter got the attention of *La Opinión*'s José Hernandez Llergo, who penned two columns defending the Mexican boxers.[36] Ortega told Llergo he felt personally attacked and demoralized and was ready to return to Mexico.[37] Boxing promoter George Parnassus convinced Ortega to stay and prepare to fight against welterweight champion Jackie Wilson for a bigger cause—to raise money for an Allied victory. Parnassus publicized the Wilson-Ortega fight as the first army benefit boxing event in Los Angeles featuring Hollywood celebrities such as Jack Benny and Mickey Rooney.[38] The match raised over fifteen thousand dollars for the Volunteer Army Canteen Service.[39] Although Ortega lost the match, he displayed his patriotic duty and "proved himself a capable opponent," showing the *Los Angeles Daily News* that he indeed belong in the ring and in American society.[40]

Besides challenging negative portrayals in the sports pages, CCLAY pushed city officials and the police department to hire more Mexican Americans. On November 14, 1941, Manuel Cardona, a Mexican American playground supervisor, approached CCLAY to complain about Hollenbeck Division police officers physically attacking five boys, who were "all good boys and not members of any gang whatsoever."[41] Ruiz complained to the police chief but received no response, and within a year Cardona resigned in protest. In February 1942 a group of sixty Mexican American youth signed and presented a petition to the Department of Playground and Recreation demanding that Evergreen Playground director Coffin and his assistant be removed for causing "friction and discontent."[42] They complained about obtaining referees and transportation services for their scheduled sporting events. The petitioners argued that "this playground always bustling with activity" under the previous supervisor (Cardona), but "now they're very few leagues inadequately organized and overrun by troubles."[43] CCLAY discussed the petition and assigned José E. Ruiz to investigate the matter further. After spending four days in the playground, Ruiz agreed with the petitioners that "younger groups of boys were very dissatisfied with the present personnel and would not attend the playground at all, they would rather hang out across the street in a little lunch stand where beer and wine is sold."[44] Ruiz interviewed one Mexican American boy who requested to check out a basketball, but "because Mr. Coffin did not like the way he asked for the basketball he proceeded to grab the boy by the arm causing the boy to have pain for several days."[45] Ruiz concluded that Coffin was causing physical harm and keeping Mexican American youth away from the playground, thus "raising the juvenile delinquency rate in the district."[46] In response, Ruiz wrote letters to the head of the Department of Playground and Recreation recommending the firing of Coffin and hiring of Mexican American playground staff at Evergreen and other playgrounds in East Los Angeles.[47] Despite these measures, there was no response from city recreation officials. It is very unlikely they heeded CCLAY demands because four years later Ruiz made the same recommendation when he joined the Citizens Committee for Latin-American Youth and the Los Angeles Youth Project.[48]

Despite CCLAY's advocacy for hiring culturally competent recreation employees, a close examination of the Los Angeles Board of Playground and Recreation Commissioners' (LABPRC) minutes revealed recurring confrontations between Mexican American youth and European American supervisors at playgrounds and swimming pools. At Pecan Playground, for example, supervisor Marks reported on the "Mexican problem" to LABPRC explaining why they "found it necessary to eject a Mexican boy from the gymnasium for continued misconduct."[49] At El Sereno Playground, the supervisor blamed five Mexican boys for "causing trouble" and starting a fight with playground boys until "the police apprehended the Mexicans and held them for questioning."[50] Reports of increased juvenile delinquency extended to Mexican American girls according to Stephen Keating, secretary of the Citizens Committee for Latin-American Youth, a separate group appointed by the Los Angeles County Board of Supervisors.[51] Keating urged the LABPRC "to hire additional women directors for those playgrounds which do not have them at present so that a well-rounded program of activities may be presented all these [recreation] centers."[52] CCLAY's prominently male leadership ignored female athletes and focused all of its efforts on curbing juvenile delinquency among young men.

CCLAY faced an uphill battle convincing the American public that not all Mexican American youth were "Pachucos or Pachucas."[53] The sensationalist coverage of the Pachuco Problem in the mainstream press forced them to redirect their efforts against the media and away from more structural factors.[54] Civic organizations and middle-class liberal reformers approached CCLAY with proposed remedies to the Pachuco Problem. After a series of violent attacks on Mexican American youth in the summer of 1943 that became known as the Zoot Suit Riots, Christine Sterling approached CCLAY with her "Club Los Pachucos" proposal.[55] Sterling, considered the "Mother of Olvera Street" for converting the Los Angeles Plaza into a Mexican marketplace and tourist destination, proposed to build a recreation center with a dance floor, clubroom, and boxing ring in the basement of a building at Macy and Alameda streets. She recruited friend Joe Salas, a former Olympic silver medalist, to oversee the youth boxing program and Baby Arizmendi to offer some lessons and motivation.[56] Rival "Pachuco gangs" would settle their differences, according to one reporter, "with boxing gloves instead of razors and broken beer bottles."[57] CCLAY expressed reservations about the name because "the name would tend to confuse an already delicate state of affairs . . . it is impolitic to use it as a boys club name." In this racialized polarized climate, the club name would further stigmatize Mexican American youth and inhibit their integration into American society. When Sterling asked the attendees if they preferred "Club Olvera" at the November 11, 1943, opening, they responded "Los Pachucos."[58] The youth rejected middle-class social reformers' attempts to control them and instead reclaimed their name, identity, and dignity. After three months, Sterling had had enough with "old gang animosities" that flared up and burglaries that had left her disillusioned, so she closed the club.[59] The failed Club Pachucos experiment relied on donations and volunteers without the support of CCLAY and city officials and thus was another example of piecemeal liberal reformist efforts that failed to combat the root causes of juvenile delinquency. After the war, CCLAY ceased to function due to a lack of financial support from the City Council, leaving other organizations to carry the load of promoting sports.

BATTLE FOR HOME PLATE: *MUJERES* PLAYING SOFTBALL

The temporary absence of men during World War II allowed Mexican American women to enter the workplace and attain more economic independence. With more money to spend, they engaged in a wide range of wartime leisure activities, from attending dance halls and movie houses to forming social clubs.[60] One of these was the Señoritas United Service Organizations (USO), which according to historian Elizabeth Escobedo "signified both a promotion of ideals of upright American patriotism and an emphasis on their distinct Mexican heritage and cultural difference."[61] Many so-called Rosita the riveters also showed their patriotism and hybrid identity by competing in women's sports leagues, particularly in softball and baseball.[62] Take for example the 1942 Las Gallinas (the chickens) from East Chicago's Indiana Harbor, a competitive team that attracted large crowds at their raucous games that sometimes "ended up in fist fights."[63]

Although the system of chaperonage that forced Mexican women to be accompanied by men in public had declined by World War II, it remained alive in the sports world.[64] Most women's teams were coached and managed by men, and they often could play only if they were in the company of their brothers or fathers. Maggie Salazar Guzman had more freedom to play softball from her overly protective parents. In fact, on game day her mother made sure her uniform was clean and ironed before the team carpool arrived. Born in Irwindale, California, Guzman started playing at the age of fourteen in 1943 with the support of her mother and lukewarm support from her father, who worked long hours at the railroad yard. "Nobody stole second base from me," claimed catcher Maggie Salazar Guzman, who played catcher for the semiprofessional Baldwin Park Royals.[65] She learned how to catch from Coach Luis Ruelas, a former catcher who formed a softball team of Mexican girls from the neighborhood. A newspaper headline in the *Baldwin Park Tribune* described her as "little Salazar with her atomic tag will get them out on second."[66] She learned how to give the correct signals to the pitcher by judging how and where the batter stood. She caught for her favorite pitcher, Velia Silva, who also played for the Royals. "The harder she pitched, the more noise my glove made, the more I wanted to play. The more it gave me the strength to play."[67] Guzman was one of few Mexican Americans on the Royals, but quickly made interracial friendships and helped the team win the 1947 league championship. After winning the title, teams from Azusa and Monrovia requested to "borrow" her, but she remained loyal to the Royals.

On one occasion she substituted for a men's softball team when they were short of players. The team uniform was royal blue satin with "BP" emblazoned on the jersey. Guzman was the only player with long pants, however, because the catcher had to squat repeatedly. The Manning Brothers Rock and Sand Company sponsored her equipment and travel expenses. She fondly remembers traveling outside the state to Arizona, Mexico, and Canada for the first time. At an exhibition game in Mexicali, she used her bilingual skills to translate for her Anglo teammates. Although she was not paid, she did receive a payment of eighty dollars for an exhibition game at Atkins Park in Burbank, where the entrance fee was two dollars per person. And at this same ballpark Guzman met her future husband. When he was on leave from the U.S. Air Force, he would frequently watch her play at Atkins Park until he got the nerve to ask her out. After they married, he continued to support her athletic career, but her mother-in-law from Mexico disapproved, maintaining that women's softball would compete with her traditional gender role as wife and mother. But Guzman adamantly claimed that she was able to find a good balance between her job, family, and softball. After raising eight children and working full-time as a nurse, she retired, though this did not stop her from coaching and teaching her grandchildren how to play ball.[68] Playing softball made her visible in the community, and being both

FIGURE 6.1. The North Hollywood Vixies in 1949 at Las Palmas Park in San Fernando. Ramona Valenzuela is standing third from right. (Courtesy of Connie Lugo Ferrer and Latino Baseball History Project, Pfau Library, CSU San Bernardino)

a catcher and a captain of the team taught her leadership skills that she applied to a successful nursing career.

Mexican American women used sports participation to redefine gender roles within the family and community. Growing up in the Mexican neighborhood of Orcasitas in North Hollywood, Ramona Valenzuela found more freedom playing on a women's softball team during wartime.[69] "My mom thought I was a tomboy," admitted Valenzuela. "She would tell me that I could play, only if I cleaned the house beforehand."[70] After completing her domestic chores, she got together with friends to play softball at North Hollywood High School's baseball field. In 1945, she recruited ten to twelve girls from the neighborhood and high school to join the North Hollywood Vixies (see Figure 6.1). She proposed the name of Vixies because all her teammates could run like female foxes. Coach Carlos Lugo taught players how to bat, field, and pitch at Orcasitas ballpark, constructed on a vacant lot on the corner of Stagg Street and Irvine Avenue.[71] Chelo Martinez managed the team's schedule and helped them find a sponsor. Bob's Cleaners of North Hollywood became the team's main sponsor for equipment and uniforms, including a customized black-and-white jacket emblazoned with each player's name on the left side. The Vixies traveled in the manager's pickup truck around the San Fernando Valley to play against their main rival, the San Fernando Blue Jays. This rivalry sometimes erupted into fights. Valenzuela recalled how after they defeated the Blue Jays, the 1948 San Fernando Valley Women's Softball League champions, the losers threw rocks at them while they sat on the back of their truck. Nobody was seriously hurt, but she blamed a few "mean" Blue Jays players. "They had better-looking jackets and more sponsors than our team [Vixies]," admitted Valenzuela, "so they thought of themselves as being better than us."[72] As the team's top pitcher and captain, she would tell her teammates to ignore the "poor losers." Valenzuela's story reveals how class differences permeated women's softball teams, as evidenced through their home ballpark, uniforms, and equipment. The team disbanded in 1951 when more and more players got married and began raising families. Valenzuela, however, continued pitching for other teams, even after she married. Notably, she even pitched for an all-black softball team where she made interethnic friendships.

Mexican American women's softball helped bridge ethnic differences throughout the Southwest, a region still divided and segregated along racial lines even when wartime unity was needed for a U.S. victory. Rosa Duran and Evelyn Silvas, sisters who grew up in Richmond, California, and worked in the shipyards during World War II, remembered how they were not allowed to attend dances but could travel and play in a summer softball league in Arizona.[73] Duran recalled, "We could get together as a Mexican team. There was also a black team. Then the others were mixed."[74] As more Mexican Americans enrolled in high school during the 1940s, they began to meet other ethnic groups through the Girls Athletic Association (GAA). The National Section on Women's Athletics organized GAA chapters in high schools throughout the country to encourage female students to participate in after-school sports and physical activities through "play days."[75] The play day concept was an attempt to deemphasize competitive sports for women because of the potential for sexual exploitation, commercialism, and "masculinization."[76] At Oxnard High School, Ernestina Navarro served as the vice president of GAA while she learned how to play basketball, volleyball, and speedball (soccer) after school hours. This allowed her to meet new friends from diverse ethnic backgrounds and become involved in student service clubs. Because she was discouraged from competing and playing aggressively in basketball, she decided to play softball. "I always loved playing sports and I never let anything discourage me," asserted Navarro, who at fifteen learned how to play fast pitch, considered the most competitive form of softball.[77] Her teammates bestowed on her the nickname of Ernie, which she proudly adopted. After pitching for an all-Mexican girls' softball team, she joined the Cotler's Girls in the Ventura County Girls Softball League.[78] Cotler's Clothing Store in Oxnard sponsored their uniform and equipment in return for advertising their business. Navarro played every position, but because she had a strong throwing arm, she was mainly featured in center field. The *Oxnard Press-Enterprise* praised Navarro's ability to hit with power, "smashing three home runs, drive in six runs and whip Somis, 14–3."[79] Navarro's hitting, and pitching helped her team win the 1949 county league title. When they lost their sponsor, the team changed to the Oxnard Merchanettes with new coach Bud Newman. Adding "ette" to the end of a name was a common practice among women's softball to emphasize their femininity.[80]

Each player on the Merchanettes was required to secure her own merchant sponsor. Navarro acquired Diener's Clothing store, and they paid for her custom-designed royal blue satin uniform with her name sewn on. She did not mind wearing kickers for sliding but disagreed with other restrictions: "We were not allowed to wear cleats. And we were not allowed to wear caps because they felt we may trip over the other foot and hurt ourselves or drop our hats running and forget about the game."[81] The restrictions did not apply to men's softball, how-ever, revealing the gendered assumptions that women could not play but could simply dress fashionably well. Navarro recalled her best game: "I hit three homeruns against the Moorpark team, and a male fan gave me five dollars and that was a lot of money, even though I refused, he insisted. He said that he had never seen women hit home runs in one game."[82]

The Culver City softball team attempted to recruit Navarro because of her athleticism, but her parents did not want her to play far away. Redlands Univer-sity even offered her a scholarship, but she declined because of family obliga-tions. Rather, she continued to play for the Oxnard Merchanettes until 1955, all while raising a family, attending community college, and working for an optom-etrist office and school district. The sporting arena allowed for cross-cultural interactions and interracial romances that might not otherwise have occurred. As one of few Mexican American girls on her teams, Navarro found acceptance by Anglo and black teammates due in part to her athletic abilities.[83] This con-trasted with opposing players who taunted her because of her race. Navarro recalled one incident: "A white girl in the opposing team would single me out while playing. She kept yelling at me, 'Oh here comes the little Hershey,' are you going to melt today.'"[84] This racist comment did not bother Navarro. As a young girl growing up in rural Texas, she had faced blatant forms of racism, but her mother taught her not to stoop to their level and to rise above and appreciate racial and ethnic differences. She met her husband Masayuki "Butch" Hosaki while watching him play in the Nisei baseball league. Their mutual love for sports brought them together, and even after marriage they continued to play, this time teaming up in bowling tournaments. Navarro won several bowling champion-ships in Ventura and Los Angeles counties.[85]

Another standout player from the Ventura County Girls Softball League was Agnes Trejo, who led her Oxnard team to many victories. F&O Cleaners spon-sored the team and advertised their business on the uniform. Trejo already played softball for her Oxnard High School softball team but wanted to continue playing in the off-season, so she showed up for tryouts. She surprised the coach and the other girls on the squad with her pitching abilities and was immediately offered a spot on the team. Showcasing her pitching talent, Trejo led her team-mates to many victories around Ventura County (see Figure 6.2).[86] The team,

FIGURE 6.2. Agnes "Aggie" Trejo is prepared to pitch for the Oxnard F & O Cleaners softball team, 1947. (Courtesy of Irene Castellanos and Latino Baseball History Project, Pfau Library, CSU San Bernardino)

which was later renamed the Patio Girls, played throughout Ventura County, often defeating other women's teams. No one questioned the decision to include the only Mexican girl in the team. But as Trejo's daughter recalled, she did feel some discomfort and "was afraid to speak Spanish for fear of being ridiculed through she was fluent."[87] Trejo occupied a middle space within the softball world and learned to navigate multiple aspects of her mestiza identity.[88] Consequently, Trejo used her biculturalism and bilingualism to become a successful business owner catering to both Mexican and Euro-American customers. She also became the madam president of the Fraternal Order of the Eagles 232 as well as a member of the Veterans of Foreign Wars Ladies Auxiliary, Fleet Reserve Association Ladies Auxiliary, and American Legion Auxiliary.

Mexican American women got behind the plate and served as female umpires. Emma Galvan was one of few female umpires in southern California.[89] Born and raised in the Casa Blanca neighborhood of Riverside, California, she started pitching for an all-boys team. As a teenager, she played alongside her sisters, Stella and Kinny, with the Casa Blanca Busy Bees. There she perfected her pitching and became virtually unhittable.[90] Besides playing softball, she worked full time at the National Orange Company Packing House and became a truck driver for Hunter Douglas Production Company during World War II. After the war, Galvan was considered one of best hurlers in fast-pitch softball and was recruited by several southern California teams. From 1950 to 1953, she pitched for the Magnolia Maids of Riverside for four seasons. According to the *Riverside Daily Press*, "the 23-year old pitching star will spearhead the club's attack against El Monte. She is believed to be the best hurler in the loop."[91] In another stellar pitching performance, Galvan struck out seventeen hitters to defeat the Highland Pirates.[92] When she did not play, she worked as an umpire for the Pony League. In 1954, she fell ill and died within a year, at the young age of 28. Her obituary stated, "She was regarded as one of the best arbiters in the [Pony] league. She was the only woman ump and had intended to return again this season until she became sick."[93] Years later, the Inland Empire Hispanic Chamber of Commerce honored Galvan as a local sports hero and inducted her into the Hispanic Hall of Fame.[94]

As softball continued to thrive during World War II, Mexican American women began joining professional teams and leagues. One of these was Amelina "Amy" Peralta, who developed a deceptive windmill pitching style that helped the Phoenix Ramblers win three national titles.[95] After graduating high school in Tempe, Arizona, with athletic accolades, Peralta joined the Ramblers in 1937 as an outfielder, batted cleanup, and was quick around the bases. She soon switched to the mound and became one of the best pitchers in softball, with an overall record of 670 wins and 150 losses, 300 shutouts, 20 no-hitters, and 80 one-hitters. Her stellar pitching during the 1940 season helped the Ramblers win a championship—the state's first title in any professional sport. Softball scholarship and media coverage failed to mention Peralta's Mexican American identity.[96] Sportswriters constructed specific gender and racial ideologies about Latina softball players based on their physical appearance rather than their specific skills. In *The Softball Story*, Morris Bealle described Peralta as "a full blooded Indian girl with a blazing fast ball."[97] The English-language newspaper coverage of Peralta referred to the star pitcher by her Americanized name Amy and racialized her athletic ability.[98] For example, one sportswriter described Peralta as a "Shining light of the 16-girl squad is dark-complexioned Amelina Peralta, who pitched to fame last year."[99] Another sportswriter attributed her pitching prowess to her masculine "husky" body shape.[100]

In 1957, the American Softball Association selected Peralta as one of four founding members of the Softball Hall of Fame. The softball magazine *Balls and Strikes* profiled her hall-of-fame career and corrected her mistaken ethnic identity.[101] "Amy is a native Arizonian and of purest Mexican descent. She has no Indian ancestry. She is extremely proud of her family background."[102] She attributed her athletic success to her family and community. During the off-season, Peralta helped organize youth recreational programs in Tempe's Mexican community that included Mexican music and dancing.[103] Reflecting on her twenty-year career with the Peterson, Brooks, Steiner and Wist Supply Company (PBSW)Ramblers of Phoenix, Peralta wrote, "Softball did a great deal for me in travel, health, experience, social adjustment and just pure joy of competition."[104] Peralta inspired women in the Mexican American Movement organization that profiled her in their magazine. *The Mexican Voice* praised the eighteen-year-old Peralta who helped her Tempe team win the Arizona championship. Peralta recounted how barnstorming across the country led her to meet baseball and boxing celebrities. At the Softball National Tournament in Chicago, she proudly stated, "Among the forty-three states represented there, I was the only Mexican."[105] Amy Peralta inspired Mexican American women in Southern California like Valentina Hernandez to continue playing softball despite the racial, class, and gender barriers they encountered.

Like Phoenix, Southern California also produced strong women's fastpitch softball teams that competed at the highest levels and barnstormed across the country for tournament play.[106] These teams included Mexican American women on their rosters. "They held their own," declared Carlos Salazar, referring to his older sisters, Margaret and Eleanor, who played for the Pasadena Ramblers from 1944 to 1949. "My sisters played as good as men, they use to wear maroon shorts and got strawberries [bruises] from sliding."[107] They learned to hit, catch and pitch from their father, David Salazar, veteran El Paso Shoe Store pitcher discussed in chapter 3. The Salazar sisters thrived as student athletes at Pasadena's John Muir Technical High School, the same high school that produced Jackie Robinson, the first African American to play major league baseball.

In 1944, Hollywood actress Gladys Lloyd recruited a group of women war workers to form a softball team to entertain servicemen stationed at California's desert training bases.[108] Soon thereafter this group became the Pasadena Ramblers and hired Mark Nottingham as coach and manager. Nottingham recruited All-American softball catcher Nina Baziak away from a Hollywood team to serve as captain because she was "one of the best feminine backstops in the game."[109] That same year, the Salazar sisters joined the Ramblers and helped the team win the Southern California Girls Softball Association's championship. The next year the Desert Battalion Program hired the Ramblers to play against men's softball teams at military camps "as part of an entertainment and moral building program."[110] Camp Roberts attracted its largest crowd to date—seventy-five hundred—reportedly because some did not "believe the girls can play ball against a men's club" and others because "there are gals to look at."[111] When the Ramblers played against the Palm Springs Army airbase team, fans were "over-awed by the band of ball that the girls played especially the All-American catcher, Nina Baziak and the cute little shortstop, Salazar."[112] After Saturday games they attended USO dances as special guests, replacing their cleats with dancing shoes. It was at the USO dances that Margaret and Eleanor met their future military husbands. As Elizabeth Escobedo has argued, Mexican American women creatively used USO dances to engage in cross-cultural romances and other respectable forms of rebellion to gain autonomy.[113]

The sports media portrayed the Ramblers players as sexual objects while overlooking their athletic competence. This prompted Baziak to respond in a local Pasadena newspaper that her players were not only athletically talented but also "respectable" and patriotic. This attempt to uplift their reputation by engaging in patriotic activity is a type of softball activism. She asserted, "The Ramblers, who do everything male diamondeers do except chew tobacco; have the greatest array of talent and most ambitious schedule in the 11-year history of the club."[114] The Ramblers demonstrated their patriotism by playing at military camps and participating in wartime work. Every morning the Salazar sisters boarded a shuttle bus to Long Beach, where Margaret worked as a riveter and Eleanor as an office secretary. They continued playing after marriage and in 1948 left their husbands and young children behind to barnstorm with Karl's Shoe Store's softball team across several western states.[115]

Eleanor's son Darrell Evans recalled how "when I was six weeks old, my mother left me with my grandmother because she had to play a series of games in Arizona."[116] Twenty-two years later, Evans made his debut with the Atlanta Braves; he was a strong defensive player and home run hitter for twenty years. He added, "Mom played catch with me when Dad was at work. . . . My mother retired when I was about 10, but I remember watching her and my aunt play. They were the two best players on the team."[117] Darrell credited his mother with having a large impact on his professional baseball career. He admitted, "I know it's usually a different situation in most families, but we followed Mom around the countryside to watch her play."[118] For the Salazar sisters, the ability to travel and play softball during and after World War II signaled a small shift in gender roles for Mexican American women, but breaking the glass ceiling of professional baseball proved more difficult.

PLAYING HARDBALL IN *A LEAGUE OF THEIR OWN*

When the U.S. government drafted men into military service, baseball rosters were depleted, threatening cancelation of Major League Baseball games. To keep the sport alive during wartime, American women stepped up to the plate and joined the All-American Girls Professional Baseball League (AAGPBL). The 1992 film *A League of Their Own* chronicled the first season of this league that had been long forgotten by the American public.[119] In 1943, Chicago Cubs owner Philip Wrigley financed a female professional softball league to entertain baseball fans while the men were away serving in World War II.[120] Wrigley's new league capitalized on the popularity of women's softball leagues across the country, but he considered the sport too masculine, so he emphasized femininity more than athleticism. For example, Wrigley required women to wear short skirts, attend charm school, wear lipstick on the field, and emphasize their sex appeal to increase gate receipts. As one player stated, "[Wrigley] wanted no tomboys. So many thought of girls as tomboys because we played wherever we could and with boys."[121] While male fans came to "check out the girls," these players showed off their athletic skills and proved they were serious baseball competitors on the diamond. One male baseball manager was so impressed with his Grand Rapids Chicks team that he admitted to his mother that "it ain't the [player's] femininity that gets me. It's their skill."[122] By 1948, the league conformed to major league standards using hardballs, overhand pitching, and a 120-game schedule. At its peak in 1948, the AAGPBL fielded ten teams located throughout the Midwest and attendance reached almost one million spectators.[123] In 1954, however, with only five teams remaining, declining attendance, diminished press coverage, and television broadcasting only men's sports, the league folded.

The mainstream success of *A League of Their Own* sparked renewed interest in women's baseball history by scholars and journalists.[124] In celebrating the AAGPBL's history, however, scholars have ignored the racial and sexual politics of the league.[125] In addition, the concept of the "the All American Girl" is taken for granted as referring to heterosexual white women. Wrigley prohibited "short-haired, mannishly dressed toughies" on his league and expected "nothing but healthy, wholesome 'all-American' girls."[126] The film erased the presence of lesbians, including the league practice of expelling women who were perceived as lesbian.[127] One lone scene in the film did acknowledge the existence of black women who played baseball but were shunned by white-only leagues. Since they had "no league of their own," according to Amira Rose Davis, the only option for African American women was to join professional Negro leagues despite opposition from sportswriters, players, and coaches.[128] Sports historian Mario Longoria has done extensive research on Latina presence in the AAGPBL, and only recently have sportswriters followed with individual player profiles.[129]

Eleven Latina ballplayers, two Mexican Americans born in the United States and nine born and raised in Cuba, received more acceptance compared to black women, thus occupying an in-between racial position within the AAGPBL. Isabel "Lefty" Alvarez was one of nine Cuban women recruited after 1947, the year that the league held its first spring training camp in Havana, Cuba. In fact, Isabel's mother encouraged her to practice pitching with the visiting ballplayers, and after impressing the Chicago Colleens' coach, she was offered a contract.[130]

Alvarez and other Cuban players encountered language and cultural barriers, but they comforted each other and rode the bus together whenever possible.[131] Before the Cubans joined the AAGPBL, however, Mexican Americans were already playing big league baseball. The Spanish-language press reported, "The League has some Hispanic ladies ... These girls who have distinguished themselves in the game, especially as pitchers."[132] Two Mexican American women from Los Angeles joined the ranks of the AAGPBL starting in 1946, when Helene Machado joined the Peoria Redwings and Margaret Villa signed with the Kenosha Comets. Machado grew up in Culver City and at nine years old played with her four brothers and cousins on a team managed by her father, Porfirio. The AAGPBL recruited her at the age of seventeen, but her father refused to allow her to leave home. "My father wouldn't let me go. He was very strict. He said I had to be 21 to play."[133] When she reached that age in 1946, she joined the AAGPBL and traveled to spring training in Havana. After a successful season with the Redwings, batting .407 and becoming a fan favorite, a year later she was traded to the Fort Wayne Daisies. Machado did not finish the 1947 season, however, because she returned home to help her family when her father became gravely ill. Unlike Machado, Margaret Villa lasted five seasons with the Kenosha Comets and, besides being an outstanding athlete, used her bilingual skills to act as an unofficial ambassador during AAGPBL's postseason exhibition tours in Latin America.

Margaret "Marge" Villa grew up on a ranch in Montebello, the third of four children of Jay and Eva Villa. She played ball with her younger brother and was encouraged by her father who was a big baseball fan. She preferred to be outdoors away from household chores. As she told one interviewer, "When World War II came, my brothers went into the service, and I tagged along with my dad, hunting, and fishing, anything to get out of the kitchen."[134] At fourteen years old, she joined the Orange County Lionettes, one of the best fast-pitch softball teams in California. Her mother thought she was too young to play with older girls, but she held her own on the diamond, playing alongside future softball hall-of-famers like Bertha Ragan.[135] Her father watched her Lionettes games closely, especially the 1938 championship game at Wrigley Field in front of twenty thousand fans. With America's entry into World War II, she worked as an inspector at the U.S. Rubber plant to help with the family income. Villa first heard about the women's professional league through Bill Allington and Johnny Rawlings, who managed several softball teams that she played against, and although she was offered a contract for the 1943 inaugural season, she could not leave her job until after the war.[136]

In 1945, Villa joined the spring training camp at Pascagoula, Mississippi, and then was assigned to the Kenosha Comets on the Wisconsin shores of Lake Michigan. She started out as a catcher for the first season—the first-string player had broken her arm—until she stubbed her thumb and switched to her regular position of shortstop. For five seasons, Marge became an all-around good player, finishing with a batting average of .209 and 168 RBIs. By the end of the first season, Villa set three league records for the most RBIs (9), total bases (11) and most advanced bases (23) in a single game (see Figure 6.3).[137] The *Kenosha Evening News* reported on her rising popularity: "True to her Spanish ancestry, Margaret decided it was about time fans should take note of her playing ability and applauding her with 'Viva Villa.'"[138] Mainstream English-language newspapers identified Villa as Spanish American rather than of Mexican origin, partly because the 1940 U.S. Census Bureau used "Spanish mother tongue" to classify this population. This racial classification allowed Mexican-origin players to transcend racial barriers in ways that black players could not. This did not mean, however, that racialization of Latinas did not occur in women's professional baseball.[139]

The sports press racialized Villa and other Latina players in the AAGPBL, but not white and European American players. Sportswriters referred to Villa as Marge, Maggie, or Poncho. The misspelled term Poncho referenced the notorious Mexican Revolution leader Poncho Villa who had invaded Columbus, New Mexico, and evaded capture by the U.S. Army. She preferred the nickname Marge and reluctantly accepted Poncho because of her fighting spirit on the field, but rejected the more feminine Maggie. The press also referred to her as a "peppery youngster," the "cute Montebello brunette," and the "little California Villa . . . braids her hair with pig-tails."[140] It was not only her ethnicity and physicality but also her femininity that became the focus of sportswriters. One article described her defiance against a male umpire: "She turned around and with a truly feminine approach questioned his judgment . . . with a look that only a woman can give a man." This was enough for the umpire, who then coldly stared at her and called her Maggie. The umpire then warned her, "If you turn around again,

FIGURE 6.3. Margaret "Marge" Villa Cryan played for the Kenosha Comets of the All-American Girls Professional Baseball League from 1946 to 1950. (Courtesy of the Montebello Historical Society)

I'm going to pull those pigtails. Villa never said a word the rest of the afternoon." The umpire received letters from husbands across the country asking for the "secret formula on how a man can make a woman shut up the first time."[141] Sexist attacks on outspoken women like Villa sought to keep them in line and silence them. Off the field, they were counseled by female chaperones.

Each team was required to have a female chaperone to enforce moral conduct rules and approve players' living quarters. According to AAGPBL rules each player had to follow the "femininity principle" that required them to attend charm school where they learned how to apply makeup and dress in feminine attire, how to behave in public, and how to charm a date.[142] One Associated Press photograph with the caption "Goils Will Be Goils" featured Marge Villa and her teammate brushing their hair in front of the mirror.[143] "But both are women and that means a dab of lipstick and an extra curl or two before doing anything—even playing a rip-roaring game of ball."[144] Susan Cahn argues that "by promoting women's baseball as a spectacle of feminine 'nice girls' who could 'play like a man,' the AAGPBL did as much to heighten the cultural dissonance between masculine athleticism and 'feminine' womanhood as it did to resolve it."[145] There existed a racialized component to this gender binary, however. For example, when Comets coach Chet Grant was suspended for seven days after a blowup with an umpire, he promoted Villa as team captain and interim coach in charge of practices and game lineups.[146] This experience gave her an inside look at league operations and salary contracts. Villa recalled, "I got paid about $200 a week, and when I found out someone was getting a little more than me and not playing as many games. I went right up to the front office and said I wanted a raise . . . I didn't mess around. I told them I was going home unless they gave me one because I have been playing a lot longer and they were sitting on the bench yet making more money because their fathers were lawyers and negotiated their contract."[147] Player salary inequity also angered Helene Machado, who recalled, "I was their best hitter and getting $75 a week. . . . Then I found out a girl sitting on the bench was making $125."[148] Despite the league's mandated femininity principle and pay inequity, Villa used this athletic opportunity to develop leadership and bilingual skills, complete her education, travel, and pursue other athletic endeavors.[149]

Compared to their male counterparts, Mexican American female athletes had limited opportunities to travel abroad. Villa and Machado competed in international exhibition games in Cuba and Latin America, allowing them to develop their own sporting networks in the diaspora. In 1947, the AAGPBL teams held spring training in Havana, attracting seventy-five thousand fans and outdrawing the Brooklyn Dodgers.[150] "Thousands of fans stop in their daily toil to shout, whistle and applaud the girls," reported the *Kenosha Evening Press*, and at the Gran Stadium, "the ardent Cuban fans applaud every catch and every good fielding play made."[151] Villa enjoyed playing in Havana, and because of her fluent

FIGURE 6.4. Margaret "Marge" Villa Cryan (in front, second from right) barnstorming in South America with teammates from the All-American Girls Professional Baseball League, 1949. (Courtesy of the National Baseball Hall of Fame and Museum)

Spanish she served as the interpreter for her team and league.[152] Betty Luna Hill recalled that Villa was very helpful to her teammates because she could speak Spanish.[153] Two years later, Villa joined the AAGPBL team on an eight-week exhibition tour to Central and South America (see Figure 6.4).[154] "Knowing Spanish was the big deal," admitted Villa, "we went to homes of dignitaries and dictators that lived like kings. The crowds at our games were almost 90 percent men, and I wondered where the women were?"[155] Villa's team were special guests at the home of Nicaraguan dictator General Anastasio Somoza, whose guests had been "awe-struck with the ability of feminine diamond gals."[156] General Somoza responded to the exhibition by declaring his interest "to import a Yankee manager to reach the young women of his country and teach them how to play this new game."[157] Somoza hoped the Latin American tour would inspire girls to play ball. Villa recalled, "I got to know a Cuban girl who really wanted to learn the game. Her family thanked me for inspiring her to play the game."[158]

After playing exhibition games throughout South and Central America, Villa returned to Kenosha for her last season. At the end of the 1950 season, she retired from the AAGPBL and returned to Montebello to help her parents with the ranch. Four years later, she married Daniel Cryan, a dentist, and had two children. In 1988, Marge and former players of the AAGPBL were inducted into the Baseball Hall of Fame in Cooperstown, New York. An active grandmother, Marge enjoys golfing and pitching batting practice for her grandsons. Villa describes her grandsons' passion for the game: "My glove and ball is sitting right by their front door so when they hear me drive up, I can't even go inside without them wanting to play ball."[159] Villa and Machado represented the formation of a new sporting identity among Mexican American female athletes who challenged racial, class, and gender barriers during the 1940s. Mexican American "sportswomen" should be recognized as part of the sporting Mexican diaspora not only for their athletic achievements, but also for advancing gender equality in sports and making great strides in women's history, sport history, and Latina history.

MEXICAN ATHLETIC UNION

By America's entry into World War II, the Mexican Athletic Union (MAU) rivaled the Mexican Athletic Association of Southern California (MAASC) as the leading sports organization in the Mexican American community. Both organizations agreed to settle their differences and combine forces to fight juvenile delinquency by expanding sports activities. MAASC agreed to organize the annual track and field event at the LA Coliseum, adult basketball tournaments, tennis matches, and swim meets. MAU took over organizing American football games, men's and women's softball, amateur boxing bouts, and junior basketball tournaments.[160] When MAASC disbanded in 1942, MAU took over organizing sports activities during World War II.[161] MAU modeled itself after the Amateur Athletic Union (AAU), the nation's governing body of amateur sports, by registering athletes, sanctioning games, and cooperating with schools and city parks and recreation departments to secure playing facilities.[162] Ray Sánchez and Pedro Aguilar Despart led MAU in a new direction by forging a closer relationship with northern Baja California's Department of Physical Education and organizing cross-border sporting events.[163]

Ray Sánchez was born in Arizona and raised in Los Angeles, where he attended Belmont High School.[164] In high school, Sánchez was an all-star athlete playing basketball, running track, and serving as baseball captain.[165] In 1931 Sánchez founded Club Atletico México with Pablo Ortiz and Arturo Flores at Evergreen Playground and coached several basketball teams that toured throughout Mexico.[166] As a former MAASC member, he developed relationships with Mexican government officials to enlist his teams in international basketball competitions. He got involved with the Democratic Party and campaigned for the re-election of President Roosevelt through his basketball team, "On with Roosevelt."[167] After leaving MAASC for MAU, Sánchez organized the annual basketball tournament and solicited *La Opinión* to donate the trophy to the winning team (see Figure 6.5).[168] In 1943, he joined the Army Air Forces and two years

FIGURE 6.5. *Sports Page* (December 4, 1948) photo of Ray Sánchez (left side, front row) displaying the winning trophy donated by *La Opinión* newspaper with the "Halcones" team that won the 1947 Mexican Athletic Union basketball tournament. (Courtesy of Bobby Recendez and Latino Baseball History Project, Pfau Library, CSU San Bernardino)

later returned to Los Angeles to opened a sports equipment business, College Athletic Company, at 365 College Street. This location also served as the headquarters of the MAU. To promote his business and MAU, he wrote for the *Sport Page* in exchange for free advertisements.[169]

Born in 1906 to an Italian immigrant father and Mexican American mother, Pedro Aguilar Despart grew up in Los Angeles.[170] He worked part-time at the family liquor store on Spring Street and played sports at the nearby Downey Recreation Center. Despart was a sport enthusiast who had received honors for high academic marks and track and field records at Lincoln High School. After graduation, he received a baseball scholarship to Arizona State University.[171] After returning to Los Angeles, he handled publicity for the Gutierrez Circus Company while also playing for the Belvedere Bus Lines team. In 1936, he used his position to raise funds for their championship MAASC basketball team to travel to compete in Mexico.[172] In 1938, Despart received the support of the Federation of Spanish-American Voters of California to run for the California State Assembly but lost to John Pelletier.[173] MAASC members elected Despart as president in 1939, and within a few months he diversified its sports offerings with tennis, swimming, football, wrestling, and amateur boxing.[174] Despart forged close ties with Mexico's sports federations by cosponsoring exhibitions and hosting visiting athletes. After resigning from MAASC in 1940, he collaborated with Ray Sánchez to form the MAU.[175] That same year, Despart recruited Armando "Cisco" Cisneros, former Loyola University football player, to serve as commissioner of a new football league and the "Tortilla Bowl."[176]

Pedro Despart came up with the idea of the Tortilla Bowl during a 1939 meeting with Armando Rodriguez, director of physical education for northern Baja California. He outlined the plan for "organized athletic competition between teams representing the Republic of Mexico and Mexican teams form the southwestern part of the United States."[177] Despart explained that all-star football teams organized on both sides of the border would inaugurate a cross-border competition. Before they competed against Mexico, however they needed to organize their own team. Despart instructed coach "Chickie" Hernandez to organize football players from local high schools and colleges under the name Mexican All-Stars.[178] The first annual Tortilla Bowl scheduled for January 7 at White Sox Park featured the Mexican All-Stars against the Ross Snyder Bulldogs. Under coach Busch Manson, the Bulldogs joined the semipro Municipal Football Association in 1936 and consisted of the star African American high school football players.[179] After rain forced a one-week postponement, *La Opinión* reported it was a "good game" because despite the odds against the Mexican All-Stars they surprised everyone by holding the Bulldogs to a scoreless tie until the fourth quarter, when the Bulldogs scored a touchdown and won 7–0.[180]

Under Despart's leadership the MAU took over the organizing of the 1941 Tortilla Bowl under Armando Cisneros and with the help of Juan Carmona from Occidental College and Sal Mena from USC. For the second annual game the MAU organized a six-team football league, with the winner competing against the Bulldogs in the Tortilla Bowl on January 5, 1941.[181] At a planning meeting, coaches agreed to allow only two non-Mexican football players per team. The All-Star team would be composed of players from six teams and would compete against other teams in Southern California and Mexico.[182] To generate publicity for the new football league, Cisneros organized a double-header between La Purisima and the Verduga Knights, followed by a matchup between Boliver A.C. and Watts Cardinals.[183] Cisneros assigned University of Southern California's Salvador "Sal" Mena, who had gained notoriety after helping his team win the 1939 national championship at the Rose Bowl, to officiate the opening.[184] During the second annual Tortilla Bowl, the newly selected Mexican All-Stars were better prepared after two months of playing in the new football league under Cisneros.[185] Despite their preparation, the Bulldogs dominated the Mexican All-Stars by a score 25–0.[186] Despart's plan for a cross-border competition for American football failed to garner enough support in Mexico compared to baseball.

Because Los Angeles teams could not afford to travel to Mexico City, they made short, single-day trips to the Mexican border to play against teams from Mexicali

FIGURE 6.6. Pedro Aguilar Despart (center with tie) with the San Fernando Missions team after winning the 1941 Mexican Athletic Union baseball championship at White Sox Park. (Courtesy of Sandi Villanueva Naiman and Latino Baseball History Project, Pfau Library, CSU San Bernardino)

and Tijuana. The MAU coordinated a cross-border baseball competition between Los Angeles and Mexican border cities. For example, the San Fernando Missions competed against the Mexicali Mayas in a best-of-three championship series called the Inter-Californias International Championship.[187] On March 2, 1941, MAU announced the opening of a six-team baseball tournament with the winner playing against northern Baja California's champion team, La Maya.[188] The San Fernando Missions won the MAU league championship by defeating the Villa Stars on March 16, 1941 (see Figure 6.6). The first game took place at White Sox Park, with the remaining games at Hidalgo Park in Mexicali. The handbill featured the team lineup, and photos of General Ignacio Beteta, Mexico's national director of physical education, Governor Culbert Olson, Mayor Fletcher Bowron, the Mexican consul, and Professor Armando Rodriguez, director of physical education in northern Baja California.[189]

La Opinión announced that the most important baseball game of the 1941 season begins today between "two strong Mexican teams of the Californias."[190] Pedro Despart introduced the teams' lineups and the government dignitaries, Hollywood actor Crispin Martin and other special guests. But the preliminary game was more exciting than the boring game in which San Fernando defeated La Maya by a score of 12–8, with many errors on both sides.[191] The second game in Mexicali was more captivating, with the Maya team seeking a rematch: "Not only to raise more morale among our athletes, but also for our Mexicali residents. We will all do our part to achieve the desired victory over the San Fernando Mission."[192] Despite

Mexicali's high expectations, San Fernando Missions defeated the Mayas 10–5 and received the Inter-California Championship trophy.[193]

More broadly, Mexican Americans kept professional baseball a alive during World War II as nearly a thousand minor and major league players joined the U.S. armed forces.[194] President Roosevelt encouraged the continuation of professional baseball to boost soldier morale. To overcome a player shortage, team owners began to recruit from the Caribbean and Latin America.[195] With the help of scout Joe Cambria, the Washington Senators developed a pipeline of Cuban, Puerto Rican, Venezuelan, and Mexican ballplayers.[196] Former second baseman with the Philadelphia Phillies Jose "Chile" Gomez rejoined the major leagues in 1942 by signing with the Washington Senators.[197] He lasted only one season, however; after that his batting average declined.[198] Another factor for the attrition of players was the likelihood that they could become "involved in immigration technicalities and end up in the Army."[199] Jesus Sandoval Flores encountered such a dilemma. Born in Guadalajara, Flores migrated with his family to La Habra, California, at eight years old, when he started playing baseball, first for La Habra Juveniles, then pitching for the Pacific Coast League's Los Angeles Angels. In 1942, the Chicago Cubs called him up for a brief stint, but he then returned to the Angels for the rest of the season. A year later, the Cubs sold Flores to the Philadelphia Athletics, where he pitched for five seasons.[200] The *New York Times* praised the "Mexican Rookie" for pitching thirty-two innings with only eleven hits and three runs allowed.[201] Although Flores never served in the military, he did his part by recording a Spanish-language radio broadcast to encourage South American countries to remain loyal to the Allies during wartime.[202] *La Opinión's* sports page and Mexican American sporting organizations celebrated Flores's baseball career by reprinting articles on his major league accomplishments and awarding a special trophy in his honor.[203] During the offseason, the MAU recruited Flores to coach La Habra's softball team for the inaugural 1941 season of the Southern California Mexican Softball Association.[204] After retiring in 1955, Flores continued to coach and manage teams until 1961, when he became a full-time scout for the Minnesota Twins covering southern California and the U.S.-Mexican border.

The MAU organized men's basketball tournaments and league play at local high school and YMCA gyms during the 1941 season.[205] The war interrupted league play when players were drafted in the military. To keep the sport alive, veteran basketball player José Placencia recruited the remaining players onto a new team. Placencia, who helped Mexico win a bronze medal at the 1936 Olympics in Berlin, formed the Mexican All-Stars to compete in the Amateur Athletic Union (AAU) Basketball League. In 1942, the power forward became the AAU top scorer with eighty-four points during the season and was runner-up for three more seasons.[206] Using his Americanized name of Joe Placentia, the *Los Angeles Times* referred to him as an "eagle-eyed forward" and his team as the "speedy Mexican

All-Stars."[207] The Mexican All-Stars played against military base and defense plant teams throughout Southern California. This team helped to boost soldier morale and prove their patriotism through basketball while claiming both their Mexican and American identities.[208]

After the U.S. government instituted the Selective Training and Service Act of 1940, which required all male citizens between the ages of twenty-one and forty-five to register for the draft, the reality started to sink in for Mexican American athletes that they could be selected. After all, by 1940 people of Mexican descent were twice as likely to be born and raised in the United States than not. MAU athletes left their sport to join approximately half a million Mexican Americans for military service. On October 19, 1941, President Roosevelt selected Despart's lottery number (158) in the national draft, making him one of the first Angelenos drafted in World War II.[209] Sánchez wrote to CCLAY members with a special request "to contribute to the financial stability" of MAU.[210] To make matters worse, Ray Sánchez reported that one of the teams for the MAU Basketball Carnival had to pull out because they lost three of their players to military service.[211] To recognize Despart for all his efforts to promote sports across borders, Mexico's physical education director General Beteta awarded him with a "beautiful diploma" because "in Mexico we recognize and [have] taken into account the work developed by *Mexico de afuera* athletes like Mr. Despart."[212] After Despart departed for military training, Sánchez took over the everyday operations of the MAU for the remainder of 1943 until he was called to active duty. With nobody left to lead the MAU, though, they had to postpone all sports programs until the end of the war.

The MAU established a working relationship with the Mexican American Movement (MAM), an organization composed of second-generation Mexican Americans dedicated toward promoting education for their political and economic advancement.[213] Formally incorporated in 1942, MAM emerged from the YMCA Committee on Mexican Work and Mexican Youth Conferences and published the *Mexican Voice* newspaper to promote its message of "progress through education."[214] MAM also promoted sports among Mexican American youth as a means of gaining organizational and leadership skills.[215] Many MAM members were former high school and college athletes, such as Bert Corona, who had earned a basketball scholarship to USC, and Juan Acevedo, former MAASC secretary and UCLA track athlete who also designed the front covers of *Mexican Voice*. Manuel Ceja and Félix Gutiérrez served as sport editors for the paper, writing profiles of athletes who excelled in high school and college sports and selecting all-star teams in basketball and football.[216] After listing the athletic accomplishments in football, basketball, and track and field, Gutiérrez concluded, "As you can see by these examples, we Mexicans are as good athletes as any other race! Let's follow the examples of these champions of our race! They know that to be champions, they must train hard—no smoking, drinking; regular hours and clean fun. One slip in this schedule—and flop."[217]

After World War II, MAM members formed a new newspaper called *Forward* to reach a broader audience about the postwar challenges facing Mexican Americans and to provide updates for the MAM chapters in Southern California. *Forward* published updates on Mexican American athletes who earned a spot on all-star teams, obtained a college scholarship, and won the MAU league championship.[218] One article profiled the work of the MAU "to promote athletics among Mexican American youth throughout the California."[219] The article highlighted the MAU-sponsored track and field festival at Compton Junior College: "When an all-star combination of Southern California Mexican-American ability was matched against the National University of Mexico . . . the All-Star team won."[220] Although MAM's publications praised the athletic talent of Mexican American boys and men, rarely were girls and women athletes mentioned, except softball pitcher Amelina Peralta.

Not all MAM leaders discouraged women from sport participation. MAM leader Gualberto "Bert" Valadez grew up with a single mother, got married, and raised five daughters, and these strong women in his life helped to change his belief about female sport participation. He also learned about the health benefits of women's athletics in physical education classes at UC Berkeley. After graduation in 1938, Valadez moved to Placentia to start his new job at La Jolla Junior High, where he taught Spanish and physical education. He recalled, "I coached track and field, basketball and baseball and other sports that help to keep kids in school."[221] Some of his former female students approached him to coach a new softball team. They selected the name Kats, borrowed from the Jazz world because it made them look "hip and cool." It was not easy raising money and finding a sponsor for team uniforms and equipment, but according to Valadez "the girls took a collection in the stands and bought me the jacket."[222] The team comprised Mexican American and Anglo girls from the Atwood, Richfield, and La Jolla neighborhoods.[223] They played on a lighted diamond so they could practice in the evenings. According to Valadez, "We were one of the few Hispanic communities to have lights. We immediately organized softball teams; these softball teams played there at night. They'd invite teams from other cities to come and play under the lights."[224] The lighted field combined with the interethnic interactions on and off the field allowed Mexican American women to expand their networks outside of Placentia and Orange County.

Like MAASC and MAM, MAU excluded women from participation in leadership positions within the organization, as reflected in their executive and advisory boards.[225] Since the inception of the Inter-Californias sporting exchange, MAU leaders excluded female athletes from international competition.[226] In outlining their 1948 goals, MAU leaders perpetuated the ideology of male privilege and dominance. As one MAU leader put it, "The ideals of the UMA are not only to spread the sport spirit in Southern California but also to obtain through international competitions a more intimate union with our *brothers* of Baja California, and later with the other sections of Mexico, and then with others countries of the Latin America."[227] The sports pages reaffirmed the idea that Mexican American women should play only "feminine sports." Cuban American sports journalist Jess Losada prescribed for women the outdoor sports of tennis, golf, swimming, yachting, lacrosse, and skating, all of which "will help conquer their beauty and grace."[228] The only MAU-sponsored sporting events in which female athletes participated were tennis and marathons. In its first annual crosstown race from Downtown Los Angeles to Belvedere Park—measuring five and a half miles— the MAU celebrated the husband and wife who finished in first place in forty-one minutes and second place in fifty-two minutes, respectively.[229] Sánchez waited at the finished line to award the trophy to the husband and wife.[230]

EL MAESTRO DE LA RAQUETA IN A WHITE SPORT

After MAASC dissolved, MAU took over organizing tennis tournaments that included men's and women singles and doubles competition at Evergreen Playground courts.[231] The winners then traveled to Mexicali and Tijuana to compete for the Inter-Californias tennis title.[232] The 1947 men's singles match featured eighteen-year-old Richard "Pancho" González against Fernando Isaís, the defending champion for three consecutive years.[233] Isaís was also an eight-time national horseshoe pitching champion and founding secretary of the Mexican Tennis Club, who boasted about having never lost a tennis match against González. "Ricardo González has yet to beat Fernando Isaís," asserted La Opinión. "The MAU has much to be proud of when its champion Isaís competes against González who was named the future champion of the world by the white tennis establishment."[234] When Los Angeles Tennis Club (LATC) owner Perry Jones banned González from playing tournaments because he had quit going to school, González headed to the public tennis courts at Exposition Park, Griffith Park, and Evergreen Playground (see Figure 6.7). After spending fifteen months in the U.S. Navy, he returned to Los Angeles to play in MAU-sponsored tennis tournaments. When Jones finally allowed González to compete in Southern California Tennis Association tournaments, he took the white tennis establishment by storm, defeating the national junior champion and earning the eighth spot in the U.S. Lawn Tennis Association's national rankings before the 1948 national championships.

On September 19, 1948, González shocked the tennis world when he defeated South African Eric Sturgess in straight sets, 6–2, 6–3, 14–12, becoming the new national champion. The next day, La Opinión printed the headline "Gonzalez, New Champion of Tennis" on its sport page and announced, "The triumph of Gonzalez was one of the greatest and most amazing successes in the annals of this white sport."[235] La Opinión sports columnist Rodolfo García reminded readers, "González is Mexican—because he is a son of Mexican parents. He is Mexi-

FIGURE 6.7. Richard "Pancho" Gonzalez on the practice court. Sept. 29, 1949. (Courtesy of the *Los Angeles Herald Examiner* Photo Collection, Los Angeles Public Library)

can because it does not matter where he is born—at 20 years of age, he has achieved an amazing career in the history of white tennis."[236] He was *El Maestro de la Raqueta* (master of the tennis racket) according to *La Opinión* because he conquered the "white sport" of tennis. Tennis has long been associated with country clubs, exclusive, white upper-class membership, a strict code of etiquette, and even attire that reinforces class and racial privilege. Even though LATC allowed Richard González to play after a four-year suspension, he did not always feel welcome in the locker room. González recalled feeling like an "outsider" at the LATC. "I found not one familiar face as I started for the locker room. No one smiled at me. No one even talked to me."[237]

Inclusion did not always lead to equitable treatment. González also had to defend himself against the English-language print media's racialized and gendered constructions of him as a "bad boy" of tennis.[238] González was very media savvy, however, often criticizing reporters for negative portrayals and mischaracterizations. In *Man with a Racket*, González admitted, "I read the write ups. Every guy does, no matter how earnestly some might tell you that they don't. But ever since the time of my suspension for playing hooky, when some writers branded me as anything from a 'juvenile delinquent' to 'Public Enemy No. 1,' I stopped believing everything I read in the papers."[239] In contrast, the Spanish-language print media portrayed him as a sports star and role model for Mexican American youth. In Mexico, González was considered a national hero, and the Mexican government attempted to recruit him for their Davis Cup team. Before he rejected Mexico's offer, however, he used the media controversy as leverage to get U.S. tennis officials to select him for the U.S. Davis Cup team.[240]

Upon González's return to Los Angeles, the MAU was the first organization to invite the tennis star to their basketball league's opening game.[241] MAU leaders reminded attendees about how their tennis tournaments helped González to reach the highest level of the sport and achieve the number-one ranking. As their honored guest, they paid tribute to their "number one athlete" who represented "an unparalleled example to our youngsters who aspire to be in a better and more prominent position."[242] That same week, González received an award from the Helms Athletic Foundation.[243] Founded in 1936, this foundation brought together various English-language newspaper sports editors to select and award trophies to the best teams and athletes from Southern California. *La Opinión* reflected on the racial significance of the Helms award for Greater Mexico: "This award represents something important for all Mexicans that were born in this country and those that reside here and struggle daily against [racial] prejudices." González's victory challenged the racial stereotypes of Mexican athletes as short, weak, and physically inferior. González's athletic achievement also instructed Mexican American youth to follow a similar path. According to *La Opinión*, the case of González was an example for Mexican youth, who at twenty years old had already obtained financial security with a perseverance and talent and reached a place where he could determine his own successful future. He was the example for youngsters of Mexican origin.[244] Sports columnists promoted a middle-class ideology of "racial uplift" by instructing youth that through moral refinement and hard work they could advance socially and economically.[245]

The following year, González won his second national title and silenced critics who argued that he was a one-hit wonder. *La Opinión*'s Rodolfo García considered González a "champion of the world" like how a boxer claims the world title after winning a championship fight.[246] He added that he should be regarded "equally, in tennis. The one who wins the national championship is really the champion of the world, since United States produces the best tennis players in the world."[247] Years later, when González was losing to Jack Kramer on the world professional tour, *La Opinión* sportswriters encouraged readers to attend his matches in Los Angeles because "by having Mexican fans maybe his luck [against Kramer] will change."[248] In front of six thousand spectators at the Pan Pacific Auditorium, González played one of his best matches and defeated Kramer in three sets.[249] Kramer and González continued their bitter rivalry during their professional tour around the world that sometimes spilled into personal confrontations. The biggest affront to González came when Kramer "whitened" his image with blonde hair and lighter skin on the front cover of a 1959 tennis program.[250]

Years later, González reflected on his considerable impact on Mexican American youth.[251] "The favoring of one group of persons over another was something I wasn't conscious of for many years," admitted González.[252] When a Texas restaurant denied him service because of its "No Mexicans served here" sign, he became more aware of racial discrimination. After returning to Los Angeles, González met with Mexican American leaders like Ignacio Lopez, publisher of *El Espectador*, and Los Angeles City Council member Edward Roybal to gain a better understanding of how institutional racism had affected Mexican American youth. "They cry for recognition," González concluded, "a life without restrictions, equal rights, to find employment with chances for advancement. When they can't find a place in the American way of life, they are forced to resort to their own groups, their own behavior patterns which are neither American nor Mexican."[253] González helped break the color barrier in tennis and used his celebrity status to open access to the sport for more Latino/as and African Americans.

DEPORTES IN POSTWAR AMERICA

After World War II, Mexican American veterans returned to civilian life desperate to find employment, pursue an education with the G.I. Bill of Rights, and return to the playing field. One basketball team called itself the Mexican American Veterans, or Los Vets, and competed in the MAU basketball league.[254] The Vets lost a hard-fought game for the 1947 season title against the Azusa Dons. The Dons represented the MAU against Tecate Cerveceros (Brewers) for the Inter-Californias basketball title.[255] The Cerveceros defeated the Dons 73–31, and Mexican boxer Enrique Bolaños awarded the trophy to the winning team in front of hundreds of spectators at the Loyola High School gym.[256] Present at the ceremonies were Ray Sánchez and Pedro Despart, who returned to Los Angeles to help rebuild MAU with a renewed focus on organizing cross-border tournaments, awarding trophies, and recruiting Hollywood celebrities to attend games.[257] To increase participation, MAU leaders awarded the *La Opinión* trophy to the winners of the basketball tournament in Mexicali and the softball tournament in Tijuana.[258] The MAU exhibited the trophies at a department store window in Downtown Los Angeles days before Mexican Independence Day festivities "to illustrate to the Mexican colony the intense work that the Mexican Athletic Union has carried out to develop the interest and the fondness of the Mexican youth, who have responded in an active and enthusiastic way."[259]

Mexican Americans in other cities of the Southwest used basketball as vehicle to attend college and advocate for civil rights. In *When Mexicans Could Play Ball*, historian Ignacio García described how coach William "Nemo" Herrera led the Sydney Lanier High School basketball team, the Voks, to regional and state titles during World War II.[260] The players not only excelled in basketball but also overcame racial and class barriers to show they could play and win. Under Herrera's mentorship, they learned lifelong lessons on and off the court that enabled many to become successful middle-class professionals and political leaders. Joe Bernal remembered how Herrera was more like a father figure to the young boys, encouraging them to pursue a college education. This was not easy because of the extreme poverty and acts of racial discrimination they faced daily. Winning was the best way to combat racism, according to Herrera, even when they faced a size disadvantage. Bernal recalled that "in basketball, we just outran them . . . the short team can sometimes beat the tall team because they can run up and down the court much easier."[261] Bernal heeded Herrera's advice and after serving in the U.S. Army used the G.I. Bill to attend Trinity University, later becoming a schoolteacher and administrator. Later in the 1960s, Bernal turned to electoral politics to advocate for bilingual education and voting rights in the Texas legislature.

As more Mexican American women attended high school in the postwar years, they participated in sports through the Girl's Athletic Association. Lupe Anguiano, a civil rights and women's rights activist, developed her leadership and organizing skills while playing sports in high school and college. After her family moved from La Junta, Colorado, to Saticoy, California, she attended third grade in a segregated school for migrant kids who were dismissed in the afternoon to pick walnuts. She and her sister attended Ventura High School and were the first in the family to graduate. In an interview, Anguiano proudly declared that "I was a letterwoman too."[262] When asked to clarify what she meant by the term—commonly applied to men who perform at a high level in high school sports—she responded by recounting all the sports she played. "I was very good in all sports. . . . I played soccer, which was known as speedball at that time, I was very good at baseball and basketball. I earned my letters." At Ventura College she continued her involvement in sports through the Women's Athletic Association. Anguiano was one of few Mexican American women in college during the late 1940s, a topic that awaits more research.[263] After graduation, Anguiano pursued a long career fighting for social justice, from leading the grape boycott campaign

FIGURE 6.8. Manuel "Midget" Martinez published and edited the *Sport Page* in the 1940s and 1950s. (Courtesy of Bobby Recendez and Latino Baseball History Project, Pfau Library, CSU San Bernardino)

in Michigan to attending the first International Women's Conference in Mexico City, helping single mothers find work, and advising presidents on Latino and women's issues. When I asked her what she learned from playing sports, she reflected that "if you are playing sports you just fit in anywhere."[264] Playing sports taught her to expand her social network and gave her the confidence to become a leader and take on new challenges in life.

Sports journalism became one of the ways that Mexican Americans raised their voice about discrimination, culture, and identity. Manuel "Midget" Martinez founded the *Sport Page* immediately after the 1941 Cinco de Mayo athletic event organized by the MAASC (see Figure 6.8).[265] Tired of the misleading coverage or complete lack thereof of Mexican and Mexican American athletes from mainstream newspapers, Martinez turned to sports journalism to provide a counternarrative of their athletic ability.[266] Born and raised in Watts, California, Martinez lost his parents at an early age, so he sold newspapers and learned to box to defend his newspaper corner against competitors.[267] After winning the 1931 Newsboys flyweight title, he earned a spot on Mexico's Olympic boxing team. After competing in the 1932 Olympic Games, Martinez became a professional boxer with over two hundred fifty fights, and although he never won a title he was considered "Hollywood Legion Stadium's most valuable and popular

Mexican fighter."[268] After retiring in 1937, Martinez became a boxing trainer at the Belle Martell Arena and organized amateur boxing tournaments for MAASC and MAU before he switched to sports journalism.[269]

During World War II the *Sport Page* devoted much of its coverage to Mexican American athletes who joined the U.S. armed forces to demonstrate their patriotism. The headline at the bottom of each page encouraged readers to "Send it to a Man you Know in the Forces." While recovering at a convalescent ward from war injuries, Raul Morin contributed cartoons and stories to the *Sport Page* that inspired his future book on Mexican American soldiers, *Among the Valiant.*[270] In 1946 they devoted a special issue to "proudly pay high tribute to all the Latins fighting for Uncle Sam."[271] The front page listed the names of "Boys in the Army" for boxing, basketball, football, and track and field. Female athletes were excluded from the listing nor recognized for serving in the military. The editor published a photo of his younger brother Danny Martinez—in a navy uniform, no less—who fought twelve amateur boxing fights before enlisted in the navy. Martinez admitted, "These five years have been a struggle, but the SPORT PAGE thinks it has accomplished their goal, that [is] to serve and help you—the Mexicans of southern California."[272] Despite financial problems, the *Sport Page* continued to create a positive image of Mexican American athletes in the postwar years, advocating for their full participation in American sports.

The *Sport Page* resembled the *Mexican Voice*, for its focus on discrimination, identity, education, and civil rights.[273] Published in English on Saturdays, the newspaper charged one dollar for six months and could be delivered by mail or purchased at sporting events. It offered extensive coverage of Mexican and Mexican American athletes, teams, and leagues to demonstrate their contribution to American sports. The small staff covered boxing, baseball, football, basketball, and wrestling as well as local news about social clubs, food, music, and entertainment. In 1947, the newspaper sponsored the All-Latin Annual Basketball Tournament and invited readers to submit their team's entry by filling out a blank form.[274] The *Sport Page* promoted and honored the best Mexican-origin athletes in their respective sports through their annual all-star team selections. This was modeled after the Helms Athletic Foundation to honor the foremost amateur athletes in football and basketball. For example, every year the staff asked readers to select the best Latino football players from local high schools and colleges in Southern California.[275] According to Martinez, "More than 600 Mexican football gridders, who participated in football this year, will be looking forward to the SPORT PAGE's annual All-Latin Selection for this year's eleven." He reminded readers that the "All-Latin eleven that merits the honor and respect of all of us."[276] The *Sport Page* honored the eleven football players with a gold medal at a dinner celebration. This tribute according to *Sport Page* was as an "act of justice" for Mexican-origin athletes who had lacked recognition from the mainstream sporting press and sports organizations in Southern California.[277]

The *Sport Page* profiled high school student athletes to attract attention from college coaches. Martinez wrote that "it is interesting to note that each year more and more of our Mexican boys are striving towards a higher education, which in the future will result in better leadership for our younger ones." These profiles contrasted the sensational images of Mexican American youth as pachucos and zoot suiters that dominated the front pages of the mainstream press. Two baseball athletes from Santa Paula, California, were featured in the June 19, 1948, issue because they opted to remain at Pepperdine University instead of accepting offers to play in Mexico. "For the past three years, a pair of chicanos have been the mainstays on Pepperdine's Baseball Team, with Rudy Victoria on the mound and Gilbert Asa stopping them behind the plate."[278] Martinez emphasized the importance of using their athletic scholarship to complete their degree. For this reason, he praised Humberto Lopez, who earned a track scholarship to the University of California, Berkeley. "Humberto does not confine all his talents to running as he is also an outstanding student in the field of Chemistry."[279]

Besides coverage of sporting events, the *Sport Page* raised civil rights problems affecting the Mexican community. For example, Martinez pressed elected officials to resolve the police brutality problem facing Mexican American youth. He reported on how two activists campaigned for an elected official who "had promised to appoint some of the local Chicanos to the police department." However, to his dismay they received only a three-month appointment, prompting him to print the words "Politicians, Phooey!"[280] The *Sport Page* continued to hold city officials accountable for not providing adequate recreational facilities for Mexican American youth. When the Mexican boys' softball league faced a shortage of sporting equipment the *Sport Page* stepped in to help by cosponsoring a fund-raiser with Carmelita Provision Company. Baseball editor Saul Toledo encouraged readers to "get behind this good cause and show the rest of the world that our race can take care of its own."[281] Martinez was also critical of the sports industry for not providing adequate medical care of injured and disabled athletes. Again, the *Sport Page* mobilized support for boxer Perfecto Lopez and baseball player Richard Maldonado who both went blind in separate accidents. Martinez encouraged readers to "help out our countrymen that are in need."[282] Fans could attend a dinner fund-raiser in their honor or purchase a discounted newspaper subscription from them.[283]

A closer examination of the articles and cartoons in the *Sport Page* revealed a problematic gender bias in its exclusive coverage of men's sports. Mexican American women appeared in beauty shop, cafe, and restaurant advertisements. For example, a Club Brazil ad featured a nearly topless woman sitting on a coconut holding a cocktail.[284] The place where women were frequently mentioned was in the "Café Society" section that covered the local music and entertainment scene. In a review of Daven's café, the *Sport Page* recommended dinner only to meet "the popular little girl" of Carmen "who is very good cook and you will enjoy some of her food."[285] After attending a boxing match, the newspaper recommended El Popo Club to listen to the best Latin music bands and meet the "most beautiful waitresses ready to serve you."[286] The newspaper suggested that women belonged in the kitchen, restaurants, or nightclubs to serve men, not on the diamond.

The *Sport Page* frequently used the terms "Latin" or "Chicano" when writing about athletes. Take for example Saul Toledo's baseball column where he cites a scheduling conflict between two baseball leagues over the use of Evergreen baseball diamond. Toledo refused to take sides and urged team managers to resolve their differences. Toledo reminded both leagues that fans "hope to see the best of the Latin baseball talent perform. Well we all know that we have more than nine outstanding Chicano baseball players in Muny [municipal] competition and, therefore we must make arrangements so that all Mexican players have an opportunity to play."[287] Since not all players were of Mexican descent, Toledo used a pan-Latino label to promote league unity.[288] Toledo also referred to ballplayers of Mexican descent born and raised in the United States as "Chicanos." Even though the term is used as a referent to the 1960s generation that fought for civil rights, the word was appropriated in the 1930s and 1940s by sports journalists to refer to younger Mexican American athletes. The *Sport Page* fostered the creation of forge hybrid identities in the sporting Mexican diaspora.

In 1950, *Sport Page* teamed up with *La Opinión* to form the Mexican Sports Writers Association (MSWA) to provide professional development opportunities and encourage younger Mexican Americans to pursue sports journalism (see Figure 6.9).[289] More importantly, the MSWA sought to pay tribute to the legendary sport stars of Greater Mexico. On November 25, 1951, the MSWA honored five of the "most famous Mexican boxers in fistic history of Los Angeles."[290] *La Opinión* conducted a citywide poll to generate the final list. The lengthy poll resulted in 14,395 votes for Enrique Bolaños, considered "the most popular modern-day Latin fighter," followed by 4,966 for Bert Colima, considered the "most popular of yesteryear," then Manuel Ortiz, former bantamweight champion of the world, who received 1,125 votes, and 1,004 votes for Alberto "Baby" Arizmendi, who had been declared "the Mexican boxer with the greatest all-time record." Additionally, Art Aragon received 674 votes and was declared the "best Mexican boxer of today."[291] The special tribute attracted more than three hundred boxing fans at Club Zarape on Sunset Boulevard, with MSWA member Gabriel "Hap" Navarro as master of ceremonies and featuring entertainment by Joaquin Garay, Rodolfo Hoyos, and Ruben Reyes (see Figure 6.10).[292] MSWA president Aurelio Garcia Jr. expressed his appreciation to "the top five Mexican fighters of all time," because "they dedicated the best year of their lives to the grilling and devastating processes of training and then fighting for purses which so many times do not even go to cover the most indispensable needs of their profession"[293] A photo of the five honorees with their trophies was featured in

FIGURE 6.9. Founding members of the Los Angeles Mexican Sports Writers Association. From Left to Right, Rodolfo García, Gabriel "Hap" Navarro (standing), Manuel "Midget" Martinez, Salvador Hernández Rojas (center), unknown persons standing on right, Luis Magaña is signing the official constitution next to Aurelio Garcia II. (Courtesy of the Lozano family/La Opinion Collection, The Huntington Library, San Marino, CA)

the *Los Angeles Times*, *La Opinión*, and *Sport Page*.[294] Mexican sportswriters recognized the importance of celebrating Mexican prizefighters as part of a larger struggle to challenge negative stereotypes about Mexican athletes and demand equitable treatment from the U.S. sporting press.

CONCLUSION

On September 16, 1951, *La Opinión* published a special anniversary edition with the sports page celebrating the "Golden Era of Sports" in Greater Mexico.[295] The newspaper listed baseball and boxing as the most popular sports, with their selection of sport heroes that produced a large fan base. One of these sports heroes was Bert Colima, the "unforgettable idol of idols" who retired on the same day as the newspaper's founding, who led the boxing list. Colima's name was followed by Alberto "Baby" Arizmendi, Rodolfo Casanova, Kid Azteca, Juan Zurita, Alfredo Gaona, David Velasco, Bobby Pacho, Art Aragon, and Ricardo Lemos. Atop the

FIGURE 6.10. Five famous Mexican boxers honored by the Los Angeles Mexican Sports Writers Association at Club Zarate on November 25, 1951. From left to right, Bert Colima, Art Aragon, Enrique Bolaños, Manuel Ortiz and Alberto Arizmendi. (Courtesy of the Lozano family/La Opinion Collection, The Huntington Library, San Marino, CA)

baseball list were the Almada brothers, Luis and Melo, followed by Jesus Flores and Joe Gonzalez, all of them starting their playing career at White Sox Park and ultimately reaching the major leagues. This list of all-male athletes was considered the "Idolos Mexicanos" (Mexican idols) in the eyes of both the local Mexican community and the Mexican nation.[296] Throughout the Mexican diaspora, newspaper coverage of these athletes presented a counternarrative to the negative stereotypes perpetuated by American writers and physical educators. This retrospective edition, however, erased female athletes from their shared memory, and their histories continue to be in the shadows of dominant historical narratives.

This chapter demonstrated that Mexican American women became empowered through sports—albeit limited to softball, baseball, tennis, and basketball—during the first half of the twentieth century and argued that Mexican American women adopted a "sportswoman" identity by developing senses of physical confidence and empowerment. Mexican American women used sports to exercise, travel, socialize, and develop their own networks of support. Compared to their male counterparts, female athletes had limited travel opportunities to develop transnational networks, yet they still managed to do so. These women challenged gender, class, and racial barriers imposed by dominant ideologies and institutions to create spaces of empowerment on the diamond and on the court. These sportswomen were forerunners to the women's movement and civil rights era that helped lead to the 1972 passing of Title IX, a landmark federal law that seeks to end sex discrimination and advance gender equity in athletics and sports programs.

Marge Villa's baseball tour throughout Latin America demonstrated the important role of women in the making of a sporting Mexican diaspora. Before the Cubans stepped foot on the diamond, there was the five-foot, two-inch Mexican American from Southern California who caught the eye of an AAGPBL scout. Villa joined the Kenosha Comets in 1946 and traveled throughout Latin America on a baseball exhibition tour.

In the postwar years, the MAU replaced MAASC as the leading sports organization in the region and state. MAU offered returning veterans opportunities to return to the basketball court, diamond, and tennis court. MAU's leaders Pedro Despart and Ray Sánchez forged transnational ties with northern Baja California's Physical Education Department to organize cross-border baseball, softball, basketball, and boxing competitions. MAU was effective in recruiting Hollywood celebrities to publicize sporting events and secured business sponsorships for championship trophies. In addition, MAU worked closely with *La Opinión* sportswriters, Midget Martinez's *Sport Page*, and MAM to advocate for more sports and recreational opportunities and to advance a broader civil rights agenda in Greater Mexico. MAU was not shy about highlighting the athletic talent of Mexican American athletes like boxer Manuel Ortiz, pitcher Jess Flores, and tennis champion Richard "Pancho" González. González emerged from the Los Angeles public tennis courts to become a national tennis champion and role model to Mexican American youth. González helped to integrate the sport and encourage more people of color to play this traditionally white sport.

CONCLUSION

After living in Washington State for almost a decade, I could not wait to return to Dodger Stadium. So when my cousin organized a family reunion there on July 31, 2013, I was the first to sign up. Returning to Dodger Stadium brought back fond memories of Dodger Dogs, picturesque views of the Downtown skyline and sunset over palm trees, and the electrifying atmosphere of playing against the Yankees. Upon my return, what surprised me most was the increased Latino/a fan base, which in 2015 reached 2.1 out of 3.9 million fans. Latin music was now blasting from the loudspeakers and rowdy fans were cheering for their favorite Latino Dodger. I was astonished by how many fans were wearing "Los Doyers" T-shirts. A new generation of Latino fans have appropriated the mispronunciation of "Dodgers" by their immigrant parents and claimed it for their team. By 2013, the management of the Dodgers had jumped on this nostalgia and trademarked the hybrid word in an effort to sell more merchandise.

When I joined the faculty of California State University Channel Islands (CSUCI) in 2008, I became involved with the Latino Baseball History Project (LBHP) and got a chance to meet my baseball hero. In 2016, Fernando Valenzuela dropped by unannounced at a Latino baseball community event at Mitla Café, San Bernardino's oldest Mexican restaurant that had inspired Glen Bell to found Taco Bell and where patrons joined baseball players for a postgame meal. Everyone was excited to hear from Fernando, who spoke about the significance of preserving the history of Latinos in the national pastime. Organized by the Smithsonian Institution's National Museum of American History and California State University San Bernardino, this event sought to collect stories, photos, and artifacts for a national exhibition on the history of U.S. Latinos and Latinas in baseball.

When it was my turn to shake his large hand and pose for a photo with him, I told him how much he inspired me and my immigrant family to work hard and excel in school, especially when my coach told me I was no good at playing ball. He smiled and nodded approvingly at my choice. Fernando Valenzuela taught me to feel proud about being both Mexican and American without having to sell my cultural soul. When I met Fernando, he spoke English yet was very proud of his Mexican heritage. He confirmed for me that I did not have to run from my Mexican heritage but should embrace it, while also embracing American culture and, especially, its favorite pastime. Fernando made it okay for many of us to be Doyers fans. He also helped open doors for other Latino Dodgers such as Nomar Garciaparra and Manny Ramírez, who launched the Mannymanía phenomenon. And today we have Adrián González, who helped spearhead the "Ponle Acento" campaign in 2015 to add the correct accents and tildes to the names of Latino players on their jerseys. Major League Baseball accepted the demand and even put an accent on its own logo. As for the future? Julio Urías, another left-handed pitcher from Sonora, burst onto the scene on May 27, 2016, at the same age as Valenzuela. We love to think Urías, a twenty-year-old prodigy, is destined to become a future star. Yet for some of us Fernando Valenzuela will always remain the first.

While most people remember Valenzuela, the dazzling left-hander from Sonora who became one of the best pitchers of the 1980s, few remember names such as Melo Almada, Chile Gomez, Joe Gonzalez, and Jess Flores, big leaguers from the 1930s and 1940s. Even fewer remember the minor leaguers and semiprofessionals like Alonzo Orozco, Dave Salazar, Ernie Salazar, Lakes Lagunas, and many others who have made important contributions to the national pastime. To recover the baseball legacy of these relatively unknown ballplayers is one of the reasons that the LBHP exists today. In 2005, historians Richard Santillan and Francisco Balderrama collaborated with librarian César Caballero and museum curator Terry Cannon to organize the first Mexican American baseball exhibition at Cal State Los Angeles.[1] Since then, LBHP has relocated to Cal State San Bernardino's library, where scholars have hosted player reunions, first-pitch ceremonies, public symposia, and photo collection events as well as publishing over twenty-five books under the Mexican American Baseball series.[2] The LBHP has tapped into memories of surviving ballplayers who are now in their eighties and nineties to receive long-overdue recognition from families, museums, libraries, historical societies, and the academic community.

In 2015, I collaborated with curator Anna Bermúdez from the Museum of Ventura County and CSUCI student Juan Canchola-Ventura to uncover a rich history of Mexican American baseball in Ventura County.[3] Because historians have been slow to recognize women's participation in sports, I wanted to ensure they were represented in this public history project. On March 2, 2015, I organized an exhibition and panel discussion with Mexican American women who played softball and baseball in the 1940s and 1950s and tested and redefined gender norms within their family and community. During the panel eighty-four-year-old Ernestina "Ernie" Navarro Hosaki shared memories of playing for the Oxnard Merchanettes: "When someone told me that I threw like a girl . . . I took it as a compliment since I had a strong arm and could throw out runners."[4] Also on the panel was ninety-two-year-old Margaret "Marge" Villa Cryan, who started playing with the Orange Lionettes and later joined the All-American Girls Professional Baseball League. Villa Cryan recalled, "Women at that time were not looked at as a sportsman because we were supposed to be ladies, but I was far from being a lady. I started playing baseball with my older brothers and never stopped."[5] Both proudly embraced the "sportswomen" label, one that recognizes their multilayered identity and struggles to find opportunities to play ball.[6] Listening in the audience were young Latina girls from local softball teams who were inspired by Navarro and Villa. After the panel, they patiently waited in line to meet them and get their baseball autographed. These female athletes not only defied traditional gender roles—precisely through their athletic participation—but also helped advance gender equity in sports at all levels.

When I asked Jessica Mendoza to write the foreword to our book, she graciously accepted despite her busy broadcasting duties as the new ESPN baseball analyst.[7] On August 25, 2015, Mendoza became the first woman to call an ESPN MLB game. To have a Latina calling national games for a major men's sport (instead of being a sideline reporter) was a major step in the right direction for gender equity in sports. The backlash came quick, however, like a mean fastball aimed at the batter. Mike Bell, a popular Atlanta sports radio host, bluntly stated, "Really? A women's softball slugger as guest analyst on MLB Wildcard Game? Once again ESPN is too frigging cute for their own good." He continued, "You guys are telling me there isn't a more qualified baseball player ESPN can use, than a softball player? Gimme a break!" Bell referred to Mendoza as "Tits McGhee." In response to Bell's comments, Mendoza followed Michelle Obama's dictum, "When they go low, we go high." Mendoza related to the media, "At the end of the day, I don't care about ignorant people. It's one thing if he attacks me because he didn't like the job I did. That, I can understand." The backlash against Mendoza reveals the deeply entrenched sexism in sports that continues to reify baseball as a "man's sport."[8]

Mendoza is not only a pioneer for women's sports, education, and human rights but also a staunch advocate for Latina girls playing sports. As an inductee into the International Latin Sports Hall of Fame, she speaks publicly about the importance of family in encouraging Latinas to play sports. Mendoza wrote, "Growing up with my father, Gil Mendoza meant spending hours on baseball fields when he was the head coach at Moorpark College. I felt a great comfort with my dad and sensed early on his deep passion for the game. His love of the game closely entwined his Mexican heritage and upbringing."[9] In an interview, Mendoza discussed the importance of fighting against gender barriers that hold Latinas back from participation in sports: "I find that there are still a lot of traditional cultural roles for females—a lot of pressure for young girls to be around the family, help with siblings, help with meals, be kind of the rock of the household rather than doing extracurricular activities like sports."[10] Although it is common to blame the family for a lack of Latina sports participation, research-

ers have found that when school officials and coaches have made efforts to educate parents about the long-term academic and health benefits of sports for Latina
girls, the families have often supported their daughters' athletic pursuits.[11]

THE MAKING OF A SPORTING MEXICAN DIASPORA

In this book I have argued that Mexican-origin males and females in the United
States have used sports to empower themselves and their communities by developing and sustaining transnational networks with Mexico. I have used the concept
of diaspora to frame the sporting experiences of Mexican nationals, Mexican
immigrants, and Mexican Americans as they forged identities, communities, and
networks across the U.S.-Mexico border. The rise of global sports has increased
attention to the migration of sports talent from third world to first world countries. Major sports leagues in first world countries recruit players from third
world countries to strengthen their domestic teams, thus producing what John
Bale has termed a "brawn drain."[12] In order to understand the international
migration of sport talent into and out of Latin America, sport historian Joseph
Arbena reminds us, "it [is] important to study the dynamics from both sides,
that is, both the forces which push sports figures out of their home country and
those complementary forces which pull them to other lands."[13] National borders
cannot keep athletes from competing abroad in an era when global sports is a
multibillion-dollar industry. In *Globalizing Sport*, historian Barbara Keys asserts
that the 1930s was a critical period for the United States, Germany, and the Soviet
Union in taking sports to a global level.[14] I would add that Mexico also sought
to use the 1932 Olympic Games and its connection with México de afuera sporting organizations to promote national ideologies at home and abroad and move
to global prominence in the international arena.

For the purposes of this study, I prioritized five dimensions that make up the
sporting Mexican diaspora. The first dimension focuses on the U.S. imperial
hegemony over Mexico that has led to physical, political, and economic displacement of the Mexican diaspora. This neocolonial relationship has influenced
Mexico's sports development from the YMCA movement in the early 1900s to
Good Neighbor sports diplomacy during World War II. The YMCA used sports
and physical education in an attempt to convert Mexican middle-class males
into muscular Christians. This effort was partially successful. While some YMCA
secretaries advanced into leadership positions within the organization, others
took advantage of these sport programs for empowerment of younger members
in their community. The YMCA-led Mexican Youth Conferences in Southern
California became the forerunners of the Mexican American Movement that
encouraged members to improve themselves through education and athletics.

During World War II, the Office of Inter-American Affairs Sports Office used
a "soft power" approach to further U.S. political and economic dominance over

Mexico and Latin America. For example, the office sent U.S. college football coaches to teach "good sportsmanship" to Mexican university students. Instead of accepting the desired message of U.S. government officials, Mexican athletes took advantage of the coaching missions, sporting exchanges, and touring opportunities to show off their athletic talent. Through their participation in U.S.-sponsored goodwill sports programs, Mexicans helped grow and expand the sporting Mexican diaspora. The uneven sports development in both countries has meant that athletes receive better coaching and training in the United States compared to Mexico. Despite more sports opportunities in the United States, Mexican immigrants and Mexican Americans have encountered racial prejudice and discrimination on the playing field, in stadiums, and in the sporting press.

The second dimension considers the importance of diasporic sporting networks necessary for economic and emotional survival. These networks extended beyond the local and national levels, allowing athletes and touring teams to crisscross countries to compete in international sporting exchanges. The Mexican Athletic Association of Southern California (MAASC) and the Mexican Athletic Union (MAU) were two Southern California organizations that forged transnational ties with Mexico's sport federations.[15] In many ways, these amateur athletic organizations acted like hometown associations where Mexican men used sports organizations to enhance their political status in relation to the Mexican state.[16] These amateur sports organizations built a transnational network of coaches, managers, promoters, fans and athletes that linked the development of sports in Los Angeles and Mexico. Both organizations pressed government officials, from the city to federal level, to offer more sporting opportunities for Mexican youth to prevent juvenile delinquency. This transnational sporting network was a lost opportunity for the American sports industry. U.S. professional sport teams failed to recruit and develop Mexican talent. Not until the 1980s, when Fernando Valenzuela appeared on the sports scene, did the U.S. sports industry begin to take notice.

These transnational sporting networks shaped political activism. Unlike the iconic black power salute at the 1968 Olympic Games, Mexican and Mexican Americans established grassroots activist organizations focused on individual and collective empowerment to challenge systems of oppression. The great majority of athletes played amateur sports for their neighborhood club, community group, and city league and in the process learned good teamwork, leadership, and sportsmanship, skills transferable to other areas in life. For example, former UCLA track runner and MAASC secretary Juan Acevedo became the first Latino appointed to the California Youth Authority. MAU president Pedro Despart organized cross-border sports competitions that helped to extend his political network when he ran for the California State Assembly. The synergy of sports, politics, and culture enabled Mexican-origin athletes to challenge constraints imposed on their lives and in so doing redefine political claims to freedom and equality. As George Lipsitz reminds us, "The capacity to envision places where everybody can be somebody can be of tremendous value to everyone in this society."[17]

The third dimension conceptualizes sports as a racial project in which the federal government, the sports industry, sportswriters, and city officials played significant roles in the racialization of Mexican athletes. I have shown how Mexican prizefighters navigated an increasingly rigid U.S. immigration regime that prohibited border entry because they supposedly threatened the livelihood of Euro-American boxers. U.S. immigration officials also accused Mexican prizefighters of using "fraudulent contracts" to enter the U.S. boxing arena. Additionally, crossing the U.S.-Mexico border was not easy for Mexican baseball players who were suspected of violating immigration law. This did not stop barnstorming teams from finding opportunities to play ball across borders and producing some of the best Mexican baseball players who entered the U.S. major leagues. In other words, "brown" athletes threatened white hegemonic masculinity and could not be trusted in the sporting world. This pattern continues today, with Dominican baseball players accused of using "forged birth certificates" or Mexican boxers blamed for using performance-enhancing drugs to increase their chances of winning. Considered neither white nor black, Mexican-origin athletes occupied an in-between racial position within the U.S. sports industry. Under certain circumstances they could use their mixed background and legal classification as white to gain access to the sporting world. But the great majority of Mexican athletes were placed in a "brown" category according to their nationality, citizenship, and race.[18]

While sports has actively contributed to racial formation of Mexican athletes, it can also be used to challenge and transform the foundations of racial formation in American society. Mexican athletes used their performance and celebrity status to challenge prevailing racial assumptions about their community and nation. Furthermore, Mexican and Mexican American sportswriters played a crucial role in crafting a "counternarrative," projecting positive images of athletes and teams representing their community and nation. The *Sport Page* and the Mexican Sportswriters Association pushed back against negative portrayals of Mexican athletes and highlighted the athletic achievements of the Mexican diaspora as a step toward racial equity.

The fourth dimension includes the relationship between masculinity, femininity, and sporting cultures in the lives of Mexican male and female athletes in order to understand how they negotiated gender identities in the sporting world. The YMCA encouraged Mexican and Mexican American boys and men to embrace a "muscular Christian" ideology through physical education and sports. Mexican-origin YMCA leaders rejected the religious message but welcomed the sporting opportunities to affirm and assert a respectable masculinity and leadership conferences to advance racial solidarity in an effort to achieve equality.

Mexican and Mexican American boxers negotiated a range of masculinities from a rough masculinity that emphasized roughness and violence inside the ring and hypersexualized treatment of women outside the ring to a more respectable masculinity that emphasized self-discipline, compassion, and familial and community responsibilities.

Mexican women negotiated a range of sporting femininities from a respectable heterosexual form to a marginalized muscular form that associated them with lesbian sexuality. Compared to their male counterparts, Mexican women faced real gender barriers and limitations, which make their athletic achievements ever more remarkable. They did more than compete, however; they used sports to expand their social network and develop cross-cultural relationships. In this process, they helped redefine gender roles within their families and communities and the sporting world. This sporting network, however, was constrained by familial pressures and patriarchal forces that limited their freedom to travel outside of their hometowns. There were some exceptions, like Marge Villa Cryan, a light-skinned Mexican American who could pass as white and join the All-American Girls Professional Baseball League (AAGPBL). With family support she was allowed to travel to Latin America on a barnstorming exhibition tour. The AAGPBL insisted that female players maintain sexualized femininity on and off the field for male spectators. The male sporting world was more comfortable with women in auxiliary roles as spectators, girlfriends, and "baseball widows" who looked after homes and children while their husbands practiced or traveled for competitions. More threatening were Mexican female boxers like Margarita "La Maya" Montes, who displayed a "muscular femininity" that prompted the Mexican government to ban women's boxing for over fifty years. Nevertheless, Mexican-origin women were both supporters of and participants in the making of a sporting Mexican diaspora

The fifth and last dimension includes the diasporic consciousness that informed the construction of hybrid sporting identities. As I have shown, Mexican athletes in the United States were not fully accepted in either country but rather occupied an in-between zone of ambiguity, creativity, and hybridity. When Mexican American peloteros and peloteras faced racial restrictions and segregation in ballparks in the United States, they journeyed to Mexico, where they could reclaim their roots. They were welcomed for their talent and skills but sometimes were criticized for not speaking Spanish or being a "pocho or pocha," an Americanized Mexican who forgot their heritage. These and many other athletes discovered and embraced the cultural dimensions of their Mexicanness at home and abroad. In other words, they can enter and exit a Mexican identity depending on the sociohistorical circumstances and end up creating new hybrid identities. The term "Chicano" was one of these labels that young Mexican American athletes were starting to embrace in the 1930s and 1940s, even though it did not become popular until the 1960s. The Spanish-language sporting press referred to young male athletes of Mexican descent as "Chicanos" or "Chicanitos." These athletes navigated the cultural tensions within a sporting world that emphasized American values and norms while also maintaining aspects of Mexican culture and identity in the diaspora.

Much work remains to be done on the intersections of sports and diaspora in relation to the Mexican population. More research is needed on Mexican female athletes at the national and international level to better understand their sporting identities.[19] Additionally, when most people think about the most popular sport in Mexico, they consider soccer or *fútbol*. While it is true that fútbol is wildly popular today, this was not always the case. More research is needed on the early history and development of fútbol in Greater Mexico. Another area that needs further exploration is the role of coaches. Today, most people know of Tom Flores, who led the Oakland Raiders to a Super Bowl title, and Ozzie Guillén, who brought Chicago a World Series title, but few know the history of Latino/a coaches in high school, collegiate, and amateur sports. While many recognize Sal Castro as an inspiring teacher and important leader of the Chicano/a student movement, they often forget that he was also a playground supervisor, coach, and athletic director. He coached a Little League baseball team in his early years and as a high school athletic director coached students and athletes to run for leadership positions and organize a mass walkout. Coaches teach more than the fundamentals of the sport, instilling lessons about discipline, fairness, leadership, and teamwork that become instrumental to success in life.

TOWARD A SPORTING LATINO DIASPORA

Although Latinos and Latinas have been at the core of the American sporting landscape, their history and contributions have not been fully recognized. As the Latino/a population continues to grow, their numbers have not translated into power and influence in U.S. professional sports. The 2017 Major League Baseball season had the highest ever percentage of Latino players at 31.0 percent.[20] While the Latinization of baseball has reached the players, it has not reached into the managerial and front office levels.[21] In boxing, Latinos have produced a long line of champion fighters, with over two hundred coming from Mexico. The Latinization of boxing is reflected in both the Latino dominance in the lighter weight categories and pay-per-view ratings.[22] Latina boxers have also entered the ring despite facing numerous obstacles to train and get on televised boxing cards.

In the past three decades soccer has finally emerged in the United States, growing in parallel with the U.S. Latino population. The hosting of World Cup in 1994 was a big factor, but so was the fact the over 85 percent of the U.S. Latino population originated from countries where soccer was the dominant sport. This change has affected my family, including the younger generation preferring youth soccer over baseball and watching and cheering for the Mexican national team (El Tri) in big soccer tournaments (World Cup, Copa America, Gold Cup), my father religiously following Mexico's premier soccer league, Liga Mexicana, and my older brother travels with his soccer-loving friends to every World Cup to cheer for El Tri. However, the rapid growth of the Latino population and of soccer has also brought out nativist forces, intent on cracking down on illegal immigration on the soccer fields. For example, in A Home on the Field, Paul Cuadros writes about his high school soccer team in North Carolina, which faced initial resistance from school officials, athletes, and the local population until the Jets won the state championship.[23] Additionally, in 2008 Immigration and Customs Enforcement (ICE) officials detained Latino soccer players en route to their games in Prince William County, Virginia, thus forcing the cancelation of league matches.[24] This is happening not only in areas unaccustomed to immigration and soccer but also in Southern California. Costa Mesa city leaders encouraged their police force to check players' legal status and fine groups playing pickup soccer without a permit.[25] Although Latino fans have been the driving force for soccer's popularity in the United States, they have not been well represented on U.S. professional team rosters and coaching staffs. In 1978, former soccer coach Horacio R. Fonseca called out U.S. professional soccer's "Anti-Latino Game Plan" by pointing out that only a select few Latino players are selected to the national team despite a large untapped soccer talent in the Latino community.[26] Fonseca's early warning continues to fall on the deaf ears of U.S. soccer officials.[27] While Major League Soccer improved to over 20 percent of Latin American players in 2016, the U.S. national team has consistently missed out in recruiting Latino players. Soccer America's Paul Gardner recently criticized U.S. soccer's failure to acknowledge the Latino presence and warned that "a well-organized nationwide system that virtually ignores homegrown Latino talent is asking for trouble. Not only is it absurdly self-defeating, it smacks of discrimination, and it provides significant backing for the view that Latino soccer counts for little and can be ignored."[28]

The so-called pay to play system in American soccer and failure to send scouts to Latino neighborhood parks are to blame for the lack of Latino players. Parents cannot afford to pay thousands of dollars for their kids to play on elite club soccer teams. While U.S. soccer scouts skip over Latino neighborhoods, their Mexican Football Federation counterparts have traveled north to recruit Mexican American players with dual citizenship.[29] Take for example Edgar Castillo, who was born and raised in Las Cruces, New Mexico, and now plays in Liga Mexicana. In a New York Times interview, Castillo disgruntledly admitted, "It would have been nice to be from the U.S. and play for the U.S. . . . I was wondering what the U.S. was thinking, why they were not calling me."[30] Because of U.S. soccer's failure to tap into homegrown Latino talent, many are now finding opportunities in Mexico. Mexican American female soccer players are also finding more opportunities in Mexico, helping its national team qualify for the 2012 FIFA Women's World Cup.[31]

Recently Mexico's secretariat of foreign affairs created the Program for Mexican Communities Abroad to cultivate and nurture long-term relations with the Mexican diaspora in the United States.[32] The program sponsors sports activities like soccer, basketball, and baseball "as a way to bring families together, stimulate sharing, and keep young people healthy and out of trouble."[33] From March 29 to April 4, 2010, Mexico's sports minister organized the Sports Games for Mexicans Abroad in Los Angeles in search of potential Olympic athletes with family links to Mexico who could represent Mexico at the Olympic Games.[34] In 2008 when Mexican Olympians came home from Beijing with only three medals, only one more than in 1932, the Mexican government made recruiting athletes in the Mexican diaspora a priority. While some critics argue that U.S.-born athletes who compete in Mexico are turning their backs on their country, this is not the case. In sports participation, Mexican-origin athletes occupy an "in-between" position, often with dual citizenship that allows them to navigate multiple cultures and contexts, creating hybrid sporting identities within the sporting diaspora.

In a 2016 *Rolling Stone* article, Juan Vidal asked, "Why Does American Sports Have a Latino Problem?"[35] Vidal cited a Nielsen report that found that 94 percent of Latino males are sports fans and 56 percent are avid fans and are likely to attend a sporting event at least once a week.[36] Although Latinos make up a large fan base in basketball and football, they are not reflected on team rosters. Although college enrollment figures have gradually increased for Latinos, they remain concentrated in community colleges where sports scholarships are not available. An innovative and more intentional approach is needed to increase the numbers of Latinos in competitive sports. The one professional sport without a Latino presence is certainly tennis.

At Washington State University I started researching the history of Richard "Pancho" González and realized that in order to fully understand his life story I also needed to play tennis.[37] So I found a retired WSU tennis coach to give me lessons at his home court. Over time I gradually improved and fell in love with recreational tennis. Since 2008, I have been a member of the U.S. Tennis Association (USTA) and play weekly with my team, the Mission Oaks Warriors. I wish I could have started earlier, but in high school I was discouraged from playing tennis because it was too expensive, too white, and too unmanly. I believed all these misconceptions until González taught me otherwise.

Growing up in a working-class Mexican American family, González had no formal tennis coaching, trained only at public courts, and despite being barred from junior tournaments, still managed to win back-to-back national titles. Indeed, he could have won more if he had not turned pro so early. Because Grand Slam tournaments were reserved for amateurs, González joined the pro tour and barnstormed across the globe to support his young family. He dominated the sport of tennis, winning 124 ATP professional tournaments and holding the number-one world ranking between 1952 and 1961. He displayed a competitive drive and self-confidence that resembled that of the heavyweight boxer Muhammad Ali. "I'll play any one of them any day of the week, and I'll bet on myself," declared González to the *Los Angeles Times*, adding that "I'm willing to play them any place, any time and for whatever they want—if they dare."[38] He broke the stereotype of the servile Mexican that irritated the tennis establishment. He was dismissed by tennis promoters including Jack Kramer, who doctored González's image in a tennis program booklet so he appeared white with blond hair.[39] When the Open Era arrived in 1968, González was forty years old and was inducted into the International Hall of Fame, but rather than sit on the sidelines he returned to play in Grand Slam tournaments. On June 25, 1969, González defeated Charlie Pasarell in one of the longest and most memorable matches in Wimbledon history, lasting five hours and twenty minutes and spanning 112 games. After retiring in 1974, González accepted a coaching job at Caesar's Palace in Las Vegas, and on July 4, 1994, he died of stomach cancer. Although his competitive zeal and the longevity of his playing career make this Mexican American athlete a strong candidate for one of the greatest tennis players of his era, recognition from the sports world is long overdue.

Today, when I ask people to identify a U.S.-born Latino professional tennis player, most respond with a blank face. However, they can identify top-ranked players from Spain, Argentina, Brazil, Chile, Colombia, and Ecuador. Despite the popularity of tennis in Latin America and Spain as well as the international stardom of Rafael Nadal, the fast-growing demographic in the United States is still not represented in professional tennis.[40] An important distinction between Latin American and U.S.-born Latino tennis players is necessary, however. Unlike Latin American players who learn the sport in their home country, Latinos/as who are born or raised in the United States encounter multiple obstacles. According to the Pew Research Center, Latinos make up 57 million or 17 percent of the U.S. population, but their numbers in American tennis remain staggeringly low to nonexistent.[41] Filling this void requires a new approach toward finding Latino and Latina talent. As Patrick McEnroe, director of player development for the USTA, frankly stated, "We should have huge numbers of Hispanic kids playing tennis in places like Miami, Southern California, New York, and Chicago, and we do not. Those kids are playing soccer and other sports. My guess is it's an economic issue, and cultural issue. We are doing much better with African Americans and Asian-Americans."[42] This bewilderment stems from the missing history of Latinos and Latinas in tennis. I hope this book has helped correct this omission.

Sports continues to be an important area in fostering a sense of community across borders, despite strict immigration policies. In the award-winning documentary *Sixth Section* (2003), a group of Mexican migrants in Upstate New York feverishly worked overtime to raise money to build a baseball stadium three thousand miles away in their hometown of Boquerón, near Puebla, Mexico.[43] These transnational migrants raised over fifty thousand dollars for a two-thousand-seat stadium, even though strict immigration laws prevented them from returning to play or watch a game there. To them, this baseball stadium meant more than a recreational or entertainment venue; it became a symbol of public recognition and a means toward forging a transnational identity across borders.

U.S.-Mexico relations are becoming increasingly strained with President Donald Trump's repeated attacks against Mexican immigrants as criminals, rapists, and drug dealers, threatening the future of the sporting Mexican diaspora. Trump's proposal—building a wall along the U.S.-Mexico border—will hurt plans for U.S. professional league expansion into Mexico. Professional Mexican soccer players would prefer to play on top European soccer clubs rather than on Major League Soccer teams where they may not feel welcome. Trump's draconian immigration enforcement and detention and deportation policies have led to the separation of mixed-status families, hindering their full integration into American society.[44] As a result, these policies will hamper the efforts of the U.S. sports industry to recruit future Latino and Latina athletes and efforts to increase their fan bases.[45] The prospects of finding and developing a future Leo Messi in the Mexican diaspora look grim under this presidency. The broader tensions in the Trump era have infected high school football games. At an Orange County football game between a predominantly white Aliso Niguel high school and a predominately Latino high school in Santa Ana erupted into racial tension.[46] The Santa Ana principal accused Aliso Niguel's fans of racism by intimidating his team with signs that read "We Love White" and "Build the Wall," with fans chanting "USA," "USA" during the game. Unfortunately, pro-Trump signs have become the new norm at sporting events where fans can express racist signs and chants without consequences. The Santa Ana team threatened to walk off the field if the chants did not stop. Taking their cue from Colin Kaepernick, who sparked the NFL player movement against police brutality, Latino/a athletes are finding ways to resist on and off the field. To show solidarity with black football players, Latino football players have begun kneeling during the playing of the national anthem.[47]

ACKNOWLEDGMENTS

Every weekend I played sports at Arroyo Verde Park in Ventura, California with my brothers and cousins. My parents encouraged us to join Little League Baseball, even though they could not attend because of their labor-intensive jobs. To be honest, I was not a very good ballplayer compared to my older brother who continued playing in high school, but this did not keep me from being a baseball fan, especially when Fernando Valenzuela burst onto the scene, forever changing my view of Latinos in sports. Sports was not on my academic radar. For my dissertation I focused on the labor and leisure experiences of Mexican immigrants and their descendants in the southern California citrus town of Corona, California. However, when conducting oral history interviews, I kept hearing more and more about their playing or attending baseball and softball matches. This prompted me to devote a chapter to sports and baseball clubs in my first book.

When researching my first book, I interviewed Ray Delgadillo who told me about how his professional baseball career abruptly ended in Mexico when he was drafted into the U.S. military during World War II. He decided to play in Mexico because he faced racial discrimination on the U.S. baseball diamonds. When he tried out for a professional baseball team, he was told that he excelled in all areas of the game, but because he was "Mexican" and "too small" he was denied a contract. Instead, he played professional baseball in Mexico for two seasons until he was drafted. He continued playing while stationed in Australia, New Guinea and the Philippines. After the war, he joined the Riverside City College Tigers, becoming one of the most skilled players on the team. Delgadillo's story encouraged me to rethink the national pastime beyond national borders.

I traveled to Mexico City during my sabbatical to find more information about Mexico's sports history. Guided by the pioneering work of late Joseph Arbena and suggestions from Keith Brewster, I found information in the presidential files at the Archivo General de la Nación, the newspaper collection at Hemeroteca and consular documents at the Secretaria de Relaciones Exteriores. During my research trip I was accompanied by WSU colleagues Luz Maria Gordillo and E. Mark Moreno who helped me navigate the research permits and transportation to AGN. *Mil gracias* to uncle J. Encarnacion "Chonito" Alamillo and cousins Mario and Gerardo who fed me at their popular restaurant, Quesadillas la Abuelita Coni Polanco. I owe a debt of gratitude to Romeo Guzman and Alina Méndez who put aside their own research to help me find additional documents at SRE and Hemeroteca. Thank you to historian Miguel Esparza for sharing his research on Mexico City baseball.

In the United States, this book benefited from the invaluable assistance of librarians and archivists. Shirley Ito graciously helped me find material at the LA84 Foundation's large sports library collection. Ryan Bean and the friendly staff at the Kautz Family YMCA Archives at the University of Minnesota helped me locate materials on YMCA's International Work in Mexico. Thanks also to Linnea M. Anderson, archivist at the Social Welfare History Archives at the University of Minnesota. Finding information on YMCA's work with Mexican immigrants proved more difficult, however. Thankfully, Becky Ruud at the Wardman Library at Whittier College allowed me access to the uncatalogued collection of the Pacific Southwest Area Council of YMCAs. Little did I know that I would find important information about sports in the Immigration and Naturalization Service (INS) Records the National Archives in Washington, D.C. Thanks to Bill Creech for helping access immigration records. Nancy Liliana Godoy-Powell and Christine Marin at Chicano/a Research Collection at Arizona State University were very helpful in finding more information on women softball players. Ruth McCormick at the Riverside Public Library helped with research on Emma Galvan. Many thanks to Corey Schroeder, interlibrary loan librarian at Broome Library, who fulfilled all my requests in timely fashion and tolerated my overdue returns. Monica Pereira secured a quiet space in the Broome Library for me to write and helped to check the accuracy of my sources. To find photographs and images was not easy; I had to rely on the expertise of archivists across the country. Thank you to Jon Reed at the Montebello Historical Society, who shared photographs of Marge Villa Cryan. Special thanks to Xaviera S. Flores archivist and librarian at UCLA Chicano Studies Research Center for fulfilling my last-minute requests. Jackie Beckey was helpful in finding images from their collections at the Huntington Library. I'm grateful for the generosity of Mario Longoria, who shared his photos and documents of the All-American Girls Professional Baseball League. Thanks to Eduardo B. Almada, who graciously shared his photo collection of his father. A big thanks to Jorge Moraga, who took time from his own research to locate player files for me at the National Baseball Hall of Fame.

When I returned to southern California, I became part of the Latino Baseball History Project (LBHP), a grassroots documentation project that seeks to collect, preserve, and promote the rich history of Latinos and Latinas in baseball and softball. Thanks to Richard Santillán, Francisco Balderrama, Terry Cannon, and César Caballero for inviting me to join the advisory board. Richard has been incredibly supportive of this book by sharing contacts and research, and inviting me to join player reunions and panel discussions. It has been a pleasure working with Teresa Santillan, Tomas Benítez, Al Ramos, Rod Martinez, Maria García, Sandra Uribe, Chris Docter, Manuel Veron, Mark A. Ocegueda and Monserrath Segura, who helped me tremendously with leads and photos for this book. Special thanks to Anna Bermúdez and Juan J. Canchola-Ventura for being wonderful collaborators on local exhibits and coauthors of two books. Thank you, Erin Curtis, at LA Plaza de Cultura y Artes and curators Margie Salazar-Porzio and Steve Velasquez at the National Museum of American History for inviting me to consult on their Latino baseball exhibitions. I am grateful to students Maria Marzicola, Rafael Gonzalez, Daisey Valadez-Miguel, and Gabriela Jasso, who assisted with conducting oral history interviews and curating an exhibition on Mexican American Women in Baseball and Softball. Thanks to Jessica Mendoza for supporting this exhibition and writing a foreword to the Ventura County baseball book.

I was able to meet former players and their families who opened their homes to me for an interview or answering my questions. Thanks go to Ernestine "Ernie" Navarro Hosaki, Margie Villa Cryan, Valentina Hernandez, Ramona Valenzuela, Maggie Salazar, Carlos Salazar, Robert Lagunas Jr., Guadalberto Valadez, and Lupe Anguiano, Elisa Orozco-O'Neil, and Angie Salazar-Capela, and Alonzo "Al" Orozco.

This book would not have been possible without the support of my colleagues for their engaging conversations and critical feedback. For their intellectual support and mentorship, I thank Gilbert González, Raul Fernandez, Jeff Garcilazo, Rodolfo Torres, Vicki Ruiz, Antonia Castañeda, Mario García, Carlos Cortes, Pedro Castillo, Al Camarillo, Devra Weber, Douglas Monroy, Zaragoza Vargas, Tomás Almaguer, Emilio Zamora, José Limón, David Montejano, George Lipsitz and who helped mentor me in the world of academia. Betsy Jameson has been an incredible mentor, always supporting my scholarship and encouraging me to take up leadership positions in western history. I was fortunate to have Matt Garcia as series editor, for providing critical feedback that helped strengthen the manuscript. Adrian Burgos Jr. encouraged me to pursue the transnational dimensions of sports. Mark Dyreson offered important feedback on the Olympic Games. Lorena Oropeza helped sharpen my ideas and arguments. George Sánchez invited to speak with his seminar on global baseball. Elizabeth Escobedo provided invaluable feedback on Mexican American female athletes. Rudy Mondragon offered invaluable feedback on my boxing chapter. Chris Bolsmann invited me to present in his Sports Studies Seminar Series that helped me sharpen my argument. Priscilla Leiva provided insightful feedback on my introduction. Thanks also to sports scholars who supported this book include Samuel Regalado, Jorge Iber, Arnoldo de León, Ignacio García, Luis Alvarez, Frank Guridy, John Bloom, Bernardo Ramirez Rios, Louis Moore, Jennifer Doyle, Michael Willard, and Krista Comer.

I am grateful for my colleagues at Washington State University who first encouraged me to pursue a study on Latino/as in sports. Thank you, Linda Heidenreich, Francisco Tamayo, Lisa Guerrero, David J. Leonard, C. Richard King, Carmen Lugo-Lugo, Thabiti Lewis and Victor Villanueva. Other colleagues across the country offered comments, suggestions and questions—and most of all encouragement, including but not limited to Gabriela Arredondo, Kelly Lytle Hernández, Miroslava Chávez-García, Verónica Castillo-Munoz, Theresa Gaye Johnson, Ralph Armbruster-Sandoval, Dolores Inés Casillas, Michael Innis-Jiménez, Lilia Fernandez, Abigail Rosas, Ana Rosas, Lydia Otero, Gilda Ochoa, Tomas Summers Sandoval, Alexandro Gradilla, David James Gonzalez, Sergio Gonzalez, Felipe Hinojosa, Rudy Guevara, Mario Sifuentez, Jimmy Patiño, Max Krochmal, Josh Sides, Mireya Loza, Mike Amezcua, Steve Pitti, Elliott Young, Gerado Cadava, Rosina Lozano, Lori A. Flores, Margie Brown-Coronel, Miriam Pawel, Erika Perez, Debbie Kang, Karen Leong, Matt Basso, Laura Barraclough, Ana Sánchez-Muñoz, Enrique Buelna, Katherine Ramirez, Alison Rose Jefferson, Jerry Gonzalez, Ernie Chavez, Ricky Rodriguez, Dionne Espinoza, Esther Hernandez, Anthony Macias, Cynthia Orozco, Monica Perales, Gabriela González, Raul Ramos, John Mckiernan-Gonzalez, Omar Valerio-Jimenez and Tiffany Gonzalez.

Mil gracias to my *hermano* Estevan Rael y Gálvez, who offered his home to me, whether in Washington, D.C., or Santa Fe, and has inspired me with his wisdom and creativity. Natalia Molina, is another longtime friend who generously shares archival sources, invites me to campus talks and conference panels, and provides constructive feedback on my scholarship. Thanks to my dear friend Wilson Chen, who has supported my scholarship since graduate school and continues to join me in foodie excursions and is always welcoming, along with Jane Hseu and Kaya Chen, when I visit Chicago.

The staff at Rutgers University Press has been great to work with. Leslie Mitchner believed in this book project and kept checking in on my progress. Nicole Solano has kept me on track and shepherded me through the process. Thanks to Jordan Beltran Gonzalez who worked his copyediting magic and helped me with the appendix.

For the last decade, I have had the pleasure of working among incredible colleagues at California State University Channel Islands (CUSCI) in Camarillo, CA. I'm lucky to work with colleagues who believe in making CSUCI a truly Hispanic *Serving* Institution. Frank Barajas helped recruit me to CSUCI and since then has been a constant source of support in building Chicano/a Studies, collaborating on equity issues on campus, and offering thoughtful feedback on my writing. I am fortunate to have Jennie Luna and Nicholas Centino as amazing colleagues who are dedicated to our students and building a vital and dynamic Chicano/ Studies Department. Much gratitude to Amanda Sanchez, Alison Potter, Christy Teranishi Martinez, Georgina Guzmán, Raul Moreno Campos, Julia Ornelas-Higdon, Theresa Avila, Kathleen Contreras, Julia Balén, Marie Francois, and Jim Meriwether for their support and contributions to my department. Thanks also to Stephen Clark, LaSonya Davis, Antonio Jiménez Jiménez, Kaia Tollefson, Selenne Bañuelos, Geoffrey Buhl, Jorge Garcia, Mary Adler, Cindy Weyls, Karina Chavarria, Luis Sanchez, Dennis Downey, Amanda Quintero, Monica

Rivas, Michelle Hasendonckx and Rosario Cuevas, as well as other colleagues across campus, who offered encouragement and inspiration. I received financial support from California State University Channel Islands through mini-grants, sabbatical, faculty writing retreats that helped me make progress on the book.

Outside of campus, I met some wonderful people playing adult recreational tennis. I want to thank my Camarillo Warriors teammates for inviting me to play, trusting me to be their captain, and encouraging me to write about tennis in the book.

Finally, I would like to thank my family for their love and support. To my father, José Alamillo, who taught me to value of history by listening to his stories and for making me the sports fan I am today. To my mother, Rosa Alamillo, who is always there to feed me and nourish me with love and kindness. To my siblings, Esteban, Yolanda, Esaul, Rafael, and Angelica, for their love and support. Since I moved back to Ventura County, I have been blessed to reconnect with my extended family of uncles, aunts, and cousins. Thanks to Joey De Leon who encouraged me to add a personal touch to the book; to Rick and Cesar who always invite me to watch a Dodgers game or boxing match; to Antonio and Mary Cabral for their hospitality and encouraging me to preserve our family history; and to Libia Gil and Rick Hanks for their generous support and encouragement. This book would not have been possible without the support of my wife, Leilani, who is my best friend, partner and coparent. She keeps me grounded, challenges my ideas, sustains me and always reminds me of what is important— *familia*. Finally, I need to thank my kids, Lorenzo, Maya. and Danilo, for their patience and support while writing this book. They have grown into smart, kind, and compassionate young adults. They make me proud to be their *papi*.

An earlier iteration of chapter 4 was published as "Playing Across Borders: Transnational Sports and Identities in Southern California and Mexico, 1930–1945," *Pacific Historical Review* 79, no. 3 (2010): 360–392.

NOTES

INTRODUCTION

1. José M. Alamillo, "Fernando, Los Doyers, and Me," *La Vida Baseball*, April 2017, www.lavidabaseball.com/fernando-valenzuela-dodgers-latinos/.
2. David Reyes, "Latino Heroes: The Few and Far Between," *Los Angeles Times*, August 5, 1983, B1.
3. Ibid., 3.
4. David La France, "A Mexican Popular Image of the United States through the Baseball Hero, Fernando Valenzuela," *Studies in Latin American Popular Culture* 4, no. 1 (1985): 14–23.
5. José M. Alamillo, "Beyond the Latino Sports Hero: The Role of Sports in Creating Communities, Networks, and Identities," in *American Latinos and the Making of the United States: A Theme Study* (Washington, DC: National Park Service Advisory Board, 2013), 161–183.
6. On the historiography of African Americans in sports from the 1800s to the present, see Jeffrey Sammons, "Race and Sport: A Critical, Historical Examination," *Journal of Sport History* 21, no. 3 (Fall 1994): 203–278.
7. Edwin Henderson, *The Negro in Sports* (Washington, DC: Association for the Study of Negro Life and History, 1939); Harry Edwards, *The Revolt of the Black Athlete* (New York: Free Press, 1969). See also Rob Ruck, *Sandlot Seasons: Sport in Black Pittsburgh* (Urbana: University of Illinois Press, 1987); David K. Wiggins, *Glory Bound: Black Athletes in White America* (Syracuse, NY: Syracuse University Press, 1997); David Wiggins and Patrick Miller, *Sport and the Color Line: Black Athletes and Race Relations in Twentieth-Century America* (New York: Routledge, 2004); William Rhoden, *Forty Million Dollar Slaves: The Rise, Fall and Redemption of the Black Athlete* (New York: Crown, 2006); Louis Moore, *We Will Win the Day: The Civil Rights Movements, The Black Athlete and the Quest for Equality* (Westport, CT: Praeger, 2017).
8. Alan Klein, "Towards a Transnational Sports Studies," *Sport in Society* 10, no. 6 (November 2007): 885.
9. Wray Vamplew, "The History of Sport in the International Scenery: An Overview," *Revista Tempo* 17, no. 34 (May 2013): 461–462. The lone exception is Alan Klein's *Baseball on the Border: A Tale of Two Laredos* (Princeton, NJ: Princeton University Press, 1997).
10. Ben Carrington, *Race, Sport and Politics: The Sporting Black Diaspora* (Thousand Oaks, CA: Sage, 2010); Thomas Carter, *In Foreign Fields: The Politics and Experiences of Transnational Sport Migration* (London: Pluto, 2011); Theresa Runstedtler, *Jack Johnson, Rebel Sojourner: Boxing in the Shadow of the Global Color Line* (Berkeley: University of California Press, 2012); Damion Thomas, *Globetrotting: African American Athletes and Cold War Politics* (Urbana: University of Illinois Press, 2012); Janelle Joseph, *Sport in the Black Atlantic: Crossing and Making Boundaries* (London: Bloomsbury, 2015); Lara Putnam, "The Panama Cannonball's Transnational Ties: Migrants, Sport, and Belonging in the Interwar Greater Caribbean," *Journal of Sport History* 41, no. 3 (Fall 2014): 401–424.
11. Carrington, *Race, Sport and Politics,* 55; Paul Gilroy, *The Black Atlantic: Modernity and Double Consciousness* (Cambridge, MA: Harvard University Press, 1993).
12. Américo Paredes, *Folklore and Culture on the Texas-Mexican Border,* ed. Richard Bauman (Austin: University of Texas Press, 1993), xi.
13. Ramón Saldívar, *The Borderlands of Culture: Américo Paredes and the Transnational Imaginary* (Durham, NC: Duke University Press, 2006).

14. Ibid., 22–23; Américo Paredes, "El Cowboy Norteamericano en el Folklore y la Literatura," *Cuadernos del Instituto Nacional de Antropología* 4 (1963): 227–240.

15. José Limón, *American Encounters: Greater Mexico, the United States, and the Erotics of Culture* (Boston: Beacon, 1998); Hector Calderón, *Narratives of Greater Mexico: Essays on Chicano Literary History, Genre and Borders* (Austin: University of Texas Press, 2004); José David Saldívar, *Trans-Americanity: Subaltern Modernities, Global Coloniality and the Cultures of Greater Mexico* (Durham, NC: Duke University Press, 2011); David P. Sandell, *Open Your Heart: Religion and Cultural Poetics in Greater Mexico* (Notre Dame, IN: University of Notre Dame Press, 2015); Alan Eladio Gómez, *The Revolutionary Imaginations of Greater Mexico: Chicana/o Radicalism, Solidarity Politics, & Latin American Social Movements* (Austin: University of Texas Press, 2016). Edward J. McCaughan, *Art and Social Movements: Cultural Politics in Mexico and Aztlán* (Durham, NC: Duke University Press, 2012); Colin Gunckel, *Mexico on Main Street: Transnational Film Culture in Los Angeles before World War II* (New Brunswick, NJ: Rutgers University Press, 2015).

16. The lone exceptions are Alan Klein's *Baseball on the Border*; Ignacio M. García, *When Mexicans Could Play Ball: Basketball, Race, and Identity in San Antonio, 1928–1945* (Austin: University of Texas Press, 2013); Jorge Iber, Samuel O. Regalado, José M. Alamillo and Arnoldo de León. *Latinos in U.S. Sport: A History of Isolation, Cultural Identity, and Acceptance* (Champaign IL: Human Kinetics, 2011)

17. Although their article was written over twenty years ago, many of the points raised by Elliot Gorn and Michael Oriard still apply today. See Gorn and Oriard, "Taking Sports Seriously," *Chronicle of Higher Education*, March 24, 1995, A52. For a more recent assessment of sports historiography, see Amy Bass, "State of the Field: Sports History and the 'Cultural Turn,'" *Journal of American History* 101 (June 2014): 148–172.

18. Samuel Regalado, "Invisible Identity: Mexican American Sport and Chicano Historiography," in *Mexican Americans and Sports: A Reader on Athletics and Barrio Life*, ed. Jorge Iber and Samuel Regalado (College Station: Texas A&M Press, 2007), 243.

19. Adrian Burgos Jr., *Playing America's Game: Baseball, Latinos, and the Color Line* (Berkeley: University of California Press, 2007).

20. Carol Griffing McKenzie, "Leisure and Recreation in the Rancho Period of California, 1770 to 1886" (PhD diss., University of Southern California, 1974), 153–182.

21. Joseph Arbena, "Sport, Development, and Mexican Nationalism, 1920–1970," *Journal of Sport History* 18, no. 3 (1991): 354.

22. Eric Hobsbawm, *Nations and Nationalism since 1780* (Cambridge: Cambridge University Press, 1991), 143.

23. Thomas A. Guglielmo, "Fighting for Caucasian Rights: Mexicans, Mexican Americans, and the Transnational Struggle for Civil Rights in World War II Texas," *Journal of American History* 92, no. 4 (March 2005): 1231.

24. Michael Omi and Howard Winant, *Racial Formation in the United States*, 3rd ed. (New York: Routledge, 2015), 13.

25. Ben Carrington, *Race, Sport and Politics*, 66.

26. Ibid., 66.

27. Luca Bifulco and Mario Tirino, "The Sports Hero in the Social Imaginary, Identity, Community, Ritual and Myth," *Imago: A Journal of the Social Imaginary*, no. 2 (July 2018): 9–25.

28. George Lipsitz, *How Racism Takes Place* (Philadelphia: Temple University Press, 2011), 73–94.

29. Natalia Molina, "The Relational Turn in Chicana/o History," *Pacific Historical Review* 82, no. 4 (2013): 520–541. See also Natalia Molina, Daniel Martinez Hosang, and Ramón A.

Gutiérrez, *Relational Formations of Race: Theory, Method, and Practice* (Berkeley: University of California Press, 2019).

30. Molina, "Relational Turn in Chicana/o History," 522.

31. Michael Messner, *Power at Play: Sports and the Problem of Masculinity* (Boston: Beacon, 1995).

32. Susan Cahn, *Coming on Strong: Gender and Sexuality in Twentieth-Century Women's Sports*, 2nd ed. (Urbana: University of Illinois Press, 2015), 302.

33. Jennifer Hargreaves, *Sporting Females: Critical Issues in the History and Sociology of Women's Sports* (New York: Routledge, 1994), 169–172.

34. For more critical interpretations of Latino masculinity, see Maxine Baca Zinn, "Chicano Men and Masculinity," *Journal of Ethnic Studies* 10, no. 2 (1982): 29–44; Lionel Cantu, "Entre Hombres/Between Men: Latino Masculinities and Homosexualities," in *Gay Sexualities*, ed. Peter Nardi (Thousand Oaks, CA: Sage, 2000), 224–246; Aída Hurtado and Mrinal Singha, *Beyond Machismo: Intersectional Latino Masculinities* (Austin: University of Texas Press, 2016).

35. On masculinity in baseball, see Alan Klein, "Dueling Machos: Masculinity and Sport in Mexican Baseball," in *Masculinities, Gender Relations and Sport*, ed. Jim McKay, Michael A. Messner, and Don Sabo (Thousand Oaks, CA: Sage, 2000), 67–85; José M. Alamillo, "Mexican American Baseball: Masculinity, Racial Struggle and Labor Politics in Southern California, 1930–1950," in *Sports Matters: Race, Recreation and Culture*, ed. Michael Willard and John Bloom (New York: New York University Press, 2002), 86–115. On masculinity in boxing, see Gregory Rodríguez, "Boxing and Masculinity: The History and (Her)story of Oscar de la Hoya," in *Latino/a Popular Culture*, ed. Michelle Habell-Pallan and Mary Romero (New York: New York University Press, 2002), 252–268; Fernando Delgado, "Golden But Not Brown: Oscar de la Hoya and the Complications of Culture, Manhood and Boxing," *International Journal of the History of Sport* 22, no. 2 (March 2005): 196–211.

36. Susan Birrell, "Women of Color, Critical Autobiography, and Sport," in *Sport, Men, and the Gender Order: Critical Feminist Perspectives*, eds. Michael Messner and Donald Sabo (Champaign, IL: Human Kinetics, 1990), 195.

37. Katherine Jamieson, "Occupying a Middle Space: Towards a Mestiza Sport Studies," *Sociology of Sport Journal* 20, no. 1 (2003): 1–16. Women of color athletes are only beginning to receive more scholarly attention. See Jennifer Lansbury, *A Spectacular Leap: Black Women Athletes in Twentieth Century America* (Fayetteville: University of Arkansas Press, 2014); Linda Peavy and Ursula Smith, *Full Court Quest: The Girls of Fort Shaw Indian School Basketball Champions of the World* (Norman: University of Oklahoma Press, 2008); Nicole Willms, *When Women Rule the Court: Gender, Race and Japanese American Basketball* (New Brunswick, NJ: Rutgers University Press, 2017).

38. Some exceptions include Katherine Jamieson, "Advance at Your Own Risk: Latinas, Families, and Collegiate Softball," in Iber and Regalado, *Mexican Americans and Sports*, 213–232; Paul Cuadros, "We Play Too: Latina Integration through Soccer in the 'New South,'" *Southeastern Geographer* 51, no. 2 (2011): 227–241; Kat D. Williams, "Sport 'A Useful Category of Historical Analysis': Isabel 'Lefty' Alvarez: The Rascal of El Cerro," *International Journal of the History of Sport* 29, no. 5 (April 2012): 766–785.

39. Emma Perez, *The Decolonial Imaginary: Writing Chicanas into History* (Bloomington: Indiana University Press, 1999), 81.

40. James Clifford, "Diasporas," *Cultural Anthropology* 9, no. 3 (1994): 312.

41. Stuart Hall, "Cultural Identity and Diaspora," in *Colonial Discourse and Postcolonial Theory*, ed. Patrick Williams and Laura Chrisman (New York: Columbia University Press, 1994), 402.

42. Gloria Anzaldúa, *Borderlands/La Frontera: The New Mestiza* (San Francisco: Aunt Lute Books, 1987).

43. George J. Sánchez, *Becoming Mexican American: Ethnicity, Culture and Identity in Chicano Los Angeles, 1900–1945* (New York: Oxford University Press, 1993).

44. Douglas Monroy, *Rebirth: Mexican Los Angeles from the Great Migration to the Great Depression* (Berkeley: University of California Press, 1999).

45. Bloom and Willard, *Sports Matters.*

46. C. L. R. James, *Beyond a Boundary* (London: Stanley Paul, 1963).

47. Bill Simons, "Nelson Mandela, Arthur Ashe and the Transformative Power of Sports," *Inside Tennis* 32, no. 6 (September/October, 2013): 9.

48. For example, see the popular book by Dave Zirin, *What's My Name, Fool? Sports and Resistance in the United States* (Chicago: Haymarket Books, 2005).

1. *DEPORTES*, AMERICANIZATION, AND MEXICAN SPORTING CULTURE

1. Lamberto Álvarez Gayou set a record in the low hurdles and pole vault and later became captain of the gymnastic team at Mexico City's YMCA. Jo Grossman, "Mexico Athletics Booming," *San Diego Sun*, April 19, 1933, 5.

2. Lamberto Álvarez Gayou, "Sport in Latin America," *Pan American Union Bulletin* 60, no. 9 (September 1926): 888.

3. Lamberto Álvarez Gayou, "Los Mexicanos Que Han Triunfado y Siguen Triunfando Actualmente en Las Arenas de Estados Unidos," *El Heraldo de Mexico*, November 1, 1927, 8; Lamberto Álvarez Gayou, "El Boxeo Is Boosted in Mexico These Days," *Seattle Daily Times*, August 7, 1929, 23.

4. "Plan Extensive Mexico Sports Program," *San Diego Evening Tribune*, July 8, 1930, 27.

5. "Latin-American Olympiad Considered for Tijuana," *Miami Daily News-Record*, August 27, 1930, 8.

6. "Tom Akers, "Talking It Over," *San Diego Evening Tribune*, August 12, 1931, 17.

7. Lamberto Álvarez Gayou, "Mexico's Youth Is Building for Future in Athletics; 'True Sportsmanship' Goal," *San Diego Evening Tribune*, August 26, 1931, 21.

8. "Gayou—Man of the Hour," *Los Angeles Times*, April 23, 1933, E3.

9. Irving Eckhoff, "Mexican Youth Headed for Sports Limelight," *Los Angeles Times*, January 22, 1933, E3.

10. "Lo Que Espera Mexico de Sus Nuevos Jefes," *La Opinión*, April 24, 1933, 7.

11. "Wallace to Bring New Athletic Plan to U.S.," *San Francisco Chronicle*, December 9, 1940, 11.

12. Lamberto Álvarez Gayou, "Physical Education for Pan-American Cooperation," *Journal of Health and Physical Education* 13, no. 5 (June 1942): 356–357.

13. Gerald Gems, *The Athletic Crusade: Sport and American Cultural Imperialism* (Lincoln: University of Nebraska Press, 2006).

14. Gilbert González, *Culture of Empire: American Writers, Mexico, and Mexican Immigrants, 1880–1930* (Austin: University of Texas Press, 2004), 44.

15. Stuart Chase, *Mexico: A Study of Two Americas* (New York: Macmillan, 1931), 206–207.

16. Lewis Spence, *Mexico for the Mexicans* (New York: Charles Scribner's Sons, 1918), 108.

17. Wallace Thompson, *The Mexican Mind: A Study of National Psychology* (New York: Little, Brown, 1922), 97.

18. Ibid., 99.

19. David Pletcher, *Rails, Mines, and Progress: Seven American Promoters in Mexico, 1867–1911* (Ithaca, NY: Cornell University Press, 1958).

20. William Beezley, *Judas at the Jockey Club and Other Episodes of Porfirian Mexico* (Lincoln: University of Nebraska Press, 1987), 13–66.

21. Quote is from the September 12, 1896, issue of the *Mexican Sportsman*, reprinted in Javier Bañuelos Rentería, *Cronica del Futbol Mexicano: Balon a Tierra (1896–1932)* (Mexico City: Editorial Clio, 1998), 13.

22. Beezley, *Judas at the Jockey Club*, 58.

23. Ibid., 58.

24. C. Howard Hopkins, *History of the YMCA in North America* (New York: Association Press, 1951), 349; Glenn Avent, "A Popular and Wholesome Resort: Gender, Class and the Young Men's Christian Association in Porfirian Mexico" (master's thesis, University of British Columbia, 1996), 7.

25. The YMCA opened other branches in Mexico including Monterrey (1904), Chihuahua (1907), and Tampico (1918). Kenneth Scott Latourette, *World Service: A History of Foreign Work and World Service of the Young Men's Christian Association of the United States and Canada* (New York: Association Press, 1957), 226–227.

26. G. I. Babcock, "Report Letter No. 1," December 20, 1902, Mexico City, box 1, folder 2, Records of YMCA International Work in Mexico, Kautz Family YMCA Archives, University of Minnesota (hereafter YMCA Mexico Archives).

27. "A Good Investment: Young Men's Christian Association of Mexico City," Pamphlet, 1902, 6, box 17, folder 1, YMCA Mexico Archives.

28. "Sicursal Mexicana," YMCA Brochure, April 1905, 5, box 17, folder 1, YMCA Mexico Archives.

29. This five-story building also included a weight room, gymnasium, swimming pool, showers, dormitories, restaurant, library, and recreation room. "Diaz Also Opens Y.M.C.A.," *New York Times*, September 11, 1910, C4. See also Elmer Johnson, *The History of the YMCA Physical Education* (New York: Association Press, 1979), 164–165.

30. The concept of "muscular Christianity" became an integral part of YMCA's physical education programs overseas. See Clifford Putney, *Muscular Christianity: Manhood and Sports in Protestant America* (Cambridge, MA: Harvard University Press, 2001).

31. "La Asociacion: Annual Prospectus of the Mexico City Y.M.C.A.," 1911, 44, box 17, folder 1, YMCA Mexico Archives.

32. Johnson, *History of the YMCA Physical Education*, 166–167.

33. G. I. Babcock, "Mexico, Our Nearest Mission Field," in *The Red Triangle in the Changing Nations* (New York: Association Press, 1918), 97.

34. "What $100,000 Would Do for Mexico," Brochure, 1920, box 15, folder 17, 3–4, YMCA Mexico Archives.

35. "The YMCA in Mexico and West Indies," Brochure, 1919, box 2, folder 14, YMCA Mexico Archives. Reverend James Naismith, an instructor at the International YMCA Training School (later renamed Springfield College), is credited with inventing the sport of basketball in an indoor gym during a cold winter when restless college men needed to burn off energy. See James Naismith, *Basketball: Its Origins and Development* (New York: Association Press, 1941).

36. "YMCA in Mexico and West Indies."

37. Oscar Castillon, "Sobre La Marcha," *La Prensa*, October 28, 1943, 7.

38. P. W. Wilson, "The Renaissance in Mexico," *Association Men*, June 1926, 489.

39. "Sees Mexico as Friendly," *New York Times*, June 14, 1919, 3.

40. The 1,313 members comprised one-half Mexican and one-half foreigners of twenty or more nationalities. Richard Williamson, "The Association and the Revolution," ca. 1915, 1, box 1, folder 8, YMCA Mexico Archives.

41. Norman Hayner, "Mexicans at Play, a Revolution," *Sociology and Social Research* 38, no. 2 (November–December 1953): 80–83; *Constitution of the United Mexican States, 1917, Article 4 (as amended)* (Washington, DC: Pan American Union, 1961), 10.

42. Oscar F. Castillon, "Physical Education in Mexico," *Journal of Health and Physical Education* 5, no. 5 (May 1934): 12. See also Maurice A. Clay, "Physical Education in Mexico," in *Physical Education around the World*, ed. William Johnson (Indianapolis: Phi Epsilon Kappa Fraternity, 1928), 34–45; Christopher Grenfell, "Physical Education in Mexico, 1867–1972" (master's thesis, University of California, Los Angeles, 1973), 24–38.

43. Thomas Benjamin, *La Revolución: Mexico's Great Revolution as Memory, Myth, & History* (Austin: University of Texas Press, 2000), 126; Patrice Elizabeth Olsen, *Artifacts of Revolution: Architecture, Society, and Politics in Mexico City, 1920–1940* (Lanham, MD: Rowman & Littlefield, 2008), 52.

44. Joseph Arbena, "Sport, Development, and Mexican Nationalism, 1920–1970," *Journal of Sport History* 18, no. 3 (1991): 350–364.

45. Keith Brewster, "Patriotic Games: The Role of Sport in Post-Revolutionary Mexico," *International Journal of the History of Sport* 22, no. 2 (March 2005): 139–157. See also Miguel Lisbona Guillén, "Mejorar La Raza: Cuerpo y Deporte en El Chiapas de la Revolución Mexicana," *Relaciones Estudios de Hisoria y Sociedad* 27, no. 105 (2006): 60-106.

46. "Annual Report Letter of Richard Williamson, General Secretary, Young Men's Christian Association, Mexico City, Mexico for the Year Ending September 30, 1918," box 2, folder 13, YMCA Mexico Archives.

47. In 1910, Mexico City Association's Physical Department recruited fourteen members through its Leaders Corps with the aim of developing "native secretaries" to take on leadership positions in Mexico's YMCA branches. Jess T. Hopkins, "Confidential Report on Mexico from Visit of May and June, 1918," box 2, folder 13, 1–5, YMCA Mexico Archives.

48. Johnson, *History of the YMCA Physical Education*, 165.

49. Ibid.; "Engagement Party," *Springfield Union*, May 13, 1914, 10.

50. "Annual Report for the Year Ending September 30, 1918," E. C. Aguirre, Physical Director, Mexico City, box 2, folder 13, 3, YMCA Mexico Archives.

51. Gail Bederman, *Manliness and Civilization: A Cultural History of Gender and Race in the United States, 1880–1917* (Chicago: University of Chicago Press, 1995).

52. "Annual Report for the Year Ending September 30, 1918," 10.

53. Ibid., 9.

54. The brochure's front image featured two muscled basketball players of equal size shaking hands—the dark-haired man on the left represented the Mexico team, and a blonde Euro-American man on the right represented the U.S. team. Mexico Red Triangles International Friendship Tour Brochure, 1924, box 15, YMCA Mexico Archives.

55. "Letter to John Manley from Enrique Aguirre," December 17, 1923, box 2, folder 15, YMCA Mexico Archives.

56. "Mexican Five to Appear Here with Boro Club," *Brooklyn Daily Eagle*, January 13, 1924, 44; "Mexican Five Plans Trip, Basketball Team to Invade U.S. for Extended Tour," *New York Times*, December 23, 1923, 19.

57. Enrique Aguirre, "Origen de los Juegos Deportivos Centro-Americanos," *La Prensa*, August 12, 1926, 8; Enrique Aguirre, "Mexico City Attacks Its Leisure Time Program," *Recreation* 25, no. 8 (November 1931): 431–433. See also Richard V. McGehee, "The Origins of Olympism in Mexico: The Central American Games of 1926," *International Journal of the History of Sport* 10, no. 3 (December 1993): 313–332.

58. "Mexican Girls Not Anxious to Indulge in Athletic Games," *Bisbee Daily Review*, July 21, 1921, 9.

59. Carl Lumholtz, *Unknown Mexico: A Record of Five Years' Exploration of the Western Sierra Madre*, vol. 1 (New York: Charles Scribner's Sons, 1902), 293–294.

60. Darcy Plymire, "The Legend of the Tarahumara: Tourism, Overcivilization and the White Man's Indian," *International Journal of the History of Sport* 23, no. 2 (March 2006): 154–166.

61. Mark Dyreson, "The Foot Runners Conquer Mexico and Texas: Endurance Racing, Indigenismo, and Nationalism," *Journal of Sport History* 31, no. 1 (Spring 2004): 1–31.

62. Ibid.; Antonio Lavin Ugalde, *México en Los Juegos Olímpicos, MCMLXVIII*. (Mexico City: Asociación Nacional de Periodistas, A.C., 1968), 18–20.

63. Enrique Aguirre, "Values through Sports," in *Development of Human Values through Sports*, ed. Reuben Frost and Edward Sims (Springfield, MA: Proceedings of National Conference on Development of Human Values through Sports, 1974), 19–24.

64. Keith Brewster, "Redeeming the Indian: Sport and Ethnicity in Post-revolutionary Mexico," *Pattern of Prejudice* 38, no. 3 (2004): 213–231.

65. Oscar Castillón, "Physical Education in Mexico," *Journal of Health and Physical Education* 5, no. 5 (May 1934): 14.

66. Oscar Castillón, "La Mujer en el Deporte," *La Prensa*, March 18, 1926, 8; Oscar Castillón, "La Mujer en el Deporte," *El Heraldo de México*, January 16, 1926, 5; Oscar Castillón, "La Mujer en el Deporte," *El Heraldo de México*, October 24, 1925, 5.

67. Oscar Castillón, " La Vida Deportiva en Monterrey, Evolucion Atletica de la Mujer Regiomontana," *La Prensa*, June 26, 1926, 7.

68. "The YMCA in Mexico," *Latin American Bulletin of Springfield College* 3, no. 1 (1928): 7.

69. Ibid., 7.

70. Ibid., 7.

71. Nancy Boyd, *Emissaries: The Overseas Work of the American YWCA, 1895–1970* (New York: Women's Press, 1986), 97–118.

72. "Senorita Landazuri to Talk on Mexico at Student Forum Lunch," *Daily Northwestern*, July 23, 1926, 1.

73. Mireya Medina Villanueva and Marisol Pedraza Luevano, "Women and Sport in Mexico," in *Women and Sport in Latin America*, ed. Rosa López de D'Amico, Tansin Benn, and Gertrud Pfister (New York: Routledge, 2016), 144–157; Maria Monserrate Sanchez Soler, ed., *Formando el cuerpo de una nación: El deporte en el México postrevolucionario (1920–1940)* (Mexico City: Consejo Nacional para la Cultura y Las Artes, Instituto Nacional de Bellas Artes, Museo Casa Estudio Diego Rivera y Frida Kahlo, 2012).

74. Claire Brewster and Keith Brewster, "Women, Sport, and the Press in Twentieth-Century Mexico," *International Journal of the History of Sport* 35, no. 10 (2018): 1–20.

75. Clay, "Physical Education in Mexico," 36; Grenfell, "Physical Education in Mexico," 42–43.

76. Rudolph Muller Lopez, "History of Physical Education and Sports in Mexico" (master's thesis, Claremont Graduate School, 1953), 46–52.

77. Mary Kay Vaughan, "Nationalizing the Countryside: Schools and Rural Communities in the 1930s," in *The Eagle and the Virgin: Nation and Cultural Revolution in Mexico, 1920–1940*, ed. Mary Kay Vaughan and Stephen E. Lewis (Durham, NC: Duke University Press, 2006), 157–175.

78. Mónica Lizbeth Chávez González, "Construcción de la nación y el género desde el cuerpo: La educación física en el México posrevolucionario," *Descatos*, no. 30 (May–August 2009): 43–58.

79. "Como Cultiva Mexico Ahora Los Deportes," *La Opinión*, August 17, 1934, 7.

80. Brewster and Brewster, "Women, Sport, and the Press."

81. Ibid., 9.

82. Ignacio Herrerías, "Buena Disciplina Tienen Los Atletas en Centro-America, Chabelita Silva Cuenta Como Pasan las Horas Nuestros Deportistas," *El Continental*, March 20, 1935, 5.

83. *The First International Recreation Congress Proceedings, July 23–29, 1932, Los Angeles, CA* (Washington, DC: National Recreation Association, 1933), 110–112. See also "Triunfa La Mujer en Los Deportes," *La Prensa*, February 1931, 26.

84. Fray Nano, "Mucha Falta ha al Deporte Mexicano el Ing. Marte Gomez," *Afición*, November 30, 1934, 1.

85. Bederman, *Manliness and Civilization*, 170–215.

86. Theodore Roosevelt, "Value of an Athletic Training," *Harper's Weekly* 37 (December 23, 1893): 1236.

87. Américo Paredes," The United States, Mexico and Machismo," *Journal of the Folklore Institute* 8, no. 1 (June 1971), 34.

88. Bederman, *Manliness and Civilization*, 193.

89. Jorge Iber, Samuel Regalado, José M. Alamillo, and Arnoldo De León, *Latinos in U.S. Sport: A History of Isolation, Cultural Identity and Acceptance* (Champaign, IL: Human Kinetics, 2011), 71–76.

90. Gilbert González, "Racial Intelligence Testing and the Mexican People," *Explorations in Ethnic Studies* 5, no. 5 (July 1982): 36–49; Carlos Kevin Blanton, "From Intellectual Deficiency to Cultural Deficiency: Mexican Americans, Testing and Public School Policy in the American Southwest, 1920–1940," *Pacific Historical Review* 72 (2003): 39–62; Miroslava Chávez-García, "Intelligence Testing at Whittier School, 1890–1920," *Pacific Historical Review* 76, no. 2 (2007): 193–228.

91. Lynn Couturier, "The Influence of Eugenics Movement on Physical Education in the United States," *Sport History Review* 36, no. 1 (May 2005): 21–42.

92. Alexandra Minna Stern, *Eugenic Nation: Faults and Frontiers of Better Breeding in Modern America* (Berkeley: University of California Press, 2005); Nancy Stepan, *The Hour of Eugenics: Race, Gender and Nation in Latin America* (Ithaca, NY: Cornell University Press, 1991).

93. Silvana Vilodre Goellner, "Body, Eugenics and Nationalism: Women in the First Sport and Physical Education Journal Published in Brazil (1932–1945)," *International Journal of the History of Sport* 31, no. 10 (2014): 1278–1286.

94. Elmer Mitchell, "Racial Traits in Athletics," *American Physical Education Review* 27, no. 3 (March 1922): 93–99; Elmer Mitchell, "Racial Traits in Athletics," *American Physical Education Review* 27, no. 4 (April 1922): 147–152; Elmer Mitchell, "Racial Traits in Athletics," *American Physical Education Review* 27, no. 5 (May 1922): 197–206.

95. Elmer Mitchell, "Racial Traits in Athletics," *American Physical Education Review* 27, no. 3 (March 1922): 94.

96. Elmer Mitchell, "Racial Traits in Athletics," *American Physical Education Review* 27, no. 4 (April 1922): 148, 150.

97. Elmer Mitchell, "Racial Traits in Athletics," *American Physical Education Review* 27, no. 5 (May 1922): 201–202.

98. See, for example, Frankling Paschal and Louis Sullivan, "Racial Difference in the Mental and Physical Development of Mexican Children," *Comparative Psychology Monographs* 3 (1925): 1–76; Helen Irene Hyde, "Comparison of the Physical Characteristics of American, Mexican and Japanese School Children" (master's thesis, University of Southern California, 1928), 7–8.

99. For an early critique of the "Mexican problem," see Carey McWilliams, *North from Mexico: The Spanish-Speaking People of the United States* (New York: Praeger, 1948), 188–205.

100. See also Gilbert González, *Chicano Education in the Era of Segregation* (Philadelphia: Balch Institute for Ethnic Studies, 1990); George J. Sánchez, *Becoming Mexican American: Ethnicity, Culture and Identity in Chicano Los Angeles, 1900–1945* (New York: Oxford University Press, 1993); Matt García, *A World of Its Own: Race, Labor, and Citrus in the Making of Greater Los Angeles, 1900–1970* (Chapel Hill: University of North Carolina Press, 2001); Natalia Molina, *Fit to Be Citizens? Public Health and Race in Los Angeles, 1879–1939* (Berkeley: University of California Press, 2006); Stephanie Lewthwaite, *Race, Place, and Reform in Mexican Los Angeles* (Tucson: University of Arizona Press, 2009).

101. González, *Culture of Empire*, 128–152.

102. Robert McLean, *That Mexican! As He Really Is, North and South of the Rio Grande* (Chicago: Fleming H. Revell, 1928), 126.

103. Robert McLean, *The Northern Mexican* (New York: Home Missions Council, 1930), 17.

104. Emory Bogardus, "The Mexican Immigrant," *Sociology and Social Research* 5–6 (1927): 483.

105. Daniel Russell, "Problems of Mexican Children in the Southwest," *Journal of Educational Sociology* 17, no. 4 (December 1943): 216–222.

106. Albert F. Cobb, "Comparative Study of the Athletic Ability of Latin-American and Euro-American Boys on a Junior High School Level" (master's thesis, University of Texas, 1952), 54–56.

107. Katherine Murray, "Mexican Community Service," *Sociology and Social Research* 17 (July–August 1933): 547–548.

108. Cleofas F. Muci, "A Survey of Participation in Athletics by Mexican American Boys" (master's thesis, Kansas State Teachers College, 1965), - 37.

109. Ibid.

110. Ed Horner, "A Recreation Director in a Mexican-American Community" (master's thesis, University of California, Los Angeles, 1945), 41.

111. Ibid., 42.

112. Ibid., 45.

113. Ibid., 47.

114. Mario T. García, "Americanization and the Mexican Immigrant, 1880–1930," *Journal of Ethnic Studies* 6, no. 2 (Summer 1978): 19–34; George Sanchez, *Go After the Women: Americanization and the Mexican Immigrant Women, 1915–1929*, no. 6 (Stanford, CA: Center for Chicano Research Working Papers, 1984); Gilbert González, "The Americanization of Mexican Women and Their Families during the Era of De Jure School Segregation, 1900–1950," in *Social and Gender Boundaries in the United States*, ed. Sucheng Chan (Lewiston, NY: Edwin Mellen Press, 1989), 55–79.

115. Gilbert González, *Labor and Community: Mexican Citrus Worker Villages in Southern California County, 1900–1950* (Urbana: University of Illinois Press, 1994), chap. 4; Lewthwaite, *Race, Place, and Reform*, chap. 4; James William Cameron, "The History of Mexican Public Education in Los Angeles, 1910–1930" (PhD diss., University of Southern California, 1976), chap. 4.

116. For a contemporary research study, see Monika Stodolska and Konstantinos Alexandris, "The Role of Recreational Sport in the Adaptation of First Generation Immigrants in the United States," *Journal of Leisure Research* 36, no. 3 (2004): 379–413.

117. Richard Knapp and Charles Hartsoe, *Play for America: The National Recreation Association, 1906–1965* (Arlington VA: National Recreation and Park Association, 1979); Carey Goodman, *Choosing Sides: Playground and Street Life on the Lower East Side* (New York: Schocken Books, 1979); Dominick Cavallo, *Muscles and Morals: Organized Playgrounds and Urban Reform, 1880–1920* (Philadelphia: University of Pennsylvania Press, 1981).

118. Al Goldfarth, *100 Years of Recreation and Parks, City of Los Angeles* (Los Angeles: Department of Recreation and Parks, 1988), 9.

119. Los Angeles Playground Commission, "1906 Annual Report," 42, box C-2012, Department of Playground and Recreation Collection, City Archives, Los Angeles (hereafter LADPR Records); Marlou Belyea, "The Joy Ride and the Silver Screen: Commercial Leisure, Delinquency and Play Reform in Los Angeles, 1900–1980" (PhD diss., Boston University, 1980), 47–49.

120. Bessie Stoddart, "Recreative Centers of Los Angeles, California," *Annals of the American Academy of Political and Social Science* 35, no. 2 (March 1910): 218.

121. Frances M'Crillis "Our Grounds Best in West," *Los Angeles Times*, March 7, 1909, H13.

122. Mark Wild, *Street Meeting: Multiethnic Neighborhoods in Early Twentieth Century Los Angeles* (Berkeley: University of California Press, 2005), 102.

123. By 1910 there were four playgrounds with eighteen supervisors with an average attendance of thirty thousand children per month, and reaching fifty thousand during summer months. "Appropriation Much Desired," *Los Angeles Times*, April 29, 1910, 112. By 1917 there were eleven playgrounds with a total attendance of 585,192, and each one was equipped with play structures, play fields, and a club house with structured games and athletic programming. See "A Community Survey Made in Los Angeles City" (Sacramento: Commission of Immigration and Housing of California, 1917), 28–29.

124. David G. García, *Strategies of Segregation: Race, Residence, and the Struggle for Educational Equality* (Berkeley: University of California Press, 2018), 27–28.

125. Victor von Borosini, "Our Recreation Facilities and the Immigrant," *Annals of the American Academy of Political and Social Science* 25, no. 2 (1910): 141–151; "Americanization! What Is the Secret?," *Playground*, May 1921, 147–150.

126. "Playgrounds Crime Cure," *Los Angeles Times*, July 11, 1926, B1.

127. Burton Hunter, *The Evolution of Municipal Organization and Administrative Practice in the City of Los Angeles* (Los Angeles: Parker, Stone & Baird, 1933), chap. 6. Since the public schools began to pay more attention to physical education, Hjelte began to develop adult recreation programs that included "gymnasium classes for house-wives in the mornings, evening gymnasium classes for men and women, bowling, pool and billiards, entertainments, dramatics, community singing." 1925–26 Annual Report, Department of Playground and Recreation, 6–9, box C-2012, LADPR Records.

128. George Hjelte, *Footprints in the Park* (Los Angeles: Public Service Publications, 1977), 102–107; Susan Diane Hudson, "George Hjelte: Recreation Administrator" (PhD diss., University of Utah, 1974), chap. 4; George Hjelte, "Public Recreation in Los Angeles," *Civic Affairs*, March 1938, 3–8.

129. "City Recreation Director Declares Supervised Play Must Be Public Concern," *Los Angeles Times*, January 5, 1935, A6.

130. 1929 Annual Report, Department of Playground and Recreation, 33, box C-2012, LADPR Records. See also Lawrence Culver, *The Frontier of Leisure: Southern California and the Shaping of Modern America* (New York: Oxford University Press, 2010), 65–66.

131. According to Carey Goodman, "Through the establishment of playgrounds where trained directors formalized play, institutionalized hierarchy, legitimized external control and rewards, and mandated repressed sexuality, the elite was able to 'Americanize' the immigrants and teach them such attitudes as would be beneficial towards maintaining the status quo." See Goodman, *Choosing Sides*, 165.

132. On the relationship between nationalism and American sports, see Steven Pope, *Patriotic Games: Sporting Traditions in the American Imagination, 1876–1926* (New York: Oxford University Press, 1997).

133. 1928–1929 Annual Report, Department of Playground and Recreation, 3, box C-2012, LADPR Records.

134. 1926–1927 Annual Report, Department of Playground and Recreation, 33, box C-2012, LADPR Records.

135. The first municipal associations were the Municipal Baseball Association and Municipal Tennis Association, and in 1930 five new ones were formed, including the Municipal Archery Association, Municipal Football Association, Municipal Horseshoes Associations, and Japanese Baseball Association. The Mexican Athletic Association does not appear until April 1932. 1930 Annual Report, Department of Playground and Recreation, 23, box C-2012, LADPR Records.

136. 1930–1932 Annual Report, Department of Playground and Recreation, 23–24, box C-2012, LADPR Records.

137. "Vote Drops City's Pool Racial Case," *Los Angeles Times*, July 4, 1931, A1; Culver, *Frontier of Leisure*, 68–69. Segregation of swimming pools also existed in Pasadena. See Howard Shorr, "Thorns in the Roses: Race Relations and the Brookside Plunge Controversy in Pasadena, California, 1914–1947," in *Law in the Western United States*, ed. Gorden Morris Bakken (Lincoln: University of Nebraska Press, 2000), 522–528.

138. Rena Blanche Peek, "The Religious and Social Attitudes of the Mexican Girls of the Constituency of the All Nations Foundation in Los Angeles" (master's thesis, University of Southern California, 1929), 50.

139. Horner, "Recreation Director," 41.

140. Vicki Ruiz, *From Out of the Shadows: Mexican Women in Twentieth-Century America* (New York: Oxford University Press, 1998), 52.

141. 1928–1929 Annual Report, Department of Playground and Recreation, 33, box C-2012, LADPR Records.

142. Mildred Van Werden, "Girls' and Women's Activities in Los Angeles," *Playground & Recreation* 24, no. 8 (November 1930): 437; Lynn Couturier, "'Play with Us, Not Against Us': The Debate about Play Days in the Regulation of Women's Sports," *International Journal of the History of Sport* 25, no. 4 (2008): 421–442.

143. *Todays Leisure Magazine*, 1938, Department of Playground and Recreation, 29, box C-2012, LADPR Records.

144. Mina Carson, *Settlement Folk: Social Thought and the American Settlement Movement, 1885–1930* (Chicago: University of Chicago Press, 1990); Gerald Gems, "The Rise of Sport at a Jewish Settlement House: The Chicago Hebrew Institute, 1908–1921," in *Sports and the American Jew*, ed. Steven Riess (Syracuse, NY: Syracuse University Press, 1998), 146–159; Gerald Gems, "Sport and the Americanization of Ethnic Women in Chicago," in *Ethnicity and Sport in North American History and Culture*, ed. George Eisen and David Wiggins (Westport, CT: Greenwood, 1994), 177–199; Linda Borish, "Settlement Houses to Olympic Stadiums: Jewish American Women, Sports and Social Change, 1880s–1930s," *International Sports Studies* 21, no. 1 (2001): 5–24.

145. Steven Reiss, *City Games: The Evolution of American Urban Society and the Rise of Sports* (Urbana: University of Illinois Press, 1989), 164–167.

146. Gabriela Arredondo, *Mexican Chicago: Race, Identity and Nation, 1916–1939* (Urbana: University of Illinois Press, 2008), 86; David Badillo, "Incorporating Reform and Religion: Mexican Immigrants, Hull-House and the Church," in *Pots of Promise: Mexicans and Pottery at Hull House, 1900–1940*, ed. Cheryl Ganza and Margaret Strobel (Urbana: University of Illinois Press, 2004), 35–65.

147. As a research assistant to economist Paul S. Taylor, Jones conducted one of the first surveys of the Mexican population in Chicago. See Anita Jones, "Conditions Surrounding Mexicans in Chicago" (PhD diss., University of Chicago, 1928); Anita Jones, "Mexican Colonies in Chicago," *Social Science Review* 2, no. 4 (December 1928): 579–597.

148. Anita Jones also worked briefly at the Rusk Settlement House in Houston where she taught English classes to Mexican women. María Cristina García, "Agents of Americanization: Rusk Settlement and the Houston Mexicano Community, 1907–1950," in *Mexican Americans in Texas History*, ed. Emilio Zamora, Cynthia Orozco, and Rodolfo Rocha (Austin: Texas State Historical Association, 1999), 133.

149. Founded in 1914 at 1809 National Avenue by sisters Helen and Mary Marston. Cynthia Shelton, "The Neighborhood House of San Diego: Settlement Work in the Mexican Community, 1914–1940" (master's thesis, San Diego State University, 1975), 92–104.

150. Maria E. García, *La Neighbor: A Settlement House in Logan Heights* (San Diego: San Diego Printers, 2017).

151. Ibid., 10–26.

152. Ibid., 42–44. See also Maria García, "The History of Neighborhood House in Logan Heights: Americanization through Baseball," *San Diego Free Press*, April 4, 2015, http://sandiegofreepress.org/2015/04/the-history-of-neighborhood-house-in-logan-heights-americanization-through-baseball/.

153. "Some of San Diego's Future Baseball Stars," *San Diego Union*, June 28, 1928, 19.

154. Alan McGrew, "Bill Breitenstein," *San Diego Union*, August 6, 1924, 6.

155. Molina, *Fit to Be Citizens?*

156. William Munro, "Settlement Work Begun among Mexicans in 1914," *Pasadena Star News*, October 12, 1937, 5. See also Anna Christine Lofstedt, "A Study of the Mexican Population in Pasadena, California" (master's thesis, University of Southern California, 1922), 33–34.

157. "Neighborhood Settlement Annual Report," 1927, 6, box 49, folder: Los Angeles Settlement Houses, National Federation of Settlements Records, Social Welfare History Archives, Minneapolis, MN.

158. "La Novena 'Neighborhood' Ira a San Diego el Domingo," *La Opinión*, August 3, 1832, 4.

159. "Neighborhood Settlement Annual Report."

160. Susan Cahn, *Coming on Strong: Gender and Sexuality in Twentieth-Century Women's Sports*, 2nd ed. (Urbana: University of Illinois Press, 2015), 66.

161. YWCA, The International Institute of the YWCA (Los Angeles: Young Women's Christian Association [YWCA] of Los Angeles Collection, 1924), box 10, folder: brochures, Special Collections, Oviatt Library, California State University Northridge.

162. Mary Ritchie, "Where 1000 Would be Super-Girls is Biggest Adamless Eden of West, L.A. YWCA Excels in Sports," Los Angeles Record, January 9, 1920, 3.

163. YWCA, Keeping Fit Through Exercise, (Los Angeles: Young Women's Christian Association [YWCA] of Los Angeles Collection, 1922, 2, box 11), folder: brochures, Special Collections, Oviatt Library, California State University Northridge.

164. Valerie J. Matsumoto, *City Girls: The Nisei Social World in Los Angeles, 1920–1950* (New York: Oxford University Press, 2014), ch. 1; Adrienne Lash Jones, "Struggle Among Saints: African American Women and the YWCA, 1870–1920" in *Light in the Darkness: African Americans and the YMCA, 1852–1946*, eds. Nina Mjagkij and Margaret Spratt (Louisville: University of Kentucky Press, 2003), 160–187.

165. "Mexico Honors Retired El Paso Educator," *El Paso Herald-Post*, June 15, 1959, 21.

166. Mario García, *Desert Immigrants: The Mexicans of El Paso, 1880–1920* (New Haven, CT: Yale University Press, 1981), 221–222.

167. Servando I. Esquivel, "The Immigrant from Mexico," *Outlook*, May 19, 1920, 131.

168. Monica Perales, *Smeltertown: Making and Remembering a Southwest Border Community* (Chapel Hill: University of North Carolina Press, 2010), 80–81.

169. "To Those Interested in the Town and Country Work of the YMCA and Residing on the Pacific Coast from F. P. Knapp," San Francisco, June 15, 1934, YMCA Pacific Southwest Area Collection, Wardman Library Special Collections, Whittier College, Whittier, CA.

170. Richard Williamson, "Mexican Y.M.C.A. Program for California," May 17, 1935, YMCA Pacific Southwest Area Collection.

171. The use of "Whither Bound" was to pose the question of where Mexican boys were going in life, and only by embracing Protestant values will they find direction and purpose. "YMCA Committee on Mexican Work Brochure," ca. 1930s, YMCA Pacific Southwest Area Collection.

172. Nina Mjagkij, *Light in the Darkness: African Americans and the YMCA, 1852–1946* (Louisville: University of Kentucky Press, 2003).

173. Douglas Flamming, *Bound for Freedom: Black Los Angeles in Jim Crow America* (Berkeley: University of California Press, 2005), 263.

174. "Mexican Colony Holds Banquet," *Van Nuys News*, April 1934, 1.

175. Gualberto Valadez, "Mexican Y Club," *Mexican Voice*, July 1939, 12.

176. David James González, "Battling Mexican Apartheid in Orange County, CA: Race, Place, and Politics, 1920–1950" (PhD diss., University of Southern California, 2017).

177. Juan Acevedo, "Mexican Y Club," *Mexican Voice*, July 1939, 13.

178. Sánchez, *Becoming Mexican American*, 255–264.

179. Federico Allen Hinojosa, *El Mexico de afuera* (San Antonio, TX: Editado de Artes Graficas, 1940).

180. For works that have explored the process of becoming Mexican within a U.S. context, see Douglas Monroy, *Rebirth: Mexican Los Angeles from the Great Migration to the Great Depression* (Berkeley: University of California Press, 1999); Arredondo, *Mexican Chicago*; F. Arturo Rosales, "Shifting Self Perceptions and Ethnic Consciousness among Mexicans in Houston, 1908–1946," *Aztlan: Journal of Chicano Studies* 16, nos. 1–2 (1987): 71–94; Roberto Álvarez, "*Los Re-Mexicanizados*: Mexicanidad, Changing Identity and Long-Term Affiliation on the U.S.-Mexico Border," *Journal of the West* 40, no. 2 (Spring 2001): 15–23.

181. Monroy, *Rebirth*, 45–48.

182. Maggie Rivas-Rodriguez, "Ignacio E. Lozano: The Mexican Exile Publisher Who Conquered San Antonio and Los Angeles," *American Journalism* 21, no. 1 (Winter 2004): 75–89.

183. Francisco Medeiros, "*La Opinión*, a Mexican Exile Newspaper: A Content Analysis of its First Years, 1926–1929," *Aztlan: Journal of Chicano Studies* 11, no. 1 (1980): 65–87.

184. Ignacio F. Herrerías, "Comentarios Deportivos," December 1, 1926, 6.

185. Fray Nano, "Cuales Son Las Probabilidades de Triunfo que Tiene Mexico," *La Opinión*, March 23, 1935, 5.

186. Herrerías was tragically killed in 1944 by an employee during a bitter strike between his newspaper *Novedades* and its employees. "Mexican Publisher Killed by Striker," *Abilene Reporter-News*, April 4, 1944, 15.

187. Rafael Ybarra, "Marginando los Deportes," *La Opinión*, August, 28, 1932 5. Other sportswriters included Francisco Costello, Fulgencio "Fistiana" Corral, Aurelio García, Gabriel "Hap" Navarro, Alfonso Arias, Julio Muñoz, Gil Castro, Ildefonso Franco Jr., Salvador Hernandez Rojas, and Manuel "Midget" Martinez.

188. Translated in English as "In the Tangle of Sport" column. "Nuevo Redactor Depotivo de *La Opinión*," *La Opinión*, November 24, 1933, 7.

189. "Makanazo Se Despide de Todos sus Compañeros!," *La Opinión*, April 25, 1943, 5. *Hoy* magazine was the forerunner to *Siempre!*, one of the most influential Latin American magazines in Mexico City. See John Mraz, *Nacho Lopez, Mexican Photographer* (Minneapolis: University of Minnesota Press, 2003), chap. 2.

190. On "racial uplift" ideology, see Kevin Gaines, *Uplifting the Race: Black Leadership, Politics and Culture in the Twentieth Century* (Chapel Hill: University of North Carolina Press, 1996).

191. Luis Magaña, "Cincuenta Anos De Existencia en la Tierna Edad de Luis Magaña nació La Opinión," *La Opinión*, September 16, 1976, 6, sec. 2.

192. "Se Formo Nuevo Club Deportivo en Los Angeles," *La Opinión*, September 25, 1932, 4.

193. Luis Magaña, "Cincuenta Anos de Existencia," *La Opinión*, Special 50th Anniversary ed., September 16, 1976, sec. 6, 2.

194. Rigoberto Cervantez, "La Leyenda de Luis Magaña: 'El Dorian Grey' del Boxeo Celebra 90 anos de fructifera existencia," *La Opinión*, January 2, 2000, 5C.

195. Armando Benitez, "La Historia del Olympic Auditorium: Luis Magaña, Mister Olympic, habla de suses remembranzas," *La Opinión*, February 21, 1994, 1C.

196. Ibid., 1C.

197. David Avila, "Boxer Aragon and Promoter Magaña Made LA History," *Los Angeles Times*, April 1, 2008, C10.

198. Rodolfo García, "Esquina Neutral," *La Opinión*, Special 50th Anniversary ed., September 16, 1976, sec. 6a, 8.

199. Samuel Regalado, "Read All About It! The Spanish Language Press, the Dodgers, and the Giants, 1958–1982," in *Mexican Americans and Sports: A Reader on Athletics and Barrio Life*, ed. Jorge Iber and Samuel Regalado (College Station: Texas A&M University Press, 2007), 145–159.

200. Medeiros, "*La Opinión*, a Mexican Exile Newspaper," 79.

201. Raul Tovares, "*La Opinión* and Its Contribution to the Mexican Community's Adaptation to Life in the U.S.," *Latino Studies* 7, no. 4 (2009): 480–498.

202. José Pages Llergo, "The Organization of Sports Clubs Is Missing in Los Angeles," *La Opinión*, December 28, 1930, 4.

203. Nancy Aguirre, "Porfirista Femininity in Exile: Women's Contributions to San Antonio's *La Prensa*, 1913–1929," in *Women of the Right: Comparisons and Interplay across Borders*, ed. Kathleen M. Blee and Sandra McGee Deutsch (University Park: Pennsylvania State University Press, 2012), 151.

204. "Triunfan Los Deportes en Las Mujeres," *La Opinión*, April 4, 1927, 7. The term is the female counterpart to "machismo" that refers to women displaying masculine or tomboyish behavior or a butch lesbian.

205. "Los Deportes le Conservan su belleza," *La Prensa*, March 27, 1926, 2; "Los Deportes Ayudan a La Mujer a Ser Bella," *La Opinión*, April 12, 1942, 5.

206. "La Mujer en el Deporte, es muy Notable," *El Heraldo de México*, June 6, 1925, 6.

207. José Amaro Hernández, *Mutual Aid for Survival: The Case of the Mexican American* (Malabar, FL: Robert Krieger, 1983); José Rivera, *Mutual Aid Societies in the Hispanic Southwest: Alternative Sources of Community Empowerment* (Albuquerque: University of New Mexico Press, 1984).

208. Nelson Pichardo, "The Establishment and Development of Chicano Voluntary Associations in California, 1900–1930," *Aztlan: Journal of Chicano Studies* 19 (1992): 106.

209. Albert Camarillo, *Chicanos in a Changing Society: From Mexican Pueblos to American Barrios in Santa Barbara and Southern California, 1848–1930*, repr. ed. (Dallas: Southern Methodist University Press, 2005), 152.

210. Kaye Lynn Briegel, "Alianza Hispano-Americana, 1894–1965: A Mexican American Fraternal Insurance Society" (PhD diss., University of Southern California, 1974). There were over twenty-five AHA lodges in Los Angeles County, each with its own elected officers and members, including women who were admitted after 1913 but denied leadership positions. See Pichardo, "Establishment and Development," 123–128.

211. "Los Miembros Fundadores de La Asociacion Deportiva Hispano-Americana en 'La Opinión,'" La Opinión, May 1, 1927, 1.

212. Ibid.

213. "Smokers" were boxing matches with musical and dance performances. "El Primer 'Smoker' de la Asociación Deportiva se Efectuará el Martes," La Opinión, May 14, 1927, 7; "El Baile del Deportista Sera El 26," La Opinión, August, 27, 1927, 9.

214. "Hoy en la Noche se Tributara Un Homenaje a Bert Colima," La Opinión, May 26, 1927, 8; "15 Diplomáticos en La Fiesta de la Deportiva," La Opinión, July 22, 1927, 7; "Se Conmemora el Décimo Aniversario de la Iniciación Pugilística de Colima," La Opinión, August, 9, 1927, 7; "Gran Festiva Prepara La A.D.H.A.," La Opinión, July 18, 27, 7.

215. The ADHA gymnasium included a boxing ring in the center surrounded by weightlifting equipment, punching bag, balancing rings, and swinging apparatus. "Con una Ovación fue Aprobada la labor de la Mesa Directiva de la A.D.H.A.," La Opinión, September 25, 1927.

216. Iber et al., Latinos in U.S. Sport, 95. On José Torres, see La Opinión 75th Anniversary ed., September 16, 1976, 6, box 43, folder 3, Lozano Family/La Opinión Collection, Huntington Library, San Marino, CA.

217. José Torres, letter to editor Rafael Ybarra, "Marginando Los Deportes," La Opinión, January 17, 1933, 6.

218. "El Equipo Asociacion Deportiva Hispano-Americana en Buen Juego," La Opinión, September 20, 1927, 7.

219. Joseph Rodríguez, "Becoming Latinos: Mexican Americans, Chicanos, and the Spanish Myth in the Urban Southwest," Western Historical Quarterly 29 (Summer 1998): 165–185.

220. "Listos Para La Temporada de Futbol, 1929–1930 Y Todos Propuestos a Retener el Campeonato," La Opinión, September 21, 1929, 9.

221. "Los Futbolistas Del Hispano Americano Iran a Mexico," La Opinión, February 10, 1929, 6.

222. Rafael Ybarra, "Marginando Los Deportes," La Opinión, January 17, 1933, 6.

223. "Del Los Primeros El Club Deportivo Pan Americano," photograph in La Opinión 75th Anniversary ed., September 16, 1976, 6.

224. Juan Gómez-Quiñones, "Piedras contra la luna: México en Aztlán y Aztlán en México: Chicano-Mexican Relations and the Mexican Consulates, 1900–1920," in Contemporary Mexico: Papers of the IV International Congress of Mexican History, ed. James W. Wilkie, Michael C. Meyer, and Edna Monzón de Wilkie (Berkeley: University of California Press, 1976), 494–527; Francisco Balderrama, In Defense of La Raza: The Los Angeles Mexican Consulate and the Mexican Community, 1929 to 1936 (Tucson: University of Arizona Press, 1982); Gilbert González, Mexican Consuls and Labor Organizing: Imperial Politics in the American Southwest (Austin: University of Texas Press, 1999).

225. "El Cónsul de Mexico En Los Angeles Lanzara la Primera Bola en El Parque White Sox," La Opinión, February 17, 1929, 6.

226. The Consular Club developed a rivalry against the Office of Hunting and Fishing club in the sport of bowling. "El Consulado en Juego vs Caza y Pesca," La Opinión, November 22, 1934, 7.

227. Balderrama, In Defense of La Raza, 44–45.

228. Telegram by Consul Rafael de la Colina, August 15, 1931, Protección a Mexicanos del Consulado en Los Angeles, El Ecervo Histórico Diplomático de Secretaría de Relacionese Exteriores, Mexico City.

229. Fiesta Annual Mexicana Program, box IV-657-8, Protección a Mexicanos del Consulado en Los Angeles. Other clubs included Circulo Cosmopolita, Club Atletico y Sociol Atenas, Club Social Imperio, Casino A.R.C., Club Victoria Mutalista, Club Recreativo Olimpia, Club

Cultural Benito Juarez, Club Artistico y Social Rivoli, Logia Juventud Latina 222 A.H.A., Club Atletico Mexico, and Club Atletico y Social Zaragoza.

230. "Letter to Serectario de Relaciones Exteriores from Rafael de la Colina, Consul de Mexico," January 19, 1932, box IV-657-8, Protección a Mexicanos del Consulado en Los Angeles.

231. Ibid. On the parade, see Ignacio Herrerías, "Por El Mundo del Deporte," *La Opinión*, May 5, 1932, 7.

232. Lamberto Álvarez Gayou, "A National Sports Program," *Journal of Health and Physical Education* 14, no. 1 (January 1943): 6.

2. *EL BOXEO*, IMMIGRATION, AND THE "GREAT BROWN HOPE"

1. Jonathan Snowden, "Civil War: Chavez-De la Hoya and the Latino World's Great Divide, 20 Years Later," *Bleacher Report*, June 6, 2016, https://bleacherreport.com/articles/2640463-civil-war-chavez-de-la-hoya-and-the-latino-worlds-great-divide-20-years-later.

2. Ibid.

3. Gail Bederman, *Manliness and Civilization: A Cultural History of Gender and Race in the United States, 1880–1917* (Chicago: University of Chicago Press, 1995), 8.

4. Michael T. Isenberg, *John L. Sullivan and His America* (Urbana: University of Illinois Press, 1988), 293.

5. Theresa Runstedtler, *Jack Johnson, Rebel Sojourner: Boxing in the Shadow of the Global Color Line* (Berkeley: University of California Press, 2012), 18.

6. Jeffrey Sammons, *Beyond the Ring: The Role of Boxing in American Society* (Urbana: University of Illinois Press, 1988), 73.

7. Kath Woodward, *Globalizing Boxing* (Oxford: Bloomsbury, 2015).

8. Matthew Taylor, "The Global Ring? Boxing, Mobility, and Transnational Networks in the Anglophone World, 1890–1914," *Journal of Global History* 8 (2013): 231–255.

9. Meg Frisbee, *The Cultural Battles over Heavyweight Prizefighting in the American West* (Seattle: University of Washington Press, 2018).

10. Jack London, "The Mexican," in *Sporting Blood: Selections from Jack London's Greatest Sports Writing*, ed. Howard Lachtman (Novato, CA: Presidio Press, 1981), 123–153.

11. Betty Lou Young, *Our First Century: The Los Angeles Athletic Club, 1880–1980* (Los Angeles: LAAC Press, 1980), 31–32.

12. Louis Moore, *I Fight for a Living: Boxing and the Battle for Black Manhood, 1880–1915* (Urbana: University of Illinois Press, 2017), 80–88.

13. Ibid., 145–153.

14. Jay Davidson, "Battling Nelson and Herrera Are Matched," *Los Angeles Herald*, March 22, 1906, 6.

15. "Many Offers for Herrera," *Los Angeles Times*, January 16, 1906, 9; "Sporting Expert Finds Some New Facts about Aurelio Herrera," *Bakersfield Californian*, June 14, 1916, 7; "Much Vaulted Fistic Battle Ends in a Miserable Fizzle," *Los Angeles Herald*, May 26, 1906, 5.

16. "Herrera Makes His Statement," *Los Angeles Herald*, June 3, 1906, 6.

17. Dewitt Van Court, *The Making of Champions in California* (Los Angeles: Premier Printing, 1926), 78–79.

18. Although Mexicans had access to citizenship and were legally constructed as "white" after the 1848 Treaty of Guadalupe Hidalgo, they were treated socially as nonwhite and racially inferior. In other words, according to legal historian Laura Gomez, Mexicans became a "wedge racial group" between whites and blacks. Laura Gomez, *Manifest Destinies: The Making of the Mexican American Race* (New York: New York University Press, 2007), 5.

19. Joseph Salas interview by George A. Hodak, April 1987, An Olympian's Oral History, Transcript, 2–3, Amateur Athletic Foundation of Los Angeles (LA84 Foundation), Los Angeles.

20. William D. Estrada, "The Triumph of Joe Salas: First Latino Olympian," *Caminos*, January 1984, 29–30.

21. Ibid., 29–30.

22. Salas interview, 7.

23. "Olympic Auditorium Opens Its Doors Tonight," *Los Angeles Times*, August 5, 1915, 9.

24. Tracy Callis and Chuck Johnston, *Boxing in the Los Angeles Area, 1880–2005* (Victoria, BC: Trafford, 2009), 19–55.

25. Emory Bogardus, *The City Boy and His Problems* (Los Angeles: House of Ralston, 1926), 86.

26. Emory Bogardus, *The Mexican in the United States* (Los Angeles: University of Southern California Press, 1934), 60.

27. Ibid., 59.

28. Ibid., 60.

29. Gregory Rodríguez, "Palaces of Pain–Arenas of Mexican-American Dreams: Boxing and the Formation of Ethnic Mexican Identities in Twentieth Century Los Angeles" (PhD diss., University of California, San Diego, 1999), 45.

30. Bogardus, *City Boy and His Problems*, 86.

31. Bert W. Colima, *Gentleman of the Ring: The Bert Colima Story* (Long Beach, CA: Magic Valley, 2009), 1–13.

32. Ignacio F. Herrerías, "La Pelea de Vernon Fue Sensacional," *La Opinión*, February 9, 1927, 1, 7.

33. "Declaraciones de Bert Colima," *La Opinión*, February 9, 1927, 1.

34. Colima, *Gentleman of the Ring*, 89.

35. "Colima Trains Amateurs," *Los Angeles Times*, March 8, 1932, 29.

36. Callis and Johnston, *Boxing in the Los Angeles Area*, 54.

37. "Los Mejores Boxeadores Mexicanos se Presentan Hoy en la Noche en el Main Street Athletic Club," *La Opinión*, April 6, 1927, 8.

38. Luis Magaña, "Cincuenta Años de Existencia," *La Opinión*, September 16. 1976, 6th sec., 3.

39. "Kid Cupido, Vencedor de Bert Colima," *El Heraldo de México*, February 5, 1926, 1; "Colima y Su Heredera," *El Heraldo de México*, December 14, 1927, 1.

40. "Una Medalla a Ramon Novarro y Diploma a Bert Colima Dara La As. Deportiva H. Americana," *El Heraldo de México*, August 9, 1927, 1.

41. "El Famoso Boxeador Mexicano Bert Colima Participara en la Fiesta del Jueves próximo," *El Heraldo de México*, August 12, 1924, 1.

42. "Bert Colima Estuvo Ayer En Nuestra Redacción," *El Heraldo de México*, August 14, 1924, 1.

43. "Bert Colima saluda al los o aficionados de este país," *Excélsior*, March 12, 1926, 1; Servando Ortoll, *Bert Colima: Relámpago de Whittier* (México City: La Dulce Ciencia/Conaculta, 2013), 89.

44. Colima, *Gentleman of the Ring*, 79–80.

45. Marco Antonio Maldonado and Ruben Amador Zamora, *Pasión por Los Guantes: Historia del box Mexicano I, 1895–1960* (México City: Clio, 1999), 28.

46. "Colima Gets Decision over White in México," *New York Times*, October 8, 1929, 21. Fray Nano is quoted in Servando Ortoll, "Bert Colima: El Principe de Mejico," *Esquina Boxeo*, September 1, 2012, 9.

47. Karly Taube and Marc Zender, "American Gladiators: Ritual Boxing in Ancient Mesoamerica," in *Blood and Beauty: Organized Violence in the Art and Archaeology of Mesoamerica and Central America*, ed. Heather Orr and Rex Koontz (Los Angeles: Cotsen Institute of

Archaeology Press, 2009), 161–220; William Beezley, *Judas at the Jockey Club and Other Episodes of Porfirian Mexico* (Lincoln: University of Nebraska Press, 1987), 31–35.

48. Paul Vanderwood, *Satan's Playground: Mobsters and Movie Stars at America's Greatest Gaming Resort* (Durham, NC: Duke University Press, 2010), 73–74.

49. Maldonado and Zamora, *Pasión por Los Guantes*, 42.

50. Ibid., 43.

51. "Mexico Seeks Aid in Boxing Cleanup," *Californian*, May 15, 1925, 6.

52. Paul Hopwood, "Mexico Boxing Notes," *Ring*, February 1925, 35.

53. "Mexico City Notes," *Ring*, November 1929, 37.

54. Richard McGehee, "The Dandy and Mauler in Mexico: John, Dempsey, et al., and the Mexico City Press, 1919–1927," *Journal of Sport History* 23, no. 1 (Spring 1996): 20–33.

55. Runstedtler, *Jack Johnson, Rebel Sojourner*, 224.

56. Don Cee, "Mexico Notes," *Ring*, January 1926, 42.

57. See, for example, the white boxer image on the front cover of *Revista de Revistas: El Semanario Nacional* in Maria Monserrate Sanchez Soler, *Formando el cuerpo de una nación: El deporte en el México postrevolucionario (1920–1940)* (Mexico City: Consejo Nacional para la Cultura y Las Artes, Instituto Nacional de Bellas Artes, Museo Casa Estudio Diego Rivera y Frida Kahlo, 2012), 52.

58. Rodolfo García, "Esquina Neutral," *La Opinión*, Special 50th Anniversary ed., September 16, 1976, sec. 6a, 8.

59. Ibid., 8.

60. Alexandra Minna Stern, "From Mestizophilia to Biotypology: Racialization and Science in Mexico, 1920–1960," in *Race and Nation in Modern Latin American*, ed. Nancy P. Appelbaum (Chapel Hill: University of North Carolina Press, 2003), 194–195.

61. "Eduardo Huaracha," in *Manuel Gamio: El Inmigrante Mexicano La Historia de su Vida, Entrevistas Completas, 1926–1927*, ed. Devra Weber, Roberto Melville, and Juan Vicente Palerm (Mexico City: México Secretaria de Gobernación, Instituto Nacional de Migración, 2002), 267–269.

62. Eduardo Huaracha "Tomara Parte En le Gran Picnic de la Corte Columbus 102," *El Heraldo de Mexico*, August 16, 1928, 6.

63. "El Caballero Huaracha Demostrará Mañana en la Noche su Agresividad," *La Opinión*, September 14, 1928, 4; "Un Púgil Mexicano, el Caballero (Eduardo Huaracha) aspira al campeonato mundial que ostenta Delaney," *La Prensa*, February 16, 1927, 8.

64. Lamberto Álvarez Gayou, "Los Mexicanos Que Han Triunfado y Siguen Triufando Actualmente en Las Arenas de Estados Unidos," *El Heraldo de México*, November 1, 1927, 1.

65. Lamberto Álvarez Gayou, "El Boxeo Is Boosted in Mexico These Days," *Seattle Daily Times*, August 7, 1929, 23.

66. "México City to Stage Its First Title Bout," *Brooklyn Daily Eagle*, September 7, 1929, 9.

67. Antonio Lavín U, *México en Los Juegos Olímpicos* (Mexico City: Asociacion Nacional de Periodistas, A.C., 1968), 15–25.

68. Hortensia Moreno, "Women Boxers and Nationalism in Mexico," in *Sports and Nationalism in Latin/o America*, ed. Hector Fernandez L' Hoeste, Robert McKee Irwin, and Juan Poblete (New York: Palgrave Macmillan, 2015), 181–199.

69. Ibid., 187; Diane Hofner Samphire, "Mazatlán's Famous Feminist: La Maya," *VidaMaz*, May 4, 2018, https://vidamaz.com/2018/05/04/mazatlans-famous-feminist-la-maya/.

70. Raul Talán, *En El 3er Round* (Mexico City, 1952), 171–174.

71. Ripley, "Believe It or Not," *Muscatine Journal and News Tribune*, August 6, 1931, 3.

72. Moreno, "Women Boxers and Nationalism in Mexico," 181. This ban remained until 1999 when Laura Serrano brought a lawsuit against Mexico City's boxing commission.

73. Maldonado and Zamora, *Pasión por Los Guantes* Mexico, 46–47. Jimmy Fitten was often referred to as the Tex Rickard of Mexico and often compared to Frank Churchill, the American boxing promoter in the Philippines who "imported" Filipino boxers to fight in the United States.

74. Alan Ward, "On Second Thought," *Oakland Tribune*, April 1, 1956, 10.

75. Ibid., 10.

76. Maldonado and Zamora, *Pasión Por Los Guantes*, 44–45.

77. Mae Ngai, *Impossible Subjects: Illegal Aliens and the Making of Modern America* (Princeton, NJ: Princeton University Press, 2004).

78. Natalia Molina, "In a Race All Their Own: The Quest to Make Mexicans Ineligible for U.S. Citizenship," *Pacific Historical Review* 79, no. 2 (May 2010): 167–201.

79. Ibid.

80. Francisco Balderrama, *Decade of Betrayal: Mexican Repatriation in the 1930s*, rev. ed. (Albuquerque: University of New Mexico Press, 2006).

81. The four main racial scripts include the "Birds of Passage" or "Mexican Invaders," the "Deportable Mexican," "Violence as Discourse" and "Whiteness." Natalia Molina, *How Race Is Made in America: Immigration, Citizenship, and the Historical Power of Racial Scripts* (Berkeley: University of California Press, 2014).

82. Helen Delpar, *The Enormous Vogue of Things Mexican: Cultural Relations between the United States and Mexico* (Tuscaloosa: University of Alabama Press, 1992).

83. William Estrada, *The Los Angeles Plaza: Sacred and Contested Space* (Austin: University of Texas Press, 2008).

84. Colin Gunckel, *Mexico on Main Street: Transnational Film Culture in Los Angeles before World War II* (New Brunswick, NJ: Rutgers University Press, 2015).

85. Maldonado and Zamora, *Pasión por Los Guantes*, 32.

86. Douglas Monroy, *Rebirth: Mexican Los Angeles from the Great Migration to the Great Depression* (Berkeley: University of California Press, 1999), 59.

87. Rodriguez, "Palaces of Pain," 63.

88. "Whose Built-Up Is It, Kid Mexico's or Bert Colima's," *Los Angeles Times*, May 10, 1925, A5.

89. "'Baron of Signal Hill' Ring's Kid Mexico Now Fast Hombre with $$," *Los Angeles Times*, October 25, 1949, C1.

90. "Bandit Romero Faces Gene Mullins Tonight," *Los Angeles Times*, December 14, 1929, 11.

91. Harry A. Williams, "Sport Shrapnel," *Los Angeles Times*, August 21, 1932, E6.

92. "Baby Arizmendi Back, Plans to Fight Here," *Los Angeles Times*, April 12, 1936, A11.

93. "Mexican Ring Battlers Bid for U.S. Titles," *San Bernardino County Sun*, May 29, 1934, 5.

94. "Bert Colima Se Retira de los Rings," *La Opinión*, September 16, 1926, 8. Colima made several comebacks until finally retiring in 1933.

95. "Ring Test for Mexican Boxer," *Los Angeles Times*, November 4, 1928, 21.

96. "Gold Found in Mexico Boxers," *Los Angeles Times*, November 6, 1932, E6.

97. "Hay Demanda De Mexicanos," *La Opinión*, January 31, 1933, 5.

98. Ibid.5.

99. Harold Joyce, "Hot Tamales from Mexico," *Ring*, May 1933, 30.

100. Pino Páez, *A Solas En El Altar: Vida de Rodolfo Casanova "El Chango"* (Mexico City: EDAMEX, 1997).

101. Stephen Allen, *A History of Mexican Boxing: Masculinity, Modernity and Nationalism* (Albuquerque: University of New Mexico Press), 75–83.

102. Lew Eskin, "The Amazing Kid Azteca," *Ring*, May 1959, 26.

103. "Mexican Boxing Champs Are Refused Admittance to U.S.," *Lubbock Morning Avalanche*, June 21, 1933, 22; "Casanova and Azteca Still Being Held," *Los Angeles Times*, June 23, 1933, I3.

104. Transmission of Records on Appeal, June 24, 1933, file 55836/955, 1, Records of the Immigration and Naturalization Service, RG 86, National Archives, Washington, DC (hereafter INS Records). The Board of Special Inquiry is a board set up by the Commissioner of Immigration in order to investigate all matters concerning immigration.

105. "Gallery Closes Casanova Bout," *Los Angeles Examiner*, June 18, 1933, 4.

106. Board of Inquiry Testimony of Rodolfo Casanova-Mendez, June 20, 1933, file 55836/955, INS Records.

107. Board of Inquiry Testimony of José Corona, June 21, 1933, file 55836/955, 12, INS Records.

108. Alien Contract Labor Act of 1885, chap. 164, § 1, 23 Stat. 332, 48th Congress, February 25, 1885, http://library.uwb.edu/Static/USimmigration/23%20stat%20332.pdf.

109. Krystin R. Moon, "On a Temporary Basis: Immigration, Labor Unions, and the American Entertainment Industry, 1880s–1930s," *Journal of American History* 99, no. 3 (December 2012): 771–792.

110. To All Districts Immigration and Naturalization Service from Edward Shaughnessy, Acting Commissioner, April 6, 1937, file 55880/500, INS Records.

111. Board of Inquiry Testimony of Rodolfo Casanova-Mendez, June 21, 1933, file 55836/955, INS Records.

112. Memorandum to Board of Review by G. C. Wilmoth, District Director of Immigration, El Paso District, June 26, 1933, file 55836/955, INS Records.

113. Western Union Telegram to Secretary of Labor from J. C. Russell, June 23, 1933, file 55836/955, INS Records.

114. David Leonard, *Playing While White: Privilege and Power On and Off the Field* (Seattle: University of Washington Press, 2017).

115. Francine Sanders Romero, "'There Are Only White Champions': The Rise and Demise of Segregated Boxing in Texas," *Southwestern Historical Quarterly* 108, no. 1 (July 2004): 27–41.

116. W. J. Stephens to District Director Immigration, Galveston, Texas, March 28, 1935, file 55880/500, INS Records.

117. "Mexican Boxers to Invade Los Angeles," *Bakersfield Californian*, June 16, 1933, A8.

118. "Azteca and Casanova on Spot, Rival Gymnasiums Squabble over Invading Mexican Boxers," *Los Angeles Times*, July 7, 1933, A11.

119. *Ring* 5, no. 5 (June 1935): 3.

120. Molina, *How Race Is Made in America*, 29–34.

121. "Classy Boxers Open Olympic," *Los Angeles Times*, July 11, 1933, A9.

122. "Juan Zurita Favor over Gene Espinoza in Hollywood Ring Battle Tonight," *Los Angeles Times*, January 18, 1935, A12.

123. Linda España-Maram, *Creating Masculinity in Los Angeles's Little Manila: Working-Class Filipinos and Popular Culture, 1920s–1950s* (New York: Columbia University Press, 2006), 92.

124. "Kennedy May Referee Casanova—Dado Battle," *Los Angeles Times*, November 9, 1932, 26.

125. Ibid. 26.

126. "Classy Boxers Open Olympic," *Los Angeles Times*, July 11, 1933, A9.

127. Salvador Baguez, "On the Outside Looking In," *Los Angeles Times*, June 22, 1933, A9.

128. "Scrappers Still 'Out' at Border," *Los Angeles Times*, June 22, 1933, A9.

129. "El Martes Se Enfrentaran Los Paisanos," *La Opinión*, July 9, 1933, 7.

130. "Es Probable Que Se Pida Una Prorroga," *La Opinión*, June 22, 1933, 7.

131. "Olympic to Hold Show if Azteca Freed Today," *Los Angeles Times*, June 24, 1933, 5.

132. Ed Gorey to James Farley, Western Union Telegram, June 22, 1933, file 55836/955, INS Records.

133. "Ring Stars of Mexico Due Today," *Los Angeles Times*, June 29, 1933, A11.

134. "Son Esperados Hoy Azteca y Casanovita," *La Opinión*, June 20, 1933, 7; "Los Pugilistas Estaban en El Paso Ayer en la Noche y Son Esperados en Breve," *La Opinión*, June 21, 1933, 7.

135. Rafael Ybarra, "Marginando," *La Opinión*, June 22, 1933, 7.

136. Rafael Ybarra, "Marginando," *La Opinión*, June 23, 1933, 7.

137. Fraudulent Boxing Contracts, file 56251/138, INS Records.

138. Western Union Telegram to Secretary of Labor from Dutch Meyers, June 16, 1933, file 55836/955, INS Records.

139. Colima, *Gentleman of the Ring*, 107.

140. "Por No Decir La Verdad Casanovita y Azteca No Pueden Ir a California," *El Excélsior*, June 21, 1933, 4.

141. "Se Les Niega La Entrada a Casanova y Kid Azteca," *El Excélsior*, June 22, 1933, 4.

142. "Mexico's Fistiana Has Wail, Boxers Victimized in Dollar-Land, Invaders Urged to Stay Home," *Californian*, November 18, 1932, 7.

143. "Mexican Ring Aces Robbed in U.S. Claim," *Santa Ana Register*, November 18, 1932, 12.

144. "Boxers Given Timely Advice, Mexican Sports Writer Urges Home Stay Following Loss by Baby Casanova," *San Bernardino County Sun*, November 19, 1932, 5.

145. Allen, *History of Mexican Boxing*, 113.

146. "Muchos Han Sido Pugilistas y Después Actores de Cine," *La Prensa*, June 29, 1941, 12.

147. Rodolfo García, "Esquina Neutral," *La Opinión*, December 17, 1944, 4.

148. Rodríguez, "Palaces of Pain," 75.

149. Anthony Quinn, *The Original Sin: A Self-Portrait* (Boston: Little, Brown, 1971), 148–157.

150. U.S. Department of Labor, "Report of Execution of Department Decision," June 29, 1933, Immigration and Naturalization Service, file 7001/3385, INS Records.

151. "Se Les Prepara Una Recepción en el Aeropuerto," *La Opinión*, June 28, 1933, 7.

152. "Casanova, Azteca Primed to Repel Filipino Foes," *Los Angeles Times*, July 9, 1933, D2.

153. Rafael Ybarra, "Marginando," *La Opinión*, July 7, 1933, 7.

154. "Siguelo . . . Siguelo . . . Gritaba Lupe Vélez," *La Opinión*, July 14, 1933, 4.

155. "Kid Azteca New Mexican Title Threat," *Los Angeles Times*, July 13, 1933, A9.

156. Casanova and Azteca disliked fighting abroad especially since they performed worse outside of Mexico. See Stephen Allen, "Boxing in Mexico: Masculinity, Modernity and Nationalism, 1946–1982," (PhD diss., Rutgers University, 2013), 47–48.

157. "Immigration Authorities Again Halt Baby Casanova," *Los Angeles Times*, November 20, 1933, 11; "Casanova Is Here en Route to L.A.," *El Paso Times*, November 19, 1933, 14.

158. "Entry of Boxer to U.S. Depends on Uniqueness," *El Paso Herald-Post*, November 20, 1933, 2.

159. "Mexican Army Man will Run Babe Casanova," *Nevada State Journal*, July 21, 1934, 5.

160. Allen, *History of Mexican Boxing*, 48–49.

161. "Mexico Debe Tener Un Campeon Mundial," *La Opinión*, December 3, 1933, 4.

162. Lara Putnam, "The Panama Cannonball's Transnational Ties: Migrants, Sport, and Belonging in the Interwar Greater Caribbean," *Journal of Sport History* 41, no. 3 (Fall 2014): 401–424; Enver Casimir, "A Variable and Unwavering Significance: Latinos, African Americans and the Racial Identity of Kid Chocolate," in *More Than Just Peloteros: Sport and US Latino Communities*, ed. Jorge Iber (Lubbock: Texas Tech University Press, 2014), 39–65.

163. "Shwa Gives Mexico First Boxing Title," *Brooklyn Times Union*, February 21, 1933, 13.

164. Mike Wagner, "Ex-Champ's Career Was 'Muy Grande,'" *Laredo Morning Times*, August 13, 1991, 5; Andrew Fruman, "Muy Grande Great: The Story of Battling Shaw," *Cruelest Sport*, August 21. 2013, 1.

165. "Mexicanos Que Han Estado a Punto de Conquistar el Campeonato de Su División," *La Opinión*, February 28, 1933, 7.

166. These included Aurelio Herrera, Joe Rivers, Bert Colima, and Baby Sal Soria.

167. "La Iniciación de Baby Arizmendi," *La Opinión*, May 12, 1935, 24.

168. Ralph Huston, "New Mexican Sensation," *Los Angeles Times*, February 11, 1932, A11.

169. " Mexican Fighter Keeps His Title," *Daily Capitol*, October 19, 1932, 8.

170. Daniel M. Daniel, "Mexican 'Baby Face' Seeks Fistic Heights," *Ring Magazine*, June 1932, 12.

171. Paul Lowry, "Baby Arizmendi, Mexican Hero," *Los Angeles Times*, November 22, 1932, A9.

172. There was a total of 145 published letters from February 5 to February 24, 1933.

173. "Logrará México Tener un Campeón Mundial?," *La Opinión*, February 8, 1933, 7.

174. "Envie Ud. Su Opinion Acera de La Pelea," *La Opinión*, February 10, 1933, 7.

175. "Opiniones Son . . . Opiniones," *La Opinión*, February 21, 1933, 7.

176. "Hablan Los Aficionados," *La Opinión*, February 5, 1933, 4.

177. "El Baby No Tiene Miedo Al Campeon," *La Opinión*, February 26, 1933, 4.

178. "Veinte Minutos Antes de Que Entrara al Ring, Se Hallaba Muy Enfermo en Su Vestidor," *La Opinión*, March 3, 1933, 9.

179. "Decision Met by Near Riot of Partisans," *Oakland Tribune*, March 1, 1933, 18; "Miller Wins to Keep Title: Mexicans Rain Bottles on Beaten Arizmendi," *De Moines Tribune*, March 1, 1933, 16; "Hail of Bottles Climax of Featherweight Bout," *Los Angeles Times*, March 1, 1933, A9.

180. "Miller Retains Crown in Bout with Arizmendi," *Anniston Star*, March 1, 1933, 8.

181. Harden Burnley, "Mexican Maulers," *Great Falls Tribune*, April 6, 1933, 8. King Features Syndicate distributed this cartoon.

182. "Debemos Enseñarlos a Perder en Buena Lid," *La Opinión*, March 2, 1933, 7.

183. "Mexican Boxer Held at Border," *Arizona Independent Republic*, May 6, 1933, 12.

184. "Arizmendi Hit by Ruling of Inquiry Board," *Los Angeles Times*, May 10, 1933, A9.

185. "Girl Given $3500 Betrayal Damages," *Oakland Tribune*, April 25, 1933, 3.

186. Bill Ball, "Sports Shots," *Laredo Times*, May 11, 1933, 5.

187. Several years later he admitted that he was the boy's father. "Baby Arizmendi Admits Paternity in Court Battle," *San Jose News*, June 1, 1937, 8.

188. Rafael Ybarra, "Marginando," *La Opinión*, May 11, 1933, 7.

189. "Arizmendi Admits Child Is His Son," *Stateman's Journal*, June 4, 1937, 22.

190. Werner Laufer, "Aztec Assassin," *Arizona Republic*, December 3, 1933, 14.

191. Makanazo, "En La Maraña del Deporte," *La Opinión*, December 10, 1933, 4.

192. Joseph Nichols, "Arizmendi Victor in Belloise Bout," *New York Times*, August 31, 1934, 23.

193. "Arizmendi, Campeon Mundial?," *La Opinión*, August 31, 1934, 1.

194. "Arizmendi Whips Belloise, Wins Title," *Los Angeles Times*, August 31, 1934, A9.

195. "Subí Al Ring Acordándome de mi Patria," *La Opinión*, August 31, 1934, 1.

196. "Versos Para El General Arizmendi," *La Opinión*, July 14, 1932, 7.

197. "Esta Noche Se Estrena El Hidalgo La Revista 'El Establo de Arizmendi,'" *La Opinión*, October 27, 1932, 4.

198. T. F. Franco, "Corrido del Famoso Campeon Mexicano Baby Arizmendi," in Nellie Foster, "The Corrido: A Mexican Culture Trait Persisting in Southern California" (master's thesis, University of Southern California, 1939), 125–126.

199. Ibid.

200. Américo Paredes, *Folklore and Culture on the Texas-Mexican Border*, ed. Richard Bauman (Austin: University of Texas Press, 1993).

201. "California Café" advertisement, *Sport Page*, December 26, 1946, 6.

202. "Lauro Salas and Guzman in Café Bout," *Los Angeles Times*, July 10, 1952, 67.

203. Magaña, "Cincuenta Años de Existencia," 2.

204. "Gómez Barred by U.S." *New York Times*, March 22, 1932, 27.

205. Francisco Costello, "Como Se Inició En El Baseball El Gran Jugador Mexicano José (Chile) Gómez, Segunda Base del 'Filadelfia,'" *La Prensa*, November 9, 1936, 7.

206. Gil Castro, "Como Inicio Su Carrera El Gran Pelotero Mexicano Chile Gómez, " *La Opinión*, May 13 1934, 4.

207. "Gómez Barred by U.S." *New York Times*, March 22, 1932, 27.

208. "Barnstormer to Big Leaguer" August 15, 1935, Chile Gómez Player File, National Baseball Library and Archive, National Baseball Hall of Fame, Cooperstown, NY.

3. PLAYING *BÉISBOL* ACROSS BORDERS

1. Tony Gamboa attempted to try out with the Brooklyn Dodgers but was rejected because of his Mexican heritage. Richard Santillán, Mark Ocegueda, and Terry Cannon, *Mexican American Baseball in the Inland Empire* (Charleston, SC: Arcadia, 2012), 20.

2. "Mañana es el Banquete de Los Peloteros," *La Opinión*, June 5, 1955. Those attending included Arturo Castillo, Rodrigo Castillo, Tony Gamboa, Alonzo "Pops" Orozco, Phil Speaker, Charles "Conde" Galindo, Lefty Ocampo, Albert Piña, Carlos Lima, Yamo Ornelas, Loco Soto, Spike, Eddie Lopez, Paul Ramirez, Earl Zuñiga, Earl Ramirez, Al Zuñiga, Juan Chacón, Frank Hernandez, Gordon Leach, Manuel Regalado, Joe Mitre, David Salazar, and Pete Salazar.

3. Luis Magaña, "50 años de existencia," *La Opinión*, September 16, 1975, sec. 6, 2.

4. Carlos Salazar, "*La Opinión* nació en la época de Dempsey, Casablanca y Ruth," *La Opinión*, September 16, 1975, sec. 5, 1.

5. John Virtue, *South of the Color Barrier: How Jorge Pasquel and the Mexican League Pushed Baseball toward Racial Integration* (Jefferson, NC: McFarland, 1996); Mark Ribowsky, *The Power and the Darkness: The Life of Josh Gibson in the Shadows of the Game* (New York: Simon & Schuster, 1996); Quincy Troupe, *20 Years Too Soon: Prelude to Major-League Integrated Baseball* (Los Angeles: S and S Enterprises, 1997); Monte Irvin, *Nice Guys Finish First: The Autobiography of Monte Irvin* (New York: Carroll & Graf, 1996).

6. Adrian Burgos Jr., "Learning America's Other Game: Baseball, Race, and the Study of Latinos," in *Latino/a Popular Culture*, ed. Michelle Habell-Pallán and Mary Romero (New York: New York University Press, 2002), 235.

7. Jean Hastings Ardell, *Breaking into Baseball: Women and the National Pastime* (Carbondale: Southern Illinois University Press, 2005); Mary Littlewood, *The Path to the Gold: An Historical Look at Women's Fastpitch in the United States* (Columbia, MO: National Fastpitch Coaches Association, 1998); Erica Westley, *Fastpitch: The Untold History of Softball and the Women Who Made the Game* (New York: Simon & Schuster, 2016).

8. A. G. Spalding, *Baseball: America's National Game* (San Francisco: Halo Books, 1911; repr., 1991), 9.

9. Kamar Al-Shimas (pen name for Morton F. Brand), *The Mexican Southland* (Fowler, IN: Benton Review Shop, 1922), 83.

10. William Beezley, *Judas at the Jockey Club and Other Episodes of Porfirian Mexico* (Lincoln: University of Nebraska Press, 1987), 16; William Schell, "Lions, Bulls and Baseball: Colonel R.C. Pate and Modern Sports Promotion in Mexico," *Journal of Sport History* 20, no. 3 (Winter 1993): 271–273.

11. Sullivan Holman McCollester, *Mexico, Old and New: A Wonderland* (Boston: Universalist, 1899), 31.

12. Eugene Murdock, *Ban Johnson, Czar of Baseball* (Westport, CT: Greenwood, 1982), 196–197; William Beezley, "The Rise of Baseball in Mexico and the First Valenzuela," *Studies in Latin American Popular Culture* 4 (1985): 1–14.

13. S. W. Rider, "Is Bull Fighting Losing Its Appeal in Mexico?," *Playground*, October 1923, 415.

14. Tomas Morales, "El Beisbol Mexicano a través de las décadas," in *Enciclopedia del Beisbol Mexicano*, ed. Pedro Treto Cisneros (Mexico City: Revistas Deportivas, 1994), 6–9; Alejandro Aguilar Reyes, *Un Huracán Llamado Fray Nano* (Mexico City: Universidad Anáhuac del Norte, 2013), 77–89; Miguel Esparza, "La Pugna por El Diamante: La Institucionalización del Béisbol Capitalino, 1920–1930," *Historia Mexicana*, 68, no.3 (Enero-Marzo 2019): 1075-1120.

15. Alan Klein, *Baseball on the Border: A Tale of Two Laredos* (Princeton, NJ: Princeton University Press, 1997), 47; Peter Bjarkman, *Diamonds around the Globe: The Encyclopedia of International Baseball* (Westport, CT: Greenwood, 2005), 267–276.

16. Tomás Morales, "Mexico," in *Baseball Forever/Béisbol Para Siempre*, ed. Carlos J. Garcia (Mexico City: I.E.S.A., 1978), 246.

17. Norman Hayner, *New Patterns in Old Mexico: A Study of Town and Metropolis* (New Haven, CT: College & University Press, 1966), 219. See also Seymour Menton, "Mexican Baseball Terminology: An Example of Linguistic Growth," *Hispania* 37, no. 4 (December 1954): 478–481.

18. "Los Cafés Batearon en una Entrada Para Ganar," *La Opinión*, October 7, 1944, 8.

19. William E. Wilson, "A Note on 'Pochismo,'" *Modern Language Journal*, October 1946, 345. The term referred to an "Americanized Mexican" person who cannot speak Spanish and has been disconnected from their cultural heritage.

20. "Gringo Lindo," *Newsweek*, August 14, 1944, 76.

21. Ignacio Herrerías, "Por El Mundo del Deporte," *La Opinión*, March 2, 1931, 7.

22. John Phillips, *The Mexican Jumping Beans: The Story of the Baseball War of 1946* (Perry, GA: Capital, 1997); Harold Rosenthal, "The 'War' with Mexico," *Baseball Digest*, January 1963–December 1964, 53–56; Frank Graham Jr., "The Great Mexican War of 1946," *Sports Illustrated*, September 19, 1966, 1–8; Alan Klein, "Baseball Wars: The Mexican Baseball League and Nationalism in 1946," *Studies in Latin American Popular Culture* 13 (1994): 33–54; Gerald Vaughn, "Jorge Pasquel and the Evolution of the Mexican League," *National Pastime*, vol. 12 (Washington, DC: Society for American Baseball Research, 1992), 9–13.

23. "Would Confer on Pact, Mexican Baseball Leader Ready to Meet Big Leaguers," *New York Times*, March 13, 1946, 32.

24. Mario de la Fuente with Boye De Mente, *I Like You, Gringo—But!* (Phoenix, AZ: Phoenix Books, 1972), 75.

25. Vicki Ruiz, "'Star Struck': Acculturation, Adolescence, and the Mexican American Woman, 1920–1950," in *Building with Our Hands: New Directions in Chicana Studies*, ed. Adela de la Torre and Beatríz Pesquera (Berkeley: University of California Press, 1993), 109–129.

26. Samuel Regalado, "Baseball in the Barrios: The Scene in East Los Angeles since World War II," *Baseball History* 1 (Summer 1986): 47–59; George J. Sánchez, *Becoming Mexican American: Ethnicity, Culture and Identity in Chicano Los Angeles, 1900–1945* (New York: Oxford University Press, 1993), 166; Douglas Monroy, *Rebirth: Mexican Los Angeles from the Great Migration to the Great Depression* (Berkeley: University of California Press, 1999), 46–48.

27. Mark Dyreson, "The Emergence of Consumer Culture and the Transformation of Physical Culture: American Sport in the 1920s," *Journal of Sport History* 16, no. 3 (Winter 1989): 261–281.

28. Kevin Nelson, *The Golden Game: The Story of California Baseball* (San Francisco: California Historical Society Press, 2004), 136–146.

29. "Bien Venido Babe Ruth," *El Heraldo de México*, October 24, 1924, 5.

30. Manuel Corro M., "Desarrollo del deporte desde los fabulosos anos 'veinte,'" *La Opinión*, September 16, 1976, sec. 6, 8.

31. Earl Smith, "There Was No Golden Age of Sport for African American Athletes," *Society* 37, no. 3 (March/April 2000): 45–48.

32. "*La Opinión* Es Señalado como Gran Impulsador del Deporte," *La Opinión*, May 8, 1931, 7.

33. "Cultura Fisica, Lo Que Del Deporte Piensa Las Mujeres," *La Opinión*, April 5, 1926, 7.

34. Stephanie Twin, *Out of the Bleachers: Writings on Women and Sport* (New York: Feminist Press, 1979), xxvii–xxxiv.

35. Susan Cahn, *Coming on Strong: Gender and Sexuality in Twentieth-Century Women's Sport* (New York: Free Press, 1994), 31–54.

36. "Bloomer girls" comes from the "bloomer" trousers they wore. Debra Shattuck, *Bloomer Girls: Women Baseball Pioneers* (Urbana: University of Illinois Press, 2017); Barbara Gregorich, *Women at Play: The Story of Women in Baseball* (New York: Harcourt Brace, 1993), 2–59.

37. Cahn, *Coming on Strong*, 38.

38. Ardell, *Breaking into Baseball*; Debra Shattuck, "Playing a Man's Game: Women and Baseball in the United States, 1866–1954," in *Baseball History from Outside the Lines: A Reader*, ed. John Dreifort (Lincoln: University of Nebraska Press, 2001), 195–215.

39. Vicki Ruiz, *From Out of the Shadows: Mexican Women in Twentieth-Century America* (New York: Oxford University Press, 1998).

40. José M. Alamillo, *Making Lemonade Out of Lemons: Mexican American Labor and Leisure in a California Town, 1880-1960* (Urbana IL: University of Illinois Press, 2006).

41. William Deverell, *Whitewashed Adobe: The Rise of Los Angeles and the Remaking of Its Mexican Past* (Berkeley: University of California Press, 2004), 129–171.

42. Jim McConnell, "Brickyard Team Best of the Best," *Daily Breeze*, March 19, 2012, 1.

43. Alejandro Morales, *The Brick People* (Houston: Arte Publico Press, 1988). See also the Brick People documentary produced by the University of California Television, www.youtube.com/watch?v=u3ucvoTLCF4.

44. Richard Santillán, Victoria Norton, Christopher Docter, Monica Ortez, and Richard Arroyo, *Mexican American Baseball in the San Fernando Valley* (Charleston, SC: Arcadia, 2015).

45. This scrapbook included newspaper clippings, photographs, handbills, patches, ribbons, and other memorabilia. Their daughter Elisa Orozco-O'Neil donated the scrapbook to the Smithsonian's National Museum of American History. See Al Orozco, "Orozcos Contribute Baseball Artifacts to Smithsonian," *Coastal View.com*, July 5, 2017 www.coastalview.com/sports/orozcos-contribute-baseball-artifacts-to-smithsonian/article_70d65072-61a6-11e7-bb92-f73b151346ab.html.

46. "Los Tigres de Wilmington son Derrotados por Los Zapateros," *La Opinión*, August 2, 1928, 7; "Los Zapateros de los Hermanos Castillo Derrotaron al Potente Team San Fernando Merchants," *La Opinión*, November 23, 1928, 6.

47. "Manuel Regalado McGraw Predice un Triunfo Decisivo de los Zapateros Sobre Los Huestes de Ortiz," *La Opinión*, March 31, 1929, 6.

48. "En El Primer Encuentro, Los Mexicanos Fueron Derrotados por los Petroleros y en el Segundo le Cerraron el Juego al A. M. Castle," *La Opinión*, July 8, 1929, 7.

49. Ibid.

50. Stephen Johnson III, "Rudy Regalado" (Society for American Baseball Research, 2014), http://sabr.org/bioproj/person/7db9ddf3.

51. "Los Zapateros Listos Para El Domingo," *La Opinión*, October 6, 1928, 7.

52. The team's 1926 roster included David Salazar, Alonzo "Pops" Orozco, Carlos Galindo, Carlos Lima, F. "Zurdo" (Lefty) Ocampo, Joe "Loco" Soto, Joe Quintana, Pete Salazar, Arturo Rodriguez, J. Alvarado, J. Chacón, S. Machuca, Billy Lopez, and Ray Zuñiga.

53. "Un Premio para la Novena de El Paso," *La Opinión*, February 27, 1927, 7.

54. "Los Zapateros Derrotaron a Los Tigres de Santa Monica y Ahora son Campeones de California, "*La Opinión*, October 23, 1928, 7.

55. "El Paso Shoe Store Fue Derrotado," *La Opinión*, November 7, 1927, 7.

56. "Juegos de Baseball a Beneficio de Un Jugador que Esta Inutilizado," *La Opinión*, October 8, 1926, 6.

57. "Los Zapateros se Ponen las Botas," ca. late 1920s, Scrapbook, Orozco Family Archive.

58. Richard Santillán, Camila Alva López, James Aguirre, Donna Galván and Mark R. García. *Mexican American Baseball in the San Gabriel Valley* (Charleston, SC: Arcadia, 2018), 20.

59. "Hoy Juega el Paso Shoe Store Con el Azteca en San Gabriel," *La Opinión*, December 16, 1928, 7.

60. Curtiz Marez, "Brown: The Politics of Working-Class Chicano Style," *Social Text* 14, no. 3 (Fall 1996): 109–132.

61. Richard Santillán, Christopher Docter, Anna Bermúdez, Eddie Navarro, and Alan O'Connor, *Mexican American Baseball in the Central Coast* (Charleston, SC: Arcadia, 2013), 94.

62. Cecilia Rasmussen, "A Park Where Only the Game Mattered," *Los Angeles Times*, February 22, 1998. Another White Sox Ball Park, home of the Los Angeles White Sox, a black semipro team, existed in Boyle Heights in 1920. See Glen Creason, "In the 1920s, L.A.'s All Black White Sox Had Their Own Boyle Heights Ballpark," *Los Angeles Magazine*, April 6, 2016, 1.

63. Phil Dixon and Patrick Hannigan, *The Negro Baseball Leagues: A Photographic History* (Mattituck, NY: Amereon House, 1992), 114–115.

64. Some of these teams included the Kansas City Royals and Monarchs, Philadelphia Giants, Detroit Giants, and Nashville Royal Giants. There were also all-black teams from the sandlots of Los Angeles, such as the Royal Giants, Colored Giants, Monarchs, Stars, and many others. William F. McNeil, *The California Winter League: America's First Integrated Professional Baseball League* (Jefferson, NC: McFarland, 2002), 21.

65. Harry Levette, "Nashville Royal Giants Welcomed in for Winter League," *California Eagle*, October 17, 1930.

66. Lipsitz argues that racialized social relations take on their full force and meaning when they are enacted physically in actual places, like sports stadiums. See George Lipsitz, *How Racism Takes Place* (Philadelphia: Temple University Press, 2011), 238.

67. "El Paso Jugara dos Partidos Mañana," *El Heraldo de México*, September 15, 1928, 5; "Los Ahijados de Ortiz Vence a Los Zapateros de Castillo," *La Opinión*, September 18, 1928, 7.

68. "El Cónsul De México En Los Angeles Lanzara La Primera Bola en El Parque White Sox," *La Opinión*, February 7, 1929, 7.

69. Ignacio Herrerías, "Por El Mundo Del Deporte," *La Opinión*, March 12, 1930, 10.

70. "Aplastante Triunfo del White Sox," *La Opinión*, January 31, 1927, 7.

71. "Carta Para Que La Contesten Los Zapateros y Los Tigres," *La Opinión*, October 10, 1928, 7.

72. "Los Zapateros Sostendrán Hoy un Juego de Mucha Importancia," *La Opinión*, November 18, 1928, 4.

73. "Los Zapateros de los Hermanos Castillo Derrotaron al Potente Team San Fernando Merchants," *La Opinión*, November 23, 1928, 6; "La Verdad Sobre el Ultimo Encuentro Entre Las Novenas El Paso Shoe Store y West Side Merchants," *El Heraldo de México*, November 27, 1928, 4.

74. "El Paso Store Dispuesto a Defender Su Campeonato de Baseball de Los Angeles," *La Opinión*, January 12, 1929, 7.

75. Ibid.

76. "Hoy a la una de la Tarde se Iniciará la Temporada de Baseball en el White Sox," *La Opinión*, February 24, 1929, 6.

77. "Desde Ayer El Paso Shoe Store es Campeón de Baseball de California Por Tercera Vez Consecutiva," *La Opinión*, February 25, 1929, 7.

78. "Hoy Celebra el 5 de Mayo en El White Sox Con Una Brillante Fiesta Beisbolista," *La Opinión*, May 5, 1929, 11.

79. Ibid.

80. On the 1920s Mexican problem, see Carey McWilliams, *North from Mexico: The Spanish-Speaking People of the United States,* new ed. (New York: Praeger, 1990).

81. "Hoy Jugaran Mexicanos Contra Americanos en el Parque White Sox," *La Opinión,* March 24, 1929, 6.

82. "El Paso Shoe Store 3 Carreras, Cudahy Puritans 1 Carrera," *La Opinión,* March 25, 1929, 7.

83. Ibid.

84. "La Novena El Paso Shoe Store Jugara en el Wrigley Field," *La Opinión,* November 3, 1929, 9.

85. "Mexican Ball Team Opens Season Today," *Los Angeles Times,* November 10, 1929, E13.

86. R. Scott Mackey, *Barbary Baseball: The Pacific Coast League of the 1920s* (Jefferson, NC: McFarland, 1995), 108–122.

87. Amy Essington, "Equality on the Baseball Diamond: Integrating the Pacific Coast League, 1948–1952," *Journal of the West* 47, no. 4 (Fall 2008): 49–59; Amy Essington, *The Integration of the Pacific Coast League: Race and Baseball on the West Coast* (Lincoln: University of Nebraska Press, 2018), 47–66.

88. Andy Vargas and David Salazar joined the San Francisco Seals in 1922 and 1924, respectively; Lou Almada joined the Seattle Indians from 1929, and his brother Melo Almada joined the team in 1931. Jess Flores was the first Latino player to join the Los Angeles Angels in 1939; Manny Perez joined the Hollywood Starts in 1942. Mackey, *Barbary Baseball,* 184–185; http://baseball-reference.com.

89. Angie Salazar Capela, telephone interview by the author, January 1, 2018.

90. Regalado, "Baseball in the Barrios"; Richard Santillán, "Mexican Baseball Teams in the Midwest, 1916–1965: The Politics of Cultural Survival and Civil Rights," *Perspectives in Mexican American Studies* 7 (2000): 131–152; José M. Alamillo, "*Peloteros* in Paradise: Mexican American Baseball and Oppositional Politics in Southern California, 1930–1950," *Western Historical Quarterly* 34 (Summer 2003): 191–211; Michael D. Innis-Jimenez, "Beyond the Baseball Diamond and Basketball Court: Organized Leisure in Interwar South Chicago," *International Journal of the History of Sport* 26, no. 7 (June 2009): 906–923; Richard Santillán and Francisco Balderrama, "*Los Chorizeros*: The New York Yankees of East Los Angeles and the Reclaiming of Mexican American Baseball History," in *Endless Seasons: Baseball in Southern California,* ed. Jean Hastings Ardell and Andy McCue (Phoenix, AZ: Society for American Baseball Research, 2011), 7–13; John Fraire, "Mexicans Playing Baseball in Indiana Harbor, 1925–1942," *Indiana Magazine of History* 110 (June 2014): 120–145.

91. On the impact of the Great Depression on Mexican American, see Francisco Balderrama, *Decade of Betrayal: Mexican Repatriation in the 1930s,* rev. ed. (Albuquerque: University of New Mexico Press, 2006).

92. Charles Alexander, *Breaking the Slump: Baseball in the Depression Era* (New York: Columbia University Press, 2004).

93. "México y El Paso se Unirán para Formar un Solo Club Que Se Llamara 'México-El Paso,'" *La Opinión,* August 29, 1930, 9.

94. Sánchez, *Becoming Mexican American,* 108–125.

95. "Galindo Fue Designado Manager Del México-El Paso," *La Opinión,* September 5, 1930, 11.

96. "Galindo Gets Coaching Job at Roosevelt High," *Chino Champion,* September 13, 1929, 4; "Galindo, Former SC Sports Star, Dead," *San Bernardino County Sun,* March 1, 1968, 30.

97. Richard Santillán, Richard Peña, Teresa M. Santillán, Al Padilla, and Bob Lagunas, *Mexican American Baseball in East Los Angeles* (Charleston, SC: Arcadia, 2016), 30–31.

98. Ibid.

99. "Estos Son Los Nipones Que Trataran de Encontrar a la Bola de Fernando Barradas en el Juego Nocturno Que Habrá el Próximo Lunes Ocho en el Parque Wrigley," *La Opinión*, September 5, 1930, 7.

100. Apart from helping Mexico earn a silver medal at the 1930 Central American Games, he threw three no-hitters, earned a 1.76 ERA, and batted an average of .290 during his long career (1925–1944) in the Mexican League. Barradas was admitted to the Mexico Hall of Fame in 1939. "El Famoso Pitcher Mexicano Fernando Barradas, Héroe de los Juegos Olímpicos de La Habana," *La Opinión*, June 8, 1920, 7.

101. "Resulto Interesante La Platica Por Radio de Fernando Barradas," *La Opinión*, August 8, 1930, 9.

102. Ibid.

103. Yochi Nagata, "'The Pride of Lil' Tokio': The Los Angeles Nippons Baseball Club, 1926–1941," in *More Than a Game: Sport in the Japanese American Community*, ed. Brian Niiya (Los Angeles: Japanese American National Museum, 2000), 100–109. See also Samuel Regalado, *Nikkei Baseball: Japanese American Players from Immigration and Internment to the Major Leagues* (Urbana: University of Illinois Press, 2013), 61–68.

104. "Sin Precedente Resultó el Gran Espectáculo del Parque Wrigley," *La Opinión*, September 10, 1930, 9.

105. Ibid.

106. "Night Game Makes Big Hit," *Los Angeles Times*, September 10, 1930, 16.

107. In 1932, Fabriles changed their name to Aztecas. "Hoy Se Efectuarán Los Primeros Juegos Por La Supremacía Entre Fabriles y Mexico-El Paso," *La Opinión*, September 21, 1930, p.7.

108. Homobono Márquez was born in Arizona but relocated to Mexico to manage baseball teams comprised of Mexican and Mexican American players. With support from his close friend, President Álvaro Obregón, Márquez develop professional baseball in Mexico during the 1920s and 1930s. Ricardo Velázquez Jr, "Los Antecedentes de la Fundación de la Liga Mexicana," *Recuerdos del Diamante*, April 10, 2015, http://recuerdosdeldiamante.blogspot.com/2015/04/antecedentes-de-la-fundacion-de-la-liga.html.

109. "México-El Paso y Fabriles Conquistaron Sendos Triunfos," *La Opinión*, September 22, 1930, 7.

110. Ibid., 7.

111. "Se Vieron Bien En Su Practica Los Campeones de Fabriles," *La Opinión*, September 20, 1930, 9.

112. "México-El Paso Derroto Ayer Dos Veces a Fabriles y Gano La Serie," *La Opinión*, September 29, 1930, 7.

113. Makanazo, "En La Maraña del Deporte," *La Opinión* October 13, 1935, 5.

114. "México-El Paso Se Fue," *La Opinión*, November 23, 1930 4.

115. "Lou Almada Interview," in Mackey, *Barbary Baseball*, 184–188; David Eskenazi, "Lou, Mel—The Almada Brothers," *Sportspress Northwest*, August 28, 2012.

116. "Dos Bandas de Música lo Recibirán," *La Opinión*, December 4, 1930, 9.

117. "Gran Triunfo del a Novena Fabriles," *El Universal*, December 8, 1930, 8.

118. "El Club Fabriles Gano La Serie a México El Paso, el Domingo," *La Opinión*, December 16, 1930, 7.

119. "La Copa Rios Para El Equipo Fabriles," *El Universal*, December 15, 1930, 2.

120. Ignacio Herrerías, "Por El Mundo Del Deporte," *La Opinión*, December 19, 1930, 11.

121. "La Copa Rios Para El Equipo Fabriles," *El Universal*, December 15, 1930, 2.

122. "Ernesto Carmona Inaugura La Liga Mexicana Del Sur de California," *La Opinión*, July 4, 1932, 4.

123. "México-El Paso Gano el Primer Juego del La Liga de California," *La Opinión*, August 8, 1932, 7.

124. Ignacio Herrerías, "Por El Mundo Del Deporte," *La Opinión*, August 11, 1932, 7.

125. Invitation for banquet in honor of México-El Paso Team, 1934, Scrapbook, Orozco Family Archive.

126. Makanazo, "En La Maraña del Deporte," *La Opinión*, May 25, 1934, 7.

127. Tony Galindo, "Al Margen De La Serie Del Cananea y Hermosa-El Paso," *La Opinión*, May 25, 1934, 7.

128. Ibid., 7.

129. Handbill for Blackie's Place Banquet, July 10, 1934, Al Orozco Family Archive.

130. Virtue, *South of the Color Barrier*; G. Richard McKelvey, *Mexican Raiders in the Major Leagues: The Pasquel Brothers vs Organized Baseball 1946* (Jefferson, NC: McFarland, 2006);Cesar Gonzalez, "The Secret History of How Mexico Pushed Baseball toward Racial Integration," *REMEZCLA*, July 28, 2015.

131. Pedro Treto Cisneros, ed. *Enciclopedia del Beisbol Mexicano* (Mexico City: Revistas Deportivas, 1977).

132. Mike Downey, "California's Only a Memory: Evans Becomes a Detroiter," *Detroit Free Press*, December 18, 1983, 83.

133. Carlos Salazar, interview by the author, January 24, 2016, Altadena, CA.

134. Letter to David Salazar from Sr. Rubio, Secretario Particular del Gobernador del Estado, Sonora, Mexico April 18, 1922, David Salazar Family Archive, Altadena, CA.

135. "Sonora Baseball Team Wants Game with Local Club," *Arizona Republic*, May 16, 1922, 7; "Salazar and Scott to Play in Mexico City Ball Series," *Arizona Republic*, October 3, 1921, 7.

136. "President Obregon Loves Baseball," *El Paso Herald*, September 22, 1921, 6.

137. Letter to David Salazar from H. R. Marquez Jr., July 25, 1923, David Salazar Family Archive.

138. "David Salazar Will Hurl for 1924 Winners," *Arizona Republic*, March 10, 1925, 8.

139. "Fanning," *Arizona Republic*, July 8, 1924, 5.

140. "Two Infielders Will Join Team in Short Time," *Arizona Republic*, March 20, 1926, 12; "Parkers Bow to Locals," *Arcadia Tribune*, January 11, 1935, 2.

141. "Globe Athletic Association Disputes Claim of Phoenix Ball Club to David Salazar," *Arizona Republic*, April 1926, 9; "Globe to Protest Contests Pitched by David Salazar," *Arizona Republic*, April 4, 1926, 11.

142. Bob Ingram, "As I Was Saying," *El Paso Herald*, August 26, 1931, 14.

143. "Pete Salazar Defeats Dave in Slab Duel," *Arizona Republic*, May 17, 1930, 18.

144. "El Pitcher Ernesto Salazar fue Admitido Ayer en el Club Seattle," *La Opinión*, July 23, 1933, 4.

145. "Major Leaguers to Play Mexico's Diamond Stars," *Evening News*, June 29, 1932, 12; "Aztecas Won Three," *Brooklyn Daily Eagle*, November 29, 1935, 23.

146. "Alex Orozco Salio a Mexico Para Jugar con Los Aztecas," *La Opinión*, August 24, 1935, 7.

147. Bob Lagunas, interview by the author, March 20, 2016, Camarillo, CA.

148. *Mexia Daily News*, ca. 1920s, Bob Lagunas Family Archive.

149. "Lagunas Goes to Arizona League: Plays Here Today," *El Paso Herald*, March 23, 1929, 2.

150. Lagunas interview.

151. "Copper League Jottings," *El Paso Herald*, August 14, 1926, 5.

152. "Mexican Nine in Final Game," *Los Angeles Times*, December 1, 1940, A17.

153. "La Vida de Ramon Lagunas," *Oro Grafico Revista Quincenal*, May 1943, 28–30, Bob Lagunas Family Archive.

154. Ana Rosas, *Abrazando el Espíritu: Bracero Families Confront the U.S.-Mexico Border* (Berkeley: University of California Press, 2014).

155. Lagunas interview.

156. Clementina Duron, "Mexican Women and Labor Conflict in Los Angeles: The UGLWU Dressmakers Strike of 1933," *Aztlan: Journal of Chicano Studies* 15, no. 1 (Spring 1984): 149.

157. Vicki Ruiz, *Cannery Women, Cannery Lives, Mexican Women, Unionization, and the California Food Processing Industry, 1930–1950* (Albuquerque: University of New Mexico Press, 1987); Zaragosa Vargas, "Tejana Radical: Emma Tenayuca and the San Antonio Labor Movement during the Great Depression," *Pacific Historical Review* 66, no. 4 (November 1997): 553–580.

158. The National Softball Association was a semiprofessional organization, whereas the Amateur Softball Association promoted softball for amateurs only.

159. Morris Bealle, *The Softball Story* (Washington, DC: Columbia, 1957), 47.

160. Gai Ingham Berlage, "Transition of Women's Baseball: An Overview," *NINE: A Journal of Baseball History and Culture* 9, nos. 1–2 (Fall 2000/Spring 2001): 72–81.

161. Merrie A. Fidler, "The Establishment of Softball as a Sport for American Women, 1900–1940," in *Her Story in Sport*, ed. Reet Howell (West Point, NY: Leisure Press, 1982).

162. Bealle, *Softball Story*, 97–104; Kyle Crichton, "Not So Soft," *Collier's*, August 10, 1935, 24–38; John Morrow, "A Survey of the Present Status of Baseball and Softball in Southern California" (master's thesis, University of Southern California, 1936), 47–62.

163. Frank J. Taylor, "Fast and Pretty," *Collier's*, August 20, 1938, 38.

164. Samuel Regalado, "Incarcerated Sport: Nisei Women's Softball and Athletics during Japanese American Internment," *Journal of Sport History* 27, no. 3 (Fall 2000): 431–444; Susan Zieff, "From Badminton to the Bolero: Sport and Recreation in San Francisco's Chinatown, 1895–1950," *Journal of Sport History* 27, no. 1 (Spring 2000): 1–129.

165. Alamillo, *"Peloteros* in Paradise"; Alamillo, *Making Lemonade Out of Lemons*, 111.

166. Valentina "Tina" Hernandez, interview by the author, June 27, 2016, Lemon Grove, CA; Chris Jenkins, "Starring in Baseball Got Player Drafted," *San Diego Union-Tribune*, May 25, 2014, www.sandiegouniontribune.com/sdut-sports-military-manuel-nay-hernandez-2014may25 -story.html.

167. Hernandez interview.

168. "Welfare Scenes," *San Diego Union*, January 9, 1935, 18; "Neighborhood House Adds Worker to Staff," *San Diego Union*, October 8, 1936, 5.

169. Maria Garcia, "A History of the Neighborhood House in Logan Heights: Jane Addams and the 1930s," *San Diego Free Press*, May 17, 2014, http://sandiegofreepress.org/2014/05/a -history-of-neighborhood-house-in-logan-heights-jane-addams-and-the-1930s.

170. Cynthia Shelton, "The Neighborhood House of San Diego: Settlement Work in the Mexican Community, 1914–1940" (master's thesis, San Diego State University, 1975), 105.

171. Garcia, "History of the Neighborhood House."

172. Ibid.

173. Hernandez interview.

174. "She's a Threat at the Plate or Behind it," *San Diego Union*, July 25, 1939, 13.

175. Ibid.

176. "México-El Paso vs. Partido Liberal el Domingo Próximo," *La Opinión*, August 11, 1933, 7; "Los Políticos Son Derrotados," *La Opinión*, August 15, 1933, 7. On the PLM in Los Angeles, see Juan Gómez Quiñonez, *Sembradores: Ricardo Flores Magón y El Partido Liberal Mexicano: An Eulogy and Critique* (Los Angeles: Aztlan Publications, Chicano Studies Research Center, University of California, Los Angeles, 1973).

177. "Una Novena De Señoritas Debuta Hoy," *La Opinión*, March 11, 1934, 5.

178. Ibid.

179. Emma Perez, "A la Mujer': A Critique of the Partido Liberal Mexicano's Gender Ideology," in *Between Borders: Essays on Mexicana/Chicana History*, ed. Adelaida R. del Castillo (Encino, CA: Floricanto Press, 1990), 459–482. For more on "third space feminism" see Emma Perez, *The Decolonial Imaginary: Writing Chicanas into History* (Bloomington: Indiana University Press, 1999), chap. 3.

180. "Interés por el debut en el White Sox," *La Opinión*, April 14, 1934, 7.

181. "Una Nueva Novena Femenil Debutará en el White Sox," *La Opinión*, March 23, 1934, 7.

182. Makanazo, "En La Maraña del Deporte," *La Opinión*, April 11, 1936, 7.

183. "Un Encuentro de Mujeres en el White Sox," *La Opinión*, April 12, 1934, 7.

184. "Salazar Tirara por México-El Paso Hoy," *La Opinión*, April 15, 1834, 5.

185. "México-El Paso Venció al Hermosa, 4–3, en un juego de 13 Entradas," *La Opinión*, April 17, 1934, 7.

186. Makanazo, "En La Maraña del Deporte," *La Opinión*, April 15, 1934, 7.

187. On "Baseball Annies," see Ardell, *Breaking into Baseball*.

188. "They Started It," *California Eagle*, May 11, 1934.

189. Alison Wrynn, "Women's Industrial and Recreation League Softball in Southern California, 1930–1950" (master's thesis, California State University, Long Beach, 1989), 48.

190. "Athena Girls in Baseball Game Win," *California Eagle*, April 20, 1934, 13. See also "Un Encuentro Reñidísimo en El White Sox," *La Opinión*, April 17, 1934, 7.

191. Makanazo, "En La Maraña del Deporte," *La Opinión*, March 23, 1934, 7, emphasis added.

192. Alamillo, *Making Lemonade Out of Lemons*, 110–111. See also Alamillo, "*Peloteros* in Paradise."

193. Sandra Uribe, "The Queens of Diamonds: Mexican American Women's Amateur Softball in Southern California, 1930–1950" (unpublished manuscript).

194. Della Fonseca Ortega and Ramona Fonseca Frias, interview by Amy Kitchener, Shades of L.A. Interview Project, September 27, 1993, cassette tape 1, side A.

195. Ibid.

196. Uribe, "Queens of Diamonds," 19; Carmen Cornejo Gallegos in *Latinas in the United States: A Historical Encyclopedia*, vol. 1, ed. Vicki Ruiz and Virginia Sanchez Korrol (Bloomington: Indiana University Press, 2006), 274; Richard Santillán, Susan Leuvano, Luis Fernandez, and Angelina Veyna, eds., *Mexican American Baseball in Orange County* (Charleston, SC: Arcadia, 2013), 58–59.

197. Ramona Valenzuela Cervantes, interview by Daisey Valadez-Miguel, April 11, 2016, San Fernando, CA.

198. Bobby Vasquez and Rudy Oliva, interview by Tom Rivera, December 16, 2013, South Colton Oral History Project, California State University, San Bernardino.

199. Richard Santillán, Mark Ocegueda, and Terry Cannon, *Mexican American Baseball in the Inland Empire* (Charleston, SC: Arcadia, 2012), 33–34; Jazmine Collins, "Remembering the 1939 Latina Softball team Colton Mercury Senoritas," *Inland Empire Community News*, April 24, 2014, 1.

200. Samuel Regalado, "Las Señoritas de Glendale" (paper, North American Society for Sport History conference, Clemson, SC, May 26, 1989).

201. "La Novena de M. Regalado Jugara Hoy," *La Opinión*, April 22, 1936, 7. The barrio name Toonerville originated from "Tunaville" because of the nearby La Tuna Canyon.

202. Santillán et al., *Mexican American Baseball in Orange County*, 77.

203. The notion of "respectable femininity" was also used by Mexican American women who formed the Señoritas USO to show their wartime patriotism while maintaining their cultural roots and notion of Mexican womanhood. See Elizabeth R. Escobedo, *From Coveralls to Zoot Suits: The Lives of Mexican American Women on the World War II Home Front* (Chapel Hill NC: University of North Carolina Press, 2013).

204. Morrow, "Survey of the Present Status," 77–78.

205. "Softball Play Opens: Motion Picture Celebrities Preside over Tonight's Loyola Program," *Los Angeles Times,* April 6, 1936, 3.

206. "Snappy Spanish Señoritas Play Pelota Muy Buena," *Los Angeles Times*, April 28, 1936, A11.

207. "Glendale vs. Bell En Juego de Señoritas," *La Opinión*, May 18, 1935, 7.

208. "Las Señoritas de Glendale, En El White Sox El Domingo," *La Opinión*, May 8, 1936, 7.

209. "El Titulo de Lopez en Peligro," *La Opinión*, May 20, 1936, 7.

210. Makanazo, "En La Maraña del Deporte," *La Opinión*, April 20, 1936, 7.

211. Ibid.

212. Francisco A. Costello, "Comentarios Deportivos," *La Opinión*, April 6, 1936, 7.

213. "Un Juego de Softball en El White Sox," *La Opinión*, May 18, 1937, 7.

214. "Debutan el Domingo en White Sox," *La Opinión*, May 21, 1937, 7.

215. Makanazo, "En La Maraña del Deporte," *La Opinión*, May 23, 1937, 4.

216. "Melo Almada Ganó Su Primer Juego con México El Paso," *La Opinión*, June 15, 1931, 7.

217. "México El Paso Gano Dos Veces a Los Bomberos y Melo Almada Dio Nueve Ceros," *La Opinión*, June 29, 1931, 7.

218. On the history of Latin American players in the Pacific Northwest, see Gilberto Garcia, "*Beisboleros*: Latin Americans and Baseball in the Northwest, 1914–1937," *Columbia* 8 (Fall 2002): 8–13.

219. Eduardo B. Almada, telephone conversation with the author, January 8, 2020.

220. David Eskenazi, "Lou, Mel—The Almada Brothers," *Wayback Machine*, August 28, 2012, 11, http://sportspressnw.com/2137082/2012/wayback-machine-lou-mel-the-almada-brothers.

221. Eduardo B. Almada, *Melo Almada: 1er Mexicano En Grandes Ligas* (Hermosillo, Mexico: Impreso en Tercer Milenio, 2014), 38.

222. Lou Almada interview in Mackey, *Barbary Baseball*, 184–188.

223. Almada, *Melo Almada*, 60.

224. "Fans Will Honor Mel Tonight," *Seattle Post-Intelligencer,* August 30, 1933, 5. See also Garcia, "*Beisboleros*," 8–13.

225. José M. Alamillo, "'He Doesn't Even Look Like a Mexican': Race, Citizenship and the Transnational Baseball Career of Melo Almada," 2009, unpublished manuscript.

226. "And Now It's 'Viva Almada,'" *Los Angeles Times*, April 9, 1933, E3.

227. "Thees for You, Senor," *Los Angeles Times*, July 24, 1933, 9.

228. "Un Éxito el Homenaje a Melo Almada," *La Opinión*, July 24, 1933, 7.

229. "Almada Honored Today," *Los Angeles Times*, July 23, 1933, D2.

230. Ibid.

231. Ibid.

232. Almada, *Melo Almada*, 61–76.

233. Almada's quote was reprinted in "Las Bandas De Estado Mayor y Jazz de Policia Alegraran Los Juegos," *El Excélsior*, November 25, 1933, 4.

234. "Una Entrevista con Melo Almada," *La Prensa*, March 19, 1939, 4.

235. Dick Farrington, "A Mexican Revolution Gave Mel Almada to the Diamond," *Sporting News*, September 15, 1935, 5.

236. Bill Cunningham, "Grandstand Grandee," *Collier's*, August 24, 1935, 16.

237. On stereotypes of Mexican Americans in film and television, see Luis Reyes, "Behind the Mask of Zorro: Mexican American Images and Stereotypes in Western Films and Television," in *Mask of Zorro: Mexican Americans and Popular Media*, ed. Deena J. Gonzalez, Luis Reyes, and Raul H. Vila. (Los Angeles: Gene Autry Western Heritage Museum, 1994), 20–46.

238. Farrington, "A Mexican Revolution," 5.

239. John Fenton, "Ferrell Brothers Manufacture Win but Call on Walberg in the Ninth Frame to Sweep Series with Senators, 4–1," *Boston Herald*, April 23, 1935, 18.

240. Daniel Frio and Marc Onigman, "'Good Field, No Hit': The Image of Latin American Baseball Players in the American Press, 1871–1946," *Revista/Review Interamericana* 15, no. 2 (Summer 1980): 199–208.

241. "Big Pitcher Believed to Dislike Club," *Washington Post*, June 11, 1937, 5.

242. "Cuatro Equipos Se Enfrentarán en un Gran Festival Nocturno en el White Sox, el martes," *La Opinión*, October 22, 1933, 7.

243. "Luis Almada, con México-El Paso, se enfrenta a su Hermano Melo en el 1er Juego de la Noche hoy en el White Sox," *La Opinión*, October 24, 1933, 7.

244. "La Opinión del Cónsul de Mexico," *La Opinión*, October 22, 1933, 4.

245. Eduardo B. Almada, *Melo Almada*, 77–96.

246. "El Juez Landis Explica Por Que dio Permiso a Almada para Ir a Mexico," *La Opinión*, November 16, 1933, 7.

247. Morales, "Mexico," 245–256.

248. Ignacio Herrerías, "Impresiones de Aquí y de Allá," *El Excélsior*, November 1, 1933, 4.

249. "Entusiasta Recepción a Los Hnos. Almada," *El Excélsior*, November 24, 1933. Hosts included President Abelardo Rodríguez, Tirso Hernandez, director of physical education, and Ernesto Carmona, head of the Mexican Baseball League.

250. Ibid.

251. "Melo y Luis Almada Sacados en Hombros," *El Excélsior*, November 26, 1933, 7.

252. "Hoy Se Efectuara El Cuarto Juego de la Serie Comintra-Delta," *El Excélsior*, November 30, 1933, 7.

253. "Los Electricistas Derrotaran a Los Campeones del Comintra," *El Excélsior*, December 1, 1933, 4.

254. "Todavía Sigue El Conflicto Entre Aztecas y Delta por Los Jueces," *El Excélsior*, December 6, 1933, 4.

255. "Dificultad Con Los Empayers," *El Excélsior*, December 5, 1933, 4.

256. "La Serie Delta-Aztecas Empezara Esta Tarde en El Parque Delta," *El Excélsior*, December 7, 1933, 5; "Hoy Se Van de Mexico Los Hermanos Almada," *El Excélsior*, December 10, 1933, 4.

257. "Nuestro Beisbol Esta Como Hace Quince Años," *El Excélsior*, December 17, 1933, 4.

258. "Una Entrevista con Melo Almada," *La Prensa*, March 19, 1939, 4.

259. Henry Edwards, "Melo Almada," Dec, 8, 1935, 2, Melo Almada Player File, National Baseball Library and Archive, National Baseball Hall of Fame, Cooperstown, NY.

260. "Melo Almada Se Siente Ya Mas En Casa," *La Opinión*, May 28, 1940, 7.

261. Carlos Bauer, "A Couple of Louie Almada Stories," *Minor League Researcher Blog*. http://minorleagueresearcher.blogspot.com/2005/09/couple-of-louie-alamda-stories.html. See also Bill Nowlin, "Mel Almada" (Baseball Biography Project, 2009), 6; "Melo Almada Struck in Head by Wild Pitch," *Los Angeles Times*, April 14, 1937, A13.

262. Eduardo Almada, email communication, November 3, 2009. See also Eduardo B. Almada, *Melo Almada*, 250–51.

263. Keith Rosenblum, "Almada's Pro Debut Was First for Mexican," *Arizona Daily Star*, August 2, 1981, 5.

264. Tracy Ringolsby, "Q & A: Almada Discusses Father's Legacy," *MLB.com*, March 26, 2016. https://www.mlb.com/redsox/news/edward-almada-talks-about-mal-almada-s-legacy-c169142842.

265. "Baldomero Almada Abrió Las Puertas a Los Mexicanos En Grandes Ligas," in Cisneros, *Enciclopedia del Beisbol Mexicano*, 10.

266. "Se Reorganiza la Veterana Organización," *La Opinión*, October 13, 1935, 5.

267. Makanazo, "En La Maraña del Deporte," *La Opinión,* October 13, 1935, 5.

268. Larry Rohter, "Shrine Honors Mexican Stars," *New York Times,* June 30, 1989, A22.

4. FORGING TRANSNATIONAL SPORTING NETWORKS

1. José Arteaga, "Un Deportista Mexicano Hace Una Selección 'All Mexico' E Incluye a Los De La Costa," *La Opinión,* April 26, 1933, 4; "La 5ta Arriola Ira Mexico," *La Opinión,* April 20, 1933, 4.

2. Mario García, *Memories of Chicano History: Life and Narrative of Bert Corona* (Berkeley: University of California Press, 1994), 83.

3. Joseph Arbena, "Sport, Development, and Mexican Nationalism, 1920–1970," *Journal of Sport History,* 18, no. 3 (1991): 350–364; Rudolph Muller Lopez, "History of Physical Education and Sports in Mexico" (master's thesis, Claremont Graduate School, 1953), 75–83.

4. Mexia's office was located inside the Los Angeles Chamber of Commerce building. The Mexican Olympic Committee of Los Angeles comprised Joaquin Terrazas, Mexican consul of Los Angeles; Mauricio Calderón, music promoter; Jesus Monjarás, medical doctor; Lamberto Hernández, businessman; Miguel Bracho, radio announcer; Juan Aguirre Delgado, engineer; Moises Sáenz, college professor; Miguel Ramírez, businessman; Alfonso Rojo de la Vega, businessman; and Ignacio F. Herrerias, sports writer.

5. "Aceptó el Cargo de Presidente del Comité Olimpico Mexicano-Americano, con Mucho Gusto," *La Opinión,* April 28, 1932, 7; "Confía en el Patriotismo del Pueblo Para que Estemos Bien Presentados en Los Angeles," *La Opinión,* April 29, 1932, 9.

6. "Olympic Queen Contest Grows More Intense," *Los Angeles Times,* July 8, 1932, 11.

7. "Mexican Olympic Games Athletes to Be Honored Tonight at Grand Ball by Countrymen," *Los Angeles Times,* July 23, 1932, 8.

8. "Mexicans Preparing for Games," *Los Angeles Times,* April 22, 1932, A18; "Actividades del Comite Olimpico," *La Opinión,* April 17, 1932, 4; Weekly Bulletin, April 15, 1932, 3, folder C-2010, box 70, Department of Playground and Recreation Collection, City Archives, Los Angeles (hereafter LADPR Records).

9. "Mexican Ring Trial Tonight," *Los Angeles Times,* July 11, 1932, 9.

10. "Bert Colima Will Coach Mexicans," *Los Angeles Times,* July 24, 1932, E1.

11. "El Comité Olimpico Recomienda Que Se Preparen Seriamente En El Transcurso de Esta Semana," *La Opinión,* June 6, 1932, 3.

12. Meeting minutes, Records of the Board of Playground and Recreation Commissioners, June 15, 1932, 776, folder C-0368, box 70, LADPR Records.

13. "Federal Doctor Defends Vaccination of Athletes," *El Paso Herald Post,* July 21, 1932. See also John McKiernan-Gonzalez, "Everyday Disturbances: The Olympics, 'Indian' Marathon Runners, and the Practice of Medical Inspection, 1932," *Journal of the West* 54, no. 4 (Fall 2015): 12–21.

14. Antonio Lavin Ugalde, *México en Los Juegos Olímpicos, MCMLXVIII* (Mexico City: Asociacion Nacional de Periodistas, A.C. 1968), 21–25.

15. "Women Olympic Athletes Take Limelight from Hollywood Film Beauties," *St. Louis Star and Times,* August 6, 1932, 3.

16. "Mexico Boosts Olympic Games," *Los Angeles Times,* June 11, 1932, A3.

17. Fernando Cabañas Prado won a silver medal in flyweight boxing and Gustavo Huet Bobadilla a silver medal in shooting.

18. "Mexican Caballeros Bring Color to Village," *Los Angeles Times,* July 23, 1932, 9; "Frijoles Come with Indians," *Los Angeles Times,* July 22, 1932, A10; Braven Dyer, "The Olympic Torch," *Los Angeles Times,* July 29, 1932, A14; José Pages Llergo, "El Papel de Mexico en la X Olimpiada," *La Opinión,* August 14, 1932, 1.

19. Barbara J. Keys, *Globalizing Sport: National Rivalry and International Community in the 1930s* (Cambridge, MA: Harvard University Press, 2006), 34.

20. Eriko Yamamoto, "Cheers for Japanese Athletes: The 1932 Los Angeles Olympics and the Japanese American Community," *Pacific Historical Review* 69 (2000): 399–430.

21. Irvin Eckhoff, "M'Carthy Could Defeat Carr . . . Southland Mexicans," *Los Angeles Times*, July 21, 1932, A10. The athletes included six boxers (Ray Campo, Al Romero, Ernie Jurado, Midget Martinez, Sammy Garcia, and Carl Gallardo) and five track and field runners (Alfredo Gamboa, Emilio Rodriguez, Fernando Ortiz, Pablo Ortiz, and Dick Arguello).

22. García, *Memories of Chicano History*, 85.

23. Ramón Sánchez to Abelardo Rodríguez, Presidente de la República Mexicana, October 24, 1932, Abelardo Rodríguez Papers, ALR 332.3/355, Archivo General de la Nación, Mexico City.

24. Ibid.

25. Articles of Incorporation, Southern California Mexican Athletic Association, folder, 14, box 4, MO295, 1, Manuel Ruiz Papers, Special Collections, Green Library, Stanford University, Stanford, CA (hereafter Ruiz Papers).

26. "Nombran Para La A. A. M. A 7 Consejeros," *La Opinión*, November 27, 1933, 4.

27. "La Junta Consejera de la A.A. M," *La Opinión*, November 27, 1933, 4. The Mexican American professionals included Manuel Ruiz Jr., attorney; Peter Salas, president of the Mexican Chamber of Commerce; Dr. Reynaldo Carreón, president of the Beneficencia Mexicana; Dr. José Díaz, dentist; and Mauricio Calderón, music store owner.

28. Articles of Incorporation, Southern California Mexican Athletic Association, folder, 14, box 4, MO295, 1, Ruiz Papers.

29. "El Imperio Dara Ayuda a La Asociacion," *La Opinión*, January 7, 1937, 4.

30. Between 1933 and 1936 Juan Acevedo held the city's three-mile record (17 minutes, 20 seconds). Makanazo, "En La Maraña del Deporte," *La Opinión*, November 5, 1935, 4; *La Opinión*, August 2, 1936, 4. On Acevedo's political biography, see Kaye Lynn Briegel, "The History of Political Organizations among Mexican-Americans in Los Angeles since the Second World War" (PhD diss., University of Southern California, 1967), 50–51.

31. "Se Entrena La Quinta de Sánchez," *La Opinión*, February, 16, 1936, 4.

32. "Ray Sánchez Organizador de Deportes," *La Opinión*, January 27, 1936, 4.

33. José Arteaga, "Impulso del Mexico de Afuera," *La Opinión* December 29, 1932, 4.

34. José Arteaga, "Juega En El Hollenbeck con Belvedere," *La Opinión*, November 7, 1935, 4; "José Arteaga, "El Progreso Obtenido en Basketball," *La Opinión*, November 27, 1932, 4.

35. José Arteaga, "La Opinión de Los Que Colaboran," *La Opinión*, October 30, 1932, 4; José Arteaga, "La Situación Atlética de Los Amateurs en la Colonia," *La Opinión*, October 28, 1934, 5.

36. "Centenares de Atletas Mexicanos Bajo el Estandarte de la A.A.M.," *La Opinión*, May 5, 1933, 4.

37. They included Club Oh Señor, Club Atenas, Club Iris, Club Bohemia, Club Atlético Olimpia, Club Atlético México, Club Monte Carlo, Club Bolívar, Club "On with Roosevelt," Club Arriola, Club Minerva, Club Benito Juárez, Club Aguilas Reales, Club Evergreen Knights, Club Alma Joven, Club Aztecas, and Club Moctezuma.

38. For a discussion of multiple Mexican masculinities negotiated by first- and second-generation Mexican migrants, see Robert Courtney Smith, *Mexican New York: Transnational Lives of New Immigrants* (Berkeley: University of California Press, 2006), 94–146.

39. "Contara Con El Apoyo del D. De Recreo," *La Opinión*, November 20, 1932, 4.

40. "La Asociación Atlética Mexicana Cumple su Primer Año de Vida," *La Opinión*, March 26, 1933, 4.

41. Michael Kimmel, *Manhood in America: A Cultural History* (New York: Oxford University Press, 1996), 137–141; David Whitson, "Sport in the Social Construction of Masculinity," in

Sport, Men, and the Gender Order: Critical Feminist Perspectives, ed. Michael A. Messner and Donald F. Sabo (Champaign, IL: Human Kinetics, 1990), 19–29.

42. "Ante 6,000 Personas se Desarrollaron las Competencias de Pista en la A.A.M.," *La Opinión*, May 9, 1933, 7; Gil Castro, "Los Mexicanos Triunfan en Los Deportes," *La Opinión*, March 27, 1934, 6; Rafael Ybarra," Marginando . . . ," *La Opinión*, May 4, 1933, 4.

43. "Con Un Imponente Espectáculo Atlético se Celebra el 5 de Mayo en El Sur de California," *La Opinión*, May 5, 1935, 9; "Coronación de Una Reina," *La Opinión*, May 6, 1934, 7.

44. García, *Memories of Chicano History*, 59.

45. "El Programa de Eventos Esta Listo," *La Opinión*, April 16, 1934, 7.

46. Albert F. Cobb, "Comparative Study of the Athletic Ability of Latin-American and Anglo-American Boys on a Junior High School Level" (master's thesis, University of Texas, 1952), 54.

47. "Basketball Inventor Finds Game Faster Minus Tap-Off," *New York Times*, January 12, 1930, 147.

48. Makanazo, "En la Maraña del Deporte," *La Opinión*, November 20, 1935, 4.

49. C. Villegas and Gil Castro, "Los Mexicanos 'Son Chiquitos Pero Picosos,'" *La Opinión*, April 13, 1933, 7.

50. Ignacio M. García, *When Mexicans Could Play Ball: Basketball, Race, and Identity in San Antonio, 1928–1945* (Austin: University of Texas Press, 2013).

51. "Occidental Cagers Tangle with Mexican Quintet Tonight," *Los Angeles Times*, February 8, 1937, A11.

52. "Mexicans Defeat Oxy," *Los Angeles Times*, February 9, 1937, A14.

53. Ibid.

54. "Joe Placentia Named Top A.A.U. Basketball Scorer," *Los Angeles Times*, March 2, 1942, 18.

55. "El Programa de Eventos Esta Listo," *La Opinión*, April 16, 1934, 7.

56. "Amenaza Con Retirarse El Club Minerva," *La Opinión*, December 30, 1933, 7.

57. Martha Menchaca, *Recovering History, Constructing Race: The Indian, Black, and White Roots of Mexican Americans* (Austin: University of Texas Press, 2001), 2–5.

58. Lopez, "History of Physical Education and Sports in Mexico"; Arbena, "Sport, Development, and Mexican Nationalism."

59. On the Confederación Deportiva Mexicana (CDM), see Armando Satow, *Décadas: Confederación Deportiva Mexican A.C.* (Mexico City: Confederación Deportiva Mexicana, 2003); Keith Brewster, "Patriotic Pastimes: The Role of Sport in Post-Revolutionary Mexico," *International Journal of the History of Sport* 22 (2005): 145.

60. "Mexican Youth Headed for Sports Limelight," *Los Angeles Times*, January 22, 1933, E3; Jo Grossman, "Mexico Athletics Booming, Rodriguez Doing Fine Work, Alvarez-Gayou Is Director," *San Diego Sun*, April 19, 1933, C5.

61. Lamberto Álvarez Gayou, "A National Sports Program," *Journal of Health and Physical Education* 14 (1943): 8.

62. "Gayou Praised as Pentathlon Program Advances in Mexico," *Los Angeles Times*, August 6, 1933, D4; Frank Shaw to Abelardo Rodríguez, July 14, 1934, Rodriguez Papers, ALR 332.3/187.1, Archivo General de la Nación, Mexico City.

63. "Gayou—Main of the Hour," *Los Angeles Times*, April 23, 1933, E3; Gayou, "National Sports Program," 8.

64. Mary Kay Vaughan, *Cultural Politics in Revolution: Teachers, Peasants, and Schools in Mexico, 1930–1940* (Tucson: University of Arizona Press, 1997); Maria Monserrate Sánchez Soler, ed., *Formando el cuerpo de una nación: El deporte en el México postrevolucionario (1920–1940)* (México City: Consejo Nacional para la Cultura y Las Artes, Instituto Nacional de Bellas Artes, Museo Casa Estudio Diego Rivera y Frida Kahlo, 2012).

65. Patrice Elizabeth Olsen, *Artifacts of the Revolution: Architecture, Society, and Politics in Mexico City, 1920–1940* (Lanham, MD: Rowman & Littlefield, 2008),185–187.

66. "Invitación a la A.A.M., para que Envié un Equipo a Mexico, Se La Hace La Confederación de Mexicana," *La Opinión*, March 17, 1937, 7.

67. "Cena A Dos Visitantes de Mexico," *La Opinión*, March 21, 1937, 5.

68. Ibid., 5.

69. "La Confederacion Deportiva Mexicana Admite a la A.A.M.," *La Opinión*, May 9, 1937, 7.

70. Ibid., 7.

71. "En Octobre Sera El Torneo de Campo y Pista En Mexico," *La Opinión*, October 27, 1937, 7.

72. Makanazo, "En la Maraña del Deporte," *La Opinión*, February 6, 1938, 4. See also Richard V. McGehee, "The Origins of Olympism in Mexico: The Central American Games of 1926," *International Journal of the History of Sport* 10, no. 3 (December 1993): 313–332.

73. "El Mexico de Afuera Envio Famosos Atletas a Panama," *Continental*, February 19, 1938, 8.

74. Makanazo, "El Mexico De Afuera Envió Famosos Atletas a Panamá," *El Continental*, February 10, 1938, 8.

75. The MAASC letterhead included the following inscription: "Miembro de la Confederación Deportiva Mexicana," letterhead, January 31, 1940, folder 14, box 4, MO295, Ruiz Papers.

76. Oscar Castillón, "Physical Education in Mexico," *Journal of Health and Physical Education* 5 (May 1934): 13; Theodore Allan Ediger, "Mexico, the Land of Sports," *Pan American Magazine* 3 (1930): 198–208.

77. "Informe de La Jira del Club Centinelas a La Capital," *La Opinión*, March 16, 1936, 7.

78. Some academics claimed that Mexican children were physically inferior and showed little interest in participating in sports; see Jorge Iber, "Mexican Americans of South Texas Football: The Athletic and Coaching Careers of E. C. Lerma and Bobby Cavazos, 1932–1965," *Southwestern Historical Quarterly* 55 (2002): 622–623.

79. "Mexican Athletes Given Welcome," *Los Angeles Times*, April 29, 1938, A12.

80. "Mexican Athletes Capture Medals," *Los Angeles Times*, May 10, 1938, A11.

81. "Hot Competition Looms in Meet: Local Mexican Trackmen Stronger," *Los Angeles Times*, May 5, 1939, A14.

82. "Latin Athletes Prep for Meet," *Los Angeles Times*, April 30, 1939, A14.

83. "La Asociación Atlética Invita A Altos Funcionarios de Mexico," *La Opinión*, October 19, 1938, 7.

84. Letter to State Athletic Commission by Manuel Ruiz, October 11 1938, Southern California Mexican Athletic Association, folder 14, box 4, MO295, Ruiz Papers.

85. Lázaro Cárdenas to Mexican Athletic Association of Southern California, July 14, 1939, Lázaro Cárdenas Papers, LC 532/94, Archivo General de la Nación, Mexico City; "Un Llamado a Los Púgiles Mexicanos lo hace Midget Martinez Comisionado de box Amateur de la ADM," *La Opinión*, October 29, 1939, 5.

86. Makanazo, "Los Campeones de Mexico Ganaron 5 Peleas Anoche," *La Opinión*, November 21, 1939, 7.

87. Makanazo, "En La Maraña del Deporte," *La Opinión*, November 23, 1939, 7. With Bert Colima's help, MAASC boxers Gregorio Escalona and Tony Contreras won two out of seven matches at the next international boxing tournament.

88. Natalia Molina, *Fit to Be Citizens? Public Health and Race in Los Angeles, 1879–1939* (Berkeley: University of California Press, 2006), 75–115; Marylou Belyea, "The Joy Ride and the Silver Screen: Commercial Leisure, Delinquency and Play Reform in Los Angeles, 1900–1980" (PhD diss., Boston University, 1980), 47–49.

89. Anthony Macías, "Bringing Music to the People: Race, Urban Culture, and Municipal Politics in Postwar Los Angeles," *American Quarterly* 56 (2004): 693–717.

90. "City Recreation Director Declares Supervised Play Must Be Public Concern," *Los Angeles Times,* January 5, 1935, A6. On George Hjelte, see Susan Diane Hudson, "George Hjelte: Recreation Administrator" (PhD diss., University of Utah, 1974); George Hjelte, *Footprints in the Parks* (Los Angeles: Public Service Publications, 1977).

91. "Quedo Formada La Asociacion Para Reunir a Las Quintas Mexicanas, Contara Con El Apoyo del D. De Recreo," *La Opinión,* November 20, 1932, 4.

92. "Mexico and Oxy to Play," *Los Angeles Times,* July 13, 1935, 10.

93. Makanazo, "En La Maraña del Deporte," *La Opinión,* August 19, 1935, 7.

94. Braven Dyer, "Oxy Meets Mexico in Grid Inaugural Today," *Los Angeles Times,* September 21, 1935, 7.

95. "Aztec Team Due Today," *Los Angeles Times,* September 19, 1935, A10.

96. Francisco Costello, "Universidad de Mexico 7-Occidental-26, Los Estudiantes Mexicanos Dieron Un Buen Juego Ayer," *La Opinión,* November 17, 1935, 7.

97. Francisco Costello, "Comentarios Deportivos," *La Opinión,* March 24, 1936, 7.

98. Francisco Costello, "Centinelas v. Mexico a Las 9 P.M.," *La Opinión,* December 21, 1936, 7.

99. "Declaraciones de A. Gonzalez de La A.A.M: El Comisionado de Basketball refuta al Secretario J. Ibarra Soltero," *La Opinión,* March 23, 1936, 7; Francisco Costello, "Comentarios Deportivos," *La Opinión,* March 8, 1936, 6.

100. Francisco Costello, "Una Acalorada Sesión de La Asociacion Atlética Mexicana," *La Opinión,* March 28, 1936, 7; "Se Efectuara En El Campo de La Roosevelt High, El Día 3," *La Opinión,* April 12, 1936, 7; Francisco Costello, "Comentarios Deportivos," *La Opinión,* March 30, 1936, 7; Francisco Costello, "Comentarios Deportivos," *La Opinión,* May 10, 1936, 7; Francisco Costello, "Importante Junta de La Asociacion," *La Opinión,* May 2, 1936, 7.

101. Francisco Costello, "Comentarios Deportivos," *La Opinión,* October 4, 1936, 7; Francisco Costello, "Comentarios Deportivos," *La Opinión,* December 20, 1936, 7; Makanazo, "En La Maraña del Deporte," *La Opinión,* December 4, 1936, 7.

102. "La Asociacion Atlética Mexicana hace un llamado a las Mujeres," *La Opinión,* March 13, 1939, 3.

103. Ibid.

104. "La Colonia Mexicana Invadiría el Coliseo," *La Opinión,* May 1, 1938, 4.

105. "Hay Entusiasmo En California y Mexico por La Justa Aquí," *La Opinión,* April 10, 1938, 7. Club Ideal de Señoritas formed a basketball team in 1933, followed by Alma Joven, who formed an all-female basketball team in 1936. "Ganan Las Canasteras del Club Ideal de Señoritas," *La Opinión,* March 21, 1933, 7; Francisco Costello, "Basketball Femenino Aquí," *La Opinión,* September 4, 1936, 7.

106. "Basketball Femenil en Echo Park," *La Opinión,* March 1, 1940, 4.

107. "Mexican Athletes Plan Active Year in Sports," *San Antonio Express,* February 7, 1932, 13. The Mexican West Side neighborhood has a long sports history. See Richard Garcia, *The Rise of the Mexican American Middle Class, San Antonio, 1929–1941* (College Station: Texas A&M University Press, 1991), 92–94; García, *When Mexicans Could Play Ball.*

108. "Frank Trejo," *San Antonio Light,* March 13, 1969, 46. See also Frank Trejo, "Sports Boom among Local West Siders," *San Antonio Light,* February 7, 1932, 6; Frank Trejo, "Fue Organizado un Team Femenino de Basquetbol," *La Prensa,* April 14, 1932, 6.

109. Frank R. Jasso, "El Deporte Entre Nuestra Colonia," *La Prensa,* December 26, 1937, 7.

110. Cynthia Orozco, "Regionalism, Politics and Gender in Southwest History: The League of United Latin American Citizen's Expansion into New Mexico from Texas, 1929–1945," *Western Historical Quarterly* 29, no. 1 (Winter 1998): 459–483.

111. "Brillante Jugadora," *La Prensa,* December 30, 1932, 9.

112. "El 'Lulac' Fue Vencido Anoche pro 31 a 18," *La Prensa,* January 19, 1933.

113. Pamela Grundy and Susan Shackleford, *Shattering the Glass: The Remarkable History of Women's Basketball* (New York: New Press, 2005).

114. Susan Cahn, *Coming on Strong: Gender and Sexuality in Twentieth-Century Women's Sport* (New York: Free Press, 1994), 100.

115. Ernestine "Ernie" Navarro Hosaki, interview by the author, January 4, 2015, Oxnard, CA.

116. "Baile del Club Femenino Tuesday Night," *La Prensa*, November 27, 1932, 5.

117. "El Equipo Femenino de Basketball 'Modern Maids,'" *La Prensa*, March 5, 1933, 13.

118. "Nuevo Club Femenino en San Antonio," *La Prensa*, July 14, 1931, 5; "Baile del Club Modern Maids," *La Prensa*, November 4, 1931, 6.

119. Zaragosa Vargas, "Tejana Radical: Emma Tenayuca and the San Antonio Labor Movement during the Great Depression," *Pacific Historical Review* 66 (1997): 553–580.

120. "All-Star Girl Team Chosen," *San Antonio Light*, March 26, 1933, 6.

121. "El Team Femenino de Joske, derroto al Prospect Hill," *La Prensa*, June 9, 1939, 8. On Eva Garza, see Deborah Vargas, *Dissonant Divas in Chicana Music* (Minneapolis: University of Minnesota Press, 2012), 149.

122. "Emma Tenayuca," *La Prensa*, May 3, 1937, 13.

123. "El Club Mexicano de Tennis Celebra Su Aniversario Hoy," *La Opinión*, November 3, 1940, 4.

124. Ibid.

125. "La Nueva Mesa Directiva de Los Tenistas," *La Opinión*, December 10, 1939.

126. "Llego a Caurtos de Finales El Torneo Mexicano de Tenis," *La Opinión*, September 25, 1940, 4. Some of the female players included Estela Belendez, Esperanza Aguayo, Celia Valles, and Lupe Saldaña.

127. "La Guapa Elda Peralta Dice que Quiere Ser Una de las Mejores Tenistas de Mexico," *La Opinión*, November 14, 1948.

128. Lynne Emery, "From Social Pastime to Serious Sport: Women's Tennis in Southern California in the Late 19th and Early 20th Centuries," *Californians*, November/December 1990, 38–42.

129. Francisco Costello, "Quien Es El Presidente De La Asociacion," *La Opinión* January 25, 1937, 7.

130. Historians have documented the Mexican consul's role in *México de afuera*, which included sponsoring patriotic celebrations, establishing Spanish-language libraries, forming community organizations and labor unions, and assisting repatriation efforts during the Great Depression, but they have largely ignored their role in promoting athletics. See George J. Sánchez, *Becoming Mexican American: Ethnicity, Culture and Identity in Chicano Los Angeles, 1900–1945* (New York: Oxford University Press, 1993); Francisco Balderrama, *In Defense of La Raza: The Los Angeles Mexican Consulate and the Mexican Community, 1929 to 1936* (Tucson: University of Arizona Press, 1982); and Gilbert Gonzalez, *Mexican Consuls and Labor Organizing: Imperial Politics in the American Southwest* (Austin: University of Texas Press, 1999).

131. Makanazo, "En La Maraña del Deporte," *La Opinión*, August 9, 1935, 7.

132. "El Consulado Colabora con La Asociacion," *La Opinión*, January 5, 1936, 4.

133. The consul circular was published in "A Competir En La Olimpiada Mexicana Aquí," *La Opinión*, March 27, 1938, 5.

134. "Leo Carillo Sera Maestro de Ceremonias el Día 2: Acepto La Invitación de La A.A.M.," *La Opinión*, April 25, 1937, 4.

135. "Mexican Colony to Have Fiesta," *Los Angeles Times*, April 29, 1937, A2.

136. "Cinco de Mayo Fete Colorful," *Los Angeles Times*, May 8, 1939, 3.

137. Ibid., 3.

138. "El Festival Deportivo de La Asociacion," *La Opinión*, September 4, 1939, 7.

139. "Newhall Sports Center Plans All-Day Fiesta," *Los Angeles Times*, July 31, 1939, 23; "Mexican Boxers of Past to Appear," *Los Angeles Times*, August 27, 1939, A9.

140. Douglas Monroy, *Rebirth: Mexican Los Angeles from the Great Migration to the Great Depression* (Berkeley: University of California Press, 1999), 56–57.

141. "El Torneo de Tennis de La A.A.M Es Hoy," *La Opinión*, August 11, 1935, 4. Club Ariel won both singles and doubles championship titles.

142. "Club Mexico y Club Juarez Juegan Hoy," *La Opinión*, September 1, 1935, 7.

143. "Mexican Davis Cup Team to Play Here," *Los Angeles Times*, October 1, 1939, 32.

144. "Juegan Manana Los Tennistas de Mexico En Griffith Park," *La Opinión*, September 30, 1939, 7; "Se Despiden Hoy De La Colonia Los Tenistas de Nuestro Pais," *La Opinión*, October 1, 1939, p. 7.

145. "Juegan en Griffith Park," *La Opinión*, October 1, 1939, 4.

146. "Horseshoe Champ Isais Unknown in Home City," *Los Angeles Times*, August 29, 1952, 27. Out of the thirty-six competitors, Fernando Isais won the Roland Trophy. Isais won four singles championships, including defeating the young up-and-coming tennis star Richard "Pancho" Gonzalez, in the 1942 tournament. Isais was selected to compete in the 1941 Revolutionary Games in Mexico City, but instead of pursuing a tennis career, Isais decided to compete professionally in horseshoe pitching contests, winning a total of six world championships. "Resultados de Los Eventos de La A.A.M.," *La Opinión*, September 16, 1939, 7.

147. José M. Alamillo, "Richard "Pancho" Gonzalez, Race, and the Print Media in Postwar Tennis America," *International Journal of the History of Sports* 26 (2009): 947–965.

148. Francisco Costello, "Comentarios Deportivos," *La Opinión*, February 7, 1937, 4. Special invitees included Mexican consul Renato Cantú Lara, Los Angeles mayor Frank Shaw, Los Angeles police chief James Davis, Los Angeles Coliseum director Ralph Chick, and *La Opinión* sports editor Pete Delgado.

149. "Gymnasium Proposal," June 1937, 1, folder 14, box 4, MO295, Ruiz Papers, emphasis added.

150. Ruiz to Los Angeles Board of Education, February 1, 1941, Ruiz Papers; Ruiz to Ralph Romero, February 7, 1941, Ruiz Papers.

151. Ruiz to Ralph Romero, February 7, 1941, Ruiz Papers.

152. "Se Proyecta Construir Aquí un Gimnasio Para Los Mexicanos," *La Opinión*, May 26, 1940, 7.

153. José Arteaga, "Comentarios Deportivos," *La Opinión*, June 27, 1943, 7.

154. "Pachuco" refers to Mexican American youth who developed their own subculture during the 1940s. Edward Escobar, *Race, Police and the Making of a Political Identity: Mexican Americans and the Los Angeles Police Department, 1900–1945* (Berkeley: University of California Press, 1999); Eduardo Obregón Pagán, *Murder at the Sleepy Lagoon: Zoot Suits, Race, and Riot in Wartime L.A.* (Chapel Hill: University of North Carolina Press, 2003), 126–142.

155. "Dos Congresos en Mexico? Bah! Habrá 2 Asociaciones Atléticas," *La Opinión*, August 18, 1940, 7; "Se Formo La Union Atlética Mexicana Aquí," *La Opinión*, September 4, 1940, 7; "Quedo Organizada una Union Atlética en Los Angeles," *La Prensa*, September 7, 1940, 6.

156. "Entrara En Actividad La Union Atlética Mexicana," *La Opinión*, September 29, 1940, 4.

157. "Mexican Athletic Union and Association Settle Dispute," *El Espectador*, August 13, 1941, 1. Based in Pomona, California, this weekly bilingual newspaper was published and edited by Ignacio Lopez. See Mario García, *Mexican Americans: Leadership, Ideology and Identity* (New Haven, CT: Yale University Press, 1989), 84–112.

158. "Un Llamado de Cordura a La Union y Asociacion Atlética," *La Opinión*, March 30, 1941, 4.

159. Most writings on Ruiz have focused on his organizational work with the Coordinating Council for Latin American Youth (CCLAY), Cultura Pan-Americana, Inc., and the Sleepy Lagoon Defense Committee, but scholars have neglected his early involvement in MAASC.

See Mario García, "Americans All: The Mexican American Generation and the Politics of Wartime Los Angeles, 1941–45," *Social Science Quarterly* 65 (1984): 278–289; Escobar, *Race, Police,* 203–226; and Obregón Pagán, *Murder at the Sleepy Lagoon,* 30–36.

160. Laura Gomez, "From Barrio Boys to College Boys: Ethnic Identity, Ethnic Organizations, and the Mexican American Elite: The Cases of Ernesto Galarza and Manuel Ruiz, Jr." (Stanford Center for Chicano Research Working Paper Series No. 25, 1989), 16–17; Christopher W. Wells, "Activist, Interpreter, Statesman: A Political Biography of Manuel Ruiz Jr." (honor's thesis, Williams College, 1995), 8–13.

161. Manuel Ruiz, Jr., "Latin American Juvenile Delinquency in Los Angeles—Bomb or Bubble?," *Crime Prevention Digest* 1 (December 1941): 1–10.

162. Ruiz to George Hjelte, September 4, 1940, folder 14, box 4, MO295, Ruiz Papers.

163. "Hoy Sesiona La Asociacion Atlética Mexicana," *La Opinión,* September 22, 1945, 4.

5. BECOMING GOOD NEIGHBORS THROUGH WARTIME SPORTS

1. Fray Kempis, "Baseball Makes Good Neighbors," *Modern Mexico* 15, no. 12 (May 1943): 13.

2. Letter to Lawrence Levy from John Akin, June 3, 1943, 1, National Archives and Records Administration (NARA), Office of Inter-American Affairs (OIAA) Records, RG 229, box 408; folder: Sports Baseball.

3. Edward O. Guerrant, *Roosevelt's Good Neighbor Policy* (Albuquerque: University of New Mexico Press, 1950), 1.

4. Joseph Nye, *Soft Power: The Means to Success in World Politics* (New York: Public Affairs, 2004).

5. Peter Smith, *Talons of the Eagle: Dynamics of U.S.-Latin American Relations* (New York: Oxford University Press, 2000), 81.

6. On Pan Americanism see John Barrett, "Practical Pan-Americanism," *North American Review* 202, no. 718 (September 1915): 413–423; John B. Lockey, *Pan-Americanism: Its Beginnings* (New York: MacMillan, 1920).

7. "Hoover and Stimson Urge Pan American Cooperation," *Cushing Daily Citizen,* April 14, 1931, 1. April 14th was chosen because on that date in 1890 the First International Congress of American States met in Washington, DC, to organize the Pan American Union.

8. The lone exception is Cesar Torres, "The Limits of Pan-Americanism: The Case of the Failed 1942 Pan American Games," *International Journal of the History of Sports* 26, no. 17 (2011): 2547–2574.

9. Mark Dyreson, "The Original Pan American Games? The 1937 Dallas Pan-American Olympics," *International Journal of the History of Sports* 33, nos. 1–2 (2016): 6–28.

10. "Roosevelt Endorses Pan-American Games," *Corpus Christi Caller-Times,* April 2, 1937, 1.

11. Henry McLemore, "Inter-American Sports to Breed Ill-Will, Not Love," *News Herald,* September 5, 1941, 5.

12. Ibid., 5.

13. Letter to Avery Brundage from Asa Bushnell, April 20, 1942, Record Series 26/20/837, Avery Brundage Collection Microfilm, LA 84 Foundation Sports Library, Los Angeles.

14. On soft power and sports, see Håvard Mokleiv Nygård and Scott Gates, "Soft Power at Home and Abroad: Sports Diplomacy, Politics and Peace-Building," *International Area Studies Review* 16, no. 3 (2013): 235–243.

15. Allen Woll, "Hollywood's Good Neighbor Policy: The Latin Image in American Film, 1939–1946," *Journal of Popular Film* 3, no. 4 (Fall 1974): 278–293; Ana Lopez, "Are All Latins from Manhattan? Hollywood, Ethnography and Cultural Colonialism," in *Mediating Two Worlds: Cinematic Encounters in the Americas,* ed. John King, Ana Lopez, and Manuel Alvarado

(London: British Film Institute, 1993), 404–423; Julianne Burton, "Don (Juanito) Duck and the Imperial-Patriarchal Unconscious: Disney Studios, the Good Neighbor Policy, and the Packaging of Latin America," in *Nationalisms and Sexualities*, ed. Andrew Parker et al. (New York: Routledge, 1992), 21–41; Dale Adams, "*Saludos Amigos*: Hollywood and FDR's Good Neighbor Policy," *Quarterly Review of Film and Video* 24 (2007): 289–295.

16. Barbara Keys, "Spreading Peace, Democracy, and Coca-Cola: Sport and American Cultural Expansion in the 1930s," *Diplomatic History* 28, no. 2 (April 2004): 189.

17. Darlene J. Sadlier, *Americans All: Good Neighbor Cultural Diplomacy in World War II* (Austin: University of Texas Press, 2012).

18. Gisela Cramer and Ursula Prutsch, eds., *America Unidas! Nelson Rockefeller's Office of Inter-American Affairs (1940–46)* (Madrid: Iberoamericana, 2012), 18.

19. Donald Rowland, *History of the Office of the Coordinator of Inter-American Affairs* (Washington, DC: U.S. Government Printing Office, 1947), 260.

20. Thomas Leonard, "The OIAA in Central America: The Coordination Committees at Work," in Cramer and Prutsch, *America Unidas!*, 283–312.

21. Originally established as the Office for Coordination of Commercial and Cultural Relations between the American Republics (OCCCRBAR), it later became the Office of the Coordinator of Inter-American Affairs (OCIAA) and then the Office of Inter-American Affairs (OIAA).

22. Rowland, *History of the Office of the Coordinator of Inter-American Affairs*, 260.

23. Claude Curtis Erb, "Nelson Rockefeller and United States-Latin American Relations, 1940-145," (PhD diss., Clark University, 1982), 76.

24. Rowland, *History of the Office of the Coordinator of Inter-American Affairs*, 98, 260.

25. Jeremy Goldberg, "Sporting Diplomacy," *Washington Quarterly* 23, no. 4 (2000): 63.

26. Memorandum to Carl B. Spaeth from William L. Clark, Sports, June 6, 1941, NARA, OIAA Records RG 229, box 408; folder: Sports Office.

27. Henry McLemore, "Inter-American Sports to Breed Ill Will, Not Love," *News-Herald*, September 5, 1941.

28. Ibid.

29. José Luis Ortiz Garza, "Fighting for the Soul of the Mexican Press: Axis and Allied Activities during the Second World War," in Cramer and Prutsch, *America Unidas!*, 181–203.

30. "Sports in the Hemisphere Defense Program," Agenda, June 23, 1941, NARA, OIAA Records, RG 229, box 408; folder: Sports Office.

31. "Bushnell Gets New Port; Will Direct Sports Office of Inter-American Affairs," *New York Times*, August 31, 1941.

32. "Asa Bushnell Dies in Princeton; Led College Athletic Association," *New York Times*, May 23, 1975, 51.

33. "Sports Seen as Boon to Hemisphere Unity," *New York Times*, November 2, 1941, S11.

34. "Program of the Coordinator of Inter-American Affairs: Athletic Consultants for the Other American Republics," November 2, 1941, NARA, OIAA Records, RG 229, box 429; folder: Athletic Coaches Mission.

35. Letter to Asa Bushnell from Avery Brundage, September 13, 1941, collection 26/20/837, reel 13, box 21, folder: Asa Bushnell, 1941–1945, Avery Brundage Collection Microfilm, University of Illinois Archives.

36. Letter to Avery Brundage from Asa Bushnell, September 16, 1941, collection 26/20/837, reel 13, box 21, folder: Asa Bushnell, 1941–1945, Avery Brundage Collection.

37. "Bushnell Gets New Post," *New York Times*, August 31, 1941.

38. Project Authorization, "Visit of Skiers from Chile to the United States," January 1941, NARA, OIAA Records, RG 229, box 408; folder: National Ski Association of America.

39. "Chileans Here for Ski Invasion," *Brooklyn Daily Eagle*, January 28, 1941, 15.

40. "Chilean Ski Team May Appear Here in March," *Salt Lake City Tribune*, January 8, 1941, 11.

41. "Hundreds Witness Ski Here, Senor," *North Adams Transcript*, January 23, 1942.

42. "Injuries Keep Two from Ski Meet," *The Register*, March 19, 1941.

43. Edwin Hilbert, "For Inter-American Soccer," *New York Times*, January 17, 1942, 11.

44. Burton Benjamin, "Soccer Seen as New Pan-American Sports Link," *News-Herald*, May 26, 1942, 12.

45. Louis Kaufman, Barbara Fitzgerald, and Tom Sewell, *Moe Berg: Athlete, Scholar, Spy* (Boston: Little, Brown, 1974), 135–136.

46. Kaufman, Fitzgerald, and Sewell, *Moe Berg*, 136; "Moe Berg Leaves Baseball, Now 'Good Will' Ambassador," *Albuquerque Journal*, January 15, 1941.

47. Project Authorization: Sports Survey of the Other American Republics, December 4, 1941, NARA, OIAA Records, RG 229, box 408; folder: Morris Berg.

48. Nicolas Dawidoff, *The Catcher That Was a Spy: The Mysterious Life of Moe Berg* (New York: Vintage, 1994).

49. "Sports Survey of the Other American Republics," December 4, 1941, NARA, OIAA Records, RG 229, box 408: folder: Sports Office.

50. Letter to Asa Bushnell by John M. Clark, November 1941, NARA, OIAA Records, RG 229, box 408; folder: Sports Office.

51. John Kieran, "Along Diplomatic Lines," *New York Times*, August 20, 1942, 27.

52. Letter to Carl Spaeth from John Clark, June 21, 1941, "Sports Experience of This Office," NARA, OIAA Records, RG 229, box 408: folder: Sports Office.

53. Agenda for Discussion Group Considering Sports in the Hemisphere Defense Program, June 23, 1941, 2, NARA, RG 229, box 408: folder: Sports Office.

54. Winston Guest's Preliminary Sports Program for Mexico, July 23, 1941, NARA, OIAA Records, RG 229, box 408: folder: Sports Office.

55. John Nash, "Personal Observations on U.S.A.-Latin American Sports Exchange," June 9, 1942, NARA, OIAA Records, RG 229, box 408: folder: Sports Office.

56. Project Authorization, "Tennis Team Tour of Other American Republics," September 26, 1941, NARA, OIAA Records, RG 229, box 408: folder: United States Lawn Tennis Association.

57. Elwood Cooke, "South American Tennis Tour Diary," December 1, 1941, 3, NARA, OIAA Records, RG 229, box 408: folder: United States Lawn Tennis Association.

58. "United States Players in Argentina," *American Lawn Tennis*, November 20, 1941, 4.

59. "Championship of the Argentine," *American Lawn Tennis*, December 20, 1941, 4.

60. "Good Will Tour," *United States Lawn Tennis Association Service Bulletin* 55 (February 1942): 3.

61. Letter to United States Lawn Tennis Association from Alfonso Londono, September 21, 1944, 3, NARA, OIAA Records, RG 229, box 408: folder: United States Lawn Tennis Association.

62. Caroline Seebohm, *Little Pancho: The Life of Tennis Legend Pancho Segura* (Lincoln: University of Nebraska Press, 2009).

63. Bod Considine, "The Good Will Kid," *Collier's*, September 5, 1942, 54–55; Allison Danzig, "Good Neighbor with a Racquet," *New York Times*, August 22, 1943, S2; "Good Neighbor Threat," *Florence Morning News*, September 1, 1942; "South American Net Star Makes Fans, Forget about Men Like Kovacs, Riggs," *Panama City News-Herald*, July 27, 1942.

64. A. Rojas, "Francisco (Pancho) Segura," *American Lawn Tennis*, July 1, 1944, 22; Letter to Mr. Baker from Nelson Rockefeller, October 18, 1944, 1 NARA, OIAA Records, RG 229, box 408: folder: United States Lawn Tennis Association.

65. Letter to Mr. Baker from Nelson Rockefeller, October 18, 1944, 2, NARA, OIAA Records, RG 229, box 408: folder: United States Lawn Tennis Association.

66. Letter to William Dawson from Asa Bushnell, March 17, 1942, NARA, OIAA Records, RG 229, box 434: folder: Sports.

67. "Program of the Coordinator of the Inter-American Affairs: Athletic Consultants for the Other American Republics," November 22, 1941, NARA, RG 229, box 429; folder: Athletic Coaches Mission.

68. Project Authorization, Athletics Consultants for Chile, Ecuador, Mexico, Peru and Uruguay, April, 11, 1942, NARA, OIAA Records, RG 229, box 408: folder Sports.

69. "Preliminary Report of Coaching Mission Questionnaire," February 19, 1941, NARA, OIAA Records, RG 229, box 408; folder Sports.

70. Ibid.

71. Luis Amador de Gama, *Historia Grafica del Futbol Americano en Mexico I, 1936-1945* (Mexico City: Olmeca Impresiones Finas, 1982), 8.

72. Asa S. Bushnell, "Proposal to Supply University of Mexico with Football Coach for 1941 Season," August 22, 1941, NARA, OIAA Records, RG 229, box 429; folder: Mexico Sports.

73. Ibid.

74. Project Authorization "Football Coach for University of Mexico," September 4, 1941, NARA, OIAA Records, RG 229, box 429; folder Mexico Sports.

75. Jack Starr-Hunt "Those Clever Mexican Futbolistas," *Santa Ana Register*, November 5, 1930, 9.

76. Ibid., 9.

77. "Sensible Diplomacy: Mexican Football Game So Named," *Los Angeles School Journal* 14, no. 9 (October 27, 1930): 29.

78. "Football Is Dying at Mexico U.: Lack of Finances Said Cause," *Brownsville Herald*, October 29, 1931.

79. Weekly Report, Football Coach to Mexico, October 9, 1941, NARA, OIAA Records, RG 229, box 429; folder Mexico Sports.

80. Excerpts from Reports Made to Sports Office by Bernard Hoban, Athletic Consultant and Football Coach at University of Mexico, September 27, 1941, NARA, OIAA Records, RG 229, box 408; folder: Football Coach Missions.

81. Ibid.

82. Memorandum to Carl B. Spaeth from William L. Clark, Subject Sports Program, June 6, 1941, NARA, OIAA Records, RG 229, box 408; folder Sports.

83. Letter Adolf Berle from Nelson Rockefeller, November 3, 1941, NARA, OIAA Records, RG 229, box 408; folder Sports.

84. "Louisiana Gridders Set for Mexican Game," *News-Journal*, December 30, 1941, 8.

85. The Orchid Bowl continued every New Year's Day until 1947. "Mexico Bowl Game Set," *New York Times*, October 24, 1947, 27.

86. "Louisiana College Wins Conquers University of Mexico at Football," *New York Times*, January 2, 1946, 26.

87. "Football in Mexico," Report to the Sports Office of the Coordinator of the Inter-American Affairs by Bernard A. Hoban, September–December, 1941, 4, NARA, OIAA Records, RG 229, box 408; folder: Football Coach Missions.

88. Theodore A. Ediger, "Football Play Has Arrived in Mexico," *Valley Morning Star*, December 1, 1944, 7.

89. Memorandum to Asa Bushnell from Dudley T. Easby Jr., November 21, 1941, NARA, OIAA Records, RG 229, box 408; folder: Football Coach Missions.

90. Jorge Prieto, *The Quarterback Who Almost Wasn't* (Houston, TX: Arte Publico Press, 1994), 115.

91. Ibid., 115.

92. Ibid., 134–135.

93. Jorge Iber, "On Field Foes and Racial Misconceptions: The 1961 Donna Redskins and Their Drive to the Texas State Football Championship," *International Journal of the History of Sport* 21, no. 2 (March 2004): 237–256; Jorge Iber, "Mexican Americans of South Texas Football: The Athletic and Coaching Careers of E. C. Lerma and Bobby Cavazos, 1932–1965," *Southwestern Historical Quarterly* 55 (2002): 617–633.

94. "Football in Mexico," Report to the Sports Office of the Coordinator of the Inter-American Affairs by Bernard A. Hoban, September–December, 1941, 5, NARA, OIAA Records, RG 229, box 408; folder: Football Coach Missions.

95. Ibid., 3.

96. Ibid., 3.

97. Football Coach to Mexico, Sports Office Weekly Report,1, January 22, 1942, NARA, OIAA Records, RG 229, box 408; folder: Football Coach Missions.

98. Ibid. 1.

99. Fray Kempis, *Novedades*, February 2, 1942. Cited in Weekly Report of the Sports Office, February 4, 1942, NARA, OIAA Records, RG 229, box 408; folder: Football Coach Missions.

100. Letter to Asa Bushnell from Leopoldo Noriega, April 12, 1942, NARA, OIAA Records, RG 229, box 408; folder: Football Coach Missions.

101. "Bernard Hoban No Irá a Entrenar en Mexico al Equipo de la Universidad Nacional," *La Prensa*, October 27, 1942, 5.

102. Letter to Asa Bushnell from Nelson Rockefeller, June 16, 1943, NARA, OIAA Records, RG 229, box 408; folder: Football Coach Missions.

103. Letter to Nelson Rockefeller from W. C. Longan, Coordination Committee for Mexico, August 30, 1943, NARA, OIAA Records, RG 229, box 408; folder: Football Coach Missions.

104. "Hoban Return as Mentor Is Sought," *Delta Democrat-Times*, August 8, 1944.

105. Theodore Ediger, "Football Play Has Arrived in Mexico," *Valley Morning Star*, December 1, 1944.

106. "South of the Border Gridders Need Heft, Mentor Declares," *Eugene Guard*, January 3, 1945.

107. Memorandum to Asa Bushnell from Dudley T. Easby, Jr., November 21, 1941, NARA, OIAA Record, RG 229, box 408; folder: Football Coach Missions.

108. Football in Mexico Report to the Sports Office of the Coordinator of the Inter-American Affairs by Bernard A. Hoban, September–December 1941, 7, NARA, OIAA Records, RG 229, box 408; folder: Football Coach Missions.

109. To Secretary of State, Washington, D.C., from Josephus Daniels, August 20, 1941, NARA, U.S. Embassy Records, RG 84, box 98; Volume 103: American Embassy Mexico City, 1941.

110. Ibid.

111. Andrei Markovits and Steven Hellerman, *Offside: Soccer and American Exceptionalism* (Princeton, NJ: Princeton University Press, 2001).

112. Burton Benjamin, "Soccer Is Answer in Sports for Getting Neighborly Good Will," *Standard Examiner*, June 14, 1942, B5.

113. Ibid., B5.

114. Letter to Asa Bushnell from Kenneth Holland, May 13, 1942, 1, NARA, OIAA Records, RG 229, box 429; folder: Mexico Sports.

115. Letter to Kenneth Holland from Asa Bushnell, May 7, 1942, 1, NARA, OIAA Records, RG 229, box 429: folder Mexico Sports.

116. On Club Atlante see Carlos Calderón Cardoso, *Crónica del Futbol Mexicano: Por Amor a la Camiseta, 1930–1950* (Mexico City: Clío 1998), 30–31.

117. "Mexicans to Arrive for Soccer Tour," *New York Times*, May 21, 1942, 29; William Graham, "Hold Luncheon Tomorrow for Atlante Squad," *Brooklyn Daily Eagle*, May 22, 1942.

118. Juan Arambari, "El Quipo Atlante de Mexico, fue Recibido con Altos Honores en la Ciudad de N. York," *La Prensa*, May 23, 1942, 7.

119. "Mexico's Soccer Champions Tie Metropolitan All-Stars in U.S. Tour Opener," *New York Times*, May 25, 1942, 20.

120. Abe Tuvim, "Visitors from Mexico," Letter to the Sports Editor, *New York Times*, May 23, 1942, 18.

121. Ibid.

122. Louis Effrat, "Touring Players Overcome by 2–0, Fans Storm the Field after Fistic Outburst—Order Is Restored in 20 Minutes," *New York Times*, June 8, 1942, 20.

123. "Mexican Booters Win at Baltimore," *New York Times*, May 30, 1942, 19.

124. "Mexican Soccer Team Sent Home," *Los Angeles Times*, June 11, 1942, 22.

125. Juan Aramburo, "El Equipo Atlante de Mexico, fue Recibido con Altos Honores en la ciudad de N. York," *La Prensa*, May 23, 1942, 7; "Están Bien Entrenados los del Atlante Para Jugar Hoy," *La Prensa*, May 2, 1942, 13.

126. Syde, "Temas Del Dia," *Excélsior*, November 19, 1941.

127. "Los Tenistas de Mexico, En Una Protesta," *La Opinión*, December 6, 1941, 7.

128. Syde, "Temas Del Dia," *Excélsior*, November 19, 1941.

129. Ibid.

130. Letter to Harry Pierson from Edward Trueblood, December 5, 1941, 1, NARA, U.S. Embassy Records, RG 84, box 98; Volume 103: American Embassy Mexico City, 1941.

131. "De Todo y En Todas Partes," *Excélsior*, December 9, 1941.

132. Letter to Wallace Harrison from Angel Rosas, October 27, 1942, 1, NARA, OIAA Records, RG 229, box 429: folder Mexico Sports.

133. Memo from Wallace Harrison to Kenneth Holland, November 4, 1942, 2, NARA, OIAA Records, RG 229, box 429: folder Mexico Sports.

134. Memorandum by Angel Rosas, Washington, DC, October 27, 1942, 1, NARA, OIAA Records, RG 229, box 429: folder Mexico Sports.

135. "Las Politas," en Jira por los Estado Unidos," *La Opinión*, January 15, 1943, 7.

136. "Mexican Team Stops Here," *Burlington Hawk Eye Gazette*, January 13, 1943, 8; "Mexican Girls to Play East Prairie," *Sikeston Herald*, January 29, 1943, 9.

137. "Mexico City Cage Is Swamped by Iowa Quintet," *Waco News-Tribune*, January 18, 1943, 7.

138. Rodolfo Bermejo, "La Jira de Las Politas por Los Estados Unidos," *La Prensa*, January 26, 1943, 6.

139. Norb Garrett, "Mexican Girls and SLU High Also Win; 3,115 Brave Weather," *St. Louis Star-Times*, January 20, 1943, 20.

140. Letter to Secretario de Relaciones Exteriores from Luis Fernandez MacGregor, Cónsul de Mexico, January 25, 1943, box III-642-11, Protección a Mexicanos del Consulado en Los Angeles, El Acervo Histórico Diplomático de Secretaría de Relaciones Exteriores, Mexico City.

141. "Mexica Girl Hoopers Enjoy Good Will Tour," *Lubbock Morning Avalanche*, February 9, 1943, 5.

142. Letter to Max Putzel from Asa Bushnell, May 26, 1942, 1, NARA, OIAA Records, RG 229, box 429: folder: Sports Women.

143. Letter to Mary Winslow from Mary Hall, March 30, 1942, 31, NARA, OIAA Records, RG 229, box 429: folder: Sports Women.

144. Robert Elias, *The Empire Strikes Out: How Baseball Sold U.S. Foreign Policy and Promoted the American Way Abroad* (New York: New Press, 2010).

145. Letter to Nelson Rockefeller by W. S. Link, October 20, 1942, 1, NARA, OIAA Records, RG 229, box 434: folder: Venezuela Sports.

146. Letter to Nelson Rockefeller from Charles R. Clason, May 12, 1941, 1, NARA, OIAA Records, RG 229, box 408: folder: Sports Baseball.

147. Letter to Nelson Rockefeller by W. S. Link, October 20, 1942, 2, NARA, OIAA Records, RG 229, box 434: folder: Venezuela Sports.

148. Ibid.

149. Letter to W. S. Link from Kenneth Holland, November 2, 1942, 2, NARA, OIAA Records, RG 229, box 434: folder: Venezuela Sports.

150. Letter to Nelson Rockefeller from Matthew Molanphy, May 10, 1943, 1, NARA, OIAA Records, RG 229, box 427: folder: Guatemala Sports.

151. Ibid.

152. Ibid.

153. Letter to William Harridge from John Akin, April 29, 1943, NARA, OIAA Records, RG 229, box 427: folder: Guatemala Sports.

154. Letter to Mr. Connolly from Maurice Ries, January 2, 1944, NARA, OIAA Records, RG 229, box 214: folder: Sports Films.

155. "The Ninth Inning," Poster by Lew Fonseca, 1942–1944, NARA, OIAA Records, RG 229, box 214: folder: Sports Films.

156. Letter to Lew Fonseca by Julio Enrique Monagas, June 21, 1942, NARA, OIAA Records, RG 229, box 215: folder: Sports Films.

157. Penne Bender, "'There's Only One America Now': The OIAA Film Programs in the United States," in Cramer and Prutsch, *America Unidas!*, 77–105.

158. Adrian Burgos Jr., *Playing America's Game: Baseball, Latinos, and the Color Line* (Berkeley: University of California Press, 2007), 180–181.

159. Letter to J. C. Connolly from Maurice Ries, January 12, 1944, 1, NARA, OIAA Records, RG 229, box 214: folder: Sports Films.

160. Ibid.

161. Shirley Povish, "This Morning," *Washington Post*, January 14, 1944, 13.

162. "Another Baseball Blow: Mexican League Likely to Gain Some Major League Players," *New York Times*, January 20, 1945, 14.

163. "Would Confer on Pact: Mexico Baseball Leader Ready to Meet Big Leaguers," *New York Times*, March 13, 1946, 32.

164. Jack Markow, "If *Beisbol* Should Cross the Border," *New York Times Magazine*, July 28, 1946, 15.

165. "Cuban Criticizes Chandler's Stand," *New York Times*, December 13, 1946.

166. Barbara Keys, *Globalizing Sport: National Rivalry and International Community in the 1930s* (Cambridge, MA: Harvard University Press, 2006).

6. SPORTING A NEW IDENTITY IN POSTWAR AMERICA

1. Valentina "Tina" Hernandez, interview by the author, June 27, 2016, Lemon Grove, CA.

2. On Mexican American women workers during World War II, see Sherna Berger Gluck, *Rosie the Riveter Revisited: Women, the War and Social Change* (New York: New American Library, 1987), chaps. 4, 9; Richard Santillan, "Rosita the Riveter: Midwest Mexican American Women during World War II, 1941–1945," *Perspectives in Mexican American Studies* 2 (1989): 115–147; Naomi Quiñonez, "Rosita the Riveter: Welding Traditions with Wartime Transformations," in *Mexican Americans and World War II*, ed. Maggie Rivas-Rodriguez (Austin: University of Texas

Press, 2005), 245–268; Elizabeth Escobedo, *From Coveralls to Zoot Suits: The Lives of Mexican American Women on the World War II Home Front* (Chapel Hill: University of North Carolina Press, 2013).

3. "Sheet Metalettes Take League Lead," *San Diego Union*, August 21, 1941, 17.

4. Hernandez interview.

5. Gary Bedingfield, "Manuel 'Nay' Hernandez," in *Baseball's Dead of World War II*, ed. Gary Bedingfield (Jefferson, NC: McFarland, 2010), 56–60.

6. Chris Jenkins, "Starring in Baseball Got Player Drafted," *San Diego Union Tribune*, May 25, 2014.

7. "Council Constitution," box 3, folder 15, M295, Manuel Ruiz Papers, Special Collections, Green Library, Stanford University, Stanford, CA (hereafter Ruiz Papers).

8. Mario García, "Americans All: The Mexican American Generation and the Politics of Wartime Los Angeles, 1941–45," *Social Science Quarterly* 65 (1984): 278–289; Edward Escobar, *Race, Police and the Making of a Political Identity: Mexican Americans and the Los Angeles Police Department, 1900–1945* (Berkeley: University of California Press, 1999); Eduardo Obregón Pagán, *Murder at the Sleepy Lagoon: Zoot Suits, Race and Riot in Wartime L.A.* (Chapel Hill: University of North Carolina Press, 2003), 32–35; Luis Alvarez, *The Power of the Zoot: Youth Culture and Resistance during World War II* (Berkeley: University of California Press, 2008), 67–68; Richard Griswold del Castillo, *World War II and Mexican American Civil Rights* (Austin: University of Texas Press, 2008), 86–87.

9. "Se Formo el Consejo de La Juventud," *La Opinión*, August 1, 1941, 8. Other CCLAY executive board members included Ernesto Orfila, former commander of Hollywood Post 43, Francisco Belendez, president of the Mexican Chamber of Commerce, Frank Fouce, theater owner, Jose Garduño of *La Opinión*, Al Rendón, athlete, and Rodolfo Salazar, Mexican consul of Los Angeles.

10. "Athletic Commission of the Coordinating Council of the Mexican Youth," August 14, 1941, box 3, folder 15, M295, Ruiz Papers.

11. "Acuerdo de la Asociación y Unión Atlética," *La Opinión*, August 21, 1941, 7; Gran Campaña en Los Angeles en contra La Delincuencia Juvenil por medio de Extensas Actividades Deportivas," *La Prensa*, August 25, 1941, 7. Other committee members included Daniel Galindo of the Verdugo Caballeros Youth Club (secretary), Hortensia Pérez of the Iris Club (treasurer), Manuel Cardona, assistant director of Evergreen Recreation Center, Pedro Despart, vice-president of the Mexican Athletic Union, Ignacio Durón and Tom Garcia of the Huntington Park YMCA, and Roberto Ortiz, president of the Mexican Athletic Association of Southern California.

12. Meeting Minutes, Coordinating Council of Latin-American Youth, December 7, 1942, box 3, folder 15, M295, Manuel Papers; Bert W. Colima, *Gentleman of the Ring: The Bert Colima Story* (Long Beach, CA: Magic Valley, 2009), 117.

13. Mexican girls' social clubs like the Iris Club and Alma Joven allowed their members to develop leadership skills and expand their social networks outside the home. See Escobedo, *From Coveralls to Zoot Suits*, 112–113.

14. "Rules and Regulations of the Mexican Athletic Committee of the Coordinating Council of Latin-American Youth," box 3, folder 15, M295, Ruiz Papers.

15. Makanazo, "El Deporte y La Delincuencia Juvenil Entre Los Mexicanos," *La Opinión*, August 10, 1941, 5.

16. "Gran Funcion Benefica en la Arena Eastside, el 29 Para Reunir Fondos Pro-Viaje de Los Atleteas a la Capital," *La Opinión*, October 20, 1941, 7.

17. Coordinating Council of Latin-American Youth to State Athletic Commission, October 20, 1941, folder 14, box 4, MO295, Ruiz Papers.

18. Letter to John Doyle, Eastside Arena from Manuel Ruiz, CCLAY October 20, 1941, box 12, folder 13, M295, Ruiz Papers.

19. "Un Buen Programa de Boxeo y Lucha en La Arena Eastside," *La Opinión*, October 29, 1941, 7.

20. Letter to Rodolfo Hoyos from Manuel Ruiz, CCLAY, October 22, 1941, box 12, folder 13, M295, Ruiz Papers.

21. Letter to Rodolfo Salazar from Manuel Ruiz, CCLAY Nov 1, 1941, box 12, folder 13, M295, Ruiz Papers.

22. "Irán deportistas Mexicanos de Los Angeles a participar en Mexico," *La Prensa*, October 18, 1941, 7. For more on the 1941 Revolutionary Games, see Keith Brewster and Claire Brewster, "Sport and Society in Post-revolutionary Mexico," *International Journal of the History of Sport* 26, no. 6 (May 2009):

23. Dirección General de Educación Física, *Juegos Deportivos Nacionales de la Revolución del 4 al 20 de Noviembre de 1941: Reglamento y Programa General* (Mexico City: Secretaria de Educación Pública, 1941), 7, 733–735.

24. Ibid., 7.

25. "La Delegacion Atletica de Los Angele Llego Con Tres Dias de Retraso a La Capital," *La Opinión*, November 14, 1941, 7.

26. "Sale Hoy La Delegación de Los Angeles a Mexico," *La Opinión*, November 2, 1941, 5.

27. Alvarez, *Power of the Zoot*, 71–73.

28. Christopher W. Wells, "Activist, Interpreter, Statesman: A Political Biography of Manuel Ruiz Jr." (honor's thesis, Williams College, 1995), 41.

29. Meeting Minutes, Coordinating Council of Latin-American Youth, March 3, 1942. box 4, folder 14, MO295, Ruiz Papers.

30. Letter to Manchester Boddy from Manuel Ruiz, Coordinating Council of Latin-American Youth, March 18, 1942, box 4, folder 14, MO295, Ruiz Papers.

31. Bob Hebert column, *Los Angeles Daily News*, March 9, 1942, 31.

32. Bob Hebert column, *Los Angeles Daily News*, February 19, 1942, 31.

33. "Gordon Macker Column," *Los Angeles Daily News*, March 1942, 34. Hudson failed to meet the 140-pound weight and the fight was canceled. "Cecil Hudson Rehuyó la Palea con Pedro Ortega," *La Opinión*, March 8, 1942, 4.

34. Letter to George Parnassus by Willie Ritchie, State Athletic Commission, March 11, 1942, box 4, folder 14, MO295, Ruiz Papers.

35. Letter to Manchester Boddy from Manuel Ruiz, Coordinating Council of Latin-American Youth, March 18, 1942, box 4, folder 14, MO295, Ruiz Papers.

36. Makanazo, "En La Maraña del Deporte," *La Opinión*, March 31, 1942, 7; Makanazo, "En La Maraña del Deporte," *La Opinión*, April 1, 1942, 7.

37. Ibid.

38. "Sellout Looms for Olympic Bout, Army Benefits from Wilson-Ortega Fight," *Los Angeles Times*, March 27, 1941, 26.

39. "Olympic Bout Lures Big Gate," *Los Angeles Times*, April 2, 1942, 21.

40. Cal Whorton, "Wilson Stops Ortega in Third Round of Tiff," *Los Angeles Times*, April 1, 1942, 21.

41. Letter to Chief C. B. Horrall from Manuel Ruiz, Coordinating Council of Latin-American Youth, February 14, 1941, box 4, folder 14, MO295, Ruiz Papers.

42. "Petition," February 1942, M295, box 2, folder, 12, Ruiz Papers.

43. Ibid.

44. Ibid.; Coordinating Council of Latin-American Youth to Manuel Ruiz, March 9, 1942, M295, box 2, folder 12, Ruiz Papers.

45. Ibid.

46. Ibid.

47. Meeting Minutes, Coordinating Council of Latin-American Youth, May 4, 1942, MO295, box 4, folder 14, Ruiz Papers. See also García, "Americans All," 280–281.

48. "Committee Studies Welfare Program for Latin Youth," *Los Angeles Times*, December 8, 1942, A8; "Minutes of Pacific Palisades Meeting," March 19, 1946, Los Angeles Youth Project Program Committee, 2, M295, box 4, folder 13, Ruiz Papers.

49. "Board of Playground and Recreation Commissioners Minutes," October 9, 1942, box 4, folder C-0368, 117, Los Angeles Department of Recreation Records, City Archives and Records Center, Los Angeles.

50. "Board of Playground and Recreation Commissioners Minutes," December 11, 1942, box 4, folder C-0368, 179, Los Angeles Department of Recreation Records.

51. This larger group included nine Anglo American and eleven Mexican Americans, including several CCLAY members such as Manuel Ruiz Jr., Eduardo Quevedo, Ernest Orfila, and Jose Diaz. See "Committee for Latin-American Youth Selects Manuel Ruiz Jr.," *Los Angeles Times*, December 3, 1842, 17.

52. "Board of Playground and Recreation Commissioners Minutes," May 3, 1943, box 4, folder C-0368, 327, Los Angeles Department of Recreation Records.

53. "Pachuco" or "Pachuca" is generally defined as a Mexican American youth subculture that originated in the El Paso–Ciudad Juárez area in the early 1900s. See Laura Cummings, *Pachucas and Pachucos in Tucson: Situated Border Lives* (Tucson: University of Arizona Press, 2009); Geraldo Licón, "Pachucas, Pachucos, and Their Culture: Mexican American Zoot Suiters in the United States, 1910–1955" (PhD diss., University of Southern California, 2009); Escobedo, *From Coveralls to Zoot Suits*, 17–44; Obregón Pagán, *Murder at the Sleepy Lagoon*, 36–39.

54. An estimated 3 percent of Mexican American youth were involved in so called "Pachuco gang" activity. "Delinquency War Mapped," *Los Angeles Times* April 20, 1943, 39.

55. "Meeting Minutes, Coordinating Council of Latin-American Youth," November 8, 1943, MO295, box 4, folder 14, Ruiz Papers. See also William Estrada, *The Los Angeles Plaza: Sacred and Contested Space* (Austin: University of Texas Press, 2008), 234–235.

56. Harold Mendelsohn, "Pachucos Club Formed to Give Youths Chance," *Los Angeles Times*, November 5, 1943, 21, 36.

57. "Hoodlums Attack Marines," *Lincoln Star*, November 14, 1943, 7.

58. "Club Pachucos Born with Boxing and Dancing," *Los Angeles Times*, November 12, 1943, 20.

59. Gene Handsaker, "Los Angeles 'Pachucos' Too Much Even for Mrs. Sterling," *Palm Beach Post*, January 3, 1944, 3.

60. Escobedo, *From Coveralls to Zoot Suits*, chap. 4.

61. Ibid., 104.

62. Richard Santillan, "Mexican Baseball Teams in the Midwest, 1916–1965: The Politics of Cultural Survival and Civil Rights," *Perspectives in Mexican American Studies* 7 (2000): 139–146.

63. John Fraire, "Mexicans Playing Baseball in Indiana Harbor, 1925–1942," *Indiana Magazine of History* 110 (June 2014): 139.

64. Vicki Ruiz, *From Out of the Shadows: Mexican Women in Twentieth-Century America* (New York: Oxford University Press, 1998), 51–71.

65. Maggie Salazar Guzman, telephone interview by the author, August 17, 2016.

66. "Women's Softball," *Baldwin Park Tribune*, March 2, 1944, 5.

67. Guzman interview.

68. Ibid.

69. The five-street Mexican neighborhood within North Hollywood was named after Felipe Horcasitas, who owned the land bounded by Stagg, Lankershim, Arleta, and Buckney streets.

Alejandro Murguia, *The Medicine of Memory: A Mexica Clan in California* (Austin: University of Texas Press, 2002), 38.

70. Ramona Valenzuela Cervantes, interview by Daisey Valadez-Miguel, April 11, 2016, San Fernando, CA.

71. Richard Santillan, Victoria Norton, Christopher Docter, Monica Ortez, and Richard Arroyo, *Mexican American Baseball in the San Fernando Valley* (Charleston, SC: Arcadia, 2015), 36.

72. Ibid., 36.

73. Evelyn Duran and Rosa Silvas, interview by David Washburn, 2007, transcript, Rosie the Riveter World War II American Homefront Oral History Project, Regional Oral History Office, Bancroft Library, University of California, Berkeley.

74. Ibid., 18.

75. Susan Cahn, *Coming on Strong: Gender and Sexuality in Twentieth-Century Women's Sport* (New York: Free Press, 1994), 687.

76. Lynn Couturier, "'Play with Us, Not Against Us': The Debate about Play Days in the Regulation of Women's Sport," *International Journal of the History of Sport* 5, no. 4 (2008): 421–442.

77. Ernestina Navarro Hosaki, interview by the author, January 4, 2015, Oxnard, CA.

78. "Cotler's Girls Go Wild Again," *Oxnard Press Courier*, July 13, 1949, 8.

79. "Cotler's Girls Collect 7 Homers in 21–8 Triumph," *Oxnard Press Courier*, July 12, 1949, 6.

80. Mary Littlewood, *Women's Fastpitch Softball—the Path to the Gold: An Historical Look at Women's Fastpitch in the United States* (Columbia, MO: National Fastpitch Coaches Association, 1998), 30.

81. Rhiannon Potkey, "For Love of Baseball: CSUCI Exhibit Details Hispanic Women in Game," *Ventura County Star*, March 22, 2015, 8D.

82. Ernestina Navarro Hosaki, interview by the author, January 4, 2015, Oxnard, CA.

83. The 1949 team roster included Nadine Boydston, Jeanne Aikens, Johnnie Johnston, Angie Rivera, Bobbie Milligan, Joyce Tewes, Loma Sawyer, Tila Santana, Florence Rush, and Ernie Navarro. "Cotler Girls Entertain SLO," *Oxnard Press Courier*, August 29, 1949, 3.

84. Ernestina Navarro Hosaki, interview by Maria Marzicola, April 26, 2016, Oxnard, CA.

85. "Navarro Leads Ladies League," *Oxnard Press Courier*, October 21, 1953, 8.

86. "Patio Softball Gals Face Moorpark Nine," *Oxnard Press Courier*, July 19, 1947, 4.

87. Richard Santillan, José M. Alamillo, Anna Bermúdez, Juan J. Canchola-Ventura, and Al Ramos, *Mexican American Baseball in Ventura County* (Mount Pleasant, SC: Arcadia, 2016), 28–29.

88. Katherine Jamieson, "Occupying a Middle Space: Towards a Mestiza Sport Studies," *Sociology of Sport Journal* 20, no. 1 (2003): 1–16.

89. On female umpires, see Jean Hastings Ardell, *Breaking into Baseball: Women and the National Pastime* (Carbondale: Southern Illinois University Press, 2005), chap. 6.

90. Richard Santillán, Mark Ocegueda, and Terry Cannon, *Mexican American Baseball in the Inland Empire* (Charleston, SC: Arcadia, 2012), 63.

91. "SB, Magnolia Maids Vie Tonight," *Riverside Daily News*, June 21, 1950, 18.

92. "Highland Pirates Fall to Magnolia Maids, 7–2," *San Bernardino County Sun*, July 1, 1950, 16.

93. "Pony League Umpire, Former Pitcher Dies," *Riverside Daily News*, June 11, 1955, 18.

94. "Local Heroes Honored at 4th Annual Hispanic Hall of Fame," *Inland Empire Hispanic News*, November 25, 1987, 10.

95. Laura Purcell, "The Queens and the Ramblers: Women's Championship Softball in Phoenix, 1932–1965" (master's thesis, Arizona State University, 2004).

96. Littlewood, *Women's Fastpitch Softball*, 37; Erica Westley, *Fastpitch: The Untold Story of Softball and the Women Who Made the Game* (New York: Touchstone, 2016), 84–85.

97. Morris Bealle, *The Softball Story* (Washington, DC: Columbia, 1957), 79.

98. "Arizona Girls Softball Winners," *Press Democrat,* September 21, 1948, 6; "Peralta, Evans Due for Battle," *Oregonian,* July 18, 1949, 22.

99. Jerry McLain, "Batting Averages, Not Looks, Worry Sagebrush Softball Gals," *Panama City-News Herald,* August 3, 1941, 2.

100. "Amelina Peralta Hurls Six-Hitter for PBSW Victory," *Arizona Republic,* September 11, 1940, 12.

101. "Portrait of a Hall of Famer," *Balls and Strikes,* June 1957, 3.

102. Ibid.

103. "Children Slate Exhibit, Program," *Arizona Republic,* August 30, 1945, 10.

104. Amy Peralta Shelton, "Amy Looks Back on 'Fame' Career with Ramblers," *Balls and Strikes,* June 1957, 3.

105. "Amelina Peralta," *Mexican Voice,* November–December 1939, 7.

106. Westley, *Fastpitch.*

107. Carlos Salazar, interview by the author, January 24, 2016, Altadena, CA. The Pasadena Ramblers were founded in 1934 by owner Mark C. Nottingham and managed by Lon A. Wynkoop.

108. "Girl Softball Team Gives GU Camps Lift," *Brooklyn Daily Eagle,* August 1945, 5.

109. Al Wolf, "Sportraits," *Los Angeles Times,* August 28, 1944, 11.

110. Jack Curnow, "Girl Softball Nine Plays Service Teams at Camps," *Los Angeles Times,* June 5, 1945, 17.

111. Ibid., 17.

112. "5th OUT Club Wins Game but Takes Ribbing," *Desert Sun,* August 10, 1945, 8.

113. Escobedo, *From Coveralls to Zoot Suits,* chap. 4.

114. Del Schrader, "M.C. Nottingham Ramblers Organized for '45 Season," *Pasadena Star-News,* March 6 1945, 5.

115. "Mom, Aunt Helped Coach Outfielder," *Daily Herald,* August 14, 1977, 11.

116. "His Aunt Swings a Bat," *Freeport Journal-Standard,* August 17, 1977, 16.

117. Ibid., 16.

118. Ibid., 16.

119. *A League of Their Own,* directed by Penny Marshal (Columbia Pictures, 1992).

120. Merrie A. Fidler, *The Origins and History of the All-American Girls Professional Baseball League* (Jefferson, NC: McFarland, 2006), chap. 1.

121. Karen Weller and Catriona T. Higgs, "Living the Dream: A Historical Analysis of Professional Women Baseball Players, 1943–1954," *Canadian Journal of Sport History* 23, no. 1 (1992): 50.

122. Bill Fay, "Belles of the Ball Game," *Collier's,* August 3, 1949, 44.

123. Karen Weiller and Catriona Higgs, "The All American Girls Professional Baseball League, 1943–1954: Gender Conflict in Sport?," *Sociology of Sport Journal* 11 (1994): 289–297.

124. Gai Ingham Berlage, "Women's Professional Baseball Gets a New Look: On Film and in Print," *Journal of Sport and Social Issues* 16, no. 2 (1992): 149–153.

125. Gai Ingham Berlage, *Women in Baseball: The Forgotten History* (Westport, CT: Praeger, 1994); Barbara Gregorich, *Women at Play: The Story of Women in Baseball* (New York: Harcourt Brace, 1993); Lois Browne, *Girls of Summer: In Their Own League* (New York: Harper-Collins, 1992); Sue Macy, *A Whole New Ball Game: The Story of the All-American Girls Professional Baseball League* (New York: Puffin Books, 1993).

126. Jack Fincher, "The 'Belles of the Ball Game' were a hit with their fans," *Smithsonian,* 20, no. 1 (July 1989), 92.

127. Carol Pierman, "Baseball, Conduct and True Womanhood," *Women's Studies Quarterly* 33, nos. 1–2 (2005): 68–85.

128. Amira Rose Davis, "No League of Their Own: Baseball, Black Women, and the Politics of Representation," *Radical History Review* 125 (May 2016): 74–96.

129. Mario Longoria, *Estrellas Latinas in the AAGPBL—1846–1954* (San Antonio: University of Texas–San Antonio Hispanic Research Center, 2002); Christiana Lilly, "Ysora Kinney, 79-Year Old Hospital Volunteer, Talks Pioneering Past in Women's Baseball," *Huffington Post*, May 9, 2012;www.huffingtonpost.com/2012/04/04/ysora-kinney-womens-baseball_n _1403283.html; Emalee Nelson, "Cuban Babe (Ruth): The Story of Seven Cubana Women in Professional Baseball," *Sport in American History*, October 17, 2016, https://ussporthistory .com/2016/10/17/cuban-babe-ruth-the-story-of-seven-cubana-women-in-professional -baseball/.

130. Kat Williams, "Sport: 'A Useful Category of Historical Analysis': Isabel 'Lefty' Alvarez: The Rascal of El Cerro," *International Journal of the History of Sport* 29, no. 5 (April 2012): 766–785; Terry Doran, Janet Satterfield, and Chris Stade, *A Road Well Traveled: Three Generations of Cuban American Women* (Fort Wayne, IN: Latin American Educational Center, 1988), 15–23; Gregorich, *Women at Play*, 150–157.

131. Longoria, *Estrellas Latinas*, 4–9.

132. "El Beisbol Femenino se Destacó Este Año con la Actuación de las Mexicanas," *La Opinión*, November 28, 1948, 4; "Un Tim Femenino de Béisbol se Destacó Este Año con la Actuación de Mexicanas," *La Prensa*, November 23, 1948, 5.

133. Katie Castator, "Women's Touch: Ex-Pro Ballplayer Finds Way to Hall," *San Bernardino County Sun*, October 26, 1988, 28.

134. "Marge Villa Cryan," in Jim Sargent, *We Were the All-American Girls: Interviews with Players of the AAGPBL, 1943–1954* (Jefferson, NC: McFarland, 2013), 152.

135. Bertha Ragan is profiled by Westley, *Fastpitch*.

136. "Comets Have all the Hopes, Inspirations of the Girl in the Stand," *Kenosha Evening News*, July 9, 1948, 12.

137. "Villa Claims All-Time Marks," *Racine Journal*, June 10, 1946, 12; W.C. Madden. *The Women of the All-American Girls Professional Baseball League: A Bibliographical Dictionary* (Jefferson NC: McFarland & Company, 1997), 247.

138. "Solution to Kenosha's Home Problem—California Villa!," *Kenosha Evening News*, June 12, 1946, 12.

139. Adrian Burgos Jr., *Playing America's Game: Baseball, Latinos, and the Color Line* (Berkeley: University of California Press, 2007), 1–14.

140. "Villa Claims All-Time Marks" *Racine Journal*, June 10, 1946, 12; "Ann Harnett Switches to Mound Combines with O'Hara to Win over Blue Sox," *Kenosha Evening News*, April 30, 1947, 10; Jack Geyer, "Southland Girls Dot Middle West Rosters," *Los Angeles Times*, April 14, 1949, C2.

141. "Baseball Story Turns into Pig Tale—All About Villa," *Kenosha Evening News*, June 18, 1946, 8.

142. Cahn, *Coming on Strong*, 140. See also Marilyn Cohen, *No Girls in the Clubhouse: The Exclusion of Women from Baseball* (Jefferson, NC: McFarland, 2009), chap. 4.

143. "Goils Will Be Goils," *Kokomo Tribune*, May 12, 1949, 19.

144. Ibid., 19.

145. Cahn, *Coming on Strong*, 141.

146. "Take Charge," *Kenosha Evening News*, July 30, 1948, 5.

147. Marge Villa Cryan, telephone interview with the author, March 11, 2015.

148. Castator, "Women's Touch," 28.

149. In Kenosha, Villa rented a room from a retired English professor, who tutored her so she could complete her education. Marge Villa Cryan, telephone interview with the author, March 11, 2015.

150. "Girl's League Played to 75,000 in Havana Games," *Kenosha Evening News*, May 14, 1947.

151. "Cubans Go 'Ga Ga' over Girl Players," *Kenosha Evening News*, April 30, 1947, 10.

152. "Kenosha Comet Comments from Training Camp," *Kenosha Evening News*, April 22, 1948, 20. See also Longoria, *Estrellas Latinas*, 18.

153. Betty Luna Hill is quoted in Longoria, *Estrellas Latinas*, 18.

154. "Latin American Tour for Three Members of Comets," *Kenosha Evening News*, January 27, 1949, 10. See also Fidler, *Origins and History*, 111–124.

155. Marge Villa Cryan, telephone interview with the author, March 11, 2015.

156. "Latin American Fans Cheer Girl Ball Players," *Kenosha Evening News*, February 3, 1949, 12.

157. General Somoza is quoted in Fidler, *Origins and History*, 120.

158. Marge Villa Cryan, telephone interview with the author, March 11, 2015.

159. Ibid.

160. "Acuerdo de la Asociación y Unión Atlética," *La Opinión*, August 21, 1941, 7.

161. "Actividades Deportivas de La U.A.M.," *La Opinión*, January 12, 1947, 5.

162. Robert Korsgaard, "A History of the Amateur Athletic Union of the United States" (PhD diss., Teacher's College, Columbia University, 1952).

163. "La U.A.M. Da A Conocer Sus Propósitos," *La Opinión*, August 15, 1948, 4. ;

164. US Bureau of the Census, *Sixteenth Census of the United States, 1940* (Washington, DC: National Archives and Records Administration, 1940), T627, 4,643 rolls.

165. "Manual Arts Ties Belmont Nine in Game," *Los Angeles Times*, March 19, 1926, 47.

166. Arturo Flores, "Actividades Deportivas del 'Mexico,'" *La Opinión*, March 24, 1935, 4.

167. "Se Entrena La Quinta de Sánchez," *La Opinión*, February 16, 1936, 4.

168. Ray Sánchez, "Hazard and S.F. Lions Tangle," *Sport Page*, December 4, 1948, 1.

169. "College Athletic Co." *Sport Page*, June 19, 1928, 8.

170. US Bureau of the Census. *Fifteenth Census of the United States, 1930* (Washington, DC: National Archives and Records Administration, 1930), T626, 2,667 rolls.

171. "Una Función a Beneficio de La Asociación," *La Opinión*, November 30, 1936, 7.

172. Ibid.

173. On Pedro Despart's political career, see Kenneth Burt, *The Search for a Civic Voice: California Latino Politics* (Claremont, CA: Regina Books, 2007), 16.

174. "Natación y Football en La Asociación Atlética Mexicana," *La Opinión*, July 31, 1939, 7.

175. Ibid.

176. "Mexican Athletic Union Captains to Assemble," *Los Angeles Times*, October 22, 1940, 32; "Tiene Junta La Union Atlética Mexicana, Hoy," *La Opinión*, August 25, 1946, 7.

177. "Tortilla Bowl Gridfest Planned by Mexican Group," *San Diego Union Tribune*, October 29, 1939, 49.

178. "El Juego del Tortilla Bowl Sera Reñido," *La Opinión*, November 3, 1940, 7. The Mexican All-Stars included players from Lincoln High School, Belmont High School, Cathedral High School, and Occidental College.

179. "Tortilla Bowl Grid Title at Stake Today," *Los Angeles Times*, January 7, 1940, 28; "El Juego del Tortilla Bowl," *La Opinión*, January 1, 1940, 7; "El Juego del Tortilla Bowl El Domingo," *La Opinión*, January 3, 1940, 7.

180. "Buen Juego Dieron Los 'All Stars,'" *La Opinión*, January 16, 1940, 7; "Ross Snyder Bulldogs Co.," *Los Angeles Times*, January 15, 1940, 22.

181. "Teams Clash Today in Tortilla Bowl," *Los Angeles Times*, January 5, 1941, 34.

182. "La Temporada de Football de La U.A.M.," *La Opinión*, November 4, 1940, 7. The MAU football league included Bolivar Athletic Club, La Purisima, San Fernando A.C., Verdugo Knights, Watts Cardinals, and Pacific Coast Bees.

183. "Twin Bill Features Mexican Grid Card," *Los Angeles Times*, November 10, 1940, 33.

184. "Sal Mena Smartest of Trojan Gridders," *Los Angeles Times*, May 9, 1940, 25.

185. "La Selección 'All Mexican' de Football," *La Opinión*, January 2, 1941, 7.

186. "Los Estrellas Mexicanos En Otra Derrota," *La Opinión*, January 8, 1941, 7.

187. "La Maya, De Mexicali, vs. San Fernando," *La Opinión*, March 21, 1941, 4.

188. "El Torneo de Baseball de La Union Atlética," *La Opinión*, March 2, 1941, 4.

189. The handbill is published in Santillan et al., *Mexican American Baseball in the Central Coast*, 12.

190. "Mexicali vs. Los Angeles en Juego de Baseball, Hoy," *La Opinión*, March 23, 1941, 5.

191. "Un Deslucido Encuentro en el White Sox," *La Opinión*, March 24, 1941, 8.

192. "La Maya Va En Pos De La Revancha," *La Opinión*, March 30, 1941, 7.

193. "La Victoria del San Fernando," *La Opinión*, April 3, 1941, 7.

194. Steven Bullock, *Playing for Their Nation: Baseball and the American Military during World War II* (Lincoln: University of Nebraska Press, 2004); Richard Santillan, "Mexican Americans and Military Baseball during World War II," *Journal of the West* 54, no. 4 (Fall 2015): 80–86.

195. Burgos, *Playing America's Game*, chap. 8.

196. David Evans, "Late in the Game: The Integration of the Washington Senators," *National Pastime*, no. 22 (2002): 45–49.

197. "Gomez en la Segunda Base de 'Senadores' Definitivamente," *La Prensa*, May 14, 1942, 7; "Chile Gomez Regresara a la Capital," *La Opinión*, June 17, 1942, 7.

198. Squeeze Play, "Chile Gomez Esta De Regreso Con La Novena de Puebla," *La Opinión*, October 15, 1942, 7.

199. "Latins in Majors May Play in Mexican Loop," *Pittsburgh Courier*, January 27, 1945, 12.

200. Cynthia Wilber, *For the Love of the Game: Baseball Memories from the Men Who Were There* (New York: William Morrow, 1992), 125–131; Gustavo Arellano, "Grove of Dreams: The Life and Times of Orange Picker-Turned-Big Leaguer Jesse Flores," *OC Weekly*, April 5, 2007, 14–19.

201. "Mexican Rookie Proving Sensation with Athletics," *New York Times*, May 7, 1943, 24.

202. Jim Sandoval, "Jesse Flores: From Picking in the Fields to Picking Prospects," in *Can He Play? A Look at Baseball Scouts and their Profession*, ed. Jim Sandoval and Bill Nowlin (Phoenix: Society for American Baseball Research, 2011), 132–133.

203. "Flores es ya el 'AS' de Los Pitchers en Las Mayores," *La Opinión*, May 11, 1943, 7; "La Asociación Deportiva Dara un Trofeo al Pitcher Flores," *La Opinión*, November 19, 1939, 4.

204. "Jesus Flores es el Coach de La Habra," *La Opinión*, August 21, 1941, 7.

205. "El Torneo de Basketball, de Los Mexicanos," *La Opinión*, February 16, 1941, 4; "Mexican Basketball Tourney on Tonight," *Los Angeles Times*, February 17, 1941, 21.

206. "Joe Placentia Named Top A.A.U. Basketball Scorer," *Los Angeles Times*, March 2, 1942, 16.

207. "Mexican Quintet Meets Apaches," *Los Angeles Times*, January 27, 1942, 16; "A.A.U. Cagers Collide Tonight," *Los Angeles Times*, January 26, 1946, 7.

208. "Mexican All-Stars Quintet Triumphs," *Los Angeles Times*, February 18, 1944, A7.

209. Raul Morin, *Among the Valiant: Mexican Americans in WWII and Korea* (Alhambra, CA: Borden, 1963), 25; "Latino Was First Man Drafted in World War II," *Missileer*, February 16, 1973, 4.

210. Ray Sánchez to Manuel Ruiz, October 9, 1941, M295, box 3, folder 15, Ruiz Papers.

211. "Carnaval de basketbol de la U.A.M. de Los Angeles," *La Prensa*, January 17, 1941, 7.

212. "Mexico da un diploma a Despart," *La Opinión*, March 8, 1942, 4.

213. George J. Sánchez, *Becoming Mexican American: Ethnicity, Culture and Identity in Chicano Los Angeles, 1900–1945* (New York: Oxford University Press, 1993), 255–264.

214. "What's the Voice All About," *Mexican Voice*, March 1, 1940, 14.

215. Félix F. Gutiérrez, "The *Mexican Voice* Goes to War: Identities, Issues, and Ideas in World War II–Era Mexican American Journalism and Youth Activism," in *Latina/os and World War II: Mobility, Agency and Ideology*, eds. Maggie Rivas-Rodriguez & B.V. Olguín (Austin: University of Texas Press, 2014), 115–136; Christopher Tudico, "Before We Were Chicana/os: The Mexican American Experience in California Higher Education, 1848–1945" (PhD diss., University of Pennsylvania, 2010), chap. 5; David James González, "Battling Mexican Apartheid in Orange County, CA: Race, Place, and Politics, 1920–1950" (PhD diss., University of Southern California, 2017), chap. 3.

216. "Félix Gutiérrez, "Sporting Around," *Mexican Voice*, November–December 1939, 15–16; Manuel Ceja, "Sports," *Mexican Voice*, January–February 1939, 18–20.

217. Manuel de la Raza, "Nosotros," *Mexican Voice*, July 1938, 4–5. Félix Gutiérrez often wrote under the pen name of Manuel de la Raza.

218. "M-A's Star in Basketball," *Forward*, May 8, 1947, 2; "Los Caballeros M.A.U. Casaba Champs of 1949," *Forward*, February 24, 1949, 4.

219. "M.A.U. Promotes Mexican Sports," *Forward*, February 24, 1949, 5.

220. Ibid., 5.

221. Gaulberto Valadez, interview by the author, July 21, 2005, Yorba Linda, CA.

222. Ron Gonzales, "Level Fields," *Orange County Register*, October 14, 2004, 2.

223. Richard Santillan, Susan Luevano, Luis Fernandez, and Angelina Veyna, *Mexican American Baseball in Orange County* (Charleston, SC: Arcadia, 2013), 46.

224. Gualberto Valadez, interview with Isabel Hlavac, August 16, 1995, transcript, Placentia Historical Committee Oral History Project, Center for Oral and Public History, California State University, Fullerton.

225. "La U.A.M. Da A Conocer Sus Propósitos," *La Opinión*, August 15, 1948, 4. New sport commissioners included Johnny Carmona, Ray Jauregui, Monico Medina, Terry Gonzalez, and Tommy Richardson.

226. "Habrá Intercambio Deportivo Entre Alta y Baja California," *La Opinión*, March 9, 1941, 4.

227. "Exhibición de los Trofeos de la Unión Atlética Mexicana," *La Opinión*, September 2, 1948, 7.

228. Jess Losada, "Los Deportes Ayudan a la Mujer a ser Bella," *La Opinión*, April 12, 1942, 5.

229. "Man, Wife Run One-Two in Marathon," *Los Angeles Times*, September 15, 1947, 10.

230. "Entregando El Trofeo a Los Vencedores," *La Opinión*, September 21, 1947, 5.

231. "Hoy Empieza el Torneo de Tenis," *La Opinión*, April 20, 1947, 5.

232. "Encuentros de Tenis, Hoy En el Evergreen," *La Opinión*, April 20, 1947, 5.

233. "El Tenista Gonzalez Compite Hoy," *La Opinión*, May 25, 1947, 4.

234. "Los Tenistas Isais y Gonzalez Compiten Hoy En El Evergreen," *La Opinión*, May 11, 1947, 5.

235. "Gonzalez, Nuevo Campeon de Tenis," *La Opinión*, September 20, 1948, 5.

236. Rodolfo Garcia, "Esquina Neutral," *La Opinión*, September 21, 1948, 7.

237. Cy Rice, *Man with a Racket: The Autobiography of Pancho Gonzales as told to Cy Rice* (New York: A.S. Barnes, 1959), 24–25.

238. José M. Alamillo, "Richard 'Pancho' Gonzalez, Race and the Print Media in Postwar Tennis America," *International Journal of the History of Sport* 26, no. 7 (June 2009): 947–965; José M. Alamillo, "'Bad Boy' of Tennis: Richard 'Pancho' Gonzalez, Racialized Masculinity

and the Print Media in Postwar America," in *More Than Just Peloteros: Sport and US Latino Communities*, ed. Jorge Iber (Lubbock: Texas Tech University Press, 2014), 121–143.

239. Rice, *Man with a Racket*, 53.

240. Alamillo, "'Bad Boy' of Tennis," 132–133.

241. "Mañana Empieza el Torneo de Basquetbol de la U.A.M.," *La Opinión*, November 19, 1948, 7; "Latins Hold Cage Tournament Tonight," *Los Angeles Times*, November 20, 1948, B4.

242. Mañana Empieza el Torneo de Basquetbol de la U.A.M.," *La Opinión*, November 19, 1948, 7.

243. "Porque Fue El Atleta Sobresaliente," *La Opinión*, November 21, 1948, 5.

244. "González Acabe de ser Objeto de Alta Distinción por La Fundación Atlética Helms," *La Opinión*, November 17, 1948, 7.

245. On "racial uplift" ideology, see Kevin Gaines, *Uplifting the Race: Black Leadership, Politics and Culture in the Twentieth Century* (Chapel Hill: University of North Carolina Press, 1996).

246. Rodolfo García, "Esquina Neutral," *La Opinión*, September 7, 1949, 7.

247. Ibid., 7.

248. "Ricardo Gonzalez Jugara Aqui el Lunes y Martes," *La Opinión*, January 8, 1950, 7.

249. "Pancho Tops Kramer in Three-Set Match," *Los Angeles Times*, January 11, 1950, C1.

250. Paul Teetor and Ralph Gonzales, "Viva Pancho!," *Oye Magazine* 2 (September 1994): 27.

251. Rice, *Man with a Racket*, 133–139.

252. Ibid., 134.

253. Ibid., 138.

254. "La Quinta Mexican American Vets Entrará en Acción el Domingo," *La Opinión*, January 30, 1947, 7.

255. "Campeones de la Union Atlética Mexicana," *La Opinión*, March 1, 1947, 7; "La Quinta Mexicali Apaleo a los Campeones de la Union Atlética," *La Opinión*, March 4, 1947, 7.

256. "Ecos del Juego de Basquet Mexicali-Azusa," *La Opinión*, March 9, 1947, 7.

257. "Actividades Deportivas de La U.A.M.," *La Opinión*, January 12, 1947, 5; "Impulsores del Deporte," *La Opinión*, June 1, 1947, 4.

258. "El Trofeo de La Opinión," *La Opinión*, November 16, 1947, 5; "16 Equipos Participaran en le Torneo de Softbol de la MAU," *La Opinión*, June 12, 1947, 7; "Celebration Held Today for Colton Mercuries Title Club," *San Bernardino County Sun*, July 27, 1947, 17.

259. "Exhibición de los Trofeos de la Unión Atlética Mexicana," *La Opinión*, September 2, 1948, 7.

260. Ignacio M. García, *When Mexicans Could Play Ball: Basketball, Race, and Identity in San Antonio, 1928–1945* (Austin: University of Texas Press, 2013).

261. Joe Bernal, interview by José Angel Gutiérrez, April 17, 2003, Center for Mexican American Studies Oral Histories, no. 169, University of Texas at Arlington, 15.

262. Lupe Anguiano, interview by the author, August 20, 2010, Oxnard, CA.

263. Victoria Maria MacDonald and Alice Cook, "Before Chicana Civil Rights: Three Generations of Mexican American Women in Higher Education in the Southwest, 1920–1965," in *Women's Higher Education in the United States: New Historical Perspectives*, ed. Margaret Nash (New York: Palgrave Macmillan, 2018), 233–254.

264. Anguiano interview.

265. "10,000 Personas Asistieron El Encuentro Atlético Ayer," *La Opinión*, May 5, 1941, 7.

266. The *Sport Page* office was located on 424 S. Broadway, Los Angeles. The staff included John Urdaburn, who covered boxing; Monico Medina, who wrote feature stories; Saul Toledo and Wally Poon, who covered the baseball scene; Joey Olmos, the newspaper cartoonist; and Ray Jauregui and Ray Sánchez, contributing writers.

267. Joey Olmos, "Midget Martinez," *Sport Page*, June 24, 1950, 1.

268. Ibid., 1.

269. "Bell Martell Stages Mitt Tourney Finals," *Los Angeles Times*, September 30, 1942, 30.

270. Morin, *Among the Valiant*.

271. Midget Martinez, "A Tribute to All Fighting Latins," *Sport Page*, ca. 1946, M295, box 2, folder 12, Ruiz Papers.

272. Ibid.

273. Felix F. Gutierrez, "The *Mexican Voice* Goes to War," 115–136.

274. "Sport Page All Latin Annual Basketball Tournament," *Sport Page*, February 29, 1948, 1.

275. The football selection committee included Midget Martinez, Ray Jauregui, Saul Toledo, and Raymundo Sánchez. Midget Martinez, "Latin Gridders Await Banquet," *Sport Page*, December 4, 1948, 1.

276. Ibid., 1.

277. "All-Latin Gridders to be Feted Sunday," *Los Angeles Times*, December 31, 1948, 33; "Fueron Agasajados los Futbolistas Mexicanos que se Destacaron en 1948," *La Opinión*, January 5, 1949, 7.

278. "Here and There," *Sport Page*, June 19, 1948, 1.

279. Ibid., 1.

280. Ibid., 5.

281. Saul Toledo, "Carmelita Aides Youth Clubs," *Sport Page*, February 28, 1948, 4. Carmelita sponsored the popular baseball club Los Chorizeros. Francisco Balderrama and Richard Santillan, "Los Chorizeros: The New York Yankees of East Los Angeles and the Reclaiming of Mexican American Baseball History," in *The National Pastime—Endless Season: Baseball in Southern California* (Lincoln: University of Nebraska Press, 2011), 1–13.

282. "Famous Boxer and Ball Player to Benefit from Paper Drive," *Sport Page*, December 4, 1948, 1.

283. "Lopez Benefit at Torrey's Inn," *Sport Page*, December 4, 1948, 2.

284. Club Brazil advertisement, *Sport Page*, December 28, 1946, 8.

285. "Café Society," *Sport Page*, June 19, 1948, 3.

286. "Café Society," *Sport Page*, February 28, 1948, 3.

287. Saul Toledo, "It's Better to Go Down Swinging, Than to Be Called Out on Strikes," *Sport Page*, December 28, 1946. 7,

288. Joseph Rodríguez, "Becoming Latinos: Mexican Americans, Chicanos, and the Spanish Myth in the Urban Southwest," *Western Historical Quarterly* 29 (Summer 1998): 165–185.

289. The founding members of the Mexican Sportswriters Association included Rodolfo Garcia, Luis Magaña, Aurelio Garcia Jr., Gabriel Navarro Jr., Arturo Martinez, Milton Navarrete, Héctor Abeytia, Salvador H. Rojas, Manuel "Midget" Martinez, Manuel D. Ortega, Carlos Talacón, Joey Olmos, Ralph Lincoln, and Eddie Rodriguez. See Colima, *Gentleman of the Ring*, 133.

290. "Program Set For Mexican Boxing Night," *Los Angeles Times*, November 24, 1951, B3; "Mexican Boxing Stars Honored at Dinner Fete," *Los Angeles Times*, November 26, 1951, C4.

291. Midget Martinez, "Latin Scribes Fete Ring Heroes," *Sport Page*, November 24, 1951, 1.

292. "La Afición Pugilística Rendirá Hoy Domingo Homenaje al Púgil Mexicano," *La Opinión*, November 25, 1951, 5. See also Gene Aguilera, *Mexican American Boxing in Los Angeles* (Charleston, SC: Arcadia, 2014), 32.

293. Aurelio Garcia Jr., "The Honored Fighters: A Word on the Occasion," reprinted in Colima, *Gentleman of the Ring*, 133.

294. "Mexican Boxing Stars Honored at Dinner Fete," *Los Angeles Times*, November 26, 1951, C4; "Latin Scribes Fete Ring Heroes," *Sport Page*, November 24, 1951, 1; "Un Gran Quinteto que ha Hecho Historia Pugilística," *La Opinión*, November 27, 1951, 7.

295. *"La Opinión* Nacio en la Edad Deportiva de Oro," *La Opinión*, September 16, 1951, 4.

296. "Los Idolos de los Deportistas y sus Utilidades," *La Opinión*, February 20, 1928, 4.

CONCLUSION

1. David Wharton, "The Glory of Their Times," *Los Angeles Times*, April 6, 2006, A1.

2. Vera Castaneda, "Rescued from History: The Baseball Teams of East Los Angeles," *Los Angeles Times*, January 27, 2017, www.latimes.com/books/jacketcopy/la-ca-jc-east-los-angeles -baseball-20170127-story.html.

3. Richard Santillan, José M. Alamillo, Anna Bermudez, Juan Canchola-Ventura, and Al Ramos, *Mexican American Baseball in Ventura County* (Mount Pleasant, SC: Arcadia, 2016).

4. Ernestina Navarro Hosaki, interview by the author, January 4, 2015, Oxnard, CA.

5. Marge Villa Cryan, panel discussion, California State University, Channel Islands, March 25, 2015.

6. Kat Williams, "Sport: 'A Useful Category of Historical Analysis': Isabel 'Lefty' Alvarez: The Rascal of El Cerro," *International Journal of the History of Sport* 29, no. 5 (April 2012): 766–785.

7. Santillan et al., *Mexican American Baseball in Ventura County.*

8. Karlene Ferrante, "Baseball and the Social Construction of Gender," in *Women, Media and Sport: Challenging Gender Values,* ed. Pamela J. Creedon (Thousand Oaks, CA: Sage, 1994), 238–256.

9. Jessica Mendoza, "Foreword," in Santillan et al., *Mexican American Baseball in Ventura County,* 6.

10. Aimee Crawford, "Jessica Mendoza: Hispanic Girls Moving beyond Traditional Roles, onto Field," ESPN, October 11, 2011, http://espn.go.com/blog/high-school/girl/post/_/id /334/jessica-mendoza-hispanic-girls-moving-beyond-traditional-roles-onto-field.

11. Katherine Jamieson, "Latinas in Sport and Physical Activity," *Journal of Physical Education, Recreation & Dance* 66, no. 7 (September 1995): 42–47; Vivian Acosta, "Hispanic Women in Sport," *Journal of Physical Education, Recreation & Dance* 70, no. 4 (April 1999): 44–46; *Increasing Young Latina Participation in Sports* (Los Angeles: LA84 Foundation, 2012).

12. John Bale, *The Brawn Drain: Foreign Student Athletes in American Universities* (Urbana: University of Illinois Press, 1991).

13. Joseph Arbena, "Dimensions of International Talent Migration in Latin American Sports," in *The Global Sports Arena: Athletic Talent Migration in an Interdependent World* (Portland, OR: Cass, 1994), 107. For a history of the migration of footballers from the late nineteenth century to the present day, see Pierre Lanfranchi and Matthew Taylor, *Moving with the Ball: The Migration of Professional Footballers* (Oxford: Berg, 2001).

14. Barbara Keys, *Globalizing Sport: National Rivalry and International Community in the 1930s* (Cambridge, MA: Harvard University Press, 2006).

15. Gustavo Cano and Alexandra Delano, "The Mexican Government and Organized Mexican Immigrants in the United States: A Historical Analysis of Political Transnationalism (1848–2005)," *Journal of Ethnic and Migration Studies* 33 (2007): 695–725.

16. Luin Goldring, "Gender, Status, and the State in Transnational Spaces: The Gendering of Political Participation and Mexican Hometown Associations," in *Gender and U.S. Immigration: Contemporary Trends,* ed. Pierrette Hondagneu-Sotelo (Berkeley: University of California Press, 2003), 341–358.

17. George Lipsitz, *How Racism Takes Place* (Philadelphia: Temple University Press, 2011), 244.

18. On "becoming brown" in the sporting arena, see Adrian Burgos Jr., "Latinos and Sport," in *The Routledge History of American Sport,* ed. Linda Borish, David K. Wiggins, and Gerald R. Gems (New York: Routledge, 2016), 122–133.

19. Williams, "Sport: 'A Useful Category of Historical Analysis,'" 766.

20. "MLC Race and Gender Report Card Shows Progress Still Needed," ESPN, April 18, 2017

21. Alan Klein, "Latinizing the 'National Pastime,'" *International Journal of the History of Sport* 24, no. 2 (February 2007): 296–310.

22. Benita Heiskanen, "The Latinization of Boxing: A Texas Case Study," *Journal of Sport History* 32, no. 1 (Spring 2005): 45–66.

23. Paul Cuadros, *A Home on the Field: How One Championship Soccer Team Inspires Hope for the Revival of Small Town America* (New York: HarperCollins, 2007).

24. Karin Brulliard, "Crackdown on Illegal Immigration Quiets Soccer Fields in Pr. Williams," *Washington Post*, March 12, 2008, A1.

25. "Group Disputes Costa Mesa's Stance on Immigration," *Los Angeles Times*, August 1, 2006; Paloma Esquivel and Tony Barboza, "Costa Mesa Talks Tough on Illegal Immigration, but Results Are Unclear," *Los Angeles Times*, June 5, 2010.

26. Horacio Fonseca, "Pro Soccer's Anti-Latino Game Plan," *Nuestro Magazine*, May 1978, 18–20.

27. Kim McCauley, "The 'Old Boys Club': How U.S. Soccer Ignores Talented Players from Underserved Communities," *SB Nation*, January 17, 2018.

28. Paul Gardner, "The Kinsman Interlude (Part 2): Total Failure to Acknowledge Latino Presence," *Soccer America's Soccer Talk*, December 1, 2016, 2.

29. In 1998, The Mexican Constitution was amended to confer nationality to children of Mexican-born parents.

30. Dan Frosch, "Born in the United States but Playing for Mexico," *New York Times*, July 23, 2008.

31. Kevin Baxter, "A Shot at Success across the Border," *Los Angeles Times*, January 3, 2011.

32. Carlos Gonzalez Gutierrez, "Fostering Identities: Mexico's Relations with Its Diaspora," *Journal of American History* 86, no. 2 (September 1999): 545–567.

33. Rodulfo Figureoa-Aramoni, "A Nation beyond Its Borders: The Program for Mexican Communities Abroad," *Journal of American History* 86, no. 2 (September 1999): 541.

34. Kevin Baxter, "Athletes without borders," *Los Angeles Times*, April 1, 2010.

35. Juan Vidal, "Why Does American Sports Have a Latino Problem?," *Rolling Stone*, September 16, 2016. https://www.rollingstone.com/culture/culture-sports/why-does-american-sports-have-a-latino-problem-122838/.

36. "Huddle Up: U.S. Hispanics Could Be a Boon for Nets, Leagues and Advertisers," Nielsen, October 11, 2013.

37. José M. Alamillo, "Richard 'Pancho' Gonzalez, Race and the Print Media in Postwar Tennis America," *International Journal of the History of Sport* 26, no. 7 (June 2009): 947–965. For a revised version, see José M. Alamillo, "'Bad Boy' of Tennis: Richard 'Pancho' Gonzalez, Racialized Masculinity and the Print Media in Postwar America," in *More Than Just Peloteros: Sport and US Latino Communities*, ed. Jorge Iber (Lubbock: Texas Tech University Press, 2014), 121–143.

38. "Gonzales Claims He's Still Best," *Los Angeles Times*, June 29, 1963.

39. Richard J. Gonzales, "Little Love in Tennis World for Pancho Gonzales," *Fort Worth Star Telegram*, September 30, 2001, 6E.

40. Michelle Kaufman, "Hispanic-American Void in Tennis Troubling," *Miami Herald*, September 5, 2009.

41. Jens Manuel Krogstad, "Key Facts about How the Hispanic Population Is Changing" (Pew Research Center, September 8, 2016), www.pewresearch.org/fact-tank/2016/09/08/key-facts-about-how-the-u-s-hispanic-population-is-changing/.

42. Ibid.

43. *Sixth Section*, directed by Alex Rivera (Rabble Rouser Media Inc./Second Generation Media New York, 2003); Carlos Uliese Decena and Margaret Gray, "Putting Transnationalism to Work: An Interview the Filmmaker Alex Rivera," *Social Text* 24, no. 3 (Fall 2006): 131–138.

44. Cecilia Menjivar and Andrea Gomez Cervantes, "The Effects of Parental Undocumented Status on Families and Children," *American Psychological Association News*, November 2016, www.apa.org/pi/families/resources/newsletter/2016/11/undocumented-status.aspx.

45. Emily Green, "U.S. Professional Sports Reaching Out to Mexico, Bucking Trump Nationalist Wave," *Univision News*, December 20, 2017, www.univision.com/univision-news/latin-america/us-professional-sports-reaching-out-to-mexico-bucking-trump-nationalist-wave.

46. Howard Blume, "Allegations of Racism at Orange County High School Football Game Underscore Broader Tension in the Trump Era," *Los Angeles Times*, September 9, 2018, www.latimes.com/local/education/la-me-ln-oc-football-racial-tensions-20180909-story.html.

47. Katy Steinmetz, "San Francisco High School Athletes Are Taking a Knee. And Their Community Is Backing Them," *Time*, September 23, 2016.

INDEX

ABOUT THE AUTHOR

JOSÉ M. ALAMILLO is professor of Chicana/o studies at California State University Channel Islands in Camarillo, CA. He is the author of *Making Lemonade Out of Lemons: Mexican American Labor and Leisure in a California Town* (2006) and coauthor of *Latinos in U.S. Sport: A History of Isolation, Cultural Identity, and Acceptance* (2011).